HTML 4

FOR THE WORLD WIDE WEB

VISUAL QUICKSTART GUIDE

by Elizabeth Castro

Peachpit Press

Visual QuickStart Guide
HTML 4 for the World Wide Web
by Elizabeth Castro

Peachpit Press
1249 Eighth Street
Berkeley, CA 94710
(510) 524-2178
(510) 524-2221 (fax)

Find us on the World Wide Web at: http://www.peachpit.com
Or contact Liz directly at html4@cookwood.com

Peachpit Press is a division of Addison Wesley Longman

ISBN: 0-201-69696-7

0 9 8 7 6 5 4

Printed in the United States of America

For my parents
(all four of them!)
who didn't always agree,
but who supported me anyway.

Special thanks to:

Nancy Davis, *at Peachpit Press, who I'm happy to report is not only my awesome editor, but also my friend.*

Mimi Heft, *at Peachpit Press, who carefully shepherded this book through production.*

Nolan Hester, *formerly of Peachpit Press, who helped me through the first and second editions of this book.*

Andreu Cabré *for his feedback, for his great Photoshop tips, and for sharing his life with me.*

Llumi *and* **Xixo** *for chasing cherry tomatoes and each other around my office and for helping me think up examples of HTML documents.*

And all the readers *of earlier versions of this book who took the time to write me (html4@cookwood.com) with accolades, questions, and suggestions.*

Table of Contents

Table of Contents

Chapter 16: Scripts **267**

Chapter 17: Extras **277**

Chapter 18: Publishing **289**

Table of Contents

Table of Contents

Introduction

Using the latest versions!

This book explains how to create Web pages using HTML 4 and Cascading Style Sheets, level 2, which are currently the latest versions of each.

Why would you want to publish an HTML page? Simply, to communicate with the world. The World Wide Web is the Gutenberg press of our time. Practically anyone can publish any kind of information, including graphics, sound, and even video, on the Web, opening the doors to each and every one of the millions of Internet users. Some are businesses with services to sell, others are individuals with stories to share. You decide how your page will be.

There are several programs on the market that let you create Web pages without learning HTML (Adobe PageMill, Microsoft FrontPage, Macromedia Dreamweaver, and others). However, you are limited to the features that each program is capable of producing. You can take advantage of the shortcuts provided by such an HTML editor, and then add the features it may not yet recognize by using the techniques described in this book. That way, you get the best of both worlds.

In this book, you'll find clear, easy-to-follow instructions that will take you through the process of creating Web pages step-by-step. It is perfect for the beginner, with no knowledge of HTML, who wants to begin to create Web pages.

If you're already familiar with HTML, this book is a perfect reference guide. You can look up topics in the hefty index and consult just those subjects that you need information on.

This book also boasts two online companion sites. For details, see page 21. Or write me directly at html4@cookwood.com.

HTML and the Web

Somehow, it shouldn't be surprising that the lingua franca of the World Wide Web was developed in Switzerland, which has four official state languages. Perhaps acutely aware of how difficult it is for people to communicate without a common language, the programmers at the CERN research lab created a kind of Esperanto for computers: the Hypertext Markup Language, or HTML.

HTML allows you to format text, add rules, graphics, sound, and video and save it all in a text-only ASCII file that any computer can read. (Of course, to project video or play sounds, the computer must have the necessary hardware.) The key to HTML is in the *tags*, keywords enclosed in less than (<) and greater than (>) signs, that indicate what kind of content is coming up.

Of course, HTML just looks like a lot of text sprinkled with greater than and less than signs until you open the file with a special program called a *browser*. A browser can interpret the HTML tags and then show the formatted document on screen. For more information on browsers, consult *HTML browsers* on page 20.

HTML is not just another way to create beautiful documents, however. Its key ingredient is in the first part of its name: *Hypertext*. HTML documents can contain links to other HTML documents or to practically anything else on the Internet. This means that you can create several Web pages and have your users jump from one to another as needed. You can also create links to other organizations' Web pages, giving your users access to information held at other sites.

onall1three.html

Figure i.1 *It doesn't matter if the original file is from a Windows machine (above), a Macintosh (right), or any other computer, as long as it uses HTML coding and is saved as a text-only file.*

Figure i.2 *Each computer (Unix, top left, Windows, above and Mac, left) shows the HTML code in its own way. The results are actually very similar; the differences are mostly cosmetic.*

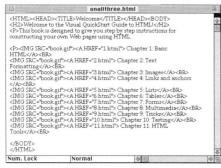

Figure i.3 *There is nothing in HTML code that cannot be expressed with simple numbers, letters, and symbols. This makes it easy for any kind of computer system to understand it.*

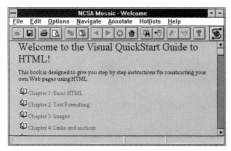

Figure i.4 *This is a browser on the Macintosh. Notice the graphic icons and different font sizes.*

Figure i.5 *This is a browser in Windows showing the same HTML document. The differences are pretty minor.*

Users vs. Programmers

Think for a minute about the wide variety of computers that exist in the world. Each and every one of them can read HTML, but they all do it in a slightly different way—according to what is allowed in their particular operating system. For example, some computers can only display text: letters and numbers, a few symbols, but no graphics or color of any kind.

On the other hand, Windows and Macintosh systems were practically created with graphics and color in mind. Even so, older machines tend to be limited to displaying 256 colors while newer machines generally are not.

In addition, the way that your visitors will connect to the Internet may affect the way their computers can view Web pages. Even a Mac user won't be able to see the graphics on your pages if she is connected to the Web through a Unix shell account, or through Telnet.

Further, there is a big difference between the visitor who connects to the Web with a slow computer, through a slow modem, and the visitor who has a direct, high speed connection and a computer that can make the most of it. The first visitor will go crazy waiting for images to download while the second may not even notice a delay.

Finally, many browsers let the surfer decide how to view certain elements on a Web page. They might be able to change the text and background colors, the text formatting, and decide whether or not to show graphics.

Users vs. Programmers

Therefore, it is important to realize that each person who looks at your page may see it in a different way, according to the kind of computer system they have, the browser they have chosen, the graphics capacity they have, the speed of their modem and connection to the Web, and the settings they have chosen for their browser.

You, as the programmer or designer of the Web page, have *limited control* over how the page actually looks once it reaches your user, the person who is seeing your page through a browser. The primary concern of HTML is that your page be understandable by any computer, not that it be beautiful.

Many people are not satisfied with this lack of control. They add special effects to their pages with nonstandard HTML that may make the pages illegible to many browsers. Or they don't use alternate text for images, making it difficult for folks with slow Internet connections or non-graphic browsers to navigate the pages.

This one is your call. You decide how universal you want your document to be. On the continuum between plain Web pages that can be read by all and beautiful Web masterpieces that can be viewed by just a few, *you* must decide where your pages will fall. You'll find a table that explains which HTML tags are part of the official specifications starting on page 316.

In this book, I refer to the person who designs Web pages as *you* (or sometimes the programmer or designer). On the other hand, the *visitor* (or sometimes *surfer)* is the person who will look at your Web pages once you've published them.

Different versions of HTML

Democracy can be a great thing: many people give their input and a consensus is reached that aims to satisfy the largest group of people. The Internet is democracy in action. While the original HTML standard was developed by CERN, new versions are hashed out through a series of online meetings open to anyone on the Internet. Then they are analyzed, discussed, decided, and published by the W3 Consortium, led by the Laboratory for Computer Science at the Massachusetts Institute of Technology (MIT) and INRIA, a French technology group, in collaboration with CERN.

There is one difficult thing about democracy, however: it's incredibly slow. So slow, that Netscape and Microsoft have often added their own proprietary extensions in order to gain followers. It has fallen to the W3C to attempt to keep all the major players happy while attempting to keep HTML free and universal. The W3C has been particularly successful with HTML 4 (the current version, and the one that this book describes), which incorporates many of the previously proprietary extensions into a shared standard. However, Netscape Communications and Microsoft continue to chafe at the bit. Currently, they are sparring over the area of dynamic HTML, or *DHTML (see page 19)*.

In this book, you will learn both standard HTML as well as the extensions developed by Netscape and Microsoft that have made these browsers so popular. Netscape extensions are marked with the Netscape Only icon while features only available for Microsoft's Internet Explorer are marked with the IE only icon **(Figure i.6)**.

Figure i.6 *HTML code that is only recognized by Netscape is marked with the N only icon (left). Code that is only recognized when viewed with Internet Explorer is marked with the IE only icon (right).*

Cascading Style Sheets

The extensions added by Netscape and Microsoft have given designers more control over the way their Web pages look, but they've also encumbered HTML and made it difficult to update and coordinate pages and sites. The answer? Cascading Style Sheets, which, according to the W3C who developed the specifications, give designers the strength they want without stripping HTML of its universality and flexibility.

In fact, the W3C has gone so far as to deprecate many popular tags. This means that the tags may disappear from future specifications of HTML but that they are still currently supported. However, since most folks still use many of the deprecated tags, I've chosen not to relegate them to a dusty corner of this book. Instead, I tell you in the text to beware. You can see which tags have been deprecated by consulting the list starting on page 316.

Cascading Style Sheets are wonderfully powerful, but they're not nearly as simple as HTML. (Therein lies the rub.) I have devoted three chapters of this book *(see pages 221–266)* to style sheets. They're all you need to create flexible, high-end pages that are easy to update and have a consistent look throughout the site.

(The specifications for Cascading Style Sheets, level 2 (CSS2), on which the information in this book is based, were in the process of being finalized at press time. You can get the latest details on style sheets at *http://www.w3.org/Style/.*)

What is DHTML?

DHTML is actually a combination of technologies used to create dynamic content on Web pages. It draws on HTML 4, Cascading Style Sheets, and usually JavaScript. These elements are supposed to work together following the rules of the Document Object Model (DOM), to change the content of a page even after it has been loaded into the browser. For example, a visitor might select an option from a menu and immediately see a picture of that item. However, Netscape and Microsoft have not come to an agreement (surprise!) about which DOM to follow, and the W3C has not yet declared an official winner. Until then, and as always, it's a good idea to test pages in as many browsers and on as many platforms as possible.

For more information on DHTML, try the W3C site: *http://www.w3.org/DOM/*, Microsoft's site: *http://www.microsoft.com/workshop/author/dhtml/*, Netscape's site: *http://devedge.netscape.com/library/documentation/dynhtml.html*, and Macromedia's site at *http://www.dhtmlzone.com*.

And XML?

HTML forms part of a larger, more powerful mark-up language called SGML. In an effort to harness the power of SGML without losing the simplicity of HTML, the W3C has developed Extensible Markup Language, or XML, that can be used to create your own mark-up languages, specifically suited to your topic. For more information, consult *http://www.ucc.ie/xml* (the XML faq) or the W3C's home page for XML at *http://www.w3.org/XML*.

HTML browsers

Perhaps the most important tool for creating HTML documents is the HTML browser. You might think that only your users need to have a browser, but you'd be wrong. It is absolutely vital that you have at least one, and preferably three or four of the principal browsers in use around the world. This way you can test your HTML pages and make sure that they look the way you want them to—regardless of the browser used.

The two most popular browsers are Netscape Communicator (used to be called Navigator) and Microsoft Internet Explorer. Both are available on a variety of platforms.

Netscape Communicator

According to the latest statistics floating around the Net, Netscape Communicator (often referred to simply as *Netscape*) still holds the lead in the browser wars (with around 60% of the Web browsing public), down from a high near 80%. Developed by some of the same engineers who created Mosaic, Netscape has distanced itself from the competition by offering non-standard features that make Netscape-enhanced pages much more attractive to the eye—if much more taxing on the modem. For more information, jump to *http://home.netscape.com* **(Figure i.7)**.

Microsoft Internet Explorer

Thanks to Microsoft's hefty public relations team as well as to Internet Explorer's solid performance and acceptance of all of HTML 4's tags plus most of Netscape's proprietary extensions, Internet Explorer is quickly becoming a viable alternative to Netscape, used by some 40% of the Web public. For more information, jump to *http://www.microsoft.com/ie/* **(Figure i.8)**.

Figure i.7 *This is Netscape Communicator 4 for Macintosh showing Netscape Communications' home page. Netscape Communicator 4 for Windows looks practically identical.*

Figure i.8 *This is Internet Explorer 4 for Macintosh showing Microsoft's Internet Explorer home page. (Internet Explorer 4 for Windows looks almost exactly the same.)*

The HTML VQS Web Site

With the Web constantly changing, it seemed most appropriate to add a dynamic element to this book: the HTML VQS Web site. In fact, there are two.

At *www.peachpit.com/vqs/html4* you can find the full Table of contents, all of the example files, an excerpt from the book, and a list (hopefully short) of errata.

At *www.cookwood.com*, you'll find a gallery of pages created by folks who have read this and earlier versions of this book, links to reviews and comments, a question-and-answer area, updates, and more.

And you can always write me directly at html4@cookwood.com with any questions, suggestions, or even complaints that you may have.

See you on the Web!

The HTML VQS Web Site

HTML Building Blocks

Tags in this book

In this book, all tags and attributes are written in ALL CAPS, and all values are shown in lowercase letters. HTML does not require this system; I use it here solely to help distinguish the tags, attributes, and values from the surrounding text in the examples.

Figure 1.1 *The anatomy of an HTML tag. Notice there are no extra spaces between the contained text and the angle brackets (greater than and less than signs).*

Figure 1.2 *Some tags can take optional attributes that further define the formatting desired.*

Writing HTML

You can create an HTML document with any word processor or text editor, including the very basic TeachText or Simple-Text on the Mac and Notepad or WordPad for Windows, both of which come free with the corresponding system software.

You can also buy a Web page editor, like PageMill or FrontPage, and then use the information in this book to tweak the page until it's exactly the way you want it. Web page editors are discussed in more detail in Appendix A, *HTML Tools*, starting on page 303.

HTML tags

HTML tags are commands written between less than (<) and greater than (>) signs, also known as *angle brackets*, that indicate how the browser should display the text **(Figure 1.1)**. There are opening and closing versions for many (but not all) tags, and the affected text is *contained* within the two tags. Both the opening and closing tags use the same command word but the closing tag carries an initial extra forward slash symbol /.

Attributes

Many tags have special *attributes* that offer a variety of options for the contained text. The attribute is entered between the command word and the final greater than symbol **(Figure 1.2)**. Often, you can use a series of attributes in a single tag. Simply write one after the other—in any order—with a space between each one.

Values

Attributes in turn often have *values*. In some cases, you must pick a value from a small group of choices. For example, the CLEAR attribute for the BR tag can take values of *left, right,* or *all.* Any other value given will be ignored **(Figure 1.3)**.

Other attributes are more strict about the *type* of values they accept. For example, the HSPACE attribute of the IMG tag will accept only integers as its value, and the SRC attribute of the IMG tag will only accept URLs for its value **(Figure 1.4)**.

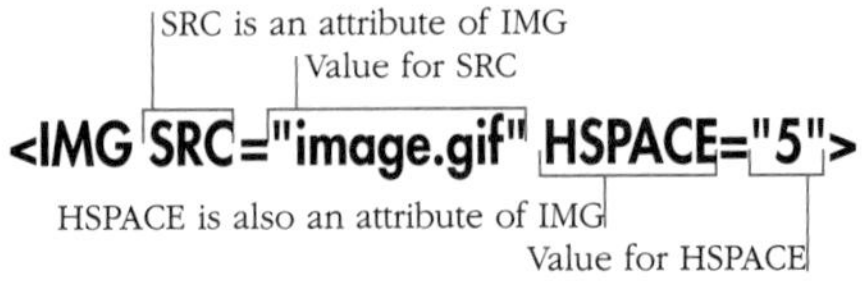

Quotation marks

Generally speaking, values should be enclosed in straight quotation marks "" (NOT curly ones ""). However, you can omit the quote marks if the value only contains letters (A–Z, a–z), digits (0–9), a hyphen (-), or a period (.). I usually use quotes around URLs to ensure that they're not misinterpreted by the server.

Nesting tags

In some cases, you may want to modify your page contents with more than one tag. For example, you may want to add italic formatting to a word inside a header. There are two things to keep in mind here. First, not all tags can contain all other kinds of tags. As a general rule, those tags that affect entire paragraphs (the W3C calls this *block-level*) can contain tags that affect individual words or letters (*inline*), but not vice versa.

Second, order is everything. Whenever you use a closing tag it should correspond to the last unclosed opening tag. In other words, first A then B, then /B, and then /A **(Figure 1.5)**.

Figure 1.3 *Some tags, like BR shown here, take attributes with given values, of which you can choose only one. You don't need to enclose one word values in quotation marks.*

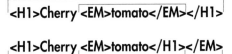

Figure 1.4 *Some tags, like IMG shown here, can take more than one attribute, each with its own values.*

Correct (no overlapping lines)

`<H1>Cherry <EM>tomato</EM></H1>`

`<H1>Cherry <EM>tomato</H1></EM>`

Incorrect (the sets of tags cross over each other)

Figure 1.5 *To make sure your tags are correctly nested, connect each set with a line. None of your sets of tags should overlap any other set; each interior set should be completely enclosed within the next larger set.*

HTML Tags

Extra returns

Figure 1.6 *Extra returns and spaces help distinguish the different parts of the HTML document in the text editor but are completely ignored by the browser.*

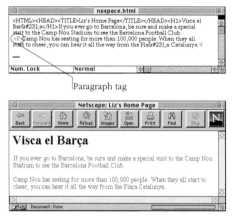

Paragraph tag

Figure 1.7 *I've removed all the returns from the document in Figure 1.6, but added a single <P> tag. The only difference in the final result is from the new tag.*

Spacing

HTML browsers will ignore any extra spaces that exist between the tags in your HTML document. You can use this to your advantage by adding spaces and returns to help view the elements in your HTML document more clearly while you're writing and designing your page **(Figure 1.6)**.

On the other hand, you won't be able to count on returns or spaces to format your document. A return at the end of a paragraph in your HTML document will not appear in the browsed page. Instead, use a P tag to begin each new paragraph **(Figure 1.7)**.

Further, you cannot repeat several P (or BR) tags to add space between paragraphs. The extra tags are simply ignored.

How do you control spacing then? Style sheets let you specify with absolute precision just how much space should go between elements in your Web page. For more information, see page 256. In addition, Netscape has developed some tags for the same purpose *(see page 93)*. You might also consult the section on pixel shims on page 97.

Tags with automatic line breaks

Block-level tags generally include automatic, logical line breaks. For example, you don't need to use a new paragraph tag after a header, since a header automatically includes a line break. In fact, you only need to insert a new paragraph tag if you're using the tag to apply styles *(see page 223)*. Some common block-level tags are P, H1, BR, UL, and TABLE.

Inline tags that affect only a few letters or words do not automatically begin on a new line. Some common inline tags are EM, B, and IMG.

Special symbols

The standard ASCII set contains 128 characters and can be used perfectly well for English documents. However, accents, curly quotes, and many commonly used symbols unfortunately cannot be found in this group. Luckily, HTML can contain any character in the full ISO Latin-1 character set (also known as ISO 8859-1). In Windows and Unix systems, simply enter the character in the usual (convoluted) way and it will display properly in the browser.

Watch out! Even though you can type special characters, accents and so on in your Macintosh and DOS based PC, these systems do not use the standard ISO Latin-1 character set for the characters numbered 129-255 and will not display them correctly in the Web page. You must enter these special characters with either *name* or *number codes* **(Figure 1.8)**.

Name codes are more descriptive (and are case sensitive), like *è* for *é* and *Ñ* for *Ñ*. However, not every character has a name code. In that case, you will need to use a number code, which is composed of an ampersand, number symbol, the character number in the Latin-1 character set and a semicolon. The number code for *é* is *é* and for *Ñ* is *Ñ*. See *Special Symbols* on page 307 for a complete listing and more instructions.

There are four symbols that have special meanings in HTML documents. These are the greater than (>), less than (<), straight double quotation marks ("), and the ampersand (&). If you simply type them in your HTML document, the browser may attempt to interpret them **(Figure 1.9)**. To show the symbols themselves, use a name or number code.

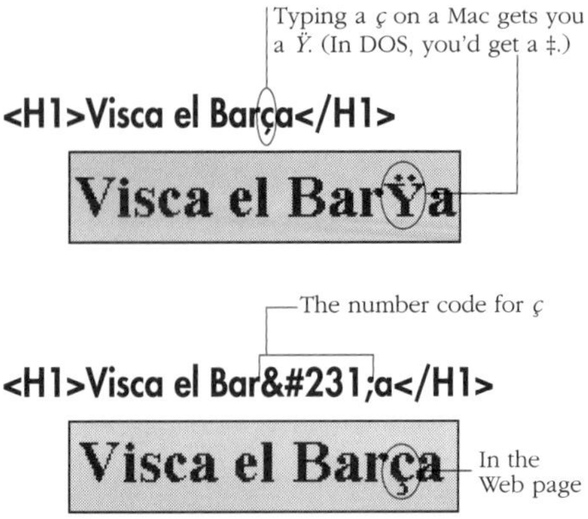

Typing a ç on a Mac gets you a Ÿ. (In DOS, you'd get a ‡.)

`<H1>Visca el Barça</H1>`

Visca el BarŸa

The number code for ç

`<H1>Visca el Bar&#231;a</H1>`

Visca el Barça In the Web page

Figure 1.8 *To display a ç properly, you must use either its number or its name. It looks awful in your HTML document, but on the Web page, where it counts, it's beautiful—on any platform.*

If you type < and > ...

Use `<BR>` for line breaks

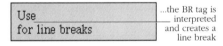

...the BR tag is interpreted and creates a line break

If you use name codes for < and >...

Use `&lt;BR&gt;` for line breaks

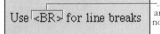

...the symbols are shown but not interpreted

Figure 1.9 *You must use name or number codes to show the symbols <, >, ", and & on your Web page. See Special Symbols on page 307 for details.*

Figure 1.10 *Your basic URL contains a scheme, server name, path, and file name.*

Figure 1.11 *A URL with a trailing forward slash and no file name points to the default file in the last directory named (in this case the* liz *directory). Some common default file names are* index.html *and* default.htm.

Figure 1.12 *When the user clicks this URL, the browser will begin an FTP transfer of the file* prog.exe.

Figure 1.13 *A URL for a newsgroup looks a bit different. There are no forward slashes after the scheme and colon, and generally, there is no file name. (Although you could add the message number or ID, a message's extremely short lifespan limits its usefulness as a link.)*

"mailto:lcastro@cookwood.com"

Figure 1.14 *A URL for an e-mail address is similar in design to a newsgroup URL (Figure 1.13); it includes the* mailto *scheme followed by a colon but no forward slashes, and then the e-mail address itself.*

"file:///Harddisk/Web/home.htm"

Figure 1.15 *To reference a file on your hard disk, use the* file *scheme. If you're on a Windows machine, specify your hard disk by letter and follow it with a vertical bar:* file:///c|/path/filename.

URLs

Uniform resource locator, or URL, is a fancy name for *address*. It contains information about where a file is and what a browser should do with it. Each file on the Internet has a unique URL.

The first part of the URL is called the *scheme*. It tells the browser how to deal with the file that it is about to open. One of the most common schemes you will see is HTTP, or Hypertext Transfer Protocol. It is used to access Web pages **(Figure 1.10)**.

The second part of the URL is the name of the server where the file is located, followed by the path that leads to the file and the file's name itself. Sometimes, a URL ends in a trailing forward slash with no file name given **(Figure 1.11)**. In this case the URL refers to the default file in the last directory in the path (which generally corresponds to the home page).

Other common schemes are HTTPS, for secure Web pages; FTP (File Transfer Protocol) for downloading files from the Net **(Figure 1.12)**; Gopher, for searching for information; News, for sending and reading messages posted to a Usenet newsgroup **(Figure 1.13)**; Mailto, for sending electronic mail **(Figure 1.14)**; and File, for accessing files on a local hard disk **(Figure 1.15)**.

A scheme is generally followed by a colon and two forward slashes. Mailto and News are exceptions; these take only a colon.

Notice that the File scheme uses three slashes. That's because the host, which in other schemes goes between the second and third slashes, is assumed to be the local computer. Always type schemes in lowercase letters.

Absolute URLs

URLs can be either absolute or relative. An *absolute URL* shows the entire path to the file, including the scheme, server name, the complete path, and the file name itself. An absolute URL is analogous to a complete street address, including name, street and number, city, state, zip code, and country. No matter where a letter is sent from, the post office will be able to find the recipient. In terms of URLs, this means that the location of the absolute URL itself has no bearing on the location of the actual file referenced—whether it is in a Web page on your server or on mine, an absolute URL will look exactly the same.

If you're referencing a file from someone else's server, you'll have to use an absolute URL. You'll also need to use absolute URLs for FTP and Gopher sites and for newsgroups and e-mail addresses—in short, any kind of URL that doesn't use an HTTP protocol.

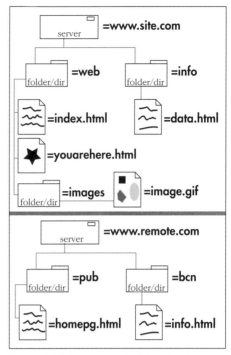

Figure 1.16 *Here is a typical, but simple representation of two servers (or hard disks), and the files that each contains. The table below shows the relative URLs for each file that you would use when writing the* youarehere.html *file. The absolute URLs shown would work in* any *file.*

File name	Absolute URL (anywhere)	Relative URL (in *youarehere.html*)
index.html	www.site.com/web/index.html	index.html
image.gif	www.site.com/web/images/image.gif	images/image.gif
data.html	www.site.com/info/data.html	../info/data.html
homepg.html	www.remote.com/pub/homepg.html	*(none: use absolute)*
info.html	www.remote.com/bcn/info.html	*(none: use absolute)*

Absolute URLs vs. Relative URLs

Inside the current folder, there's a
file called *index.html*

"index.html"

Figure 1.17 *The relative URL for a file in the same folder (see Figure 1.16) as the file that contains the link is just the file's name and extension.*

Inside the current folder
there's a folder called "images"...

"images/image.gif"

...that contains...   ...a file called *image.gif*

Figure 1.18 *For a file that is within a folder inside the current folder (see Figure 1.16), add the folder's name and a forward slash in front of the file name.*

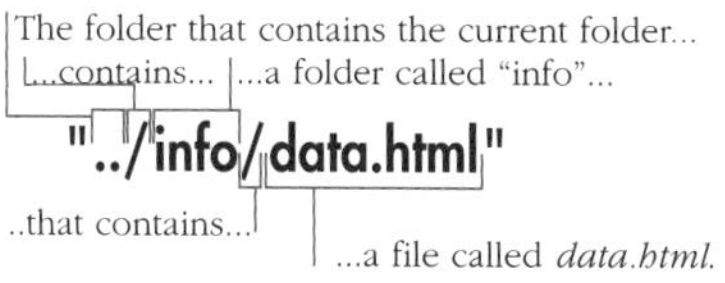

The folder that contains the current folder...
...contains...   ...a folder called "info"...

"../info/data.html"

...that contains...   ...a file called *data.html.*

Figure 1.19 *This file, as you can see in Figure 1.16, is in a folder that is inside the folder that contains the current folder (whew!). In that case, you use two periods and a slash to go up a level, and then note the subdirectory, followed by a forward slash, followed by the file name.*

Relative URLs

To give you directions to my neighbor's house, instead of giving her complete address, I might just say "it's three doors down on the right". This is a *relative* address—where it points to depends on where the information is given from. With the same information in a different city, you'd never find my neighbor.

In the same way, a *relative URL* describes the location of the desired file with reference to the location of the file that contains the URL itself. So, you might have the URL say something like "show the xyz image that's in the same directory as the current file".

Thus, the relative URL for a file that is in the same directory as the current file (that is, the one containing the URL in question) is simply the file name and extension **(Figure 1.17)**. You create the URL for a file in a subdirectory of the current directory with the name of the subdirectory followed by a forward slash and then the name and extension of the desired file **(Figure 1.18)**.

To reference a file in a directory at a *higher* level of the file hierarchy, use two periods and a forward slash **(Figure 1.19)**. You can combine and repeat the two periods and forward slash to reference any file on the same hard disk as the current file.

Generally, you should always use relative URLs. They're much easier to type and they make it easy to move your pages from a local system to a server—as long as the relative position of each file remains constant, the links will work correctly.

One added advantage of relative URLs is that you don't have to type the scheme—as long as it's HTTP.

URLs

Starting your Web Page

Every Web page has three main parts: a line that describes what *version* of HTML the page was written in, a HEAD section with information *about* the page, and a BODY with the *content* of the page. In this chapter, you'll learn how to create the foundation for each of your Web pages.

Designing your site

Although you can just jump in and start writing HTML pages right away *(see page 35)*, it's a good idea to first think about and design your site. That way, you'll give yourself direction and save reorganizing later.

To design your site:

1. Figure out why you're creating this page. What information do you want to convey?

2. Think about who your audience is. How can you tailor your content to appeal to this audience? Should you include lots of graphics or is it more important that your page download quickly?

3. How many pages will you need? What sort of structure would you like it to have? Do you want visitors to go through your site in a particular direction, or do you want to make it easy for them to explore in any direction?

4. Sketch out your site on paper—yes, with a pen.

5. Devise a simple, consistent naming system for your pages, images, and other external files.

✔ Tips

■ On the other hand, don't overdo the design phase of your site. At some point, you've got to dig in and start writing.

■ If you're not very familiar with the Web, do some surfing first to get an idea of the possibilities. You might start with Yahoo's Cool Links: *http:// www.yahoo.com/Entertainment/ Cool_Links/*.

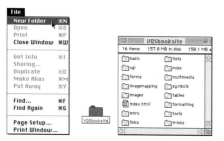

Figure 2.1 *On the Mac, select New Folder, and then give the folder a name. You can use a separate folder for each section of your site.*

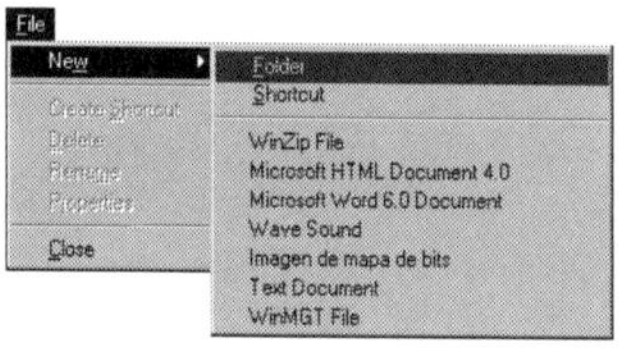

Figure 2.2 *In Windows, from the Windows Explorer, choose File > New > Folder...*

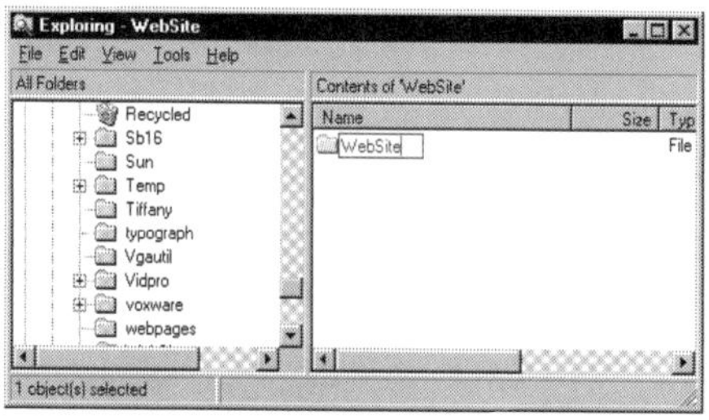

Figure 2.3 *...give the new folder a name...*

Figure 2.4 *...and then create other folders within the main folder in order to organize the pages on your Web site.*

Organizing files

Even before you start to create your files, it's a good idea to figure out where you're going to put them.

To organize your files:

1. Create a central folder or directory to hold all the material that will be available at your Web site. (On the Mac, choose File > New Folder in the Finder. On Windows, choose File > Create Directory in the Windows Explorer.)

2. Divide the central folder in a way that reflects the organization of your Web site. You may decide to create a separate folder for HTML documents, one for images, and one for other external files. If you have a large site with many pages, you may wish to divide the site into categories or chapters as I've done here, placing the images in the individual folders.

✔ Tip

■ Use simple, one-word names without symbols or punctuation for your files and folders. Use a consistent scheme of capital and small letters. This helps make your URLs easier to type and your pages easier to reach.

Organizing files

Designating a home page

A home page is the one that a user will see if they use a URL without a file name. That is, if your site's principal directory on the server is *www.site.com/flintstone/website1*, and a user points to *http://www.site.com/flintstone/website1/*, with a trailing forward slash but no file name, the browser will look for the default or home page. The most common home page name is *index.html* but this varies from server to server. Ask your ISP to be sure.

To designate one page as the home page:

1. Create the home page as described on page 35.

2. Name the file *index.html* (or whatever the default home page name is for your server).

3. Place the home page in the principal directory that contains your Web site.

✔ Tips

■ Your home page should have links to all the other information available at your Web site. Your home page should be a table of contents to your site, not just the first page.

■ If you want your users to be able to reach the other pages in your site, make your home page clean, neat, and fast **(Figure 2.7)**.

Figure 2.5 *On a Mac, create a Web page named* index.html *and place it in the main folder of the Web site.*

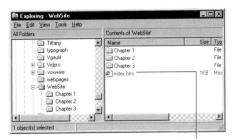

Figure 2.6 *In Windows, create a Web page called* index.htm *and place it in the main directory of the Web site.*

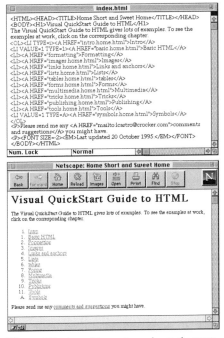

Figure 2.7 *A good home page draws the users right into the material, giving them easy, quick access to all the parts of the site.*

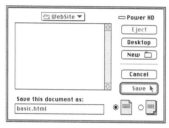

Figure 2.8 *In the text editor (this is SimpleText) choose New to create a new document. Once you've created the HTML code, choose File > Save As to save it.*

Figure 2.9 *Give the file the .htm or .html extension, choose the Text Only format (the only one available here in SimpleText), choose the desired location, and then click Save.*

Figure 2.10 *From Word-Pad (or other text editor), choose File > New. Create the Web page and then choose File > Save As.*

Figure 2.11 *Give the file the .htm or .html extension, choose Text Document under Save as type, choose the desired location, and then click Save.*

Creating a new Web page

You don't need any special tools to create a Web page. You can use any word processor, even WordPad or SimpleText, which are included with the basic Windows and Macintosh system software.

To create a new Web page:

1. Open a text editor or word processor.

2. Choose File > New to create a new, blank document **(Figures 2.8 and 2.10)**.

3. Create the HTML content as explained in the rest of this book, starting on page 37.

4. Choose File > Save As.

5. In the dialog box that appears, choose Text Only (or ASCII) for the format **(Figures 2.9 and 2.11)**.

6. Give the document the .htm or .html extension.

7. Choose the folder in which to save the Web page *(see page 33)*.

8. Click Save.

✔ Tips

- WordPad asks you what format every new document should be. Choose Text Document. It's no big deal if you don't though. You can always save the document in Text Only format as described in step 5 above.

- If you use PageMill, FrontPage, or some other Web page editor to start your pages, you can still tweak their HTML code with any text editor. Just choose File > Open from the text editor and open the file. Then use the rest of this book to create the HTML page *you* want.

Creating a new Web page

Looking at your page in a browser

Once you've created a page, you'll want to see what it looks like in a browser. In fact, since you don't know which browser your visitors will be using, it's a good idea to look at the page in *several* browsers.

To look at your page in a browser:

1. Open your browser software (Communicator, Explorer, etc.)

2. Choose File > Open, Open File, or Open Page (just *not* Open Location), depending on the browser **(Fig. 2.12)**.

3. In the dialog box that appears, find the Web page that you want to view on your hard disk **(Figure 2.14)**.

4. Click Open. The page will be displayed in the browser just as it will appear when you actually publish it on the server *(see page 289)*.

✔ Tips

■ If your Web page does not appear in the Open dialog box, make sure that you have saved it as Text Only and given it the .htm or .html extension.

■ You don't have to close the document in the text editor before you view it with a browser. This makes editing much faster—you can switch to the editor, make your changes, and then come back to the browser and click Reload to view the changes.

■ It is not necessary to publish your pages on the server before you view them. Publishing them on the server does not change them in any way (it only moves them to a new location).

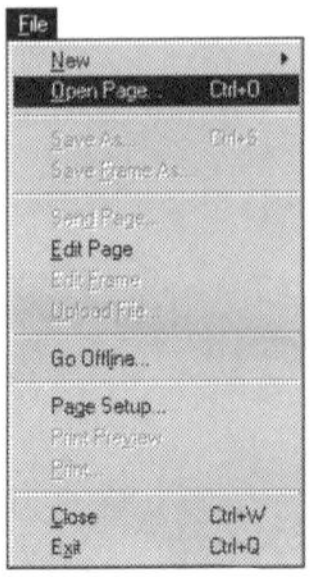

Figure 2.12 *From the desired browser (this is Communicator for Windows), choose File > Open Page. In Explorer for Windows, it's called File > Open. In Explorer for Mac, it's File > Open File.*

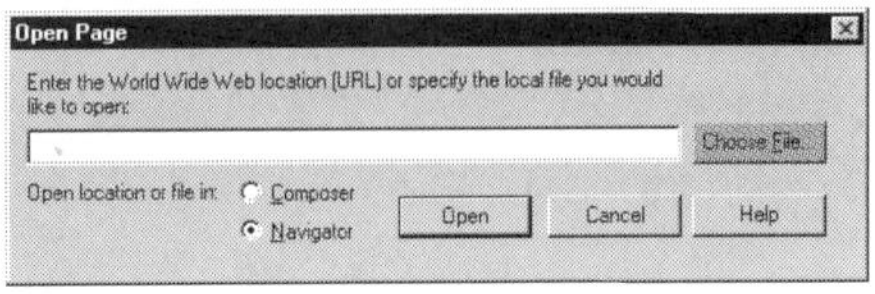

Figure 2.13 *On Windows machines, you'll get an intermediary box asking if you want to type the path in by hand. If you don't (!), click the Choose File button (in IE4, it's Browse). You'll get the dialog box shown in Figure 2.14.*

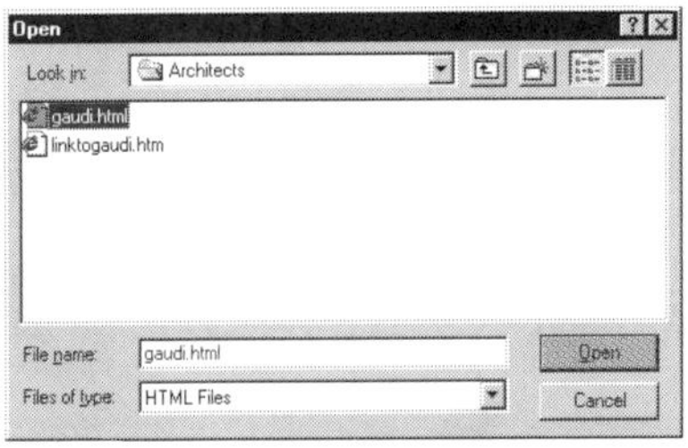

Figure 2.14 *Choose the file that you want to open and click the Open button.*

Figure 2.15 *The page appears in the browser. Give it a good look to see if it's coming out the way you planned.*

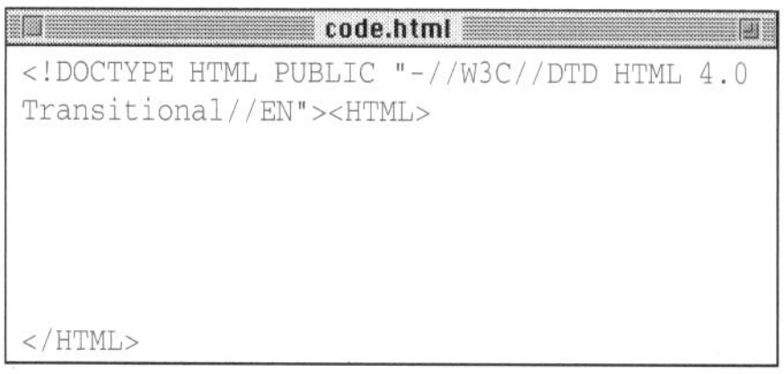

Figure 2.16 *The !DOCTYPE and HTML tags identify your document so that the browser knows what to do with it.*

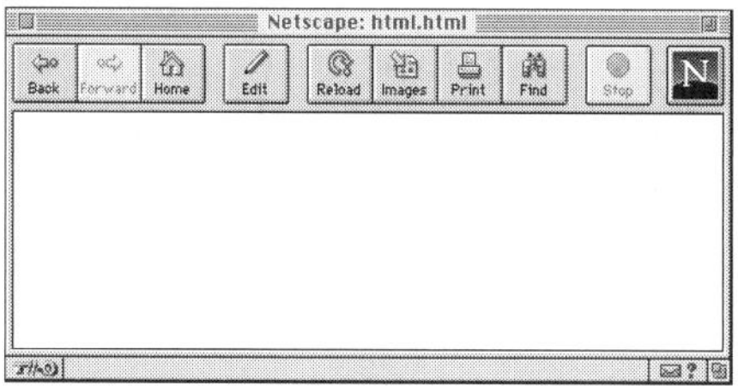

Figure 2.17 *An empty HTML document doesn't look very exciting in the browser.*

Starting your Web page

When a user jumps to the URL that corresponds to your Web page, the browser needs information right away about what kind of document it is, and how it should be displayed. You should begin every Web page with the !DOCTYPE and HTML tags.

To start your Web page:

1. Type **<!DOCTYPE HTML PUBLIC "-//W3C//DTD HTML** at the top of your Web page.

2. Type the version of HTML you're using.

   For pages that still rely on deprecated tags such as FONT and BGCOLOR, use **HTML 4.0 Transitional**.

   For pages that do not include any deprecated tags, use **HTML 4.0**.

   For pages with framesets, use **HTML 4.0 Frameset**.

   For earlier versions of HTML, type the appropriate version number (e.g., **HTML 2.0**).

3. Type **//EN"> <HTML>**.

4. Create your Web page.

5. Type **</HTML>**.

✔ Tips

■ While you can get away without either the !DOCTYPE or HTML tags, you should always include both to ensure that your page is correctly recognized, regardless of the browser used.

■ Create a template with the !DOCTYPE and HTML tags already typed in as a starting point for all your pages.

Understanding the HEAD and BODY

Most Web pages are divided into two sections: the HEAD and the BODY. The HEAD section provides information about the URL of your Web page as well as its relationship with the other pages at your site. The only element in the HEAD section that is visible to the user is the title of the Web page *(see page 39).*

Figure 2.18 *Every HTML document should be divided into a HEAD and a BODY.*

To create the HEAD section:

1. Directly after the initial !DOCTYPE and HTML tags *(see page 37),* type **<HEAD>**.

2. Create the HEAD section, including the TITLE *(see page 39).* Add META information *(see pages 290–293)* and the BASE *(see page 113),* if desired.

3. Type **</HEAD>**.

Figure 2.19 *With no title and no contents, a browser has to scrape together a little substance (in the form of a title) from the file name of the HTML document.*

The BODY of your HTML document contains the bulk of your Web page, including all the text, graphics, and formatting.

To create the BODY:

1. After the final </HEAD> tag and before anything else, type **<BODY>**.

2. Create the contents of your Web page.

3. Type **</BODY>**.

✔ Tip

■ For pages with frames, the BODY section is replaced by the FRAMESET. For more information, consult Chapter 10, *Frames.*

(sidebar) **Understanding the HEAD and BODY**

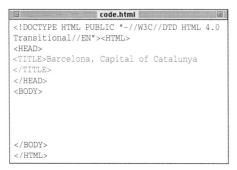

```
┌──────────────────────────────────────┐
│▤▤▤▤▤         code.html        ▤▤▤▤▤ ▣│
├──────────────────────────────────────┤
│<!DOCTYPE HTML PUBLIC "-//W3C//DTD HTML 4.0│
│Transitional//EN"><HTML>              │
│<HEAD>                                │
│<TITLE>Barcelona, Capital of Catalunya│
│</TITLE>                              │
│</HEAD>                               │
│<BODY>                                │
│                                      │
│                                      │
│                                      │
│                                      │
│</BODY>                               │
│</HTML>                               │
└──────────────────────────────────────┘
```

Figure 2.20 *The TITLE tag is the only element in the HEAD section that is visible to the user. It is a required* element.

Figure 2.21 *The title of a Web page is generally shown in the title bar of the window.*

Creating a title

Each HTML page must have a title. A title should be short and descriptive. In some browsers, the title appears in the title bar of the window; in others, the title is centered at the top of the screen. The title is used in search indexes as well as in browsers' history lists and bookmarks.

To create a title:

1. Place the cursor between the opening and closing HEAD tags *(see page 38)*.

2. Type **<TITLE>**.

3. Enter the title of your web page.

4. Type **</TITLE>**.

✔ Tips

■ There must be one and only one TITLE tag in each HTML document.

■ A title cannot contain any formatting, images, or links to other pages.

■ Don't use colons or backslashes in your titles. These symbols cannot be used by some operating systems for file names, and if someone tries to save your page as text (or source HTML), they will have to remove the offending character manually.

■ It's a good idea to use a common element to begin each page's title. For example, you could begin each page with "XYZ Company -" followed by the specific area described on that page.

■ If your title has special characters like accents or foreign letters, you'll have to format these characters with their name or number codes. Consult *Special Symbols* on page 307 for more information.

Creating a title

Organizing the page

HTML provides for up to six levels of headers in your Web page. You will seldom have to use more than three. Since headers can be used to compile a table of contents of your Web pages, you should be as consistent as possible when applying them.

To use headers to organize your Web page:

1. In the BODY section of your HTML document, type **<Hn**, where *n* is a number from 1 to 6, depending on the level of header that you want to create.

2. If desired, to align the header, type **ALIGN=direction**, where *direction* is left, right, or center.

3. Type **>**.

4. Type the contents of the header.

5. Type **</Hn>** where *n* is the same number used in step 1.

✔ Tips

■ Think of your headers as chapter names—they are hierarchical dividers. Use them consistently.

■ Headers are formatted logically: the higher the level (the smaller the number), the more prominently the header will be displayed.

■ Add a named anchor to your headers so that you can create links directly to that header from a different web page *(see page 110)*.

■ You can use styles to format headers with a particular font, size, or color (or whatever). For details, consult *Applying styles locally* on page 223.

```
code.html
<!DOCTYPE HTML PUBLIC "-//W3C//DTD HTML 4.0
Transitional//EN"><HTML>
<HEAD>
<TITLE>Barcelona, Capital of Catalunya</TITLE>
</HEAD>
<BODY>
<H1>Home of the 1992 Summer Olympics</H1>


</BODY>
</HTML>
```

Figure 2.22 *Don't repeat the information from your title in the header. The header should help organize the information on the page in sections while the title summarizes that information.*

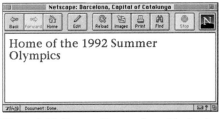

Figure 2.23 *Because Netscape has wider borders around its browser window, the header doesn't fit on one line.*

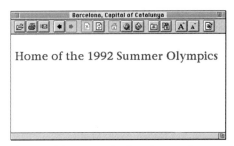

Figure 2.24 *Internet Explorer leaves a larger margin of blank space between the top of the page and the beginning of the text.*

```
code.html
<HEAD>
<TITLE>Barcelona, Capital of Catalunya</TITLE>
</HEAD>
<BODY>
<H1>Home of the 1992 Summer Olympics</H1>
Although Barcelona was transformed by the
renovation and construction projects
undertaken in preparation for the 1992
Summer Olympics, the city maintained its
cosmopolitan but friendly personality that
has enchanted visitors for more than one
thousand years.
<P>Mayor Pasqual Maragall gave the inaugural
address at the Opening Ceremonies by
offering a welcome in the four official
languages of the Summer Olympics: Catalan,
Spanish, English and French.

</BODY>
</HTML>
```

Figure 2.25 *Since headers include automatic line breaks, there is no pressing need to include a <P> before the first paragraph. You do need to insert a <P> before the second paragraph.*

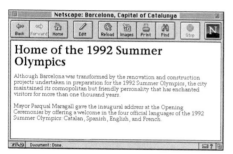

Figure 2.26 *The amount of space inserted with a <P> tag depends on the size of the text surrounding it. For more controlled spacing, see page 93.*

Figure 2.27 *Notice how the divisions from line to line are different from browser to browser (Netscape above, IE below). It is important to realize just what you can and cannot control.*

Starting a new paragraph

HTML does not recognize the returns that you enter in your text editor. To start a new paragraph in your Web page, you must use the P tag.

To begin a new paragraph:

1. Type **<P**.

2. If desired, to align the text in the paragraph, type **ALIGN=direction**, where *direction* is left, right, or center.

3. Type **>**.

4. Type the contents of the new paragraph.

5. If desired, you may type **</P>** to end the paragraph, but it is not necessary.

✔ Tips

■ The header (Hn) and horizontal rule (HR) tags include automatic paragraph markers, so you don't need to add a <P> to start a new paragraph after using them **(Figure 2.25)**. However, if you are using styles to format paragraphs, you will have to use the P tag to mark those paragraphs.

■ You can use styles to format paragraphs with a particular font, size, or color (or whatever). For more information, consult *Applying styles locally* on page 223.

■ The closing P tag *(see step 5)* comes in handy when you are trying to limit the effect of styles.

Creating a line break

When you start a new paragraph with the P tag (described on the previous page), most browsers insert a large amount of space. To begin a new line without so much space, use a line break.

The BR tag is perfect for poems or other short lines of text that should appear one after another without a lot of space in between.

To insert a line break:

Type **
** where the line break should occur. There is no closing BR tag.

✔ Tips

■ You can use special values with the BR tag for creating line breaks with text that is wrapped around images. For more information, consult *Stopping text wrap* on page 85.

■ Although you can now control spacing with much more precision thanks to style sheets *(see page 249)*, there are also some Netscape extensions for controlling the space between lines. For more information, consult *Creating indents* on page 93. You can also use a transparent image to create the proper amount of space between lines. For more information on this technique, consult *Using pixel shims* on page 97.

```
code.html
<HEAD>
<TITLE>Barcelona, Capital of Catalunya</TITLE>
</HEAD>
<BODY>
<H1>Home of the 1992 Summer Olympics</H1>
Although Barcelona was transformed by the
renovation and construction projects
undertaken in preparation for the 1992
Summer Olympics, the city maintained its
cosmopolitan but friendly personality that
has enchanted visitors for more than one
thousand years.
<P>Mayor Pasqual Maragall gave the inaugural
address at the Opening Ceremonies by
offering a welcome in the four official
languages of the Summer Olympics: Catalan,
Spanish, English and French. He said:
<P>Benvingut als Jocs Ol&#237;mpics de 1992
<BR>Bienvenido a los Juegos Ol&#237;mpicos
de 1992
<BR>Welcome to the 1992 Olympic Games
<BR>Bienvenu aux Jeux Olympiques de 1992
<P>And the crowd went wild. In lots more than
four languages.

</BODY>
</HTML>
```

Figure 2.28 *I've used a P tag to start the first line to set the group off from the remaining text. Then, each "welcome" is separated with a line break.*

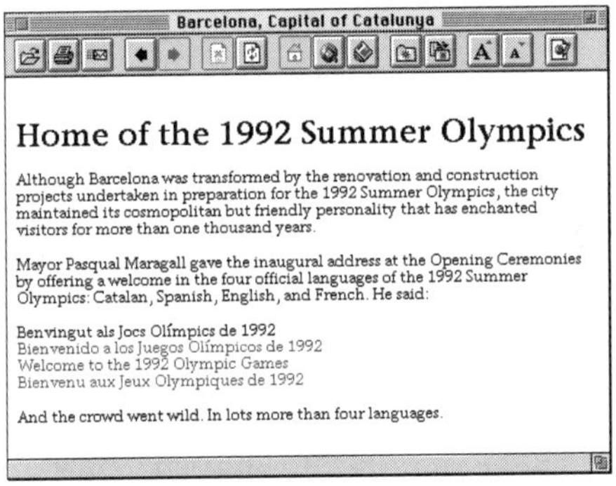

Home of the 1992 Summer Olympics

Although Barcelona was transformed by the renovation and construction projects undertaken in preparation for the 1992 Summer Olympics, the city maintained its cosmopolitan but friendly personality that has enchanted visitors for more than one thousand years.

Mayor Pasqual Maragall gave the inaugural address at the Opening Ceremonies by offering a welcome in the four official languages of the 1992 Summer Olympics: Catalan, Spanish, English, and French. He said:

Benvingut als Jocs Olímpics de 1992
Bienvenido a los Juegos Olímpicos de 1992
Welcome to the 1992 Olympic Games
Bienvenu aux Jeux Olympiques de 1992

And the crowd went wild. In lots more than four languages.

Figure 2.29 *I have to admit, I don't actually remember what Maragall said in French. Perhaps he was drowned out by the crowd and I didn't hear him...*

Creating a line break

Text Formatting

Formatting text in a Web page is much different from formatting text in any kind of desktop publishing program for one simple reason: you cannot completely control how your visitor will view the document. Some of your visitors may view your Web page with Netscape on the Mac while others may see it with Internet Explorer for Windows. Still others may use a non-graphical browser like Lynx. And some may use a hand-held device or even a TV. None of these "browsers" shows text formatting in exactly the same way.

With each revision of HTML, Web page designers get more and more control over text formatting. HTML 3.2 added several tags for changing the text's font, size, and color, among other things. And although having more control over text is nice, hand formatting each word or paragraph with its own tags and attributes can soon become very tedious.

With HTML 4 most of these tags and attributes have been deprecated in favor of style sheets that let you assign a group of characteristics to a paragraph in one fell swoop. Style sheets are wonderfully efficient and powerful.

But, to be honest, sometimes you don't need all that power. Despite the W3C's preference for style sheets, you still can choose to use local tags to apply font, colors, and size. These tags are described in detail in this chapter. If you decide to take the plunge into style sheets, consult Chapter 13, *Setting up Style Sheets*, beginning on page 223.

Text formatting

Changing the font

In order to make Web pages more universal, early versions of HTML did not allow the designer to specify a particular font. Since version 3.2, however, you can choose exactly what fonts you'd *prefer* to use. Of course, if the visitor does not have the desired fonts installed on their system, the text is rendered in the default font.

To change the font:

1. Before the text to be changed, type **<FONT FACE="fontname1**, where *fontname1* is your first choice of fonts. Type the complete name of the desired font, including the style.

2. If desired, type **, fontname2**, where *fontname2* is your second choice of fonts, should the user not have the first font in his system software. Each successive font should be separated from the previous one by a comma.

3. Repeat step 2 for each additional font choice.

4. Type **">** to complete the FONT tag.

5. Type the text that will be displayed in the given font.

6. Type **</FONT>**.

✔ Tips

■ The FONT tag is also used to change the size *(see page 47)* and the color *(see page 49)* of the text. You can combine all attributes in the same tag, e.g., **<FONT SIZE=10 FACE="Garamond Bold" COLOR="#121212">**.

■ While FONT is deprecated in HTML 4 *(see page 18)*, you can still use it. For information on using style sheets to control font usage (and to download fonts for your visitors), see page 234.

```
code.html
<TITLE>Using different fonts</TITLE>
</HEAD>
<BODY>
<FONT FACE="Lithos Black, Chicago">You can
change the font face</FONT> of just a few
letters.

<P><FONT FACE="New Century, Futura
ExtraBold">Or you can change the font face
for an entire sentence or paragraph</FONT>.

<P>If the user's browser doesn't have the
first font, it looks for the second. <FONT
FACE="Springfield, Extra Bold">If the
browser can't find any of the fonts listed,
it uses the font specified in the user's
preferences</FONT>.
</BODY>
</HTML>
```

Figure 3.1 *You may list as many fonts as you wish in each FONT tag in order of preference. Separate each choice with a comma and a space. Don't forget to add the desired style (Bold, Condensed, etc.).*

Figure 3.2 *Fonts give your page more personality. Note that only Lithos, in the first paragraph, and Futura ExtraBold—but not New Century— in the second paragraph, were available on this system. The last paragraph is displayed in the default font since neither of the special fonts chosen was available on the system.*

```
code.html
<HEAD><TITLE>Bold and Italic Text</TITLE>
</HEAD>
<BODY>
<P>Since most browsers understand <B>bold</B>
and <I>italic</I> text, sometimes it's more
predictable to use these markers instead of
the logical ones.

<P>In general, however, it's a good idea to
get into the habit of using logical
formatting.

</BODY>
</HTML>
```

Figure 3.3 *You may use bold or italic formatting anywhere in your HTML document, except in the TITLE.*

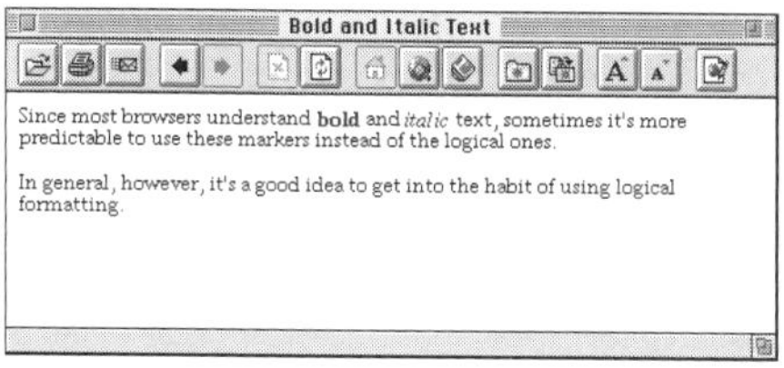

```
Bold and Italic Text
```
Since most browsers understand **bold** and *italic* text, sometimes it's more predictable to use these markers instead of the logical ones.

In general, however, it's a good idea to get into the habit of using logical formatting.

Figure 3.4 *In most browsers, the bold and italic formatting are identical to strong and emphatic formatting, respectively.*

Making text bold or italic

One way to make text stand out is to format it in bold face or italics.

To make text bold:

1. Type **<B>**.

2. Type the text that you want to make bold.

3. Type **</B>**.

To make text italic:

1. Type **<I>**.

2. Type the text that you want to make italic.

3. Type **</I>**.

✔ Tips

- You can also use the less common EM and STRONG tags to format text. These are logical formatting tags for "emphasizing" text or marking it as "strong". Generally, EM is displayed in italics and STRONG in bold. Both require opening (<EM>, <STRONG>) *and* closing tags (</EM>, </STRONG>).

- You may use CITE (the logical tag for marking citations) to make text italic, although it is less widely recognized and less widely used than the I tag.

- For more control over bold and italics, try style sheets. For details, consult *Creating italics* on page 236 and *Applying bold formatting* on page 237.

- The ADDRESS tag—old-fashioned but still legal HTML—also makes text italic, but is generally restricted to formatting the Web page designer's e-mail address.

Making text bold or italic

Choosing a default size for body text

You can select a size for all of the body text on your page with the BASEFONT tag. Then change individual sections or words with either the FONT tag or the BIG and SMALL tags.

To choose a default size for body text:

1. Type **<BASEFONT**.

2. Type **SIZE="n">** where *n* is a number from 1 to 7. The default is 3, which displays the font at the size the visitor has chosen in their browser's Fonts preferences dialog box.

✔ Tips

■ Use a slightly larger basefont in short web pages to give more importance to the whole page. Use a smaller basefont in lengthy text-intensive pages to fit more text on a page.

■ Only use one BASEFONT tag in each HTML document. The tag affects all the succeeding text. To change the font size of individual characters, use the FONT marker *(see page 47)*.

■ The BASEFONT tag has no effect on headers. Be careful, then, not to make the body text larger than the headers, or you'll confuse your readers.

■ The BASEFONT tag has been deprecated in HTML 4. To set the size of your text with style sheets, consult *Setting the font size* on page 238.

■ Some browsers support setting the default font and color with the BASE-FONT tag. Use the FACE and COLOR attributes as described on page 44 and page 50, respectively.

```
                    code.html
<BODY>
<BASEFONT SIZE="5">
<P>If you have a very short--and important-
-web page, you might want to raise the
basefont of the entire page.
<P>A value of three is the default and will
display the body text at the size specified
in the Preferences or Styles dialog box. You
may choose any value from 1 to 7.
<P><FONT SIZE="-3">You can use the &lt;FONT
SIZE="n"&gt; marker to change the font size
<EM>relative</EM> to the base font size.
</FONT>
<P>You should remember, however, that you
are messing with your user's preferences. If
she chose to display her body text at 12
points, it may annoy her to no end to have
you decide to show it to her at twice that
size.

</BODY>
```

Figure 3.5 *Don't choose a size that is too large to fit comfortably in your users' screens.*

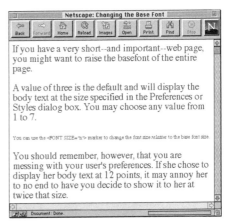

Figure 3.6 *You should have a good reason to change the default size for text. Remember that your visitors may have already chosen how they prefer to view text.*

```
                  code.html
<HTML>
<HEAD>
<TITLE>Creating a fisheye</TITLE>
</HEAD>
<BODY>
Notice that I have not used the BASEFONT
marker here, and so the base font size is set
at 3, by default.
<P>All you need to do to create a fisheye is
use change the font size for each letter
individually.<BR>
<FONT SIZE="+1">f</FONT>
<FONT SIZE="+2">i</FONT>
<FONT SIZE="+3">s</FONT>
<FONT SIZE="+4">h</FONT>
<FONT SIZE="+3">e</FONT>
<FONT SIZE="+2">y</FONT>
<FONT SIZE="+1">e</FONT>

<P>Here's another great effect:
<FONT SIZE="7">I</FONT>nitial
<FONT SIZE="7">C</FONT>aps
</BODY>
</HTML>
```

Figure 3.7 *The big differences between FONT and BASEFONT, as illustrated here, are that FONT can use relative values and depend on the BASEFONT value, and that it affects individual characters, instead of the entire page.*

Figure 3.8 *You can create some interesting effects by raising or lowering the font size of individual characters.*

Changing the text size

A particularly effective way of making your text stand out is to change the font size of a few characters or a few words.

To change the font size of one or more characters:

1. Type **<FONT**.

2. Type **SIZE="n">** where *n* is a number from 1 to 7. You may also use +*n* and -*n* to denote a value relative to the BASEFONT value *(see page 46)*.

3. Type the text whose font size you wish to change.

4. Type **</FONT>**.

✔ Tips

■ Use the FONT marker to change the font size of just a few characters or a few words. Use BASEFONT to change the font size of the whole document.

■ A value of 3 represents the size that the user has chosen for text in the Preferences dialog box or the default font size used by the browser.

■ You can make fisheye designs by changing the FONT size of each letter in a word in an ascending and then descending pattern.

■ The FONT tag is also used to change the color *(see page 50)* and typeface *(see page 44)* of individual letters.

■ The FONT tag has been deprecated in HTML 4. For more information on changing the size of text with style sheets, consult *Setting the font size* on page 238.

Using relative values to change text size

The BIG and SMALL tags change the relative size of a given word or phrase with respect to the surrounding text.

To change the font size relative to the rest of the text:

1. Type **<BIG>** or **<SMALL>** before the text that you wish to make bigger or smaller, respectively.

2. Type the text that should be bigger or smaller.

3. Type **</BIG>** or **</SMALL>** according to the tag used in step 1.

✔ Tip

■ Although the BIG and SMALL tags have not been deprecated in HTML 4, you may still want to use style sheets in order to have more control over the size of the text. For more information, consult *Setting the font size* on page 238.

```
                code.html
<HTML><HEAD><TITLE>Making text big and
small</TITLE></HEAD>
<BODY>
<H2>Growing and shrinking</H2>
Mosaic follows the HTML 3.0 standard for
increasing the font size of a page. Use the
BIG tag <BIG>to make things bigger</BIG> and
the SMALL tag <SMALL>to make things teeny
</SMALL>.
</BODY></HTML>
```

Figure 3.9 *The BIG and SMALL tags continue to form part of the standard HTML specifications.*

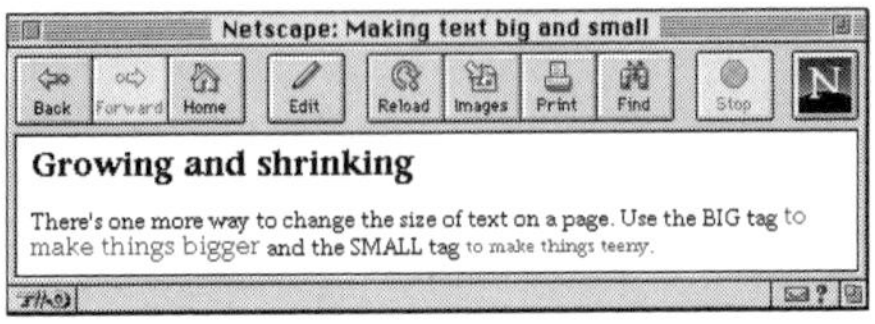

Netscape: Making text big and small

Growing and shrinking

There's one more way to change the size of text on a page. Use the BIG tag to make things bigger and the SMALL tag to make things teeny.

Figure 3.10 *In this example, the main text is displayed at the default size and the bigger and smaller text stand out nicely.*

```
                code.html
<HTML><HEAD><TITLE>Making text big and
small</TITLE></HEAD>
<BODY>
<BASEFONT SIZE=4>
<H2>Growing and shrinking</H2>
Mosaic follows the HTML 3.0 standard for
increasing the font size of a page. Use the
BIG tag <BIG>to make things bigger</BIG> and
the SMALL tag <SMALL>to make things teeny
</SMALL>.
</BODY></HTML>
```

Figure 3.11 *The only difference between this HTML document and the one shown in Figure 3.9 is the addition of the BASEFONT tag.*

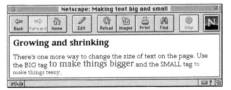

Netscape: Making text big and small

Growing and shrinking

There's one more way to change the size of text on the page. Use the BIG tag to make things bigger and the SMALL tag to make things teeny.

Figure 3.12 *With a BASEFONT of size 4, the BIG text is still bigger and the SMALL text is still smaller than the body text.*

```
                  code.html
<HTML>
<HEAD>
<TITLE>Creating Colored Text</TITLE>
</HEAD>
<BODY BGCOLOR="#000000" TEXT="#FFFFFF">
It's rather hard to demonstrate colored text
in a book with only two colors. Well, how
about white text on a colored background?
</BODY>
</HTML>
```

Figure 3.13 *Remember to select a text color that works well with your background color. (If you don't specify the background color, it will either be gray, by default, or the color the user chooses in the Preferences dialog box.)*

Figure 3.14 *Although this example is pretty basic, you can see that changing the color of your text can give your Web pages an immediate impact. You can see this page on the Web (see page 21).*

Choosing a default color for text

The TEXT attribute for the BODY tag lets you specify a default color for all of the text on the page. You can then change individual sections (or just a word or two) with the FONT tag *(see page 50).*

To choose a default color for text:

1. Inside the BODY marker, type **TEXT**.

2. Type **="#rrggbb"**, where *rrggbb* is the hexadecimal representation of the color.

Or type **="color"**, where color is one of the 16 predefined colors.

✔ Tips

■ The TEXT attribute lets you choose one color for all of the text. The FONT tag with the COLOR attribute *(see page 50)* lets you choose a color for individual letters or words and overrides the TEXT attribute.

■ See Appendix C and the inside back cover for a listing of hexadecimal values and common color representations.

■ Be sure to choose complementary colors for your background *(see page 102)* and links *(see page 123)* that work well with your body text color.

■ Check your page on a monochrome monitor before distributing it. What looks good in color may be impossible to read in grays.

■ The TEXT attribute is deprecated in HTML 4. For details on changing text color with styles, see page 241.

Changing the text color

A great way to make part of your page stand out is with color. You can change some of the text to one color and leave the rest in black. Or you can create a rainbow effect and really distract your readers.

To change the text color:

1. In front of the text whose color you wish to change, type **<FONT COLOR**.

2. Type **="#rrggbb"**, where *rrggbb* is the hexadecimal representation of the desired color.

Or type **="color"**, where color is one of the 16 predefined colors.

3. Type the final **>** of the FONT tag.

4. Type the text that you wish to color.

5. Type **</FONT>**.

✔ Tips

■ See Appendix C and the inside back cover for a listing of hexadecimal values and common colors.

■ Besides color, the FONT tag is also used to change the size *(see page 47)* and font *(see page 44)* of the text. You can change all three attributes at the same time: **<FONT SIZE=5 FACE= "Garamond" COLOR="red">**.

■ To change the color of all of the body text at once, use the TEXT attribute in the BODY tag *(see page 49)* or use style sheets *(see page 241)*.

■ The FONT/COLOR tag overrides colors specified with BODY/TEXT.

■ FONT is deprecated in HTML 4. For details on changing color with styles, consult *Setting the text color* on page 241.

```
code.html
<HTML>
<HEAD><TITLE>Changing the color</TITLE></
HEAD>

<BODY TEXT="blue">
<H1><FONT COLOR="red">Changing the color
</FONT></H1>
<P><FONT COLOR="#F1A60A">Changing font color
is cool. </FONT> <FONT COLOR="#F6E60A">You
can make your page look like a rainbow.
</FONT> <FONT COLOR="#71B30E">Of course if
you want people to actually read </FONT>
<FONT COLOR="#147CB5">what you've written,
you might be careful </FONT>
<FONT COLOR="#0D4284">about distracting with
strident color schemes.</FONT>

</BODY>
</HTML>
```

Figure 3.15 *You can use either a named color (as in the header) or a hexadecimal color (as in the paragraph) to choose a text color.*

Figure 3.16 *This text looks like a rainbow, with the header in red, and the paragraph in orange, yellow, green, blue, and violet. Really! You can see it on the Web site (see page 21).*

```
                code.html
<HTML><HEAD><TITLE>Using subscripts and
superscripts</TITLE></HEAD>
<BODY>
<H2>To the power</H2>
Use subscripts and superscripts to create
mathematical expressions like Pythagoras'
a<SUP>2</SUP> + b<SUP>2</SUP> = c<SUP>2
</SUP>, or for chemical expressions like
H<SUB>2</SUB>O.
</BODY>
<HTML>
```

Figure 3.17 *The opening SUP or SUB tag precedes the text to be affected.*

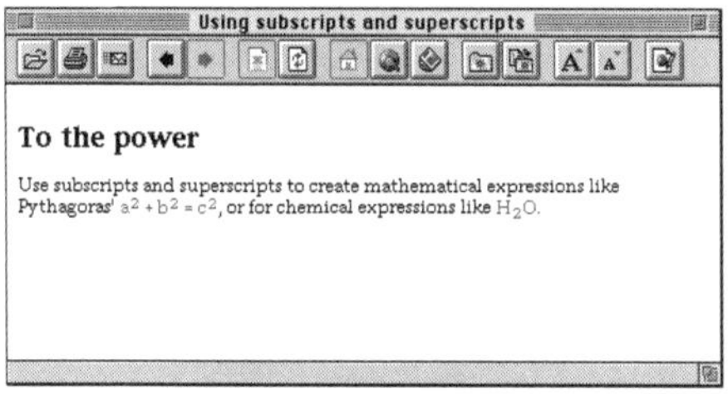

Figure 3.18 *Subscripts and superscripts are great for scientific texts and also for some foreign languages.*

Creating superscripts and subscripts

Letters or numbers that are raised or lowered slightly relative to the main body text are called superscripts and subscripts, respectively. HTML 4 includes tags for defining both kinds of offset text.

To create superscripts or subscripts:

1. Type **<SUB>** to create a subscript or **<SUP>** to create a superscript.

2. Type the characters or symbols that you wish to offset relative to the main text.

3. Type **</SUB>** or **</SUP>**, depending on what you used in step 1, to complete the offset text.

✔ Tip

■ Superscripts are the ideal way to format certain foreign language abbreviations like Mlle for *Mademoiselle* in French or 3^{a} for *Tercera* in Spanish.

Creating superscripts and subscripts

Using a monospaced font

If you are displaying computer codes, URLs, or other text that you wish to offset from the main page, you can format it with a monospaced font. There are several tags that are displayed with a monospaced font: CODE (computer code), KBD (keyboard input), SAMP (sample text) and TT (typewriter text).

To format text with a monospaced font:

1. Type **<CODE>**, **<KBD>**, **<SAMP>**, or **<TT>**.

2. Type the text that you want to display in a monospaced font.

3. Type **</CODE>**, **</KBD>**, **</SAMP>**, or **</TT>**. Use the marker that matches the code you chose in step 1.

✔ Tips

■ TT is the monospaced font marker that is used most often.

■ Remember that the monospaced font markers will not have a very dramatic effect in browsers that display all their text in monospaced fonts (like Lynx).

■ To format several lines of monospaced text, you should use the PRE marker *(see page 53)*.

```
code.html
<HTML>
<HEAD><TITLE>Using a Monospaced Font</TITLE>
</HEAD>
<BODY>

<P>Monospaced fonts are perfect for
offsetting text from the regular paragraph.
Perhaps you want to point out a command name,
or you want to use a separate font to show
the user what they should type.

<P>Here are some examples:
<P>Type <CODE>dir</CODE> to show a directory
listing of the contents of your PC.
<P>Type <KBD>Yes</KBD> at the prompt.
<P>Here is a <SAMP>sample of monospaced
text</SAMP>.
<P>Finally, the <TT>typewriter text</TT> is
the most commonly used monospaced font
marker. It's often used to simply highlight
important text, like the bold or italic
markers.

<P>Many users can choose the monospaced font
they wish to use for display in the
Preferences or Styles dialog box.

</BODY>
</HTML>
```

Figure 3.19 *There are several ways to format your text with a monospaced font. TT is the most common.*

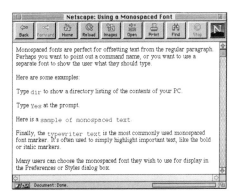

Figure 3.20 *Browsers display monospaced text in the font and size chosen for "fixed width" text in the Fonts Preferences dialog box.*

```
code.html
<HTML><HEAD><TITLE>Using preformatted text</
TITLE></HEAD>
<BODY>
<P>Here's a table that can be read with
<STRONG>ANY</STRONG> browser:
<PRE>
              Black Bears           Grizzlies
        Babies Adults Total   Babies Adults Total
Northampton   2      4     6        0      1     1
Becket        5     22    27        0      0     0
Worthington   7      5    12        2      1     3
</PRE></BODY></HTML>
```

Figure 3.21 *By using a monospaced font when writing your HTML code, you can see just how the preformatted text will appear.*

```
Using preformatted text
Here's a table that can be read with ANY browser:

              Black Bears          Grizzlies
        Babies Adults Total   Babies Adults Total
Northampton   2      4     6        0      1     1
Becket        5     22    27        0      0     0
Worthington   7      5    12        2      1     3
```

Figure 3.22 *Preformatted text is always displayed with a monospaced font.*

```
code.html
<HTML><HEAD><TITLE>Using preformatted text</
TITLE></HEAD>
<BODY>
<P>Here's a table that can be read with
<STRONG>ANY</STRONG> browser:
<PRE>
            <STRONG>Black Bears</STRONG>
<STRONG>Grizzlies</STRONG>
        Babies Adults Total   Babies Adults Total
Northampton   2      4     6        0      1     1
Becket        5     22    27        0      0     0
Worthington   7      5    12        2      1     3
</PRE></BODY></HTML>
```

Figure 3.23 *By using a monospaced font when writing your HTML code, you can see just how the preformatted text will appear.*

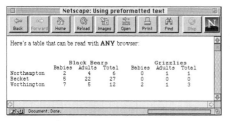

Figure 3.24 *Although the headers looked badly aligned in the HTML document (Figure 3.23), they look fine in the browser when the tags disappear.*

Using preformatted text

Usually, each browser decides where to divide each line of text, depending mostly on the window size, and eliminates extra spaces and returns. Preformatted text lets you maintain the original line breaks and spacing that you've inserted in the text. It is ideal for homemade tables and ASCII art.

To use preformatted text:

1. Type **<PRE>**.

2. Type the text that you wish to preformat, with all the necessary spaces, returns and line breaks.

3. Type **</PRE>**.

✔ Tips

■ Use a monospaced font in your text or HTML editor when composing the preformatted text so that you can see what it will look like in the browser.

■ You can insert additional formatting (like STRONG, for example) within preformatted text **(Figures 3.23 and 3.24)**. However, you should do it *after* you set up your text, since the tags take up space in the HTML document, but not in the page.

■ You can make homemade tables with preformatted text just by controlling the spaces between column entries. These tables will be readable by *all* browsers, not just the ones that currently support official tables.

Striking out or underlining text

A few browsers can display lines either through or under text. Strike out text is most useful to show revisions to text. Underlining is another way of emphasizing text.

To strike out or underline text:

1. Type **<STRIKE>** or **<U>** for strike out text and underlining, respectively.

2. Type the text that should appear with a line through or under it.

3. Type **</STRIKE>** or **</U>**.

✔ Tips

■ Both the STRIKE and U tags have been deprecated in HTML 4. There is also a shorthand S tag for STRIKE that has also been deprecated.

■ There are two new tags that are designed to strike out and underline text: DEL (for deleted) and INS (for inserted) respectively. At press time, however, only Explorer displays them correctly.

■ Although fonts and colors are letting some designers indicate links in different ways, most Web sites continue to use underlining to show links to other Web pages. You may confuse visitors by underlining text that does not bring them to a new page.

■ Lynx displays EM and STRONG text with an underline. Users may be confused by further underlining.

■ You can apply underlining, strike through, and even overlining with styles. For more details, consult *Underlining text* on page 246.

```
                code.html
<HTML>
<HEAD><TITLE>Putting Lines Through or Under
Your Text</TITLE>
</HEAD>
<BODY>
<P>Strike out text is often used by editors
to show revisions. On a web page, it might
be useful to emphasize a URL that has been
changed or removed.
<P>The URL <STRIKE>&lt;http://
www.somesite.com&gt;</STRIKE> has been
changed to <A
HREF="www.newsite.com">&lt;http://
www.newsite.com&gt;</A>

<P>Underlined text should be used sparing if
at all. It is too easy to confuse
<U>underlined</U> text with a link to <A
HREF="www.newsite.com/
underline.html">underlined</A> text. So easy
that some browsers don't recognize
underlined text.
</BODY>
</HTML>
```

Figure 3.25 *Note the use of < and > to produce the less than and greater than symbols as shown below.*

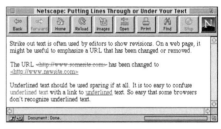

Figure 3.26 *Notice how confusing the underlined text can be, especially on a monochrome screen.*

```
┌─────────── code.html ───────────┐
│<HTML>                           │
│<HEAD>                           │
│<TITLE>Creating Blinking Text</TITLE>│
│</HEAD>                          │
│<BODY>                           │
│Blinking text is particularly useful when│
│used with an anchor. It particularly│
│attracts <A HREF="www.somesite.com/│
│mice.html"> <BLINK>mice</BLINK></A> and│
│other "pointing devices". Ooh. Doesn't it│
│just make you want to click on it?│
│</BODY>                          │
│</HTML>                          │
└─────────────────────────────────┘
```

Figure 3.27 *Although you can include an image in your blinking definition, so to speak, only the text will blink.*

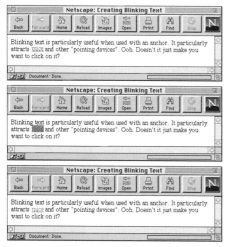

Figure 3.28 *Blinking text appears normal (top), then highlighted in a lighter shade (middle), and then normal again (bottom).*

Making text blink

Another way to make text stand out is to make it blink. You can apply the BLINK tag to anchors, links, or any important text that you have on the page.

To make text blink:

1. Type **<BLINK>**.

2. Type the text that you want to blink.

3. Type **</BLINK>**.

✔ Tips

■ You can include an image in your blinking definition, but it won't blink.

■ Blinking text is considered a bit gauche in the sophisticated world of Web design. You might want to be careful where and how much you use it.

■ Blinking text blinks in a slightly lighter shade of its normal color. A blinking URL that the user has not visited, for example, will blink in shades of blue, while normal text will blink in shades of gray.

■ You may not use blinking text in the TITLE.

■ Internet Explorer does not recognize the BLINK tag and probably never will. Could it be because the BLINK tag was one of the driving factors behind arch rival Netscape's rise to fame?

■ You can use styles to create blinking text. For more information, consult *Making text blink* on page 247.

Making text blink

Hiding text (Adding comments)

One diagnostic tool available to every HTML author is the addition of comments to your HTML documents to remind you (or future editors) what you were trying to achieve with your HTML tags.

These comments appear only in the HTML document when opened with a text or HTML editor. They will be completely invisible to visitors in the browser.

To add comments to your HTML page:

1. In your HTML document, where you wish to insert comments, type **<!--**.

2. Type the comments.

3. Type **-->** to complete the commented text.

✔ Tips

■ Comments are particularly useful for describing why you used a particular tag and what effect you were hoping to achieve.

■ Another good use for comments is to remind yourself (or future editors) to include, remove, or update certain sections.

■ View your commented page with a browser before publishing (see Chapter 18, *Publishing*) to avoid sharing your (possibly) private comments with your public.

■ Beware, however, of comments that are *too* private. While invisible in the browser, they cheerfully reappear when the user saves the page as HTML code (source).

```
code.html
<HEAD>
<TITLE>Barcelona, Capital of Catalunya</TITLE>
</HEAD>
<BODY>
<H1>Home of the 1992 Summer Olympics</H1>
<!--A little flowery, but I guess it will
do.-->Although Barcelona was transformed by
the renovation and construction projects
undertaken in preparation for the 1992
Summer Olympics, the city maintained its
cosmopolitan but friendly personality that
has enchanted visitors for more than one
thousand years.
<P>Mayor Pasqual Maragall gave the inaugural
address at the Opening Ceremonies by
offering a welcome in the four official
languages of the Summer Olympics: Catalan,
Spanish, English and French. He said:
<P>Benvingut als Jocs Ol&#237;mpics de 1992
<BR>Bienvenido a los Juegos Ol&#237;mpicos
de 1992
<BR>Welcome to the 1992 Olympic Games
<!--Find out if this is the correct French
translation-->
<BR>Bienvenu aux Jeux Olympiques de 1992
<P>And the crowd went wild. In lots more than
four languages.

</BODY>
</HTML>
```

Figure 3.29 *Comments are a great way to add reminders to your text. You can also use them to keep track of revisions.*

Figure 3.30 *The comments are completely invisible to the user when the page is viewed in a browser—unless she decides to download the source HTML.*

Creating Images

Figure 4.1 *Both of these images have exactly 18 colors and look about the same on high-end monitors. But notice how the* dither *image is full of noise and patterning (called dithering) while the* safe *image is clean and sharp. That's because the* safe *image uses browser safe colors and the* dither *image doesn't.*

Creating images for the Web is a bit different from creating images for output on paper. Although the basic characteristics of Web images and printable images are the same, five main factors distinguish them: format, color, transparency, speed, and animation.

Format

People who print images on paper don't have to worry about what their readers will use to look at the images. You do. The Web is accessed every day by millions of Macs, Windows-based PCs, Unix, and other kinds of computers. The graphics you use in your Web page should be in a format that each of these operating systems can recognize. Presently, the two most widely used formats on the Web are GIF and JPEG, with PNG gaining in popularity. Current versions of Explorer and Netscape can view all three image formats.

Color

Unlike printed images, Web images are usually viewed on a computer monitor. You knew that. But did you know that many monitors (called 8 bit) are limited to displaying 256 colors? Further, the system software and browsers reserve up to 40 colors for their own use. When displaying images on these monitors, browsers use a particular set of 216 colors (256 minus 40), often called the *browser safe palette*. If the images on your page contain more than 216 colors, or if they contain colors other than the 216 in the browser safe palette, the browser will try to combine existing colors to reproduce the missing ones (called *dithering*). The results are not always pretty **(Figure 4.1)**.

If all your visitors have 24-bit monitors, you don't have a problem. But if you want to make sure that images don't look terrible to visitors with 256-color monitors, you should restrict at least the large areas of your images to colors that belong to the browser safe palette. For details on creating images with the browser safe palette, see page 64.

Transparency

Transparency is important for two reasons. First, you can use it to create complex layouts by making one image move behind another. Second, you can take advantage of transparency to give an image a non-rectangular outline, adding visual interest to your pages **(Figure 4.2)**. Both GIF and PNG allow transparency; JPEG does not.

Speed

The fourth principal difference between Web images and printed images is that your visitors have to wait for Web images to download. (Imagine waiting for pictures to appear in your morning paper!)

How can you keep download time to a minimum? The easiest way is to use small images. The larger an image's physical size, the longer it takes to appear before your visitors' eyes. For tips on reducing your image's physical size, see page 60.

The second way to speed up download time is by compressing the image. There are three popular compression methods (that correspond to the three major formats): LZW (for GIF images), JPEG, and PNG. LZW is particularly effective for computer-generated art like logos, rendered text, and other images that have large areas of a single color. In fact, if you can reduce the number of colors in an image, LZW can often (but not always) compress the image even more. For more details on reducing colors, see page 67.

Figure 4.2 *The courthouse image's transparent background helps the image blend into the page, no matter what background color the visitor has chosen to view Web pages against. Real transparency is only available for GIF and PNG images.*

Figure 4.3 *Logotypes and other computer generated images or images with few colors are compressed efficiently with LZW and thus could be saved in GIF format. Even better at compressing images of this type is PNG format, though fewer browsers can view PNG images inline.*

Creating images

Figure 4.4 *Full-color photographs and other naturally created images, or images with more than 256 colors should be saved in JPEG format.*

JPEG, on the other hand, is better at compressing photographs and other images that have many different colors. In fact, if you blur an image, thereby creating even more colors, JPEG compression is often more effective *(see page 74)*.

Of course, each method has its drawbacks. Because LZW is patented, developers have to pay royalties on software that uses it. This is one of the principal reasons the PNG format was created. Further, GIF images are limited to 256 colors. JPEG also has two disadvantages. First, it is *lossy* compression—deciding that the eye cannot distinguish as many colors as are in your original image, it may eliminate them permanently to save space. Uncompressing the image will not restore the lost data. Second, its compression information takes up a lot of space and is simply not worth it for smaller images. For details on compressing images with JPEG, see pages 73–74.

PNG compresses better than LZW without losing information like JPEG. Its major drawback is that Microsoft and Netscape have been slow to adopt it. For details on creating PNG images, see page 76.

Another way to keep your visitors happy while they're waiting is to offer a sneak preview of what the image will look like. All three major formats offer some form of progressive display, often called *interlacing*. For details on progressively rendering images, consult pages 71, 73, and 76.

Animation

One thing you won't be seeing on paper anytime soon are moving images. On the Web, they're everywhere. For information on creating animated images, see page 72. Only GIF images can be animated.

Creating images

Making images smaller

Perhaps one of the most important improvements you can make to your page is to reduce the physical size of the images. This makes the images load more quickly and also helps visitors focus on what's really important.

To make images smaller by cropping:

1. Select the crop tool. (You may have to click the Selection tool to find it—or just press the letter C.)

2. Use the crop tool to outline the important area of your image.

3. If desired, adjust the area to be cropped by dragging the boxes around the selection border.

4. Double click in the center of the selection. The area around the selection disappears and all that's left is a lean, focused image.

✔ Tip

■ Cropping does not change the proportions of the image. It simply gets rid of the parts of the image that you (or your visitors) don't need.

Figure 4.5 *Choose the crop tool in the upper-left box of the tool palette. It may be necessary to click and hold a selection tool and then choose the crop tool from the pop-up menu.*

Figure 4.6 *Use the crop tool to select the area of the image that you want to keep. Then double click in the center of the selection.*

Figure 4.7 *This image is less than one third the size of the larger image and thus will load more than three times faster. In addition, it focuses the visitor's attention on what's important.*

Making images smaller

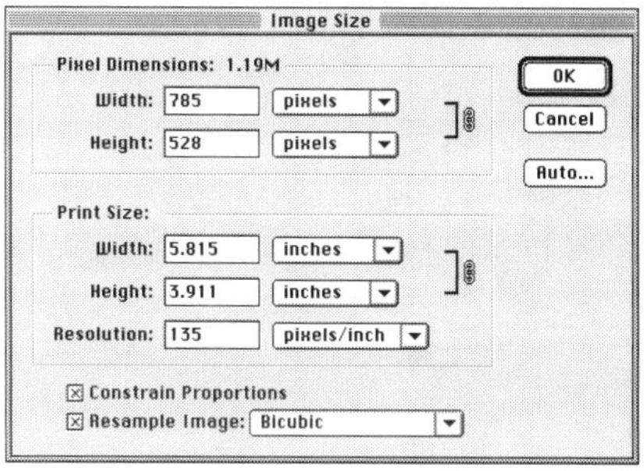

Figure 4.8 *Make sure both Constrain Proportions and Resample Image are both checked. Notice the original file size was 1.19 M!*

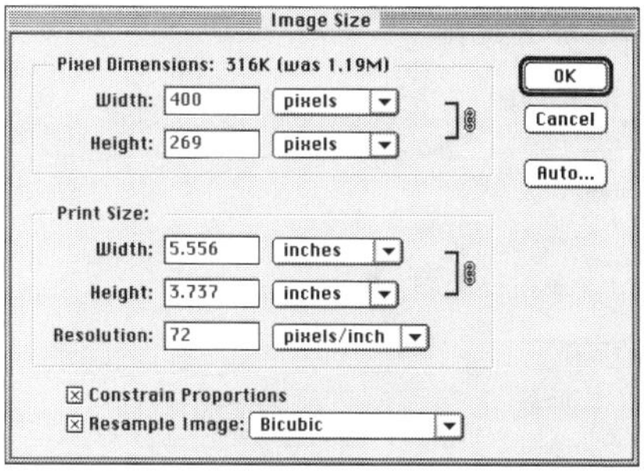

Figure 4.9 *Change the resolution to 72 and the width to 400 or less. The new file size is 316K, still huge, but much better.*

Figure 4.10 *Part of the original oversized image is shown at the top of this window. The new reduced image is shown in its entirety below.*

To make images smaller by changing the image size:

1. Choose Image > Image Size.

2. In the Image Size dialog box that appears, make sure the Constrain Proportions and Resample Image options are both checked **(Figure 4.8)**.

3. Make sure the resolution is set to 72 **(Figure 4.9)**.

4. Enter the desired final dimensions for the image.

5. Click OK. The image is resized.

✔ Tips

■ Adjusting the resolution automatically adjusts the width. If you want to create an image of a given width, adjust the resolution first and then type in the desired width.

■ Use these techniques to create icons or miniatures that point to oversized or external images *(see page 81)*. Just remember to save the icon with a different name so as not to replace the full size image.

Making images smaller

Exporting GIF images from Photoshop

Use the GIF format for logos, banners, and other computer generated images. GIF images are limited to 256 colors or less.

To export GIF images from Photoshop:

1. Create an RGB image at 72 dpi **(Figure 4.11)**.

2. Choose File > Export > GIF89a Export **(Figure 4.12)**. The GIF 89a Export dialog box appears.

3. If desired, click the Transparency Index Color box to choose how transparency will be displayed in your image. For details on creating transparency itself, see page 68.

4. If desired, choose an option in the Palette submenu or load a custom palette. For details, consult *Reducing the number of colors* on page 67.

5. If desired, click the Preview button to see how the image will appear given the palette and number of colors chosen in the previous step.

6. If desired, click the Interlaced option in the bottom left corner. For more information, consult *Interlacing GIF images* on page 71.

7. Click OK.

8. In the dialog box that appears, give the image a short name with the .gif extension **(Figure 4.14)**.

9. Click Save.

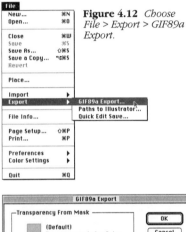

Figure 4.11 *Create an RGB image at 72 dpi. Since most monitors can't view images at higher resolutions, any higher value is just wasting bandwidth—and your visitors' time. And yes, that is a* quarter *moon.*

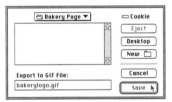

Figure 4.12 *Choose File > Export > GIF89a Export.*

Figure 4.13 *Choose the desired options in the GIF89a Export dialog box for transparency, color reduction, and interlacing.*

Figure 4.14 *Once you click OK in the GIF89a Export dialog box (Figure 4.13), the Save dialog box appears. Photoshop automatically appends the .gif extension to the name. If necessary, change the name and/or folder. Then click Save.*

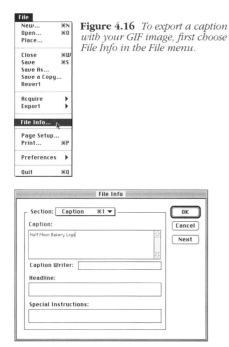

Figure 4.15 *If you have several layers in your document and only want to include some of them in the exported GIF, simply hide the unwanted ones before exporting. In this example, I've hidden the background to export just the main portion of the logo.*

Figure 4.16 *To export a caption with your GIF image, first choose File Info in the File menu.*

Figure 4.17 *Type a caption in the File Info dialog box. Then when you go to export the GIF, you'll be able to mark the Export Caption option.*

✔ Tips

■ Only the visible layers are exported. You can hide any layers that you don't want to be included in the GIF image **(Figure 4.15)**.

■ If GIF89a Export doesn't appear in your Export submenu, it's probably because you have an older version of Photoshop. For version 3.04 and later, you can download the GIF89a plug-in from Adobe (www.adobe.com). Or you can create GIF images by converting the document to Indexed-color, Grayscale, or Bitmap mode, and then saving the document in CompuServe GIF format.

■ By using the Export plug-in, you maintain the original (RGB) image as well as the new GIF image. You can return to the RGB image, modify it, and then export new GIFs as desired.

■ If your image is on a transparent layer, the Export plug-in automatically converts the transparent areas to transparency in the GIF image. For more information, consult *Creating transparency* on pages 68–69.

■ The fewer colors in your final image, the smaller it will be and the faster it will load. For details, consult *Reducing the number of colors* on page 67.

■ On the Mac, check the Export Caption option if you've added a caption to the File Info dialog box (using File > File Info) and you want to include that information with the GIF file for use with Fetch or other image cataloguing software **(Figures 4.16 and 4.17)**.

■ Since icons add to the size of your file, choose Never (under Image Previews) in the Preferences dialog box.

Using (mostly) browser safe colors

When browsers on an 8-bit monitor encounter images on a page with more than 216 colors, they automatically use a special set of colors called the *browser safe palette* to approximate the rest. The results are often less than stellar. On the other hand, if you limit yourself to 216 colors, it's hard to create soft, anti-aliased edges—which are crucial for text. A compromise is in order: browser safe colors for big areas, other colors for edges.

In order to pick browser safe colors for large areas, you'll have to load them into your Swatches palette.

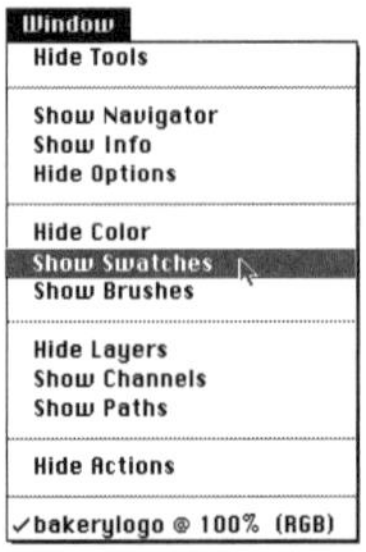

To load the browser safe palette:

1. Download the browser safe palette from the Web site *(see page 21)*.

2. Choose Window > Show Swatches to display the Swatches palette **(Figure 4.18)**. The Swatches palette appears **(Figure 4.19)**.

3. Choose Replace Swatches in the Swatches palette menu **(Figure 4.20)**.

4. In the dialog box that appears, select the palette you downloaded in step 1 and click Open **(Figure 4.21)**. The browser safe colors appear in the Swatches palette **(Figure 4.22)**.

✔ Tip

■ Choose Load Swatches in step 2 above if you prefer to *add* the browser safe colors without eliminating the existing colors in your palette.

Figure 4.18 *Choose Window > Show Swatches to display the Swatches palette on the screen.*

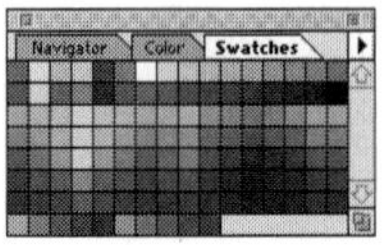

Figure 4.19 *This is the default Swatches palette. It's full of unsafe colors.*

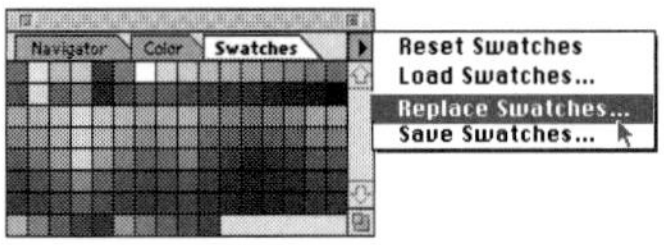

Figure 4.20 *Choose Replace Swatches from the submenu that comes off of that little arrow at the top-right corner of the Swatches palette.*

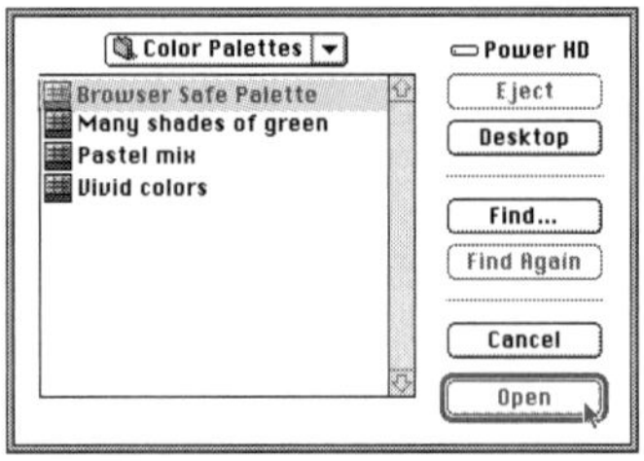

Figure 4.21 *Choose a browser safe palette and click Open. (You can find such a palette on the book's Web site—see page 21.)*

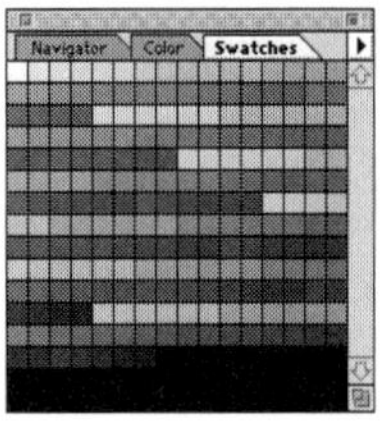

Figure 4.22 *The full set of 216 browser safe colors is displayed in the Swatches palette. You can choose any of these for the large areas of your Web images.*

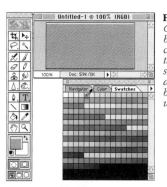

Figure 4.23 *Choose the background color from the browser safe palette and fill the background with it.*

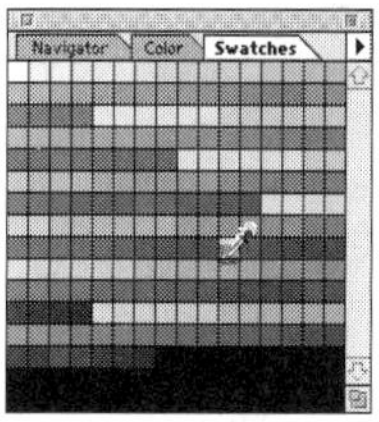

Figure 4.24 *Choose a foreground color for the text from the browser safe palette.*

Figure 4.25 *Choose the font, size, and other characteristics, type the desired text, and make sure you check the Anti-Aliased option.*

Figure 4.26 *Even though the edges are anti-aliased (and thus not browser safe) the text does not dither. It'd be perfect for a header if I cropped it a little better and wrote something useful.*

Although the example I show here is about text, you can use this technique to create any Web image. It'll look as good as possible on 8-bit monitors because most of the color is browser safe. And it'll look great on 24-bit monitors because the edges are smooth and anti-aliased.

To use (mostly) browser safe colors to create text:

1. Load the browser safe palette as described on the preceding page.

2. Create a new document in RGB mode.

3. If desired, choose a background color from the Swatches palette and fill the background with it **(Figure 4.23)**.

4. Choose a foreground color from the Swatches palette **(Figure 4.24)**.

5. Choose the type tool and click in the image where you wish to create the text. The Type Tool box appears.

6. Type the desired text and check the Anti-Aliased option **(Figure 4.25)**.

7. Click OK. The text appears in the image. Note that the body of the text (and of the background) is Web safe, while the colors used to create the smooth, anti-aliased edges are probably not.

8. Export the image to GIF as described on page 62.

✔ Tips

■ Really want to stick to Web safe colors? Don't use any anti-aliased tools, like Text, Selection, Feathering, etc.

■ Use this technique to create sharp looking headlines with unusual fonts.

Using (mostly) browser safe colors

Converting to browser safe colors

If you've already created all your images and want to make sure that they only use browser safe colors, you can load a browser safe palette and have Photoshop map the unsafe colors to the safe ones as best it sees fit.

Figure 4.27 *This is the original image, created with non browser safe colors.*

To convert to browser safe colors:

1. Download the browser safe palette from the Web site *(see page 21)*.

2. Choose File > Open to open an existing image.

3. If the image is not already in RGB mode, choose Image > Mode > RGB.

4. Choose Image > Mode > Indexed Color **(Figure 4.28)**. The Indexed Color dialog box appears **(Fig. 4.29)**.

5. In the Palette pop-up menu, choose Web. A value of 216 is automatically entered for the number of colors.

6. Click OK.

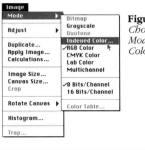

Figure 4.28 *Choose Image > Mode > Indexed Color.*

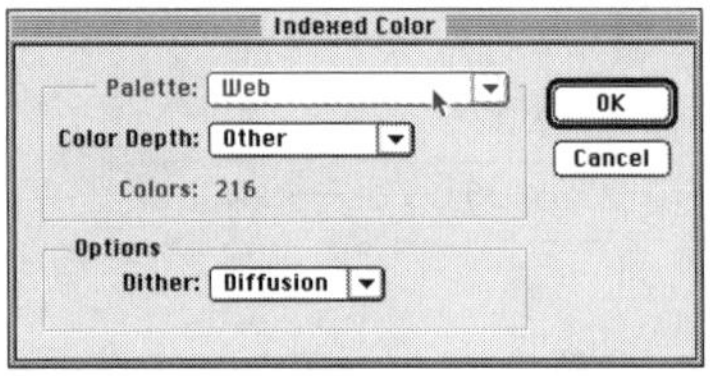

Figure 4.29 *In the Indexed Color dialog box, choose Web in the Palette menu. The Colors option will be set to 216 automatically.*

✔ Tips

■ Remember that the goal is for the visitor to see a clear, crisp image—not that the image use one set of colors or another. With that in mind, note that Photoshop may have to dither the browser safe colors to create the original ones. You may be better off just leaving the image the way it is—or creating it from scratch with browser safe colors.

■ You generally should not use this technique on photographs. Instead, use the Adaptive palette, or save them as JPEG images *(see page 73)*.

Figure 4.30 *The quality of the results depends on the colors you originally chose for the image. If Photoshop has to heavily dither browser safe colors to simulate the original ones, you may be better off not changing the colors at all.*

Figure 4.31 *Choose Adaptive for Palette and then enter the desired number of colors in the Colors box. Finally, click the Preview button to see how the illustration will look on the page.*

Figure 4.32 *With only eight colors, the dithering is very obvious. Click OK to go back to the GIF89a Export dialog box and try another value.*

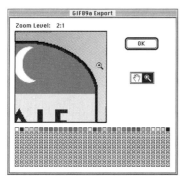

Figure 4.33 *A value of 32 considerably reduces the amount of colors—with minimal dithering.*

Reducing the number of colors

Whether or not you've decided to keep to browser safe colors, you can make compression more efficient by reducing the number of colors in your GIF images. And better compression means faster loading.

To reduce the number of colors in an image:

1. Open an RGB image with Photoshop.

2. Choose Export GIF89a in the Export submenu under the File menu.

3. Choose Adaptive in the Palette pop-up menu **(Figure 4.31)**.

4. Enter the desired number of colors in the Colors box.

5. Click Preview to see how the image will look with this number of colors **(Figures 4.32 and 4.33)**. Use the magnifying glass and the hand to examine the image carefully. Click OK to return to the main dialog box.

6. Repeat steps 4–5 until you find the least number of colors you can live with.

7. Click OK and save the document.

✔ Tips

■ If the image is already in indexed color and you wish to reduce the colors further, you have two choices. Either convert the document to RGB mode and then follow the steps above, or convert the image to RGB mode and then choose Image > Mode > Indexed Color and enter a smaller number of colors under Resolution in the dialog box that appears.

■ If you're going to save the image as JPEG, reducing the number of colors results in *larger* files *(see page 74).*

Reducing the number of colors

Creating transparency

With Photoshop's Export GIF89a plug-in, you can make any part of a GIF image transparent so that it blends almost seamlessly with the page. You can create your image on a transparent layer, make one or more colors transparent, or you can create an extra channel and make *it* transparent.

To make a layer transparent:

1. Open an RGB image in Photoshop.

2. Select the part of the image that you wish to export **(Figure 4.34)**.

3. Choose Copy in the Edit menu. Then choose Paste Layer **(Figure 4.35)**.

4. Hide or eliminate all layers except the transparent one **(Figure 4.36)**.

5. Continue from step 2 on page 62.

To make certain colors transparent:

1. Create or open an indexed-color image in Photoshop.

2. Choose GIF89a Export in the Export submenu in the File menu.

3. In the dialog box that appears, choose the eyedropper and click the color(s) in the image that you want to make transparent **(Figure 4.37)**. You can also click colors in the color table below the image. Hold down Option (Mac) or Alt (Windows) as you click to restore colors to their original state.

4. The transparent areas of the image are displayed in the color shown in the Transparency Index Color box. Click in the box to change the color.

5. Click OK and give the file a name.

Figure 4.34 *Select the part of the image that you wish to export as a GIF image.*

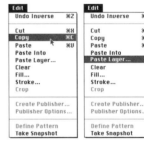

Figure 4.35 *Choose Copy in the Edit menu (left). Then choose Paste Layer in the Edit menu (right).*

Figure 4.36 *Hide all the layers except the transparent one by clicking on the eye icon to the left of the layer name. Note that transparency in Photoshop is displayed with a checkerboard (left).*

Figure 4.37 *If you export an indexed-color image, you can choose which colors should be transparent by clicking them with the eyedropper. Hold down Option (Mac) or Alt (Windows) to restore colors to their original state. (Note that the moon, because it is white like the background, is also made transparent.)*

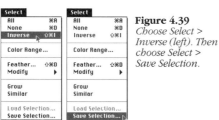

Figure 4.38 *Select the part of the image that you want to make transparent. In this example, the white background is selected but the white moon is not.*

Figure 4.39 *Choose Select > Inverse (left). Then choose Select > Save Selection.*

Figure 4.40 *In the Save Selection dialog box, choose New in the Channel menu and click OK.*

Figure 4.41 *Choose the desired channel in the Transparency From submenu. The transparent areas will be shown with the color chosen in the Transparency Index Color box. Notice that the moon will* not *be transparent, even though it is the same color as the rest of the transparent area (the background).*

Photoshop also lets you make certain areas transparent, regardless of their color. This is ideal for creating a transparent background without knocking out similar colors in the body of the image.

To make a selection transparent:

1. Create or open an indexed-color image in Photoshop.

2. Select the part of the image that you want to make transparent (**Fig. 4.38**).

3. Choose Select > Inverse (**Fig. 4.39**).

4. Choose Select > Save Selection (**Figure 4.39**).

5. In the Save Selection dialog box that appears, choose New from the Channel menu and click OK (**Figure 4.40**).

6. Deselect everything.

7. Choose Export GIF89a in the Export submenu under File.

8. In the dialog box that appears, choose the channel number in the Transparency From submenu (**Figure 4.41**). Press Option (Mac) or Alt (Windows) if you want to invert the selection.

9. Click OK and give the file a name.

✔ Tips

■ Any part of an image that you mark as transparent is replaced by the color specified in the Transparency Index Color box. This is one reason it's better to use the Export option and leave the original image intact.

■ To ensure that anti-aliased edges look good, make sure the image's original background color (now transparent) matches the page's background color.

Creating transparency

Creating fake transparency

Fake transparency means making the image's background the same color as the background of your page so that the image blends in as if the background were transparent.

To fake transparency by making the background a solid color:

1. Open the image in Photoshop, or another image editing program.

2. Use the lasso and other selection tools to select everything except the background **(Figure 4.42)**.

3. Select Inverse in the Selection menu to select only the background **(Figure 4.43)**.

4. Click the Background color control box to set it to the desired color.

5. Press Delete to change the color of the selected area (the background) to the current background color **(Figure 4.44)**.

6. Save the image.

✔ Tips

- Make sure you choose a browser safe color for the background. Otherwise, it will dither and look bad. For more details, consult *Using (mostly) browser safe colors* on page 64.

- You can also use this method to simulate transparency in JPEG images.

- This is also a good way to prepare images for programs that only allow you to make one color transparent.

- Of course, if your visitors override the background color, the effect is lost.

Figure 4.42 *Select the image itself, using the lasso or other selection tools.*

Figure 4.43 *Choose Select > Inverse to select everything but the image, that is, to select the background.*

Background color control

Figure 4.44 *Once you've inverted the selection, click the Background color control, choose the desired background color, and then press the Delete key to change the background to one solid color, in this case, white.*

Figure 4.45 *If you are exporting a GIF image from RGB mode, the Interlaced option will appear in the bottom-left corner of the GIF89a Export dialog box.*

Figure 4.46 *If the image was in indexed color, the Interlace option appears at the right in the center of the dialog box.*

Figure 4.47 *A browser will show the interlaced image gradually, allowing the visitor to move around the page and read the text while the image comes into full view.*

Interlacing GIF images

Interlacing an image prepares it so that a browser can show it at gradually increasing resolutions. Although the initial image is blurry, the visitor does not have to wait for the finished image to appear. Instead, the visitor can scroll around the page and then return when the image is complete.

To interlace an image:

1. Open the image in Photoshop.

2. Choose Export GIF89a in the Export submenu under the File menu.

3. Check the Interlaced option in the dialog box that appears. The box is slightly different for RGB **(Fig. 4.45)** vs. indexed-color images **(Fig. 4.46)**, but the effect is the same.

4. Click OK.

5. Enter a short name and extension in the dialog box that appears.

✔ Tip

■ For information on creating JPEG images that appear gradually, similar to the interlacing effect in GIF images, consult *Creating JPEG images* on page 73.

Interlacing GIF images

Creating animated GIFs

The GIF89a format can contain several images at once which, when viewed with a browser that supports animated GIFs, are displayed one after another. You can use this feature to create slide shows or to approximate moving images. Perhaps the best tool for creating animated GIFs on the Macintosh is GIFBuilder, a freeware program developed by Yves Piguet.

To create an animated GIF:

1. Create the series of images that will form the animated GIF (**Figure 4.48**). The images can be in Photoshop, PICT, or GIF format, among others.

2. Open GIFBuilder.

3. Select all the images and drag them to the GIFBuilder window. The images will appear in alphabetical order, by default (**Figure 4.49**). You can reorder them as necessary.

4. If desired, choose Animation > Start to see a preview of your animated GIF (**Figure 4.50**).

5. If desired, choose Loop in the Options menu to determine if the animation should play once, more than once, or continuously (Forever).

6. Add new images by choosing File > Add Frame.

7. Once you are satisfied with your animated GIF, choose File > Save.

8. In the Save dialog box, give the animated GIF a name, ending with the .gif extension, and click Save (**Figure 4.51**). The new conglomerated file looks just like a regular GIF (**Figure 4.52**).

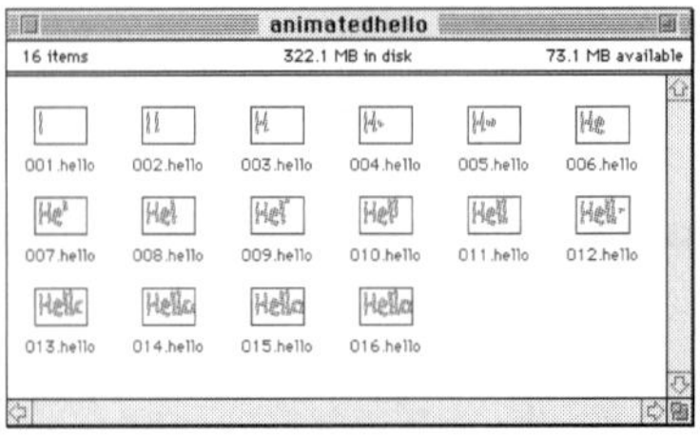

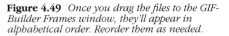

Figure 4.48 *Create the individual files in Photoshop, PICT, or GIF format. If you number them sequentially, they'll appear in order automatically in GIFBuilder.*

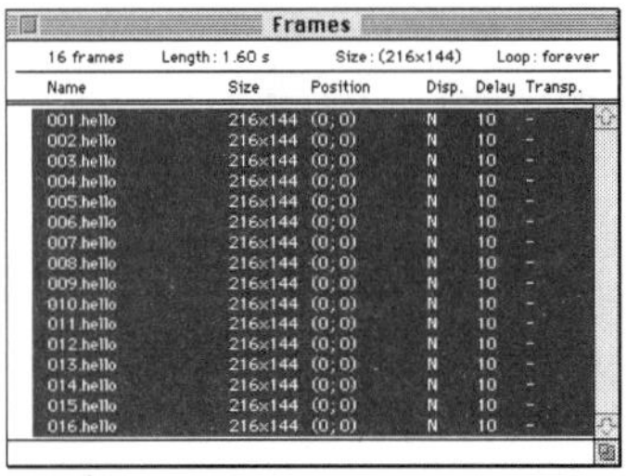

Figure 4.49 *Once you drag the files to the GIF-Builder Frames window, they'll appear in alphabetical order. Reorder them as needed.*

Figure 4.50 *Choose Animation > Start to test the animated GIF. The image appears in the Animation window. It's kind of hard to show in a book... (see page 21).*

Figure 4.51 *When you're satisfied with the animated GIF, choose Save in the File menu and then, in the Save dialog box, give the file a name, with the .gif extension. Click Save.*

Figure 4.52 *The resulting GIF image looks normal in the Finder, but it dances on any browser that recognizes the GIF89a format.*

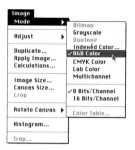

Figure 4.53 *In Photoshop, a JPEG image may be in either RGB Color or CMYK Color. However, since Web images are generally viewed on a monitor, you should use RGB mode.*

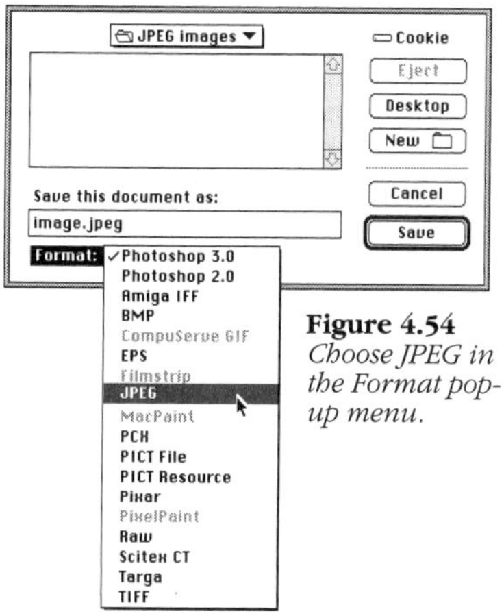

Figure 4.54 *Choose JPEG in the Format pop-up menu.*

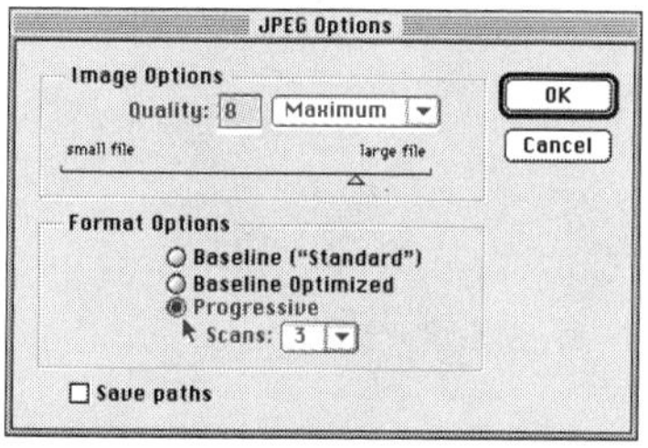

Figure 4.55 *Choose a compression quality (higher compression means less quality) and then a format option. I recommend always choosing Progressive since it always seems to result in a smaller file.*

Creating JPEG images

Use JPEG compression for photographs and for images with more than 256 colors.

To save an image with JPEG compression:

1. Open the image with Photoshop, or the desired image editing program.

2. Choose Image > Mode > RGB Color, if it's not already selected **(Figure 4.53)**.

3. Choose File > Save As.

4. In the Save As dialog box that appears, choose JPEG in the Format pop-up menu **(Figure 4.54)**.

5. Give the file a name and the .jpg or .jpeg extension, and then click Save.

6. In the JPEG Options dialog box that appears, choose the desired quality **(Figure 4.55)**.

7. If desired, choose Progressive to have the image appear gradually in the browser. You can also specify how many scans or passes it will take to display the full image.

8. Click OK.

✔ Tips

■ Because I've found that the Progressive option creates smaller images than the other options, I always choose that option when saving JPEG images—even when I don't care about progressive display.

■ You may want to experiment with different compression values until you get an image with sufficient quality at a file size you (and your visitors) can live with.

Blurring images to aid JPEG compression

Because of the way JPEG works, the softer the transition from color to color, the more efficiently the image can be compressed. So, if you blur the image slightly, you may be able to reduce the file size—and thus the load time—even further.

To blur images to aid JPEG compression:

1. Create or open the RGB image.

2. Choose Filter > Blur > Blur. The image is blurred slightly.

3. Save the image as JPEG as described on page 73.

✔ Tips

■ This is one of those cases in which a little goes a long way. You don't need to blur the image beyond recognition to get file size savings. Don't forget. You want your visitors to be able to recognize what's in the picture.

■ You have to decide if the slight loss of detail is worth faster download times and less waiting for your visitors. If all your visitors use 14K modems on 256-bit monitors, this technique may be very useful. Visitors with T1 lines on high-end systems, on the other hand, may not benefit enough from the speed improvement to make sacrificing image sharpness worthwhile.

Figure 4.56 *This is the original image. It has a file size of some 69K.*

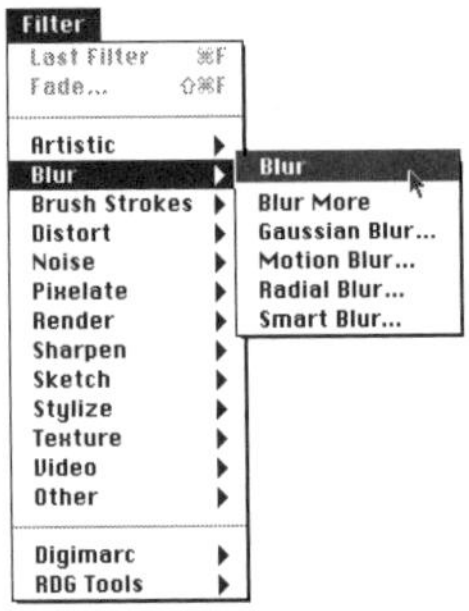

Figure 4.57 *Choose Filter > Blur > Blur to lessen the differences in the image from one area to another thereby making the compression more efficient.*

Figure 4.58 *Your visitors probably won't complain about the loss in sharpness (can you tell?) but they'll appreciate the fact that the image is now only 60K. (The image size given in the status area is the uncompressed size.)*

Figure 4.59 *Choose Image > Image Size.*

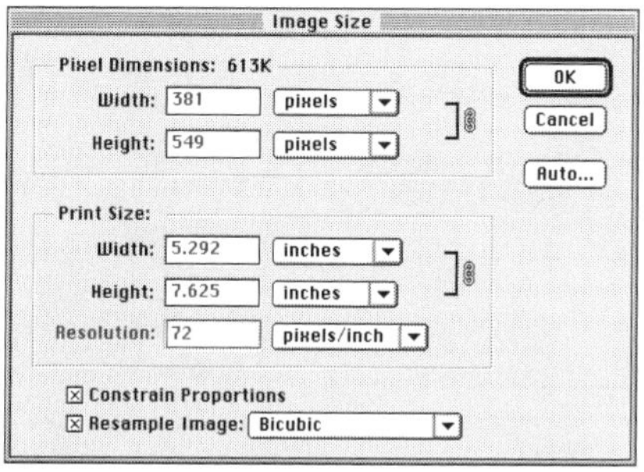

Figure 4.60 *Here you can see the original size and dimensions of the image we're going to create a low resolution version of.*

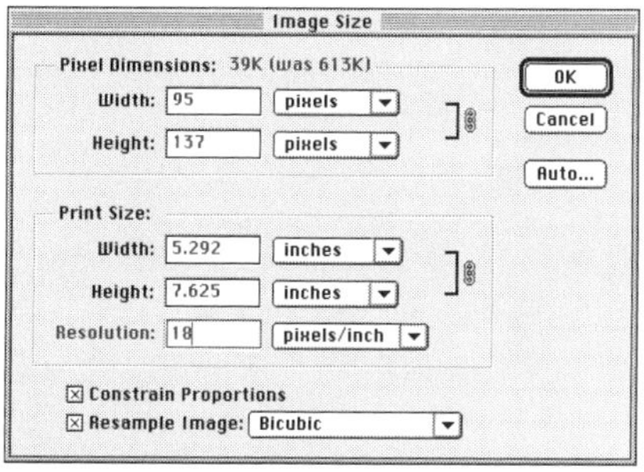

Figure 4.61 *With Constrain Proportions and Resample Image checked at the bottom of the dialog box, change the Resolution to 18. Notice that the file size shrinks to 39K but that the print dimensions remain the same.*

Creating low resolution images

If you have a lot of large images on your page, you can make life more pleasant for your visitor by creating a low resolution image that the browser can show immediately while it takes its time loading the higher resolution image.

To create a low resolution version of your image:

1. Open your image in Photoshop, or other image editing program.

2. Choose Image > Image Size **(Figure 4.59)**.

3. Check Constrain Proportions and Resample Image at the bottom of the Image Size dialog box. **(Figure 4.60)**.

4. Change the value of Resolution to 18 dpi and click OK **(Figure 4.61)**.

5. Choose File > Save As and give the low resolution image a new name.

6. Click Save.

✔ Tips

■ There is no difference between creating a low resolution image and changing the size of the image using the Width and Height fields *(see page 61)*. Changing an image's size by changing its resolution is just an easy way to reduce it evenly to half or a quarter of its original size.

■ When you insert a low resolution image on your page, you must use the WIDTH and HEIGHT attributes to specify the dimensions of *the original image* or else both the versions will appear in miniature. For more details, see page 82.

Creating PNG files

Although GIF is the most popular image format on the Web today, the W3C hopes that tomorrow everyone will be inserting PNG images on their pages. PNG (pronounced *ping*) has many advantages over GIF, not least among them the fact that its compression scheme is not patented and thus software developers can implement it for free. It also compresses more effectively than GIF, is not lossy, and allows partial transparency. Its major disadvantage is that it is relatively unknown and the major browsers have taken a while to support it. In fact, while current versions of both Explorer and Communicator view PNG images inline, they still don't support all its features.

To create a PNG image:

1. Create an RGB image.

2. Choose File > Save As **(Figure 4.62)**.

3. In the dialog box that appears, choose PNG in the Format pop-up menu and click Save **(Figure 4.63)**. The PNG Options dialog box appears.

4. If desired, choose Adam 7 to create an interlaced image **(Figure 4.64)**.

5. Click OK.

✔ Tips

■ Unfortunately, Adobe has not yet made available information about the filters offered in the PNG Options dialog box. They are for choosing different compression methods.

■ You can get more information about the PNG format on the PNG home page: *http://www.cdrom.com/pub/png/png.html*.

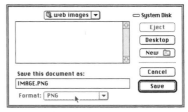

Figure 4.62 *Choose File > Save As.*

Figure 4.63 *Give the file a name and choose PNG in the Format pop-up menu. Then click Save.*

Figure 4.64 *Choose Adam 7 under Interlace to have the PNG appear gradually in your visitors' browsers.*

Creating PNG files

Using Images

Figure 5.1 *There's little on this nicely designed page besides images. Notice that even most of the text is actually GIF images. (Only real text is shown in black here.)*

Once you've created the fastest-loading, hottest-looking images you can—perhaps using the techniques in the previous chapter—you're ready to get back to HTML and get those images on your page.

Inserting images on a page

You can place all kinds of images on your Web page, from logos to photographs. Images placed as described here appear automatically when the visitor jumps to your page, as long as the browser is set up to view them.

To insert an image on a page:

1. Place the cursor where you want the image to appear.

2. Type **<IMG SRC="image.ext"** where *image.ext* indicates the location of the image file on the server.

3. If desired, type **BORDER=n**, where *n* is the thickness of the border in pixels.

4. Type the final **>**.

✔ Tips

■ Add a <P> or <BR> before an image definition to start it on its own line.

■ For information on creating images especially for Web pages, consult Chapter 4, *Creating Images.*

■ Use this technique to place GIF, JPEG, PNG, or any other kind of images that the browser recognizes.

■ Don't expect your visitors to wait more than 30 seconds to load and view your page (about 30K total with a 14.4 Kbps modem connection). To get by this limit, create miniatures *(see page 61)* of large images and let visitors choose to view the larger images *(see page 81)* only if desired.

■ You can't change the border color.

■ Images used in a link *(see page 118)* automatically have a thin, blue border. Use BORDER=0 to eliminate it.

```
                    code.html
<HTML>
<HEAD><TITLE>Inserting an Inline Image</
TITLE>
</HEAD>
<H1>Cookie and Woody</H1>
<P>Generally considered the sweetest and yet
most independent cats in the Pioneer Valley,
Cookie and Woody are consistently
underestimated by their humble humans.
Here's Cookie and Woody, exhausted after
helping us pack the last time we moved:
<P><IMG SRC="catsonbox.gif">
</BODY>
</HTML>
```

Figure 5.2 *It's a good idea to enclose the name of the image file within quotation marks, although, if the name contains only letters and numbers and one period, it's not necessary.*

Figure 5.3 *Images are aligned to the left side of the page, by default. To wrap text around an image, use the align attributes (see pages 83 and 84).*

```
                code.html
<HTML>
<HEAD><TITLE>Providing alternate text</
TITLE>
</HEAD>
<H1>Cookie and Woody</H1>
<P>Generally considered the sweetest and yet
most independent cats in the Pioneer Valley,
Cookie and Woody are consistently
underestimated by their humble humans.
Here's Cookie and Woody, exhausted after
helping us pack the last time we moved:
<P><IMG SRC="catsonbox.gif" ALT="Image of
Cookie and Woody sleeping on a box">
</BODY>
```

Figure 5.4 *If your alternate text contains one or more spaces, you must enclose it in quotation marks.*

Figure 5.5 *The alternate text will appear if the image cannot be found, if the visitor has deselected Autoload images, or if the browser does not support images.*

Figure 5.6 *On Windows machines, when the visitor points at an image with alternate text, the alternate text appears in a tool tip. This is a great way to give your visitors extra information about an image.*

Offering alternate text

Some browsers do not support images at all. Other browsers support them but the visitor may have such a slow connection that they choose not to view the images, or to load them in manually. You can create text that will appear if the image, for whatever reason, does not.

To offer alternate text when images don't appear:

1. Place the cursor where you want the image (or alternate text) to appear.

2. Type **<IMG SRC="image.ext"**, where *image.ext* is the location of the image on the server.

3. Type **ALT="**.

4. Type the text that should appear if, for some reason, the image itself does not.

5. Type **">**.

✔ Tips

■ On Windows, the text specified with the ALT tag is also used as a *tool tip*. In other words, when the visitor points at the image with the pointer, the ALT text appears **(Figure 5.6)**.

■ HTML 4 considers ALT a *required* attribute. Nevertheless, if you do forget ALT once or twice, you will not be struck with lightning. I don't think.

■ If the image is just for formatting, like a horizontal line or a bullet image, the W3C suggests you use **ALT=""**.

■ Some browsers, like Lynx, that do not support images, are used by the blind because they can read the contents of the ALT tag out loud. This is just one more reason to add alternate text to your images.

Specifying size for speedier viewing

When a browser gets to the HTML code for an image, it must load the image to see how big it is and how much space must be reserved for it. If you specify the image's dimensions, the browser can fill in the text around the image as the image loads, so that your visitors can read the page without having to wait for the images.

To specify the size of your image:

1. Open the image in Photoshop, or other image editing program.

2. Choose Image > Image Size.

3. Choose pixels for the unit of measure in both the Width and Height pop-up menus **(Figure 5.7)**.

4. Write down the values shown in the Width and Height text boxes.

5. In your HTML document where you wish the image to appear, type **<IMG SRC="image.location"**, where *image.location* is the location of the image on the server.

6. Type **WIDTH=x HEIGHT=y**, using the values you jotted down in step 4 to specify the values for *x* and *y* (the width and height of your image) in pixels. For more information on using WIDTH and HEIGHT to scale images consult *Scaling an image* on page 87.

7. Add other image attributes as desired and then type the final **>**.

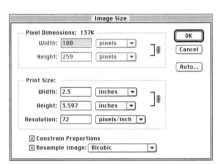

Figure 5.7 *Select pixels in the Width and Height pop-up menus and write down the values shown (in this example, 180 and 259).*

```
code.html
<H1>The Four Sisters</H1>
<P>The Four Sisters Corporaton was begun by
the previously unknown four sisters. Here's
a rare photo:
<P><IMG SRC="4sis72small.jpeg" WIDTH=180
HEIGHT=259 ALT="The Four Sisters">
<P>Beatrice, the oldest sister, shown here
on the left, is the Art Director for TFS .
She joined the corporation in 1960 and has
been one of its most ardent supporters.
Jocelyn, shown here kneeling is the
corporation's Director of Education and
```

Figure 5.8 *If you specify the exact height and width values in pixels, the browser won't have to spend time doing it and will display the image more quickly.*

Figure 5.9 *Notice that the second paragraph of text is displayed even though the image has not finished loading. This means your visitor will have something to do while they're waiting.*

```
code.html
<HTML><HEAD><TITLE>Using an icon linked to a
larger image</TITLE></HEAD><BODY>
<H1>Cookie and Woody</H1>
<P>Generally considered the sweetest and yet
most independent cats in the Pioneer Valley,
Cookie and Woody are consistently
underestimated by their humble humans.
Here's Cookie and Woody, exhausted after
helping us pack the last time we moved:
<P><A HREF="catsonbox.gif">
<IMG SRC="catsonbox.icon.gif" ALT="Image of
Cookie and Woody sleeping on a box">The full
image is 56K.</A>
</BODY>
</HTML>
```

Figure 5.10 *Remember to use the full size image in the link and the icon in the image definition.*

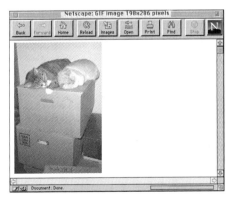

Figure 5.11 *In this example, the icon is 2K and takes 2 seconds to load. The visitor can choose to view the larger image (by clicking the icon) or to continue reading the page.*

Figure 5.12 *If the visitor clicks the icon, the browser opens a new window with the full size image.*

Linking icons to external images

If you have a particularly large image, you can create a miniature version or icon of it *(see page 61)* that displays quickly on the page and then add a link that leads the visitor to the full size image.

To link a small icon to your larger image:

1. Place the cursor in your HTML page where you wish the icon to be placed.

2. Type **<A HREF="image.location">**, where *image.location* is the location of the full sized image on your server.

3. Type **<IMG SRC="icon.location"**, where *icon.location* is the location of your icon on the server.

4. If desired, type **ALT="alternate text"**, where *alternate text* is the text that should appear if, for some reason, the icon does not.

5. Type the final **>** of the icon definition.

6. Type the label text that you wish to accompany the icon. It's a good idea to include the actual size in K of the full sized image so the visitor knows what they're getting into by clicking it.

7. Type **</A>** to complete the link to the full sized image.

✔ Tips

■ Using miniatures is an ideal way to get a lot of graphic information on a page without making your visitors wait too long to see it. Then they can view the images that they are most interested in at their leisure.

■ For more on links, see page 107.

Linking icons to external images

Using low resolution images

You can reference both high and low resolution versions of your image so that the low resolution image loads quickly and keeps the visitor's interest while the high resolution version wows your visitors, once it loads in.

To use a low resolution version of an image:

1. Create a low resolution version of your image *(see page 75)*.

2. Place the cursor where you want the full resolution image to appear.

3. Type **<IMG SRC="image.gif"**, where *image.gif* is the location on the server of the high resolution image.

4. Type **LOWSRC="imagelow.gif"**, where *imagelow.gif* is the location on the server of the low resolution image.

5. Type **HEIGHT=x WIDTH=y**, where *x* and *y* are the height and width in pixels, respectively of the original image. If you do not specify these values, browsers use the size of the low resolution image for both images.

6. If desired, type **ALT="substitute text"**, where *substitute text* is the text that will appear if the visitor can't view images with their browser.

7. Type the final **>**.

✔ Tips

- LOWSRC is not standard HTML, but both major browsers recognize it.

- There's no law that says LOWSRC has to be the same image as SRC. You can set it to some other image for a special semi-animated effect.

```
code.html
<HTML>
<HEAD><TITLE>Using a low resolution image to
speed up viewing</TITLE>
</HEAD>
<H1>The Four Sisters</H1>
<P>The Four Sisters Corporaton was begun by
the previously unknown four sisters. Here's
a rare photo:
<P><IMG SRC="4sis72.jpeg"
LOWSRC="4sis18.jpeg" WIDTH=381 HEIGHT=549
ALT="The Four Sisters">
</BODY>
</HTML>
```

Figure 5.13 *The HEIGHT and WIDTH attributes are discussed on page 80. They are necessary here to show both images at the proper size.*

Figure 5.14 *The low resolution image is replaced gradually by the higher resolution image. The callout line marks the division between the two. The status information in the lower left corner shows how much more time it will take to finish loading the high resolution image. Without the lower resolution image, the visitor would have to wait all that time before seeing anything.*

```
code.html
<HTML><HEAD><TITLE>Wrapping text around
images</TITLE></HEAD><BODY>
<IMG SRC="house.gif" ALIGN=right>
<H1>The Pioneer Valley: Northampton</H1>
This triplex on South Street is a good
example of multi-family dwellings in the
area. Built as a one family home in the 30s,
it has been converted to a three family with
separate entrances, heating and electricity.
Thanks to the area colleges, Northampton has
a booming rental industry.
</BODY>
</HTML>
```

Figure 5.15 *When you align an image to the right, you are actually wrapping text to the left (and vice versa).*

Figure 5.16 *The image is aligned to the right and the text wraps around it.*

```
code.html
<HTML><HEAD><TITLE>Wrapping text on right
side</TITLE></HEAD><BODY>
<IMG SRC="house.gif" ALIGN=left>
<H1>The Pioneer Valley: Northampton</H1>
This triplex on South Street is a good
example of multi-family dwellings in the
area. Built as a one family home in the 30s,
```

Figure 5.17 *To make the image appear on the left with the text wrapped around the right side, use ALIGN=left.*

Figure 5.18 *With the image on the left, the text wraps around on the right side.*

Wrapping text around images

You can use the ALIGN attribute (with the *left* and *right* variables only) to wrap text around an image.

To wrap text around one side of an image:

1. Type **<IMG SRC="image.location"** where *image.location* indicates the location of the image on the server.

2. *Either* type **ALIGN=left** to align the image to the left of the screen while the text flows to the right *or* type **ALIGN=right** to align the image to the right edge of the screen while the text flows on the left side of the image.

3. Add other image attributes, as described in other parts of this chapter, if desired.

4. Type the final **>**.

5. Type the text that should flow next to the image.

✔ Tips

■ Don't get confused about right and left. When you choose **ALIGN=right**, it's the *image* that goes to the right (while the text goes to the left). When you choose **ALIGN=left**, again, the image will be on the left side with the text flowing around the right side.

■ The ALIGN attribute is deprecated in HTML 4. For details on using styles to wrap text, consult *Wrapping text around elements* on page 259.

■ Why use ALIGN for wrapping text? I don't know. Personally, I'd prefer a WRAP attribute, but it doesn't exist. For more on ALIGN, see page 88.

To wrap text between two images:

1. Type **<IMG SRC="right.image" ALIGN=right>** where *right.image* indicates the location on the server of the image that should appear on the right side of the screen.

2. Type the text that should flow around the first image.

3. Type **<IMG SRC="left.image" ALIGN=left>** where *left.image* indicates the location on the server of the image that should appear on the left side of the screen.

4. If desired, type **<P>** to begin a new paragraph, that will be aligned with the image placed in step 3.

5. Type the text that should flow around the second image.

✔ Tips

- The key is to place each image *directly before* the text it should "disrupt."

- Each image will continue to push the text to one side until it either encounters a break *(see page 85)* or until there is no more text.

- Notice that in this example one of the images has a transparent background and one doesn't. You can mix all types of images on a page. For more information on creating transparency, see page 68.

- The ALIGN attribute is deprecated in HTML 4 in favor of style sheets. Styles let you control text wrap in all your images with just one step. For more information, consult *Wrapping text around elements* on page 259.

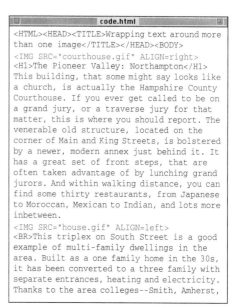

```
code.html
<HTML><HEAD><TITLE>Wrapping text around more
than one image</TITLE></HEAD><BODY>
<IMG SRC="courthouse.gif" ALIGN=right>
<H1>The Pioneer Valley: Northampton</H1>
This building, that some might say looks like
a church, is actually the Hampshire County
Courthouse. If you ever get called to be on
a grand jury, or a traverse jury for that
matter, this is where you should report. The
venerable old structure, located on the
corner of Main and King Streets, is bolstered
by a newer, modern annex just behind it. It
has a great set of front steps, that are
often taken advantage of by lunching grand
jurors. And within walking distance, you can
find some thirty restaurants, from Japanese
to Moroccan, Mexican to Indian, and lots more
inbetween.
<IMG SRC="house.gif" ALIGN=left>
<BR>This triplex on South Street is a good
example of multi-family dwellings in the
area. Built as a one family home in the 30s,
it has been converted to a three family with
separate entrances, heating and electricity.
Thanks to the area colleges--Smith, Amherst,
```

Figure 5.19 *The image always precedes the text that should flow around it.*

Figure 5.20 *The first image is aligned to the right and the text flows to its left. The next image appears after the last line of text in the preceding paragraph and pushes the following paragraph to the right.*

Wrapping text around images

```
        code.html
<HTML><HEAD><TITLE>Stopping Text Wrap</
TITLE></HEAD><BODY>
<IMG SRC="house.gif" ALIGN=right>
<H1>The Pioneer Valley: Northampton</H1>
<IMG SRC="wraplogo2.gif" ALIGN=left>
<BR CLEAR=left>
This triplex on South Street is a good
example of multi-family dwellings in the
```

Figure 5.21 *Notice the order: first comes the image of the house, then the header, then the logo, then the text.*

Figure 5.22 *The Clear=left attribute makes the text stop flowing until it reaches an empty left margin (that is, below the bottom of the left-aligned flower).*

```
        code.html
<HTML><HEAD><TITLE>Wrapping text around
images</TITLE></HEAD><BODY>
<IMG SRC="house.gif" ALIGN=right>
<H1>The Pioneer Valley: Northampton</H1>
<IMG SRC="wraplogo2.gif" ALIGN=left>
<BR CLEAR=all>
This triplex on South Street is a good
example of multi-family dwellings in the
```

Figure 5.23 *The order is the same as in the last example; only the CLEAR attribute has changed.*

Figure 5.24 *The CLEAR=all code stops the flow of text until all images have been passed.*

Stopping text wrap

A wrapped image affects all the text that follows it, unless you insert a special line break. The CLEAR attribute added to the regular BR tag indicates that the text should not begin until the specified margin is clear (that is, at the end of the image or images).

To stop the text from wrapping:

1. Create your image and the text *(see pages 83 and 84).*

2. Place the cursor where you want to stop wrapping text to the side of the image.

3. *Either* type **<BR CLEAR=left>** to stop flowing text until there are no more images aligned to the left margin.

Or type **<BR CLEAR=right>** to stop flowing text until there are no more images aligned to the right margin.

Or type **<BR CLEAR=all>** to stop flowing text until there are no more images on either margin.

✔ Tip

■ The CLEAR attribute is deprecated in HTML 4 in favor of style sheets. For information on using styles to control the text flow, consult *Stopping text wrap* on page 260.

Stopping text wrap

Adding space around an image

Look carefully at the image in Figure 5.25. If you don't want your text butting right up to the image, you can use the VSPACE and HSPACE attributes to add a buffer around your image.

To add space around an image:

1. Type **<IMG SRC="image.location"** where *image.location* indicates the location on the server of your image.

2. Type **HSPACE=x** where *x* is the number of pixels of space to add on *both* the right and left sides of the image.

3. Type **VSPACE=x** where *x* is the number of pixels of space to add on *both* the top and bottom of the image.

4. Add other image attributes as desired and type the final **>**.

✔ Tips

■ You don't have to add both HSPACE and VSPACE at the same time.

■ If you just want to add space to one side of the image, use Photoshop to add blank space to that side, and skip HSPACE and VSPACE altogether. Then, make the blank space transparent *(see page 68)*.

■ Both HSPACE and VSPACE are deprecated in HTML 4 in favor of style sheets. For more information about using styles to control the space around your images, consult *Adding padding around an element* on page 256 and *Setting the margins around an element* on page 257.

■ Explorer leaves 4 pixels to the right of the image (but not the left), by default.

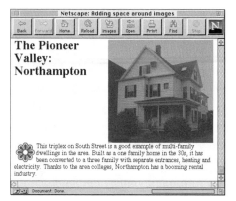

Figure 5.25 *Both Netscape and Internet Explorer have the bad habit of cramming text right up next to images. Netscape (shown) leaves no space above or below an image. Internet Explorer leaves hardly any space to either side of the image.*

```
code.html
<HTML><HEAD><TITLE>Adding space around
images</TITLE></HEAD><BODY>
<P><IMG SRC="house.gif" ALIGN=right
VSPACE=15>
<H1>The Pioneer Valley: Northampton</H1>
<P><BR CLEAR=right><IMG SRC="wraplogo2.gif"
ALIGN=left HSPACE=6>
This triplex on South Street is a good
example of multi-family dwellings in the
area. Built as a one family home in the 30s,
it has been converted to a three family with
```

Figure 5.26 *You can add either HSPACE or VSPACE, or both, to your images.*

Figure 5.27 *One of the unfortunate side effects of VSPACE is that it adds space both to the top and to the bottom of an image. Although the lower paragraph is no longer jammed against the house, the words* The Pioneer *are no longer aligned with the top of the image.*

Figure 5.28 *The image's original size is revealed in Photoshop by holding down the Option key and clicking in the lower left corner of the window.*

```
code.html
<HTML><HEAD><TITLE>Scaling an inline image</
TITLE></HEAD><BODY>
<IMG SRC="gazebo.gif" WIDTH=206 HEIGHT=290
ALIGN=right HSPACE=20>
<H1>The Berkshires</H1>
<P>Home to Tanglewood and Jacob's Pillow,
The Berkshires welcome thousands of tourists
from as far away as New York, Connecticut and
even Boston... Travelers take advantage of
the unique music, theater and dance
productions in a setting of unparalleled
```

Figure 5.29 *Use dimensions that are multiples of the original size to keep the image in proportion.*

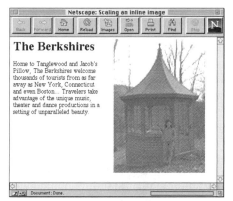

Figure 5.30 *The image quality is not great, but it loads twice as fast as a regular sized image.*

```
code.html
<HTML><HEAD><TITLE>Scaling an inline image</
TITLE></HEAD><BODY>
<IMG SRC="gazebo.gif" WIDTH=256 HEIGHT=235
ALIGN=right HSPACE=20>
<H1>The Berkshires</H1>
<P>Home to Tanglewood and Jacob's Pillow,
The Berkshires welcome thousands of tourists
from as far away as New York, Connecticut and
even Boston... Travelers take advantage of
the unique music, theater and dance
productions in a setting of unparalleled
```

Figure 5.31 *Distort images by using non-proportional values for WIDTH and HEIGHT.*

Scaling an image

You can change the size of an image just by specifying a new height and width in pixels. This is an easy way to have large images on your page without long loading times. Beware, though, if you enlarge your pictures too much, they'll be grainy and ugly.

To scale an image:

1. Type **<IMG SRC="image.location"**, where *image.location* is the location on the server of the image.

2. Type **WIDTH=x HEIGHT=y** where *x* and *y* are the desired width and height, respectively, in pixels, of your image.

3. Add any other image attributes as desired and then type the final **>**.

✔ Tips

■ Don't use the WIDTH and HEIGHT extensions to *reduce* the image size. Instead, create a smaller image. It will load faster and look better.

■ You can also use styles to control the width and height of elements. For more information, consult *Setting the height or width for an element* on page 254.

Aligning images

Perhaps, the more expected use of the ALIGN attribute is for aligning images with text. You can align an image in various ways to a single line in a paragraph. However, be careful with multiple images on the same line—different ALIGN options have different effects depending on which image is taller and which appears first.

To align an image with text:

1. Type **<IMG SRC="image.location"** where *image.location* indicates the location on the server of the image.

2. Type **ALIGN=direction** where *direction* is one of the attributes described in Figure 5.33: *texttop, top, middle, absmiddle, bottom,* or *absbottom.*

3. Add other attributes as desired and then type the final **>**.

4. Type the text with which you wish to align the image. (This text may also precede the image.)

✔ Tips

■ You may not align an image and wrap text around it at the same time.

■ Internet Explorer has trouble with aligning more than one image on a line. The results are erratic. In addition, it treats *texttop* as *top, absmiddle* as *middle* and *absbottom* as *bottom*.

■ The ALIGN attribute is deprecated in HTML 4. That means the W3C recommends you start using style sheets to control how elements are aligned on your page *(see page 258).*

```
                    code.html
<HTML><HEAD><TITLE>Aligning an image
</TITLE></HEAD><BODY>
<IMG SRC="A.gif">lign <IMG SRC="star.gif"
ALIGN="texttop"> star with texttop<P>
<IMG SRC="A.gif">lign <IMG SRC="star.gif"
ALIGN="top"> star with top<P>
<IMG SRC="A.gif">lign <IMG SRC="star.gif"
ALIGN="middle"> star with middle <P>
<IMG SRC="A.gif">lign <IMG SRC="star.gif"
ALIGN="absmiddle"> star with absmiddle<P>
<IMG SRC="A.gif" ALIGN="texttop">lign <IMG
SRC="star.gif" ALIGN="bottom"> star with
bottom/baseline<P>
<IMG SRC="A.gif" ALIGN="texttop">lign <IMG
SRC="star.gif" ALIGN="absbottom"> star with
absbottom<P>
</BODY>
</HTML>
```

Figure 5.32 *It's important to note that the letter A is an image, not an actual letter. It is aligned (by default) with the bottom of the text in the top four examples, and with the top of the text in the last two examples.*

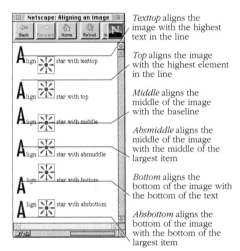

Texttop aligns the image with the highest text in the line

Top aligns the image with the highest element in the line

Middle aligns the middle of the image with the baseline

Absmiddle aligns the middle of the image with the middle of the largest item

Bottom aligns the bottom of the image with the bottom of the text

Absbottom aligns the bottom of the image with the bottom of the largest item

Figure 5.33 *There are four elements on each line: an image of the letter A, some text, a star, and some more text. The six possible alignment positions are illustrated with the star.*

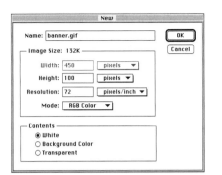

Figure 5.34 *When you create your image (here in Photoshop) make sure it is 450 pixels wide, or less.*

```
code.html
<HTML><HEAD>
<TITLE>Using a banner</TITLE></HEAD>
<BODY>
<IMG SRC="banner.gif" ALT="SE banner">
<H1>New products</H1>
<UL>
<LI>AstroFinder 3
<LI>Pleiades Expander
<LI>Southern Cross
</UL> </BODY>
</HTML>
```

Figure 5.35 *The only thing special about a banner is that it is the first element in the BODY section.*

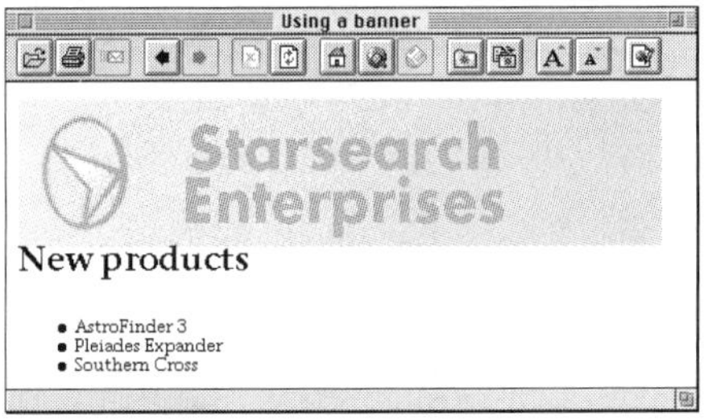

Figure 5.36 *The banner appears at the top of the page.*

Using a banner

Having a newspaper-like banner at the top of every Web page is a good way to link your pages together visually.

To place a banner at the top of each page:

1. Create an image that measures approximately 450 x 100 pixels. You can make it narrower and shorter, but you shouldn't make it much wider. Otherwise it won't fit easily on most screens **(Figure 5.34)**.

2. After converting it to indexed color, using the smallest bits/pixel ratio you can stand, save it as a GIF image.

3. Use this exact same image at the top of each of your Web pages, by typing **<IMG SRC="image.name">**, where *image.name* is the location on the server of the banner.

✔ Tips

■ By using the same image on each Web page, you create the illusion of a static banner. At the same time, since the image is saved in the cache after it is loaded the first time, it will load almost immediately onto each new page your visitor jumps to.

■ A better but slightly more complicated way to make a banner is to divide your page into two frames and place the banner in the upper frame *(see page 161)*.

Adding horizontal rules

One graphic element that is completely supported by the majority of the browsers is the horizontal rule. There are several attributes you can use to jazz up horizontal rules, although they've all been deprecated in HTML 4 in favor of styles.

To insert a horizontal rule:

1. Type **<HR** where you want the rule to appear. The text that follows will appear in a new paragraph below the new rule.

2. If desired, type **SIZE=n**, where *n* is the rule's height in pixels.

3. If desired, type **WIDTH=w**, where *w* is the width of the rule in pixels, or as a percentage of the document's width.

4. If desired, type **ALIGN=direction**, where *direction* refers to the way a rule should be aligned on the page; either *left, right,* or *center.* The ALIGN attribute is only effective if you have made the rule narrower than the document.

5. If desired, type **NOSHADE** to create a solid bar, with no shading.

6. Type the final **>** to complete the horizontal rule definition.

✔ Tip

■ All of the attributes for HR (but not the HR tag itself) have been deprecated in HTML 4. The W3 Consortium recommends using styles to decorate your horizontal rules. For more information, consult Chapter 15, *Layout with Styles.*

```
code.html
<HTML><HEAD>
<TITLE>Using horizontal rules</TITLE></
HEAD>
<BODY>
<IMG SRC="banner.gif" ALT="SE banner">
<H1>New products</H1>
<UL>
<LI>AstroFinder 3
<LI>Pleiades Expander
<LI>Southern Cross
</UL>
<HR SIZE="10" WIDTH="80%" ALIGN="center"
NOSHADE>
</BODY>
</HTML>
```

Figure 5.37 *The HR tag includes an automatic line break both before and after the rule.*

Figure 5.38 *Horizontal rules are helpful for dividing sections on your page.*

Page Layout

There are several HTML tags that apply to an entire page, instead of being limited to just a few words or paragraphs. I call these elements *page layout* features and restrict them to this chapter.

Included among these features are setting margins and columns, controlling the spacing between the elements on a page, changing the background color for the entire page, dividing a page into logical sections, positioning elements in layers, and determining when line breaks should, and shouldn't, occur.

Specifying the margins

Both Netscape and Internet Explorer add a certain amount of space, by default, between the contents of a page and the edges of the window. You can use the LEFTMARGIN and TOPMARGIN tags to specify just how much space you'd like there to be—but only IE understands it.

To specify the margins:

1. Inside the BODY tag, after the word BODY but before the final >, type **LEFTMARGIN=x**, where *x* is the width in pixels of the space between the left border of the window and the contents of the page.

2. Type **TOPMARGIN=y**, where *y* is the height in pixels of the space between the top border of the window and the contents of the page.

✔ Tips

■ The LEFTMARGIN and TOPMARGIN tags were developed by Microsoft and do not belong to HTML 4 (or any earlier version).

■ You can control the margins in both Netscape and Explorer by using styles. For more information, consult *Setting the margins around an element* on page 257.

■ Netscape always uses a value of 8 pixels for both the top and left margins. It ignores any instructions given in the LEFTMARGIN and TOPMARGIN tags.

■ You can use either the LEFTMARGIN or the TOPMARGIN tag, or both.

```
<HTML><HEAD><TITLE>Setting the margins</TITLE></HEAD>
<BODY LEFTMARGIN=0 TOPMARGIN=0>
The amount of space that Internet Explorer
leaves at the top of a page is rather
annoying. You can get rid of that space by
specifying a value of 0 for the top margin.
```

Figure 6.1 *Inside the BODY tag, type the values for LEFTMARGIN and TOPMARGIN.*

Figure 6.2 *Netscape doesn't understand the margin tags and, instead, always leaves 8 pixels at the top and left side of the page.*

Figure 6.3 *With a value of 0 for both LEFTMARGIN and TOPMARGIN, the text in Explorer is set directly in the top left corner of the page.*

```
<HTML><HEAD><TITLE>Setting the margins</TITLE></HEAD>
<BODY LEFTMARGIN=20 TOPMARGIN=20>
<P>On the other hand, maybe you like the top
margin so big. In that case, use high values
for both margin tags.
```

Figure 6.4 *Although I've chosen to use the same value for the left and top margins in both examples, you can use different values if you prefer.*

Figure 6.5 *Extra space in the margins can be handy, depending on the design of the page.*

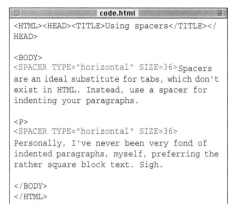

```
code.html
<HTML><HEAD><TITLE>Using spacers</TITLE></
HEAD>

<BODY>
<SPACER TYPE="horizontal" SIZE=36>Spacers
are an ideal substitute for tabs, which don't
exist in HTML. Instead, use a spacer for
indenting your paragraphs.

<P>
<SPACER TYPE="horizontal" SIZE=36>
Personally, I've never been very fond of
indented paragraphs, myself, preferring the
rather square block text. Sigh.

</BODY>
</HTML>
```

Figure 6.6 *Use horizontal spacers for indenting paragraphs, or any place you need to add an invisible, horizontal block of space.*

Figure 6.7 *Horizontal spacers are effective when viewed with Netscape.*

Figure 6.8 *Internet Explorer ignores horizontal spacers completely, aligning all text to the left. To indent text for Explorer, use pixel shims (see page 97) or styles (see page 243).*

Creating indents

You can't type a tab, or specify a tab stop in HTML documents. However, there are a number of ways to create indents for your paragraphs.

To create indents:

1. Place the cursor where you want the space to appear.

2. Type **<SPACER**.

3. Type **TYPE=horizontal**.

4. Type **SIZE=n**, where *n* is the desired indent size, in pixels.

5. Type the final **>** tag.

6. Type the text of the indented paragraph.

✓ Tips

■ You can use horizontal spaces anywhere you want, not just at the beginning of a text paragraph.

■ How much is a pixel? It all depends on the resolution of your users' screens, which is typically, but not always, 72 dpi. In this case, 36 pixels is 1/2 inch, 18 pixels is 1/4 inch. Your best bet is to be consistent on your page and/or test the result on more than one screen.

■ You can also use pixel shims *(see page 97)* or styles *(see page 243)* to create indented paragraphs.

■ IE4 still doesn't understand Netscape's SPACER tag. It probably never will.

■ For information on controlling vertical spacing, consult *Specifying the space between paragraphs* on page 95.

Creating indents (with lists)

When Netscape Gold was released, its Web page editor had one nifty feature: you could create paragraph indents that worked on most any browser. Looking at the code revealed the secret: the indents were created with lists.

To create indents with lists:

1. Place the cursor where you'd like to create indented text.

2. Type **<UL>**.

3. Type the contents of the indented text. You can type as many paragraphs as you want.

4. Type **</UL>**.

✓ Tip

■ For more control over indents, use styles *(see page 243).*

```
                    code.html
<HTML><HEAD><TITLE>Indents with lists</
TITLE></HEAD><BODY>

<H2>Sneaky ways to create indents</H2>
Using lists to create indents is not exactly
legal but it does work--in any browser. The
W3 Consortium would prefer that you use
styles. But until you do, list indents will
come in handy.
<UL>The basic technique is to create a list
for each section that you want to indent.
Don't create any list items--since they are
always marked with a bullet. Oh, and there's
no way to make hanging indents or first-line
indents. If you want to get fancy, use
styles.</UL>

</BODY>
</HTML>
```

Figure 6.9 *You can use lists (without the LI tag) to create indented paragraphs.*

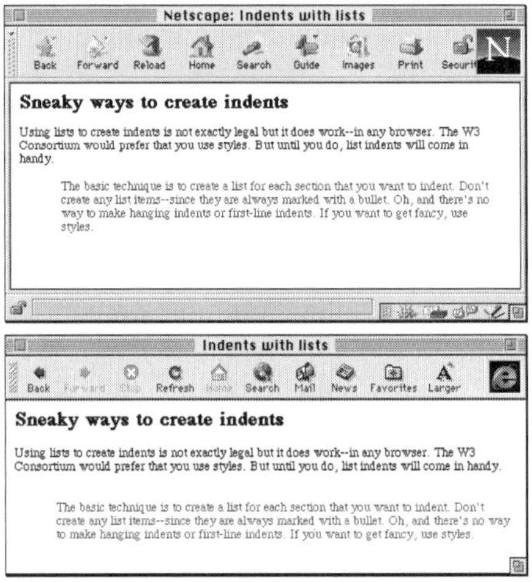

Figure 6.10 *List indents work on most browsers but they have two disadvantages: the W3C wishes you wouldn't use them and they don't offer much flexibility in the way of hanging or first-line indents.*

```
           code.html
<HTML><HEAD><TITLE>Creating space between
paragraphs</TITLE></HEAD>

<BODY>
<SPACER TYPE="horizontal" SIZE=36>Spacers
are an ideal substitute for tabs, which don't
exist in HTML. Instead, use a spacer for
indenting your paragraphs.

<SPACER TYPE="vertical" SIZE=24>
<SPACER TYPE="horizontal" SIZE=36>
Personally, I've never been very fond of
indented paragraphs, myself, preferring the
rather square block text. Sigh.

</BODY>
</HTML>
```

Figure 6.11 *Make sure you take out any P tags when using vertical spacers. Otherwise, the paragraphs will have extra space between them.*

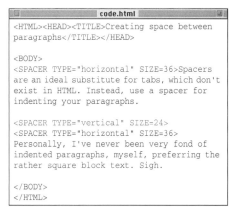

Figure 6.12 *On a 72 dpi screen, there will be exactly 1/3 inch of white space between the two paragraphs—as long as they're viewed in Netscape.*

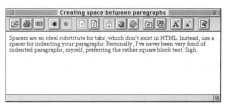

Figure 6.13 *Since we haven't used a P tag, the two paragraphs run together in Internet Explorer, which doesn't understand the SPACER tag.*

Specifying the space between paragraphs

The amount of space between paragraphs, when you use the P or BR tags, is determined by the size of the surrounding text. Larger text has larger spaces. Smaller text has smaller spaces. Netscape's SPACER tag lets you specify exactly how much space should appear between one line and another.

To specify the space between paragraphs:

1. Place the cursor between the two lines to be separated.

2. Type **<SPACER**.

3. Type **TYPE=vertical**.

4. Type **SIZE=n**, where *n* is the amount of space, in pixels, that should appear between the two lines.

5. Type the final **>**.

✔ Tips

■ The space between lines is usually specified in points, not pixels. Thanks to Steve Jobs, on most Macintosh monitors one point is almost exactly equal to one pixel. So if you want 10 points of space, use a value of 10 in step 4. Windows monitors tend to have a slightly lower resolution, and thus slightly bigger pixels. For 10 points, use 8 or 9 pixels.

■ The SPACER tag with a value of *vertical* for the TYPE attribute creates an automatic line break. You do not need to use the P tag—it will create the same amount of space it always has, in addition to the SPACER's space.

Creating blocks of space

 The SPACER tag is also useful for creating blocks of space that you can wrap text around.

To create blocks of space:

1. Place the cursor where the space should appear, before any text that will wrap around it.

2. Type **<SPACER**.

3. Type **TYPE=block**.

4. Type **WIDTH=w HEIGHT=h**, where *w* and *h* are the width and height, respectively, of the block, in pixels.

5. To wrap text around the block, type **ALIGN=left** or **ALIGN=right**, depending on which side of the block you want the text.

To align the block next to the text, without wrapping the text around it, type **ALIGN=direction**, where *direction* is top, middle, or bottom.

6. Type the final **>**.

✔ Tips

■ For more information on wrapping text, consult *Wrapping text around images* on page 83. For more information on the alignment options, consult *Aligning images* on page 88.

■ Internet Explorer does not understand Netscape's SPACER tag—and probably never will.

■ To create a *colored* block of space, use a pixel shim *(see page 97)*.

```
code.html
<HTML><HEAD><TITLE>Creating blocks of
space</TITLE></HEAD><BODY>
<SPACER TYPE="block"  WIDTH=100 HEIGHT=100
ALIGN=left>If you like to create big margins
around your text, spacers are ideal for the
job.
<P>Just use the spacer tag as if it were an
invisible image. And wrap the text right
around it as usual.
```

Figure 6.14 *When creating a block-shaped space, you have to specify the width and the height, along with an alignment, to determine where the space will appear.*

Figure 6.15 *Block shaped spaces are ideal for setting large, invisible margins—in Netscape.*

```
Creating space between paragraphs

If you like to create big margins around your text, spacers are ideal for the job.

Just use the spacer tag as if it were an invisible image. And wrap the text right
around it as usual.
```

Figure 6.16 *Again, the spacer tag has no effect in Internet Explorer.*

```
code.html
<HTML><HEAD><TITLE>Using blocks and
horizontal space</TITLE></HEAD><BODY>
<SPACER TYPE="block"  WIDTH=100 HEIGHT=100
ALIGN=left><SPACER TYPE="horizontal"
SIZE=36>If you like to create big margins
around your text, spacers are ideal for the
job.
<P><SPACER TYPE="horizontal" SIZE=36>Just
use the spacer tag as if it were an invisible
image. And wrap the text right around it as
usual.
```

Figure 6.17 *Use horizontal and block spacers to create both effects at the same time.*

Figure 6.18 *Here the entire text is offset with a block spacer while each paragraph is indented with a horizontal spacer.*

```
code.html
<HTML><HEAD><TITLE>Using pixel shims</
TITLE></HEAD><BODY>
<IMG SRC="pixelshim.gif" WIDTH=100
HEIGHT=150 HSPACE=3 ALIGN=left>If you like
to create big margins around your text,
spacers are ideal for the job.
<P>Just use the spacer tag as if it were an
invisible image. And wrap the text right
around it as usual.
<P><B>Or, perhaps better yet, use a pixel
shim. It has the advantage of being
recognized by most browsers, and you can make
it any color you want.<B>

</BODY>
</HTML>
```

Figure 6.19 *A pixel shim is nothing more than a one pixel by one pixel image, of any color you like, amplified to the desired size, and aligned as necessary.*

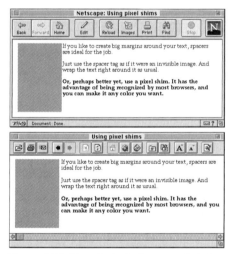

Figure 6.20 *The principal advantage of pixel shims is that they work in almost any browser. In addition, however, they are small and load quickly and they can be made any color you need. Notice, however, that Explorer (bottom) leaves more space to the right of the image than Netscape.*

Using pixel shims

A shim in the physical world is a little piece of wood (or sometimes paper) that you stick under one of the legs of your table (for example) to make it stop wobbling. A *pixel shim* is a wedge of pixels, sometimes in color, that you insert between elements on a page to shore up the balance and alignment.

To use a pixel shim:

1. Create a 1 pixel by 1 pixel GIF image in the desired color.

2. In your HTML document, type **<IMG SRC="pixelshim.gif"**, where *pixelshim .gif* is the name of the image created in step 1.

3. Type **WIDTH=w HEIGHT=h**, where *w* and *h* are the desired (not the actual) width and height, in pixels, of the desired space.

4. To wrap text around the shim, type **ALIGN=left** or **ALIGN=right**, depending on which side of the shim you want the text.

To align the shim next to the text, without wrapping the text around it, type **ALIGN=direction**, where *direction* is top, middle, or bottom.

5. Add other image attributes, as desired.

6. Type the final **>**.

✔ Tips

■ Pixel shims are recognized by most browsers since they're just images, forced to work in a new way.

■ In addition, pixel shims are tiny (and thus, load quickly) and can be made any color you want—or transparent.

Creating columns

You can divide your page into columns with a special extension that only Netscape recognizes. The extension is still pretty limited, however. First, all columns must be the same width. Second, if you make the columns too narrow, they will overlap and look horrible.

To create columns:

1. In your HTML document, type **<MULTICOL**.

2. Type **COLS=n**, where *n* is the number of columns desired. Each column will be the same size.

3. If desired, type **GUTTER=n**, where *n* is the width of the space between the columns, in pixels or as a percentage.

4. If desired, type **WIDTH=n**, where *n* is the width of the entire column set, including the gutter, in pixels or as a percentage of window size.

5. Type the final **>** to finish the column definition.

6. Create the elements (text or images) that will go into the columns.

7. Type **</MULTICOL>**.

✔ Tips

■ If you omit the WIDTH attribute, the columns will expand to fit whatever size window the user has created.

■ You can nest one set of columns with another. Simply repeat steps 1–7 when you reach step 6 of the outer set.

■ If you don't use the GUTTER attribute, Netscape automatically leaves 10 pixels between columns.

```
code.html
<H2>President Clinton wins reelection!</H2>
<FONT SIZE=-1>
<MULTICOL COLS=3 GUTTER=24 WIDTH=75%>
A multicolumn layout is typical of newspaper
articles. You start reading down the first
column and when you read the bottom, the text
starts up again at the top of the next
column. Of course, it all depends on how tall
your window is. And how is that controlled?
By the width of the columns. Netscape will
try to divide the text evenly among the
columns you've defined, making them as long
as necessary, but as even as possible.
<P>Use page breaks wherever necessary to
start a new line. Or use a line break
instead. Or insert images, or whatever.
<P>Hey, and it's only 10 am on the 5th, so
I'm not really sure what's going to happen
with the election...
</MULTICOL>
After the final multicol tag, you can go back
```

Figure 6.21 *The only required attribute in the MULTICOL tag is COLS: you must determine how many columns you want.*

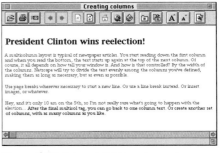

Figure 6.22 *Columns are perfect for newspaper style articles. Notice that the columns (and gutters) take up 75% of the screen, as defined in the HTML document, while the last paragraph, outside of the MUTLICOL definition, spans the entire width of the window. In addition, I've made the text one size smaller so as to better fit in the columns.*

Figure 6.23 *Internet Explorer does not recognize the MULTICOL tag. The last paragraph runs into the column text, since there was no P tag.*

```
code.html
<HTML><HEAD><TITLE>Centering text</TITLE></
HEAD>
<BODY>
<H2 ALIGN=CENTER>The Earth's Core</H2>
<CENTER>At the center of the earth, more than
6000 kilometers from the surface, the
temperature is a toasty 6500 degrees
Kelvin.</CENTER>
<P>Not bad for a little planet.
</BODY>
</HTML>
```

Figure 6.24 *Note that the header,* The Earth's Core, *is centered by the method described on page 40.*

Figure 6.25 *Although the CENTER tag has been deprecated, most browsers still support it.*

Centering elements on a page

In Chapter 2, *Starting your Web Page*, you learned how to align paragraphs and headers. There is, however, a more general centering tag that can be used with virtually any element on your page: the CENTER tag.

To center elements on a page:

1. Type **<CENTER>**.

2. Create the element that you wish to center.

3. Type **</CENTER>**.

✔ Tips

■ You can use the CENTER tag with almost every kind of HTML element, including paragraphs, headers, images, and forms, even if there is another method for centering that element.

■ For more information on aligning paragraphs, consult *Starting a new paragraph* on page 41. For more information on aligning headers, consult *Organizing the page* on page 40.

■ For information on aligning images with text, consult *Aligning images* on page 88.

■ For details on dividing your document into sections that you can then align, consult *Special tags for styles* on page 230.

■ For information on using styles to center text, consult *Aligning text* on page 245.

Centering elements on a page

Positioning elements with layers

Although they had already promised to work towards a universal standard for HTML, Netscape developed a set of proprietary tags for positioning HTML elements in early 1997. In contrast to other non-standard tags introduced by Netscape, called *extensions*, that immediately became widespread, the positioning extensions, called *layers*, have not caught on. Instead, the standard developed jointly through the W3C seems to be gaining ground *(see pages 250–253)*. Nevertheless, if you're going to be creating Web pages exclusively for Netscape users, the layer tag may still be useful.

To position elements with layers:

1. Type **<LAYER**.

2. If desired, type **ID=name**, where *name* identifies the layer to JavaScript programs.

3. Type **TOP=m**, where *m* is the number of pixels the layer's contents should be offset from the top edge of the browser window.

4. Type **LEFT=n**, where *n* is the number of pixels the layer's contents should be offset from the left edge of the browser window.

5. If desired, type **WIDTH=w**, where *w* is the width of the layer in pixels.

6. If desired, type **HEIGHT=h**, where *h* is the height of the layer in pixels.

7. If desired, type **SRC="source.html"**, where *source.html* is the initial HTML content that should appear in the layer.

```
                   code.html
<HTML><HEAD><TITLE>Positioning elements
with layers</TITLE></HEAD><BODY>

<LAYER ID=layer1 TOP=10 LEFT=50 WIDTH=100
HEIGHT=100 BGCOLOR=yellow Z-INDEX=1>
This is the very bottom layer. It's yellow.
</LAYER>

<LAYER ID=layer2 TOP=20 LEFT=60 WIDTH=160
HEIGHT=80 BGCOLOR=orange Z-INDEX=2>
This is the second layer from the bottom.
It's orange.
</LAYER>

<LAYER ID=layer3 TOP=40 LEFT=80 WIDTH=40
HEIGHT=40 BGCOLOR=black Z-INDEX=3>
<FONT COLOR=white>This is layer 3. It's
black.</FONT>
</LAYER>

<LAYER ID=layer4 TOP=70 LEFT=200 WIDTH=100
HEIGHT=100 BGCOLOR=red Z-INDEX=1>
This layer is at the same level as the first
one, that is, the bottom.
</LAYER>

<NOLAYER>
This page contains elements positioned with
layers. It only works in Netscape
Communicator 4.
</NOLAYER>
</BODY></HTML>
```

Figure 6.26 *Each layer is defined separately with its own coordinates. I've just entered plain text as the contents of each layer, but you can add any other HTML tags you like, except frames.*

Figure 6.27 *There are four layers in this example. Layers become really useful when combined with JavaScript.*

Figure 6.28 *Explorer makes a total mess of layers with content—despite the NOLAYER option.*

```
┌──────────────────────────────────────┐
│ ▢         code.html              ▢ ▢ │
├──────────────────────────────────────┤
│ <HTML><HEAD><TITLE>Positioning elements
│ with layers</TITLE></HEAD><BODY>
│
│ <LAYER ID=layer1 TOP=10 LEFT=300 WIDTH=50
│ HEIGHT=60 BGCOLOR=aqua Z-INDEX=1
│ SRC="layer1.html">
│ </LAYER>
│
│ <LAYER ID=layer2 TOP=50 LEFT=30 WIDTH=300
│ HEIGHT=80 BGCOLOR=magenta Z-INDEX=2
│ SRC="layer2.html">
│ </LAYER>
│ <NOLAYER>
│ This page contains elements positioned with
│ layers. It only works in Netscape
│ Communicator 4.
│ </NOLAYER>
│ </BODY></HTML>
└──────────────────────────────────────┘
```

Figure 6.29 *If you know Explorer users are going to try and view your page, you should use the SRC attribute in the LAYER tags to insert content and then the NOLAYER tags to alert Explorer users to the fact that they won't see the effect.*

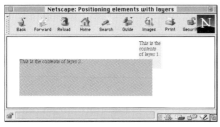

Figure 6.30 *Communicator displays the contents from the files in the SRC attribute.*

Figure 6.31 *Since Explorer completely ignores LAYER tags, it won't try to insert the content of layers defined by the SRC attribute. Instead, it simply and cleanly displays the contents of the NOLAYER tags.*

8. If desired, type **CLIP="t,l,r,b"** where *t*, *l*, *r*, and *b* are the offsets in pixels from the top, left, right, and bottom.

9. If desired, type **Z-INDEX=z**, where *z* is a number indicating the layer's level if it overlaps other layers. The higher the value of z, the higher the layer.

10. If desired, type **BGCOLOR=color**, where *color* is one of the predefined colors listed on page 311.

11. If desired, type **BACKGROUND= "image.gif"**, where *image.gif* is the image that you'd like to use for the background of the layer.

12. Type **>**.

13. Create the contents of the layer.

14. Type **</LAYER>**.

✔ Tips

- Layers are designed to be combined with JavaScript to create dynamic pages. For more information, check out *http://developer.netscape.com/ library/documentation/communica- tor/dynhtml/*. My basic examples don't quite do it justice.

- You can create content for browsers (like Explorer) that don't recognize the LAYER tags. Simply enclose it in opening and closing NOLAYER tags.

- To create relatively positioned elements (that is, elements that are offset with respect to their natural position in the flow), use opening and closing ILAYER tags instead of LAYER tags.

- Layers are not standard HTML. To precisely position elements for both Explorer and Communicator, consult Chapter 15, *Layout with Styles*.

Using background color

Tired of basic gray? The BGCOLOR tag lets you set the background color of each Web page you create.

To set the background color:

1. In the BODY tag, after the word BODY but before the final >, type **BGCOLOR="#rrggbb"**, where *rrggbb* is the hexadecimal representation of the desired color.

Or type **BGCOLOR=color**, where *color* is one of the 16 predefined colors.

2. Add other attributes to the BODY (like link and text colors) as desired.

✔ Tips

■ See Appendix C and the inside back cover for a complete listing of hexadecimal values and common color representations. Appendix C also includes a list of the 16 predefined colors.

■ For more information on setting the link colors, consult *Changing the color of links* on page 123. For more information on setting the text color, consult *Choosing a default size for body text* on page 46 or *Changing the text size* on page 47.

■ To use an image for the background, consult *Using background images* on page 103.

■ Most browsers let the user override any background color set by you, the page designer.

■ The BGCOLOR attribute has been deprecated in HTML 4. The W3C recommends using styles to control the background *(see page 262)*.

```
code.html
<HTML>
<HEAD>
<TITLE>Creating a colored background</TITLE>
</HEAD>
<BODY BGCOLOR="#FF00FF">
You can change the color of the background
of your page--but make sure your users can
still read the text on top of it. That is the
point, right?
</BODY>
</HTML>
```

Figure 6.32 *Add the BGCOLOR attribute to the BODY tag to set the background color for the page.*

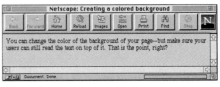

Figure 6.33 *Even though BGCOLOR has been deprecated in HTML 4, most browsers support it. Most also, however, allow the user to override such settings.*

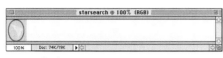

Figure 6.34 *In this example, I've created a background image that is 50 pixels high and 500 pixels wide. It compresses beautifully to less than 2K, but since browsers automatically tile images smaller than the window, it will fill the background as completely as any bigger image.*

```
code.html
<HTML><HEAD><TITLE>Using an image as a
background</TITLE></HEAD>
<BODY BACKGROUND="starsearch.gif">
<TABLE CELLSPACING="2" CELLPADDING="1">
<TR>
<TD WIDTH=50 VALIGN=TOP> </TD>
<TD VALIGN=TOP>You can also use an image for
the background. Make sure the images are as
small as possible. Your users won't wait
forever.
<P>
<H1>Starsearch Enterprises Web page</H1>
<H2>New products</H2>
<H2>Press Releases</H2>
<H2>PSO Scheduled</H2>
<H2>Job Opportunities at SE</H2>
</TD>
</TR>
</TABLE>
</BODY>
```

Figure 6.35 *To keep text from overlapping my background image along the left side, I've placed the text in a table with two columns, and left the first column empty. Notice you can't add extra image attributes (like LOWSRC) to the BODY tag.*

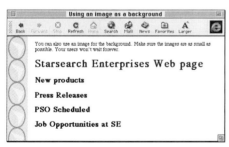

Figure 6.36 *Because the image is so wide, it does not repeat horizontally (and leaves room for text that is easy to read).*

Using background images

You can use one image as the backdrop for your entire page. *Backdrop* is the operative word here. A background image should not detract from the readability of your page, but instead make it more attractive.

To use a background image:

1. In the BODY tag at the beginning of your page, type **BACKGROUND=**.

2. Type **"bgimage.gif"**, where *bgimage.gif* is the location on the server of the image you want to use.

3. If desired, type **BGPROPERTIES= fixed** to make the image a stationary watermark.

✔ Tips

■ Take advantage of the fact that browsers automatically tile smaller images when creating your background **(Figure 6.36)**.

■ With an image editing program, try increasing the brightness and lowering the contrast to soften the background image so it doesn't distract from your page's content.

■ Save your visitor loading time by using the same background image on a series of pages. After the image has been loaded for the first page, each subsequent page uses a cached version which loads much more quickly.

■ The BACKGROUND attribute is deprecated in HTML 4. For details on using styles to create a background image, see page 262.

Chapter 6

Using block quotes

You can use block quotes to set off a section of your text—like a quotation by a famous author—from the surrounding text. As usual, different browsers display block quotes in different ways. Some center the text in an indented paragraph in the middle of the page, while others simply italicize the special text.

To create a block quote:

1. Type **<BLOCKQUOTE>**.

2. Type the desired HTML formatting for the text, like **<P>**, for example.

3. Type the text that you wish to appear set off from the preceding and following text.

4. Complete the HTML tag begun in step 2, if necessary.

5. Type **</BLOCKQUOTE>**.

✔ Tips

■ Text should not be placed directly between the opening and closing BLOCKQUOTE tags, but rather between other HTML tags within the BLOCKQUOTE tags. (However, many browsers will display a block quote correctly even if you ignore this rule.)

■ Block quotes can contain additional text formatting like STRONG or EM.

■ Explorer does not add a line break before the block quote.

■ You can also use styles to indent text on both sides. For more information, consult *Setting the margins around an element* on page 257.

```
                    code.html
<HTML><HEAD><TITLE>Creating a block quote</
TITLE></HEAD><BODY>
Sometimes I get to the point where I'm not
sure anything matters at all. Then I read
something like this and I am inspired:
<BLOCKQUOTE>
It's not hard to figure out what's good for
kids, but amid the noise of an increasingly
antichild political climate, it can be hard
to remember just to go ahead and do it: for
example, to vote to raise your school
district's budget, even though you'll pay
higher taxes. (If you're earning enough to
pay taxes at all, I promise, the school needs
those few bucks more than you do.) To support
legislators who care more about afterschool
programs, affordable health care, and
libraries than about military budges and the
Dow Jones industrial average. To volunteer
time and skills at your neighborhood school
and also the school across town. To decide
to notice, rather than ignore it, when a
neighbor is losing it with her kids, and
offer to babysit twice a week. This is not
interference. Getting between a ball player
and a ball is interference. The ball is
inanimate.
</BLOCKQUOTE>
This is from Barbara Kingsolver's brilliant
```

Figure 6.37 *A block quote can be as short or as long as you need. You can even divide it into various paragraphs by adding P tags as necessary.*

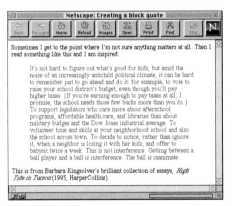

Figure 6.38 *Block quotes are generally indented from both sides.*

```
                code.html
<HTML>
<HEAD>
<TITLE>Quoting shorter passages</TITLE>
</HEAD>
<BODY>
<P>So I said <Q LANG=en>What's going on
here?</Q>
<P>I ella em va dir <Q lang=ca>Qu&egrave;
passa? Que no veus que li estic intentant
ajudar?</Q>
</BODY>
</HTML>
```

Figure 6.39 *The Q tag is for marking shorter, inline passages of text. The language code specified determines the type of quotation marks that will be used.*

Figure 6.40 *The Q tag is not yet supported by either Explorer (shown here) or Netscape, despite being part of the standard HTML 4 specifications.*

Quoting short passages of text

Block quotes, as described on the preceding page, are block-level elements, that is, they always start on a new line. HTML 4 includes a new tag for marking shorter, inline passages. Although neither Netscape nor Explorer currently supports this new tag, it may be useful for future versions.

To quote short passages of text:

1. Type **<Q**.

2. If desired, type **LANG=xx**, where *xx* is the two letter code for the language the quote will be in. This code determines the type of quote marks that will be used ("" for English, « for many European languages, etc.).

3. Type **>**.

4. Type the text to be quoted.

5. Type **</Q>**.

✔ Tips

■ Although the Q tag is part of the standard HTML 4 specifications, neither Explorer nor Communicator (version 4) supports it yet.

■ Once it's supported, use Q for phrases within a larger paragraph and use BLOCKQUOTE *(see page 104)* for entire paragraphs.

■ You can find the complete list of language codes at *http://www.sil.org/ sgml/iso639a.html.*

Controlling line breaks

You may have certain phrases in your document that you don't want separated. Or you may want to keep a word and an image together, no matter what. There are a couple of special tags for this purpose.

To keep elements on one line:

1. Type **<NOBR>**.

2. Create the text or elements that should appear all on one line.

3. Type **</NOBR>**.

To insert soft line breaks in a nonbreakable line:

In a block of nonbreakable text, as that created above, type **<WBR>** where you would allow a line break, if, and only if, the size of the user's window required it.

✔ Tips

■ Line breaks created with WBR only appear if the window is small enough to warrant them. Otherwise, the elements will not be separated.

■ Elements within NOBR tags will not be separated, unless there is a WBR tag, even if the size of the window causes them to be displayed off screen, and thus invisible to the user.

■ Unlike the NOWRAP attribute used in tables to keep a cell's contents on a single line *(see page 153)*, the NOBR tag must have an opening and closing tag and only affects the text contained within the two.

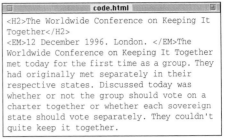

```
code.html
<H2>The Worldwide Conference on Keeping It
Together</H2>
<EM>12 December 1996. London. </EM>The
Worldwide Conference on Keeping It Together
met today for the first time as a group. They
had originally met separately in their
respective states. Discussed today was
whether or not the group should vote on a
charter together or whether each sovereign
state should vote separately. They couldn't
quite keep it together.
```

Figure 6.41 *Here is the HTML document with no control over line breaks.*

Figure 6.42 *In all browsers, the lines are divided according to the width of the window.*

```
code.html
<H2><NOBR>The Worldwide Conference on
Keeping It Together</NOBR></H2>
<NOBR><EM>12 December 1996. London. </EM>The
Worldwide Conference on Keeping It Together
<WBR>met today for the first time as a group.
They had originally met separately in their
respective states. <WBR>Discussed today was
whether or not the group should vote on a
charter together or whether each sovereign
state should vote separately. They couldn't
quite keep it together.</NOBR>
```

Figure 6.43 *The NOBR tag keeps all the enclosed elements on the same line. The WBR tag allows a line break—if necessary—depending on window size.*

Figure 6.44 *Most browsers interpret the NOBR and WBR tags correctly. Notice how the header extends beyond the width of the window, while the first line break comes before the word met which is just where the WBR was. The second line again extends beyond the width of the window, and breaks where the WBR tag is.*

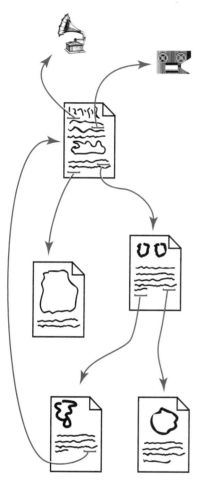

Figure 7.1 *Some of your pages may have links to many other pages. Other pages may have only one link. And still others may have no links at all.*

Links are the distinguishing feature of the World Wide Web. They let you skip from one page to another, call up a movie or a recording of Bill playing his sax, and download files with FTP.

A link has three parts: a destination, a label, and a target. The first part, the *destination*, is arguably the most important. You use it to specify what will happen when the visitor clicks the link. You can create links that show an image, play a sound or movie, download files, open a newsgroup, send an e-mail message, run a CGI program, and more. The most common links, however, connect to other Web pages, and sometimes to specific locations on other Web pages called *anchors*. All destinations are defined by writing a URL *(see page 27)* and are generally only visible to the visitor in the status area of the browser.

The second part of the link is the *label*, the part the visitor sees and clicks on to reach the destination. It can be text, an image, or both. Label text is often, but not always, underlined. The better the label, the more likely a visitor will click on it. In fact, eliciting Web visitor's clicks is an art.

The last part of the link, the *target*, is often ignored or left up to the browser. The target determines where the destination will be displayed. The target might be a particular named window or frame, or a *new* window or frame.

Creating a link to another Web page

If you have more than one Web page, you will probably want to create links from one page to the next (and back again). You can also create connections to Web pages designed by other people on other servers.

To create a link to another Web page:

1. Type **<A HREF="page.html">** where *page.html* is the URL of the destination Web page.

2. Type the label text, that is, the text that will be underlined or highlighted in blue, and that when clicked upon will take the user to the URL referenced in step 1.

3. Type **</A>** to complete the definition of the link.

✔ Tips

■ As a general rule, use relative URLs for links to Web pages on your site and absolute URLs for links to Web pages on other sites. For more details, consult *URLs* on page 27.

■ So, a link to a page at another site might look like this: **<A HREF="http://www.site.com/directory/page.html">Label text</A>** (Figures 7.5, 7.6, and 7.7).

■ You can often create a link to a site's home page by using *http://www.site.com/directory/*. The trailing forward slash tells the browser to search for the default file, usually called *index.html*, in the last directory mentioned.

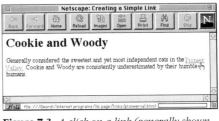

```
code.html
<HTML>
<HEAD><TITLE>Creating a Simple Link</TITLE>
</HEAD>
<H1>Cookie and Woody</H1>
<P>Generally considered the sweetest and yet
most independent cats in the <A
HREF="pioneerval.html">Pioneer Valley,</A>
Cookie and Woody are consistently
underestimated by their humble humans.
</BODY>
</HTML>
```

Figure 7.2 *Only the text within the link definition (in this case the words* Pioneer Valley*) will be clickable.*

Figure 7.3 *A click on a link (generally shown with underlined or blue text or both)...*

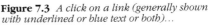

Figure 7.4 *...brings you to the associated URL.*

```
code.html
<HTML><HEAD><TITLE>Creating a link to an
absolute URL</TITLE>
</HEAD><BODY>
<H1>Cookie and Woody</H1>
<P>Generally considered the sweetest and yet
most independent cats in the <A
HREF="pioneerval.html">Pioneer Valley,</A>
Cookie and Woody are consistently
underestimated by their humble humans.
<H1>Pixel</H1>
<P>If you'd like to meet a JavaCat, check out
<A HREF="http://www.chalcedony.com/pixel/">
Pixel</A> at Tom Negrino and Dori Smith's
great site about their <A HREF="http://
www.chalcedony.com/javascript/">
<EM>JavaScript for the World Wide Web:
Visual QuickStart Guide, 2nd edition</EM>
</A>.
```

Figure 7.5 *If you're creating links to someone else's Web site, you'll have to use an absolute URL, with the http://, server, full path, and file name.*

Figure 7.6 *Links to absolute URLs don't look any different to your visitor. A click still leads to...*

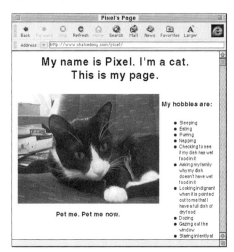

Figure 7.7 *...the destination URL on the other site.*

Now that getting people to come to your site is so important, Web link etiquette dictates that you create links not to a particular, specific page within a site, but rather to the home page of that site. A direct link, on the other hand, helps your visitor to arrive promptly at their destination. A possible compromise is to give the direct connection as well as a connection to the site's home page.

Don't make the link's label too long. If the label is part of a longer sentence, keep only the key words within the link definition, with the rest of the sentence before and after the less than and greater signs.

Don't use "Click here" for a label. Instead use the key words that already exist in your text to identify the link.

You may apply text formatting (or styles) to the label.

You can also use an image as a label. For more details, consult *Using images to label links* on page 118.

To create a link to a particular location on a Web page, use an anchor. For more details, see pages 110–111.

You can make the link appear in a given window or frame. For more information, consult *Targeting links to specific windows* on page 112.

You can create keyboard shortcuts for links. For more details, see page 116.

You can determine the tab order for visitors who use their keyboards to navigate your page. For more details, consult *Setting the tab order for links* on page 117.

Creating anchors

Generally, a click on a link brings the user to the *top* of the appropriate Web page. If you want to have the user jump to a specific section of the Web page, you have to create an *anchor* and then reference that anchor in the link.

To create an anchor:

1. Place the cursor in the part of the Web page that you wish the user to jump to.

2. Type **<A NAME="anchor name">**, where *anchor name* is the text you will use internally to identify that section of the Web page.

3. Add the words or images that you wish to be referenced.

4. Type **</A>** to complete the definition of the anchor.

✔ Tips

■ You only need to add quotation marks around the anchor name if it is more than one word.

■ In a long document, create an anchor for each section and link it to the corresponding item in the table of contents.

■ Be aware that Netscape uses the term *targets* or *named anchors* when they mean anchors, although targets are something completely different (*see page 112*).

```
code.html
<HTML>
<HEAD><TITLE>Creating an Anchor to Make a
Dynamic Table of Contents</TITLE>
</HEAD>
<H1>Table of Contents</H1>
<OL>
<LI><A HREF=#intro>Introduction</A>
<LI><A HREF=#descrip>Description of the Main
Characters</A>
<LI><A HREF=#denoue>Denouement</A>
<LI><A HREF=#climax>Climax</A>
<LI><A HREF=#conclus>Conclusion</A>
</OL>

<H1><A NAME=intro>Introduction</A></H1>
This is the intro. If I could think of enough
things to write about, it could span a few
pages, giving all the introductory informa-
tion that an introduction should introduce.

<H1><A NAME=descrip>Description of the Main
Characters</A></H1>
Frankie and Johnny are the main characters.
She's jealous, and seems to have a reason to
be. He's a sleaze, and will pay the price.

<H1><A NAME=denoue>Denouement</A></H1>
This is where everything starts happening.
Johnny goes out, without Frankie, without
even tellin' her where he's going. She's not
crazy about it, but she lets him go. A while
later, she gets thirsty and decides to go
down to the corner bar for some beer. Chat-
ting with the bartender, she learns that
Johnny has been there with no other than Nel-
lie Bly. Furious, she catches the cross town
bus to find him.

<H1><A NAME=climax>Climax</A></H1>
When Frankie gets to Nellie's house, she
looks up and sees them kissing on the balco-
ny. With tears in her eyes, she picks up her
shot gun and kills her Johnny. He falls to
the ground.

<H1><A NAME=conclus>Conclusion</A></H1>
Frankie feels bad but it's kind of late now,
and Johnny <EM>was</EM> a lech. But the po-
lice come and cart her off anyway.

</BODY></HTML>
```

Figure 7.8 *A long document like this one can be greatly helped by a dynamic table of contents. In this example, each section has its own anchor name so that a click on the corresponding item in the table of contents at the top of the page brings the visitor directly to the section they're interested in. (See Figure 7.9 and Figure 7.10 on page 111.)*

Creating anchors

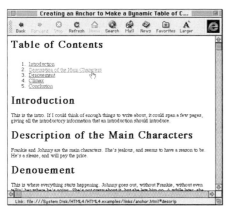

Figure 7.9 *A click in the link to the anchor brings the user...*

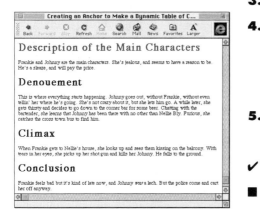

Figure 7.10 *...to the corresponding anchor farther down in the same document (as in this example) or to a specific position in a separate document.*

Linking to a specific anchor

Once you have created an anchor you can define a link so that a user's click will bring them directly to the section of the document that contains the anchor, not just the top of that document.

To create a link to an anchor:

1. Type **<A HREF="#**.

2. Type **anchor name**, where *anchor name* is the NAME of the destination section *(step 2 on page 110)*.

3. Type **">**.

4. Type the label text, that is, the text that will be underlined or highlighted in blue, and that when clicked upon will take the user to the section referenced in step 2.

5. Type **</A>** to complete the definition of the link.

✔ Tips

■ If the anchor is in a separate document, type **<A HREF="page.html#anchor-name">** to reference the section. (There should be no space between *url.address* and the # symbol.) If the anchor is on a page on a different server, you'll have to use **<A HREF= "http://www.site.com/path/page .html#anchorname">**.

■ Although you obviously can't add anchors to other people's pages, you can take advantage of the ones that they have already created. Save their documents in HTML format to see which anchor names correspond to which sections. (For more information on saving HTML code, consult *The inspiration of others* on page 278.)

Targeting links to specific windows

Targets let you open a link in a particular window, or even in a new window created especially for that link. This way, the page that contains the link stays open, enabling the user to go back and forth between the page of links and the information from each of those links.

To target links:

Within the link definition, type **TARGET= title**, where *title* is the name of the window where the corresponding page should be displayed.

✔ Tips

■ Open a link in a new window by using **TARGET=_blank**.

■ If you target several links to the same window (e.g., using the same name), the links will all open in that same window.

■ If a named window is not already open, the browser opens a new window and uses it for all future links to that window.

■ Targets are most effective for opening Web pages in particular windows or frames. However, you can also use targets for FTP or Gopher links. Targets don't make sense for e-mail or news links, since these open in different kinds of windows.

■ For more information on targeting frames, consult *Targeting links to particular frames* on page 172.

■ In fact, you can use targeted windows as a substitute for frames, which may not be supported by some browsers.

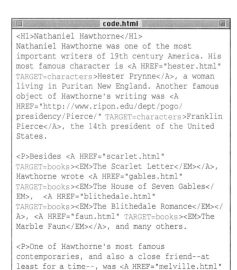

```
code.html
<H1>Nathaniel Hawthorne</H1>
Nathaniel Hawthorne was one of the most
important writers of 19th century America. His
most famous character is <A HREF="hester.html"
TARGET=characters>Hester Prynne</A>, a woman
living in Puritan New England. Another famous
object of Hawthorne's writing was <A
HREF="http://www.ripon.edu/dept/pogo/
presidency/Pierce/" TARGET=characters>Franklin
Pierce</A>, the 14th president of the United
States.

<P>Besides <A HREF="scarlet.html"
TARGET=books><EM>The Scarlet Letter</EM></A>,
Hawthorne wrote <A HREF="gables.html"
TARGET=books><EM>The House of Seven Gables</
EM>,   <A HREF="blithedale.html"
TARGET=books><EM>The Blithedale Romance</EM></
A>, <A HREF="faun.html" TARGET=books><EM>The
Marble Faun</EM></A>, and many others.

<P>One of Hawthorne's most famous
contemporaries, and also a close friend--at
least for a time--, was <A HREF="melville.html"
TARGET=friends>Herman Melville</A>. Another
```

Figure 7.11 *Add the TARGET attribute to a link to open the corresponding page in a particular window. In this example, some links will appear in the* characters *window, some in the* books *window, and still others in the* friends *window.*

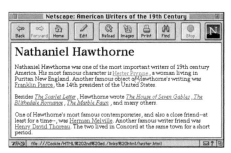

Figure 7.12 *When the visitor clicks a link with a target…*

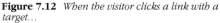

Figure 7.13 *…the corresponding page is shown in the targeted window. In this example, it's the* characters *window.*

```
code.html
<!DOCTYPE HTML PUBLIC "-//W3C//DTD HTML 3.2//
EN"><HTML><HEAD><TITLE>American Writers of the
19th Century</TITLE>
<BASE TARGET=characters>
</HEAD>
<BODY>
<H1>Nathaniel Hawthorne</H1>
Nathaniel Hawthorne was one of the most
important writers of 19th century America. His
most famous character is <A
HREF="hester.html">Hester Prynne</A>, a woman
living in Puritan New England. Another famous
object of Hawthorne's writing was <A
HREF="http://www.ripon.edu/dept/pogo/
presidency/Pierce/">Franklin Pierce</A>, the
14th president of the United States.

<P>Besides <A HREF="scarlet.html"
TARGET=books><EM>The Scarlet Letter</EM></A>,
Hawthorne wrote <A HREF="gables.html"
TARGET=books><EM>The House of Seven Gables</
EM>,   <A HREF="blithedale.html"
TARGET=books><EM>The Blithedale Romance</EM></
A>, <A HREF="faun.html" TARGET=books><EM>The
Marble Faun</EM></A>, and many others.

<P>One of Hawthorne's most famous
contemporaries, and also a close friend--at
least for a time--, was <A HREF="melville.html"
TARGET=friends>Herman Melville</A>. Another
famous writer friend was <A HREF="thoreau.html"
TARGET=friends>Henry David Thoreau</A>. The two
lived in Concord at the same town for a short
period.

</BODY>
</HTML>
```

Figure 7.14 *Use the BASE tag to set the default target (in this case the* characters *window) in order to save typing. Notice that I no longer have to specify the target for the links in the first paragraph. This document is equivalent to the one shown in Figure 7.11.*

Setting the default target

A link, by default, opens in the same window or frame that contains the link. You can choose another target for each link individually, as described on page 112, or specify a default target for all the links on a page.

To set a default target for a page:

1. In the HEAD section of your Web page, type **<BASE**.

2. Type **TARGET=title**, where *title* is the name of the window or frame in which all the links on the page should open, by default.

3. Type **>** to complete the BASE tag.

✔ Tips

■ You can override the default target specified in the BASE tag by adding a target to an individual link as described on page 112.

■ The BASE tag is optional. If you do not use it, the default target will be the window that is currently displaying the page with the link.

■ You can also use the BASE tag to set the base URL for constructing relative URLs but I frankly don't know why you'd want to do such a thing. Use **<BASE HREF="base.url">** where *base.url* is the URL that all relative links should be constructed from.

Creating other kinds of links

You are not limited to creating links to other Web pages. You can create a link to any URL—FTP or Gopher sites, files that you want visitors to be able to download, newsgroups and messages. You can even create a link to an e-mail address.

To create other kinds of links:

1. Type **<A HREF="**.

2. Type the URL:

For a link to any file on the Web, including movies, sounds, and programs, type **http://www.site.com/directory/file.ext**, where *www.site.com* is the name of the server and *directory/file.ext* is the path to the desired file, including its extension.

For a link to an FTP site, type **ftp://ftp.site.com/path**, where *ftp.site.com* is the server and *path* is the path to the desired directory or file.

For a Gopher site, type **gopher://site.edu/path**, where *site.edu* is the name of the server and *path* is the path to the desired directory or file.

For a newsgroup, type **news:newsgroup**, where *newsgroup* is the name of the desired newsgroup. For a particular message, type **news:article**, where *article* is the number (as shown in the header) of the individual article.

For a link to an e-mail address, type **mailto:name@site.com**, where *name@site.com* is the e-mail address.

For a link to a telnet site (like a library catalog), type **telnet://site**, where *site* is the name of the server you want to open the telnet connection to.

3. Type **">**.

```
code.html
<H1>Getaway Destinations</H1>
<P>There are lots of different kinds of links
that you can create on a Web page.

<P>You might want to create a link to a
directory on <A HREF="ftp://ftp2.netscape.com/
pub/communicator/4.04/shipping/">Netscape's
FTP site</A> to help visitors download the
latest version of Netscape Communicator. Or you
can point them to a specific file like the <A
HREF="ftp://ftp2.netscape.com/pub/
communicator/4.04/shipping/english/mac/PPC/
base_install/Com4.04_PPC_base.bin">Mac PowerPC
version of Communicator 4.04</A> so they don't
have to navigate the FTP site.

<P>To allow access to a <A HREF="ftp://
name:password@ftp.site.com/directory">private
FTP site</A>, you have to preface the server
name with the user name and password.

<P>Gopher sites are disappearing but there are
still an <A HREF="gopher://gopher.micro.umn.edu
:70/11/Other%20Gopher%20and%20Information%20
Servers">awful lot of them</A> you can link to.

<P>A link to an e-mail address is a great way to
elicit comments about your Web page.
Unfortunately, spammers are great at snatching
up e-mail addresses from Web pages and filling
your mailbox with non-solicited junk. Don't
think so? <A HREF="mailto:liz@cookwood.com">
Tell me</A> about it.

<P>Links to newsgroups help visitors find other
people interested in the same topic. For example,
check out the <A HREF="news:rec.pets.cats">
newsgroup for cat lovers</A>. Can you believe
there's no special section for Woody and
Cookie? If you write a particularly
scintillating message, you could create a <A
HREF="news:34F243FF.887441BD@innet.com">link
to it</A> (although messages expire really
quickly and the link will die when it does).

<P>Many libraries let you <A HREF="telnet://
208.133.228.1">log into their system</A> from
home with telnet to see if a particular book is
available or checked out. Most browsers don't
view telnet connections inline, but instead open
a helper application like NCSA Telnet.

<P>Hey, what if you just want to let your
visitors download a file that's on your server
in the same directory as your Web pages? No
problem. The link will look like any other Web
link. Here, download the Windows version of the
<A HREF="http://www.cookwood.com/cookwood/
examples/links/linkexamples.zip"> examples</A>
from this chapter.

</BODY>
</HTML>
```

Figure 7.15 *You can create a link to all different kinds of URLs.*

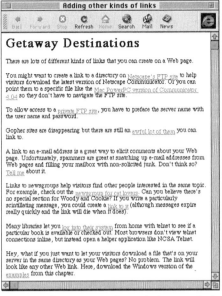

Figure 7.16 *No matter where a link goes, it looks pretty much the same in the browser window. Notice that I've tried to create labels that flow with the body of the text—instead of a lot of "click me's". These are all real links (OK, except the private FTP site). You can see where they lead by opening this page on the Web site (see page 21).*

4. Type the label for the link, that is, the text that will be underlined or high-lighted, and that when clicked upon will take the visitor to the URL refer-enced in step 2.

5. Type **</A>**.

✔ Tips

- You can create links to files on your Web site that you want visitors to be able to download. Make sure that the files are compressed in a number of formats (zipped for Windows and DOS users, stuffed for Mac users).

- You can also create links to less com-mon destinations (like WAIS servers). Just enter the URL in step 2.

- You can preface an FTP URL with **name:password@** to access a private FTP site. Beware of browsers that keep track of where you've been, however, since they'll keep track of your password as well. (For example, in Netscape, type about:global.)

- If you want to create an FTP link to a particular directory on the FTP site (as opposed to an individual file), simply use *ftp://ftp.site.com/directory*. You don't need to use the trailing forward slash. When you don't specify a spe-cific file to download, the browser automatically displays the contents of the last directory in the path.

- Not all browsers can help you follow links to non-Web destinations. If they are unable, they'll generally point you in the right direction of a helper application. For example, Netscape can't view telnet connections inline. Instead it opens a helper application like NCSA Telnet or Microsoft Telnet.

Creating other kinds of links

Creating keyboard shortcuts for links

One great new feature of HTML 4 is the ability to add keyboard shortcuts to different parts of your page, including links. Typing a keyboard shortcut for a link is the same as clicking it.

To add a keyboard shortcut to a link:

1. Inside the link's tag, type **ACCESSKEY="**.

2. Type the keyboard shortcut (any letter or number).

3. Type the final **"**.

4. If desired, add information about the keyboard shortcut to the text so that the visitor knows that it exists.

✔ Tips

■ On Windows systems, to invoke the keyboard shortcut, visitors use the Alt key plus the letter you've assigned.

■ Keyboard shortcuts don't yet work on Macs. When they do, visitors will presumably use the Command key.

■ Keyboard shortcuts that you choose may override the browser's shortcuts. If you assign a popular shortcut used in a browser to some part of your form (like S for Save), you may annoy your visitors. Keep in mind though, that at least on Windows machines, the important browser keyboard shortcuts go with the Ctrl key, not Alt.

```
                    code.html
<HTML><HEAD><TITLE>Adding keyboard shortcuts to
links</TITLE><BASE TARGET=cats></HEAD>
<BODY>
<H1>Our Cats</H1>
Each of our cats has their own home page. Click
on the corresponding link or use the keyboard
shortcut to see each one.
<BR><A HREF="woody.html" ACCESSKEY=w>Woody</A>
(Alt-W)
<BR><A HREF="cookie.html" ACCESSKEY=c>Cookie</
A> (Alt-C)
<BR><A HREF="xixona.html" ACCESSKEY=x>Xixona</
A> (Alt-X)
<BR><A HREF="llumeta.html"
ACCESSKEY=l>Llumeta</A> (Alt-L)
</BODY>
</HTML>
```

Figure 7.17 *Create a keyboard shortcut for a link by adding the ACCESSKEY attribute to its tag. The explanatory text (Alt-W, etc.) is optional but very helpful.*

Figure 7.18 *The link doesn't look any different when it has a keyboard shortcut—which is why it's important to use regular old text to tell visitors that the keyboard shortcut exists.*

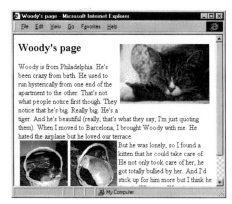

Figure 7.19 *When the keyboard shortcut is used, the link is immediately accessed (and the corresponding page is shown).*

```
code.html
<HTML><HEAD><TITLE>Adding keyboard shortcuts to
links</TITLE><BASE TARGET=cats></HEAD><BODY>
<TABLE BORDER=1 CELLPADDING=4 WIDTH=80%
ALIGN=center>
<TR ALIGN=center><TD><A HREF="toc.html"
TABINDEX=2 TARGET=info>Contents</A>
<TD><A HREF="search.html" TABINDEX=2
TARGET=info>Search</A>
<TD><A HREF="company.html" TABINDEX=2
TARGET=info>About Us</A>
</TABLE>
<H1>Our Cats</H1>
Each of our cats has their own home page. Click
on the corresponding link or use the keyboard
shortcut to see each one.
<BR><A HREF="woody.html" ACCESSKEY=w
TABINDEX=1>Woody</A> (Alt-W)
<BR><A HREF="cookie.html" ACCESSKEY=c
TABINDEX=1>Cookie</A> (Alt-C)
<BR><A HREF="xixona.html" ACCESSKEY=x
TABINDEX=1>Xixona</A> (Alt-X)
<BR><A HREF="llumeta.html" ACCESSKEY=l
TABINDEX=1>Llumeta</A> (Alt-L)
</BODY>
</HTML>
```

Figure 7.20 *This page begins with a table of general links, which, while useful, don't have anything to do with this particular page. To have the first tab result in the first "real" link being selected, I've assigned it the lowest tab index.*

Figure 7.21 *When the visitor hits the Tab key for the first time (OK, the second, see the last tip on this page), the first real link (Woody) is selected. If they hit Tab again, Cookie will be selected, and so on until after Llumeta. At that point, a tab will bring them up to the Contents link.*

Setting the tab order for links

Many browsers let users navigate through the links, image maps, and form elements with the Tab key. You can determine a custom tab order, to emphasize certain elements.

To set the tab order:

In the link's tag, type **TABINDEX=n**, where *n* is the number that sets the tab order.

✔ Tips

■ To *activate* a link the visitor must tab to it and then press Enter.

■ The value for TABINDEX can be any number between 0 and 32767.

■ By default, the tab order depends on the order of the elements in the HTML code. When you change the tab order, the lower numbered elements are activated first, followed by higher numbered elements.

■ Elements with the same tab index value are accessed in the order in which they appear in the HTML page.

■ You can take a link out of the tab sequence by assigning a negative value to the TABINDEX attribute.

■ You can also assign tab order to client-side image maps and form elements. For more information, consult *Creating a client-side image map* on page 120 or *Setting the tab order* on page 199, respectively.

■ Actually, when the visitor hits Tab for the first time, the page's URL is selected (in the Address/Location bar, even if it's hidden). The *second* time they hit Tab, the link with the lowest tab index on the page will be selected.

Setting the tab order for links

Using images to label links

In this age of graphical interfaces, people are used to clicking on images and icons to make things happen. Adding an image to a link creates a navigational button that the visitor can click to access the referenced URL. (For more information about images, see Chapter 4, *Creating Images*, and Chapter 5, *Using Images*.)

To use images to label links:

1. Type **<A HREF="destination.html">**, where *destination.html* is the URL of the page that the user will jump to when they click the button.

2. Type **<IMG SRC="image.location"** where *image.location* gives the location of the image file on the server.

3. If desired, type **BORDER=n**, where *n* is the width in pixels of the border. Use a value of 0 to omit the border.

4. Add other image attributes as desired and then type the final **>**.

5. If desired, type the label text, that is, the text that will be underlined or highlighted in blue, that when clicked upon will take the user to the URL referenced in step 1.

6. Type **</A>** to complete the link.

✔ Tips

■ If you invert steps 5 and 6, only a click on the *image* will produce the desired jump. A click on the text has no effect.

■ Use small images.

■ Clickable images are surrounded by a border with the same color as the active links (generally blue). For no border, use a value of 0 in step 3.

```
code.html
<HTML>
<HEAD><TITLE>Creating a Button (Using an Image
in a Link)</TITLE>
</HEAD>
<H1>Cookie and Woody</H1>
<P>Generally considered the sweetest and yet
most independent cats in the <A
HREF=pioneerval.html>Pioneer Valley,</A> Cookie
and Woody are consistently underestimated by
their humble humans.
<P>
<A HREF="prevpage.html"><IMG SRC=pointleft.gif
ALT="Previous page"></A>
<A HREF="nextpage.html"><IMG SRC=pointright.gif
ALT="Next page"></A>

<P><A HREF="mailto:lcastro@crocker.com"><IMG
SRC=writeletter.gif ALT="Send mail"
ALIGN=center> Send me comments</A> on this page!
</BODY>
</HTML>
```

Figure 7.22 *There is no text in the first two button links. The final </A> comes right after the image tag.*

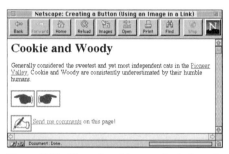

Figure 7.23 *If you do add text to the link, make sure you insert a space between the text and the image (or use HSPACE or styles to space the text, see page 86).*

Figure 7.24 *This is the original pointright.gif image. It does not have a border. Borders are automatically added in the browser to all images used to label links. You can adjust the border with the BORDER attribute in the IMG tag.*

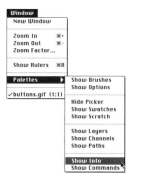

Figure 7.25 *In Photoshop, choose Show Info in the Palettes submenu in the Window menu.*

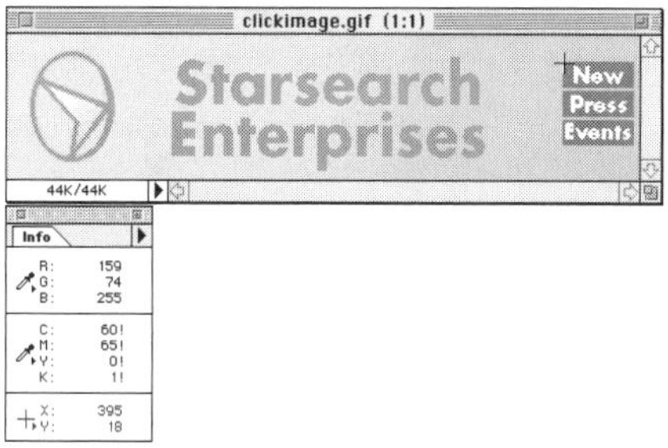

Figure 7.26 *Place the cursor in the left hand corner of the rectangle and jot down the x and y coordinates shown in Photoshop's Info palette. (In this example x=395 and y=18.)*

Dividing an image into clickable regions

A clickable image is like a collection of buttons combined together in one image. A click in one part of the image brings the user to one destination. A click in another area brings the user to a different destination.

There are two important steps to implementing a clickable image: First you must map out the different regions of your image, and second you must create a script that defines which destinations correspond to which areas of the image.

To divide an image into regions:

1. Create a GIF image, consulting Chapter 4, *Creating Images*, as necessary.

2. Open the GIF image in Photoshop or other image editing program.

3. Choose Window > Palettes > Show Info **(Figure 7.25)**.

4. Point the cursor over the top left corner of the region you wish to define. Using the Info window, jot down the *x* and *y* coordinates for that corner **(Figure 7.26)**.

5. Repeat step 4 for the bottom right corner of a rectangle, or for each point of a polygon.

✔ Tip

■ For more information on a few tools that can help you divide your image into clickable regions, consult *Image Map Tools* on page 306.

Creating a client-side image map

Image maps link the areas of an image with a series of URLs. A click in each area brings the user to a different page. There are two kinds of image maps, *client-side* and *server side (see page 122)*. Client-side image maps run more quickly because they are interpreted in your users' browsers and don't have to consult the server for each click. In addition since they do not require a CGI script, they are simpler to create, and you don't need to consult your Internet service provider, nor get their permission. But, older browsers may not understand them.

To create a client-side image map:

1. In the HTML document that contains the image, type **<MAP**.

2. Type **NAME="label">**, where *label* is the name of the map.

3. Type **<AREA** to define the first clickable area.

4. Type **SHAPE="type"**, where *type* represents the area's shape. Use *rect* for a rectangle, *circle* for a circle, and *poly* for an irregular shape.

5. For a rectangle, type **COORDS="x1, y1, x2, y2"**, where *x1*, *y1*, *x2*, and *y2* represent the upper left and lower right corners of the rectangle, as obtained on page 119, and shown in Figure 7.26.

For a circle, type **COORDS="x, y, r"** where *x* and *y* represent the center of the circle and *r* is the radius.

For a polygon, type **COORDS="x1, y1 x2, y2, x3, y3"** (and so on), giving the x and y coordinates of each point on the polygon.

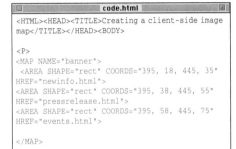

```
┌──────────── code.html ────────────┐
<HTML><HEAD><TITLE>Creating a client-side image
map</TITLE></HEAD><BODY>

<P>
<MAP NAME="banner">
 <AREA SHAPE="rect" COORDS="395, 18, 445, 35"
HREF="newinfo.html">
 <AREA SHAPE="rect" COORDS="395, 38, 445, 55"
HREF="pressrelease.html">
 <AREA SHAPE="rect" COORDS="395, 58, 445, 75"
HREF="events.html">

</MAP>
```

Figure 7.27 *You can place the map anywhere in your HTML document. Each clickable area is defined by its own set of coordinates, and has an individual URL.*

```
┌──────────── code.html ────────────┐
</MAP>

<IMG SRC="clickimage.gif" ALT="SE banner"
USEMAP="#banner" WIDTH=
"450" HEIGHT="100"  ALIGN="BOTTOM" ISMAP>
</P>

H1>Starsearch Enterprises</H1>
```

Figure 7.28 *Type the image definition in the desired place in your HTML document. The most important piece is the USEMAP=#label attribute. Don't forget the number sign (#).*

```
┌──────────── code.html ────────────┐
<IMG SRC="clickimage.gif" ALT="SE banner"
USEMAP="#banner" WIDTH=
"450" HEIGHT="100"  ALIGN="BOTTOM" ISMAP>
</P>

H1>Starsearch Enterprises</H1>

<UL>
<LI><A HREF="http://www.castro.com/lcastro/
newinfo.html">New programs</A>
 <LI><A HREF="http://www.castro.com/
lcastro/pressrelease.html">Press releases</
A>
<LI><A HREF="http://www.castro.com/lcastro/
events.html">Upcoming events</A>
<LI><A HREF="http://www.castro.com/lcastro/
infoSE.html">About Starsearch
  Enterprises</A>
</UL>
</BODY>
</HTML>
```

Figure 7.29 *Below the image it's a good idea to repeat the links in text form for those users who can't or don't want to view images. Otherwise, those users won't be able to navigate to your other pages.*

Figure 7.30 *When your users point at one of the defined areas, the destination URL appears in the status bar at the bottom of the window.*

Figure 7.31 *And if a user clicks the link, the browser will immediately display the corresponding page.*

6. Type **HREF="url.html"**, where *url.html* is the address of the page that should appear when the user clicks in this area.

Or type **NOHREF** if a click in this area should have no result.

7. Type **TARGET=windowname**, where *windowname* is the name of the window where the page should appear. For more information, see page 112.

8. If desired, add a keyboard shortcut by typing **ACCESSKEY=x** *(see page 116)*.

9. Type **>** to complete the definition of the clickable area.

10. Repeat steps 3–9 for each area.

11. Type **</MAP>** to complete the map.

12. Type **<IMG SRC="image.gif"**, where *image.gif* is the name of the image to be used as an image map.

13. Add any other image attributes.

14. Type **USEMAP="#label"**, where *label* is the map name defined in step 2.

15. Type the final **>** for the image.

✔ Tips

■ Usually, maps are in the same HTML document as the image that uses them. Internet Explorer, however, can use maps that are in an external HTML file. Simply add the full URL of that file in front of the label name: **USEMAP="map.html#label"**.

■ With overlapping areas, most browsers use the URL of the first area defined.

■ For information on using server-side image maps, see page 122.

Creating a client-side image map

Using a server-side image map

To use a server-side image map, you have to have the *imagemap* program on your NCSA HTTPd server or *htimage* on your CERN server. The program should be located in the cgi-bin directory. Ask your server administrator for help, if necessary.

To use a server-side image map:

1. In your HTML document type **<A HREF="http://www.yoursite.com/cgi-bin/imagemap**, where *imagemap* is the name of the program that interprets your set of coordinates.

2. Type **/path/coords"** (adding no spaces after step 1) indicating the path to the text file that contains the coordinates (the map) for the image.

3. Type the final **>** of the link definition.

4. Type **<IMG SRC="clickimage.gif"** where *clickimage.gif* is the image that you want your readers to click.

5. Type **ISMAP** to indicate a clickable image for a server-side map.

6. Add any other image attributes as desired and then type the final **>**.

7. Type the clickable text that should appear next to the image, if any.

8. Type **</A>** to complete the link.

✔ Tip

■ For information on creating sets of coordinates for server-side image maps, consult your Internet service provider. They'll be able to tell you what kind of server they have and in what format the coordinates should be.

```
code.html
<BODY>
<A HREF="http://www.castro.com/cgi-bin/
imagemap/lcastro/banner.map">
<IMG SRC="clickimage.gif" ALT="SE banner"
ISMAP>
</A>
<H1>Starsearch Enterprises</H1>
<UL>
<LI><A HREF="http://www.castro.com/lcastro/
newinfo.html">New programs</A>
<LI><A HREF="http://www.castro.com/lcastro/
pressrelease.html">Press releases</A>
<LI><A HREF="http://www.castro.com/lcastro/
events.html">Upcoming events</A>
<LI><A HREF="http://www.castro.com/lcastro/
infoSE.html">About Starsearch Enterprises</
A>
```

Figure 7.32 *Notice how the text-based alternate links below the image point to the same URLs as the buttons in the clickable image. This gives equal access to your users who can't see the images.*

Figure 7.33 *In Netscape, when your user points at a part of a clickable image, the cursor changes into a hand and the corresponding URL shows in the status area at the bottom of the window.*

Figure 7.34 *In Internet Explorer, the cursor changes to a hand when placed over a clickable image, but the status line does not show the particular coordinates.*

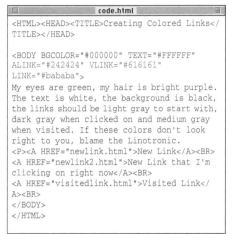

```
                    code.html
<HTML><HEAD><TITLE>Creating Colored Links</
TITLE></HEAD>

<BODY BGCOLOR="#000000" TEXT="#FFFFFF"
ALINK="#242424" VLINK="#616161"
LINK="#bababa">
My eyes are green, my hair is bright purple.
The text is white, the background is black,
the links should be light gray to start with,
dark gray when clicked on and medium gray
when visited. If these colors don't look
right to you, blame the Linotronic.
<P><A HREF="newlink.html">New Link</A><BR>
<A HREF="newlink2.html">New Link that I'm
clicking on right now</A><BR>
<A HREF="visitedlink.html">Visited Link</
A><BR>
</BODY>
</HTML>
```

Figure 7.35 *You may select a color for new links, visited links, and active links (one that is being clicked).*

Figure 7.36 *It is important to choose colors (or shades of gray, as in this example) that have enough contrast so that you can see all the items on the page, but not so much (especially with colors) as to be garish and distracting.*

Changing the color of links

The LINK markers let you change the color of links. Although certain standard link colors have already been established—like blue for links that have not yet been visited—you can use whatever color you want. Of course, folks will only click on a link if they know it's a link.

To change the color of links:

1. Place the cursor inside the BODY tag.

2. To change the color of links that have not yet been visited, type **LINK**.

   To change the color of links that have already been visited, type **VLINK**.

   To change the color of a link when the user clicks on it, type **ALINK.**

3. Type **="#rrggbb"**, where *rrggbb* is the hexadecimal representation of the desired color.

   Or type **=color**, where *color* is one of the 16 predefined colors.

4. Repeat steps 2–3 for each kind of link.

✔ Tips

■ See Appendix C and the inside back cover for a complete listing of hexadecimal values and the equivalents for many common colors.

■ Make sure you test the colors of your text, links, and background together. Also test your color page on a black and white and a grayscale monitor.

■ Be careful when choosing different colors for links from page to page. If your visitors can't tell what to click on or which pages they've already visited, they may decide not to click on anything.

Lists 8

The HTML specifications contain special codes for creating lists of items. You can create plain, numbered, or bulleted lists, as well as lists of definitions. You can also nest one kind of list inside another. In the sometimes sketchy shorthand of the Internet, lists come in very handy.

All lists are formed by a principal code to specify what sort of list you want to create (OL for ordered list, DL for definition list, etc.) and a secondary code to specify what sort of items you want to create (LI for list item, DT for definition term, etc.).

Although the W3C does not recommend the use of List codes for simply indenting paragraphs, they *are* rather handy in this regard. You can find more information about that in Chapter 6, *Page Layout*, under *Creating indents (with lists)* on page 94.

Lists

Creating ordered lists

The ordered list is perfect for explaining step-by-step instructions for how to complete a particular task or for creating an outline (complete with links to corresponding sections, if desired) of a larger document. You may create an ordered list anywhere in the BODY section of your HTML document.

To create ordered lists:

1. Type the title of the ordered list.

2. Type **<OL**.

3. If desired, type **TYPE=X**, where *X* represents the symbols that should be used in the ordered list: *A* for capital letters, *a* for small letters, *I* for capital roman numerals, *i* for small roman numerals, and *1* for numbers, which is the default.

4. If desired, type **START=n**, where *n* represents the initial value for this list item. The START value is always numeric and is converted automatically, according to the TYPE value.

5. Type **>** to finish the ordered list definition. Any text entered after the OL marker and before the first LI marker will appear with the same indentation as the first item in the list, but without a number.

6. Type **<LI**.

7. If desired, type **TYPE=X**, where *X* represents the symbols that should be used for this and subsequent list items. Changing the TYPE here overrides the value chosen in step 3.

```
code.html
<HTML>
<HEAD>
<TITLE>Creating Ordered Lists</TITLE>
</HEAD>
<BODY>
Ordered lists are the most common kinds of
lists, perfect for explaining step by step
instructions or for giving an outline
(complete with links to the corresponding
sections, if desired) for a larger document.

<H1>Changing a light bulb</H1>
<OL>
<LI>Make sure you have unplugged the lamp.
<LI>Unscrew the old bulb.
<LI>Get the new bulb out of the package.
<LI>Check the wattage to make sure it's
correct.
<LI>Screw in the new bulb.
<LI>Plug in the lamp and turn it on!
</OL>

<H1>The Great American Novel</H1>
<OL TYPE=I>
<LI>Introduction
<LI>Denouement
<LI>Climax
<LI>End
<LI>Epilogue
</OL>

</BODY>
</HTML>
```

Figure 8.1 *There is no special way to format a list's title. Just use a regular header (see page 40).*

Figure 8.2 *The first list uses the default TYPE=1 attribute to create a numbered list. The second list uses the TYPE=I to create a list headed by capital roman numerals.*

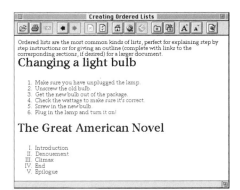

Figure 8.3 *Internet Explorer displays the numbered lists types as well as Netscape.*

8. If desired, type **VALUE=n**, where *n* represents the initial value for this list item. The VALUE is always specified numerically and is converted automatically to the type of symbol specified by the TYPE value. The VALUE attribute overrides the START value chosen in step 4.

9. Type the final **>** to complete the list item definition.

10. Type the text to be included in the list item.

11. Repeat steps 6-10 for each new list item.

12. Type **</OL>** to complete the ordered list.

✔ **Tips**

■ Keep the text in your list items short. If you have more than a few lines of text in each item, you may have better luck using headers (H1, H2, etc.) and paragraphs (P).

■ Inserting a line break (BR) in a list item breaks the text to the next line, but maintains the same indenting.

■ Text placed after the OL marker appears indented by the same amount as the following list item, but without a number or letter.

■ You may create one type of list inside another. For more information, consult *Creating nested lists* on page 131.

■ You should know that the W3C discourages the use of the START, TYPE, and VALUE attributes in favor of style sheets *(see page 265)*. However, I doubt that the major browsers will stop supporting these variables any time soon.

Creating ordered lists

Creating unordered lists

Unordered lists are probably the most widely used lists on the Web. Use them to list any series of items that have no particular order, such as hot Web sites or names.

To create unordered lists:

1. Type the introductory text for the unordered list, if desired.

2. Type **<UL**.

3. If desired, type **TYPE=shape**, where *shape* represents the kind of bullet that should be used with each list item. You may choose *disc* for a solid round bullet (the default for first level lists), *circle* for an empty round bullet (the default for second level lists), or *square* for square bullets (the default for third level lists).

4. Type **>** to finish the unordered list definition. Any text entered after the UL marker and before the first LI marker will appear with the same indentation as the first item in the list, but without a bullet.

5. Type **<LI**.

6. Type **TYPE=shape**, where *shape* represents the kind of bullet (*disc, circle,* or *square*) that should be used in this list item. You only need to specify the shape here if it differs from the one you've chosen in step 3.

7. Type **>** to finish the list item definition.

8. Type the text to be included in the list item.

9. Repeat steps 5-7 for each list item.

10. Type **</UL>** to complete the unordered list.

```
code.html
<HTML><HEAD>
<TITLE>Creating Unordered Lists</TITLE>
</HEAD><BODY>
Unordered lists are probably the most widely
used lists on the Web. Use them to list any
series of items that have no particular
order, such as hot web sites or names.

<H1>PageWhacker, version 12.0--Features</
H1>
<UL><EM><FONT SIZE=-1>New or improved
features marked with a solid bullet.
<BR>(All features may show the same bullets
in some browsers.)</FONT></EM>
<LI TYPE=round>One click page layout
<LI TYPE=disc>Spell checker for 327 major
languages
<LI>Image retouching plug-in
<LI TYPE=round>Special HTML filters
<LI>Unlimited Undo's and Redo's
<LI TYPE=disc>Automatic book writing
</UL>

<H1>The hotel offers the following
entertainment choices:</H1>
<UL>
<LI>Live music and dancing in the Starlight
Lounge
<LI TYPE=square>Midnight snacks in Balladier
Hall
<LI TYPE=disc>Free HBO and Cinemax
<LI TYPE=square>Moonlight swim in the
rooftop pool
<LI TYPE=disc>Specialty room service
<LI TYPE=square>Friday night Bingo in the
Green room
</UL>

</BODY>
</HTML>
```

Figure 8.4 *The bullets on the first level are round and solid (disc), by default, so it's not necessary to specify the TYPE unless you wish to select a different shape.*

Figure 8.5 *You can use different bullet styles to distinguish among the entries as in the first example, or to add visual interest as in the second example.*

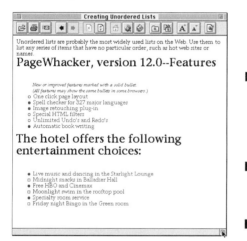

Figure 8.6 *Although many browsers understand the special bullet styles, including Internet Explorer, shown here, not all do. Either avoid giving special meaning to shaped bullets or add a text clarification.*

✔ **Tips**

■ You can use any image you want for bullets—if you use style sheets. For more information, consult *Setting list properties* on page 265.

■ Keep the text in your list items short. If you have more than a couple of lines of text in each item, you may have better luck using headers (H1, H2, etc.) and paragraphs (P).

■ Inserting a line break (BR) in a list item breaks the text to the next line, but maintains the same indenting.

■ Text placed after the UL marker appears indented by the same amount as the following list item, but without a bullet. In fact, many people use the UL marker for indenting text *(see page 94)*.

■ The TYPE marker in a list item over-rides the TYPE marker used in the unordered list definition and affects the current list item as well as any subsequent list items.

■ You may create one type of list inside another. For more information, consult *Creating nested lists* on page 131.

■ You should know that the W3C discourages the use of the TYPE attribute in favor of style sheets *(see page 265)*. However, I doubt that the major browsers will stop supporting it any time soon.

■ There is one more value possible for the TYPE attribute: *round*. However, Netscape displays it the same as circle while Explorer displays it as a square.

Creating definition lists

HTML provides a special marker for creating definition lists. This type of list is particularly suited to glossaries but works well with any list that pairs a word or phrase with a longer description. Imagine, for example, a list of Classical Greek verb tenses, each followed by an explanation of proper usage.

To create definition lists:

1. Type the introductory text for the definition list.

2. Type **<DL>**. You may enter text after the DL marker. It will appear on its own line, aligned to the left margin.

3. Type **<DT>**.

4. Type the word or short phrase that will be defined or explained, including any logical or physical formatting desired.

5. Type **<DD>**.

6. Type the definition of the term entered in step 4. Browsers generally indent definitions on a new line below your definition term.

7. Repeat steps 3-6 for each pair of terms and definitions.

8. Type **</DL>** to complete the list of definitions.

✔ Tip

■ You can create more than one DL line or more than one DT line to accommodate multiple words or multiple definitions.

```
code.html
<HTML><HEAD><TITLE>Creating Definition
Lists</TITLE></HEAD>
<BODY>
HTML provides a special marker for creating
lists of definitions. This type of list is
particularly suited to glossaries but works
well with any list that pairs a word or
phrase with a longer description. Imagine
for example a list of abbreviations, each
followed by the spelled out equivalent
<H1>Classical Greek Verb Tenses</H1>
<DL>
<DT><STRONG>Present</STRONG><BR>
<DD><EM>e.g. .luo, luomai</EM>. The present
usually shows the pure verb stem in verbs
with strong stems. In many verbs it undergoes
drastic phonetical changes due to the union
of the thematic vowels to the tense suffixes.
<DT><STRONG>Future</STRONG><BR>
<DD><EM>e.g. luso, lusomai, luthesomai</EM>.
The future has the characteristic s in
between the verb stem and the thematic
vowels, which gives: verb stem + s (-the- in
passive voice) + thematic vowel + personal
ending.
<DT><STRONG>Aorist</STRONG><BR>
<DD><EM>e.g. .elusa, eluthen, elusamen</EM>.
The aorist (from a-orizo, aoristos:
indefinite, limitless) is the equivalent to
the indefinite past in several languages.
Its main characteristic is the temporal
suffix -sa- (in the active and middle voice)
and -the- in the passive voice. The -s- from
sa may change to accomodate different stem
endings. For example: kopto = ekops (ps =
psi)a.
</DL></BODY></HTML>
```

Figure 8.7 *You may want to add formatting to your definition term to help it stand out.*

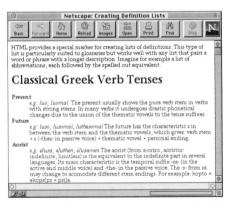

Figure 8.8 *The defined word (marked with DT) is aligned to the left. The definition (marked with DD) is indented.*

```
                code.html
<HTML><HEAD>
<TITLE>Creating Nested Lists</TITLE>
</HEAD><BODY>
Nested lists are ideal for outlines, but
don't feel limited. You can nest any list
inside any other list. Just make sure each
list has its own beginning and ending
markers.

<H1>The Great American Novel</H1>
<OL TYPE=I>
<LI>Introduction
    <OL TYPE=A>
    <LI>Boy's childhood
    <LI>Girl's childhood
    </OL>
<LI>Denouement
    <OL TYPE=A>
    <LI>Boy meets Girl
    <LI>Boy and Girl fall in love
    <LI>Boy and Girl have fight
    </OL>
<LI>Climax
    <OL TYPE=A>
    <LI>Boy gives Girl ultimatum
        <OL TYPE=1>
        <LI>Girl can't believe her ears
        <LI>Boy is indignant at Girl's
            indignance
        </OL>
    <LI>Girl tells Boy to get lost
    </OL>
<LI>End
<LI>Epilogue
</OL>
</BODY></HTML>
```

Figure 8.9 *Browsers automatically indent nested lists, but if you use tabs to indent them in your HTML document, it will be much easier to organize and set up.*

Figure 8.10 *You, the programmer, can choose the type of numbering for each level of your outline.*

Creating nested lists

You may insert one type of list into another. This is particularly useful with an outline rendered with ordered lists, where you may want several levels of items.

To create nested lists:

1. Create your first list.

2. Place the cursor inside your first list where you want your nested list to appear.

3. Create your nested list in the same way you created the regular list.

4. Continue with the principal list.

✔ Tips

- Use tabs to indent the nested list in your HTML document so that it is easier to see what you're doing. Nested lists are automatically indented by browsers.

- The numbering for nested ordered lists automatically starts at 1 unless you specify a new value with the START marker.

- The correct nesting order for TYPE markers, according to *The Chicago Manual of Style* is I, A, 1, a, 1.

- By default, the first level of an unordered list will have solid round bullets, the next will have empty round bullets and the last will have square bullets. Use the TYPE tag to specify the type of bullet you want *(see page 128)*.

Creating nested lists

Tables

There is nothing like a table for presenting complicated information in a simple way. Your visitor sees what you're getting at right away and everyone goes home happy. Too bad none of the improvements in HTML 4 make setting up tables any easier. Don't be scared off, though; the result is well worth the effort.

If tables really make you miserable, of course, you can cheat. Try the shortcut described on page 286 if you use Microsoft Word. Or if you use PageMill or FrontPage or some other Web page program, create the table in that program and then tweak the HTML code by hand afterwards as necessary.

If you are worried about visitors who use a browser that doesn't understand tables, you might consider creating hand-spaced tables with preformatted text *(see page 53)*. Tables made with preformatted text can be read with *any* browser.

Finally, don't limit your use of tables to rows and columns of numbers. Tables are a great way to divide your entire page into manageable sections that are easy to align and space. And consult Chapter 17, *Extras* for more tips on using tables in unconventional ways.

Creating a simple table

There are many kinds of tables, and even many kinds of simple tables. Here we will create a table with two columns and three rows, using the first column to contain the headers and the second column to contain the data.

To create a simple table:

1. Type **<TABLE>**.

2. Type **<TR>** to define the beginning of the first row. We will add two elements to the first row: a header cell and a regular cell. If desired, press Return and Tab to visually distinguish the row elements **(Figure 9.1)**.

3. Create a header cell in the first row by typing **<TH>**.

4. Type the contents of the first header cell.

5. Create a regular cell after the header cell in the first row by typing **<TD>**.

6. Type the contents of the regular cell.

7. Repeat steps 2–6 for each row. In this example, there are two more rows, each containing a header cell and a regular cell.

8. To finish the table, type **</TABLE>**.

✔ Tip

- If you like, you can close each cell with **</TH>** or **</TD>**. Close each row with a **</TR>**. These tags are all optional. Web editors like PageMill are diligent about using closing tags. If you need to make changes by hand, it's fine if part of the table uses closing tags and your part doesn't.

```
code.html
<HTML><HEAD><TITLE>Creating a simple table
</TITLE></HEAD><BODY><TABLE><TR><TH>
Northampton<TD>6<TR><TH>Becket<TD>27<TR>
<TH>Worthington<TD>12</TABLE></BODY></HTML>
```

```
code.html
<HTML><HEAD><TITLE>Creating a simple table</
TITLE></HEAD>
<BODY>
<TABLE>
<TR>
    <TH>Northampton
    <TD>6
<TR>
    <TH>Becket
    <TD>27
<TR>
    <TH>Worthington
    <TD>12
</TABLE>
</BODY></HTML>
```

Figure 9.1 *The only difference between the two HTML documents above is the addition of returns and tabs to visually separate the rows and row elements to help keep things straight while constructing the table. Since browsers ignore all extra spacing, both documents create the exact same Web page. (See Figure 9.2 below.)*

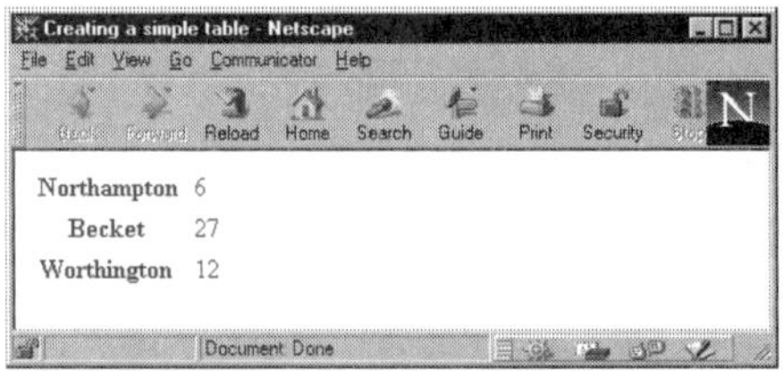

Figure 9.2 *It seems rather a lot of work for a simple table like this.*

```
code.html
<HTML><HEAD><TITLE>Putting headers across
the top</TITLE></HEAD>
<BODY>
<TABLE>
<TR>
    <TH>Northampton
    <TH>Becket
    <TH>Worthington
<TR>
    <TD>6
    <TD>27
    <TD>12
</TABLE>
</BODY></HTML>
```

Figure 9.3 *In the first row, you define all the headers. In the second row, you define all the regular cells.*

```
Putting headers across the top - Microsoft Internet Explorer
File  Edit  View  Go  Favorites  Help

Northampton Becket Worthington
      6      27      12

                            My Computer
```

Figure 9.4 *Clearly, very simple tables like these may be better off expressed in lists. However, as you will see in the following pages, there are many ways to tweak your tables to make them beautiful—and more effective.*

Putting header cells across the top

On the previous page, in our simple table, we placed the header cells along one side of the table. To have the header cells appear along the top of the table, you have to define the cells in a slightly different order.

To create a table with header cells across the top:

1. Type **<TABLE>**.

2. Type **<TR>** to define the beginning of the first row. If desired, press Return and Tab to visually distinguish the table elements.

3. Create the first header cell in the first row by typing **<TH>**.

4. Type the contents of the first header cell.

5. Repeat steps 3–4 for each header cell.

6. Type **<TR>** to begin the second row.

7. Type **<TD>** to define the first regular cell in the second row.

8. Type the cell data.

9. Repeat steps 7-8 for each regular cell.

10. To finish the table, type **</TABLE>**.

✔ Tip

■ Again, feel free to end each cell with **</TH>** or **</TD>** and each row with **</TR>**. It's completely optional.

Find extra tips, the source code for examples, and more at www.cookwood.com   **135**

Putting header cells on top and left

The objective of a table is to present complicated data in a clear way. Often you will need header cells across the top of the table *and* down the left side to identify the data being discussed.

To create a table with header cells on top and down the left side:

1. Type **<TABLE>**.

2. Type **<TR>** to define the beginning of the first row. If desired, press Return and Tab to visually distinguish the table elements.

3. Create the empty cell in the top left corner by typing **<TD>
**.

4. Create a header cell by typing **<TH>cell contents**, where *cell contents* is the data that the cell should contain.

5. Repeat step 4 for each header cell in the first row.

6. Type **<TR>** to begin the second row.

7. To define the first header on the left side, type **<TH>cell contents**, where *cell contents* is the data that the cell should contain.

8. To create a regular cell after the header cell in the second row, type **<TD>cell contents**, where *cell contents* is the data that the cell should contain.

9. Repeat step 8 for each remaining regular cell in the row.

10. Repeat steps 6–9 for each remaining row.

11. To finish the table, type **</TABLE>**.

```
code.html
<HTML><HEAD><TITLE>Putting headers on top
and left</TITLE></HEAD>
<BODY>
<TABLE>
<TR>
    <TD><BR>
    <TH>Babies
    <TH>Adults
    <TH>Total
<TR>
    <TH>Northampton
    <TD>2
    <TD>4
    <TD>6
<TR>
    <TH>Becket
    <TD>5
    <TD>22
    <TD>27
<TR>
    <TH>Worthington
    <TD>7
    <TD>5
    <TD>12
</TABLE>
</BODY></HTML>
```

Figure 9.5 *For a four row by four column table, notice that there are four sets of TR tags with four elements in each set. Once you have defined the first set, copy and paste (and edit) to create the other three.*

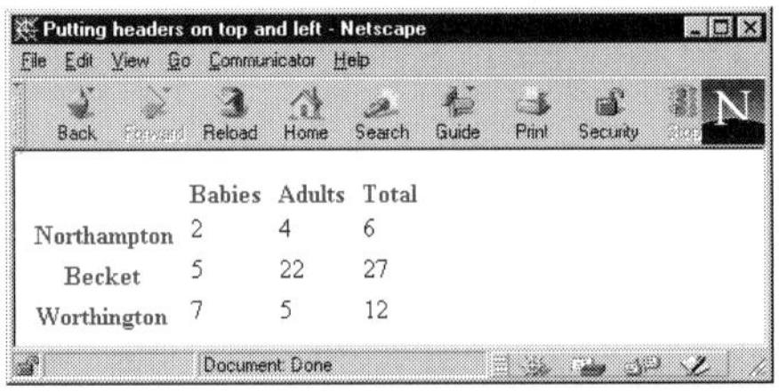

Figure 9.6 *Tables can look pretty bad without borders. (You'll add a border on page 141.)*

Putting header cells on top and left

```
┌──────────────────── code.html ──────────────────┐
│ <HTML><HEAD><TITLE>Adding a caption</            │
│ TITLE></HEAD><BODY>                              │
│ <TABLE>                                          │
│ <CAPTION ALIGN=bottom>Bear sightings in          │
│ Western Massachusetts</CAPTION>                  │
│ <TR>                                             │
│     <TD><BR>                                     │
│     <TH>Babies                                   │
└──────────────────────────────────────────────────┘
```

Figure 9.7 *You should place the caption directly after the TABLE tag.*

Figure 9.8 *Both Netscape and Internet Explorer center captions automatically and divide the lines to fit the table width, if necessary.*

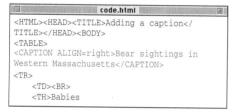

```
┌──────────────────── code.html ──────────────────┐
│ <HTML><HEAD><TITLE>Adding a caption</            │
│ TITLE></HEAD><BODY>                              │
│ <TABLE>                                          │
│ <CAPTION ALIGN=right>Bear sightings in           │
│ Western Massachusetts</CAPTION>                  │
│ <TR>                                             │
│     <TD><BR>                                     │
│     <TH>Babies                                   │
└──────────────────────────────────────────────────┘
```

Figure 9.9 *If you can be sure your visitors use Internet Explorer, you can use the ALIGN=right attribute inside your CAPTION tag to place the caption above and to the right of your table.*

Figure 9.10 *Captions aligned to the left or right are always displayed at the top of the table.*

Adding a caption

The CAPTION tag lets you attach a descriptive title to your table.

To create a caption:

1. Directly after the initial <TABLE> tag, but not inside any row or cell tags, type **<CAPTION**.

2. If desired, type **ALIGN=direction**, where *direction* is either top, bottom, left, or right.

3. Type the final **>**.

4. Type the caption for the table (in the example shown in Figure 9.8, *Bear sightings in Western Massachusetts*).

5. Type **</CAPTION>**.

✔ Tips

■ You can use styles to change the appearance of the caption.

■ There's really no reason to use **ALIGN=top**. Since that's the default, if you want the caption centered above the table, you can just leave the ALIGN attribute out altogether.

■ In Internet Explorer, the *left* and *right* values for ALIGN also place the caption above the table, but align it to the specified side (not the center). The *bottom* value always places the caption centered below the table. There is no way to place the caption at the bottom left or bottom right.

■ Netscape currently only supports the top and bottom values for ALIGN (and not right and left).

Dividing your table into column groups

There are two kinds of column groups: structural and non-structural. The former control where dividing lines, or rules, are drawn *(see page 143)*. The latter do not. Both let you apply formatting to an entire column (or groups of columns) of cells all at once.

To divide a table into structural column groups:

1. After the <TABLE> and <CAPTION> tags, type **<COLGROUP**.

2. If the column group has more than one column, type **SPAN=n**, where *n* is the number of columns in the group.

3. If desired, define the attributes for the column group.

4. Type the final **>**.

5. Repeat steps 1–4 for each column group that you wish to define.

To divide a table into non-structural column groups:

1. After the <TABLE> and <CAPTION> tags, type **<COL**.

2. If the column group has more than one column, type **SPAN=n**, where *n* is the number of columns in the group.

3. If desired, define the attributes for the column group.

4. Type the final **>**.

5. Repeat steps 1–4 for each column group that you wish to define.

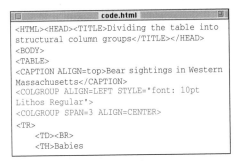

```
code.html
<HTML><HEAD><TITLE>Dividing the table into
structural column groups</TITLE></HEAD>
<BODY>
<TABLE>
<CAPTION ALIGN=top>Bear sightings in Western
Massachusetts</CAPTION>
<COLGROUP ALIGN=LEFT STYLE="font: 10pt
Lithos Regular">
<COLGROUP SPAN=3 ALIGN=CENTER>
<TR>
    <TD><BR>
    <TH>Babies
```

Figure 9.11 *This table is divided into two column groups. The first column group contains just one column (the one with the city names). It will be aligned to the left and set in 10pt Lithos Regular. The second column group spans 3 columns and its contents will be centered.*

Bear sightings in Western Massachusetts

	Babies	Adults	Total
Northampton	2	4	6
Becket	5	22	27
Worthington	7	5	12

Figure 9.12 *Netscape does not support the COLGROUP tag yet.*

Bear sightings in Western Massachusetts

	Babies	Adults	Total
NORTHAMPTON	2	4	6
BECKET	5	22	27
WORTHINGTON	7	5	12

Figure 9.13 *The first column group is now properly aligned to the left and in Lithos. The contents of the second column group (the remaining three columns) are centered.*

Dividing your table into column groups

```
                code.html
<HTML><HEAD><TITLE>Dividing the table into
non-structural column groups</TITLE></HEAD>
<BODY>
<TABLE>
<CAPTION ALIGN=top>Bear sightings in Western
Massachusetts</CAPTION>
<COLGROUP ALIGN=LEFT STYLE="font: 10pt
Lithos Regular">
<COLGROUP SPAN=3 ALIGN=CENTER>
    <COL SPAN=2>
    <COL STYLE="font-weight:900">
<TR>
    <TD><BR>
    <TH>Babies
```

Figure 9.14 *Now I divide the second column group into two separate non-structural column groups (with COL) so that I can format an entire column at a time without affecting how rules (see page 143) will be drawn.*

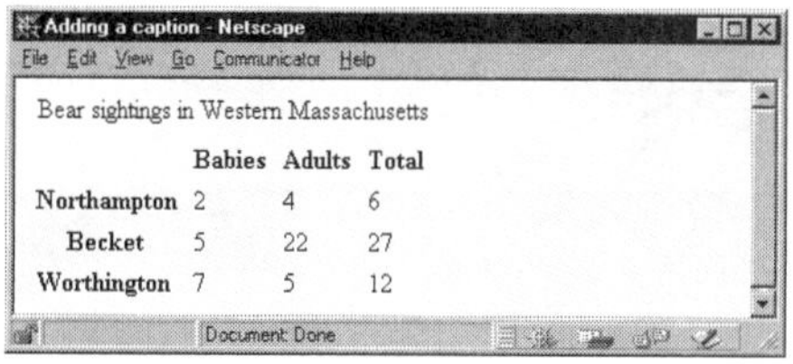

Figure 9.15 *Still no effect in Netscape.*

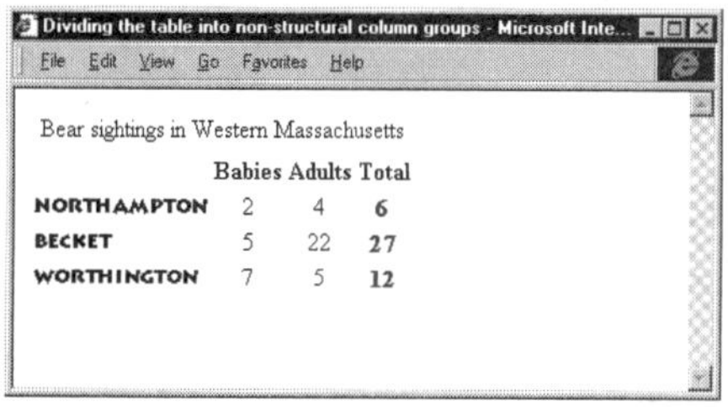

Figure 9.16 *I've used the second non-structural column group to format the last column in bold type so that the totals stand out a bit more.*

✔ **Tips**

■ Both types of column group definitions are completely ignored by Netscape.

■ Use COLGROUP when you want to determine where dividing lines (rules) should go. Use COL for *everything but* deciding where dividing lines go. For more information on drawing dividing lines, consult page 143.

■ You can use many attributes to format column groups, including BGCOLOR, STYLE, and others. For some reason, Explorer currently does not support HEIGHT.

■ You can divide COLGROUPs into COLs in order to add non-structural information (like size, alignment, etc.) to individual columns within structural column groups. Simply type the COL tag *after* the parent COLGROUP tag **(Figure 9.14)**. Note that COL tags' attributes override the attributes in the COLGROUP tag.

■ If the column group only contains one column, you don't need to use the SPAN attribute. Its default is 1.

■ Header cells—those marked with the TH tag—are not affected by the alignment specified in a column group. For more information on aligning cells, consult *Aligning the contents of cells* on page 148.

■ COLGROUP has an optional closing tag. COL has none.

Dividing your table into column groups

Dividing the table into horizontal sections

You can also mark a horizontal section of your table—one or more rows—and then format it all at once. Then draw dividing lines (rules) between sections, instead of between individual rows.

To divide the table into horizontal sections:

1. Before the first <TR> tag of the section you want to create, type **<THEAD**, **<TBODY**, or **<TFOOT**.

2. If desired, define the desired attributes for the section.

3. Type **>**.

4. If necessary, create the section's contents.

5. Close the section with **</THEAD>**, **</TBODY>**, or **</TFOOT>**.

✔ Tips

■ Netscape does not yet recognize horizontal section tags.

■ You can use many cell attributes (BGCOLOR, STYLE, etc.) to format horizontal sections of cells, but IE doesn't support HEIGHT or WIDTH.

■ Horizontal section tags go *after* column group tags *(see page 138)*.

■ Theoretically, at least one TBODY tag is required in every table. Create more than one if you like. You can only have one THEAD and one TFOOT.

■ The closing tags are optional. A section is automatically closed when you begin the next **(Figure 9.19)**.

■ For more on rules, see page 143.

```
┌─────────────────code.html─────────────────┐
<HTML><HEAD><TITLE>Dividing the table into
horizontal sections</TITLE></HEAD>
<BODY>
<TABLE>
<CAPTION ALIGN=top>Bear sightings in Western
Massachusetts</CAPTION>
<COLGROUP ALIGN=LEFT STYLE="font: 10pt
Lithos Regular">
<COLGROUP SPAN=3 ALIGN=CENTER>
    <COL SPAN=2>
    <COL STYLE="font-weight:900">
<THEAD STYLE="font: 10pt Lithos Regular">
<TR>
    <TD><BR>
    <TH>Babies
    <TH>Adults
    <TH>Total
<TBODY>
<TR>
    <TH>Northampton
    <TD>2
```

Figure 9.17 *I want the column titles in the THEAD section and the rest of the table in the TBODY.*

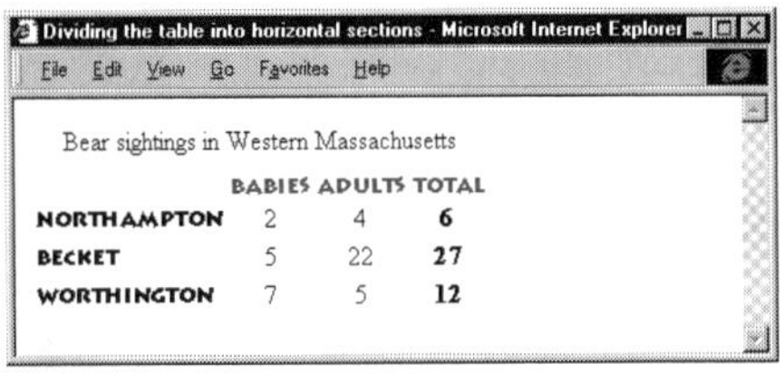

Figure 9.18 *The entire THEAD section is now formatted in Lithos Regular.*

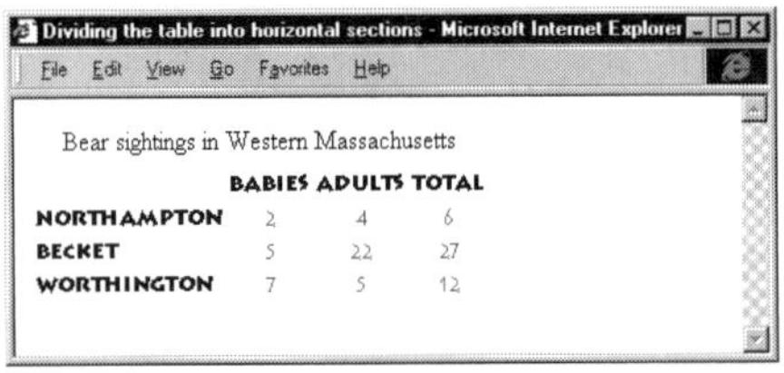

Figure 9.19 *Note that in Figure 9.17, the TBODY tag closes the THEAD tag. If it weren't there, the whole table would be considered part of the THEAD. The result is shown here—not a tragedy certainly, but notice how the entire table is now formatted in Lithos Regular (and the bold formatting specified in the COL tag has been overridden).*

```
code.html
<HTML><HEAD><TITLE>Adding a border</
TITLE></HEAD>
<BODY>
<TABLE BORDER>
<CAPTION ALIGN=top>Bear sightings in Western
Massachusetts</CAPTION>
<COLGROUP ALIGN=LEFT STYLE="font: 10pt
Lithos Regular">
<COLGROUP SPAN=3 ALIGN=CENTER>
    <COL SPAN=2>
    <COL STYLE="font-weight:900">
<THEAD STYLE="font: 10pt Lithos Regular">
<TR>
    <TD><BR>
    <TH>Babies
```

Figure 9.20 *The BORDER attribute is added to the initial TABLE tag.*

Bear sightings in Western Massachusetts

	Babies	Adults	Total
Northampton	2	4	6
Becket	5	22	27
Worthington	7	5	12

Figure 9.21 *The browser creates a shaded border (1 pixel wide, using the background color, by default) around each individual cell and around the table itself.*

	BABIES	ADULTS	TOTAL
NORTHAMPTON	2	4	**6**
BECKET	5	22	**27**
WORTHINGTON	7	5	**12**

Figure 9.22 *When you set the BORDER to 15, the external frame becomes particularly pronounced.*

```
code.html
<HTML><HEAD><TITLE>Adding a border</
TITLE></HEAD>
<BODY>
<TABLE BORDER BORDERCOLORLIGHT="#00ff00"
BORDERCOLORDARK="#189234">
<CAPTION ALIGN=top>Bear sightings in Western
Massachusetts</CAPTION>
<COLGROUP ALIGN=LEFT STYLE="font: 10pt
Lithos Regular">
<COLGROUP SPAN=3 ALIGN=CENTER>
    <COL SPAN=2>
    <COL STYLE="font-weight:900">
```

Figure 9.23 *Create a shaded border in the color of your choice—at least in Internet Explorer—with the BORDERCOLORLIGHT and BORDERCOLOR-DARK tags. Unfortunately, the result is hard to show here. Try it: It looks great.*

Adding a border

A border helps your table stand out from the rest of the text.

To create a border:

1. Inside the initial TABLE tag, type **BORDER**.

2. If desired, type **=n**, where *n* is the thickness in pixels of the border.

3. If desired, type **BORDERCOLOR= "#rrggbb"**, where *rrggbb* is the hexadecimal representation of the desired color for the border.

4. If desired, type **BORDERCOLOR-DARK ="#rrggbb"**, where *rrggbb* is the hexadecimal representation of the color that you want to use for the darker parts of the border (top and left borders of cells, right and bottom borders of the table itself).

5. If desired, type **BORDERCOLOR-LIGHT ="#rrggbb"**, where *rrggbb* is the hexadecimal representation of the color that you want to use for the lighter parts of the border (bottom and right borders of cells, top and left borders of the table itself).

✔ Tips

■ With no BORDERCOLOR tags, most browsers shade the border based on the background color. With just the BORDERCOLOR tag the table will have no shading and be a solid color.

■ The BORDERCOLORLIGHT and BOR-DERCOLORDARK tags let you create a shaded border of any color you wish. Use dark and light versions of the same color for best results.

■ For more on colors, see Appendix C.

Adding a border

Choosing which borders to display

When you use the BORDER tag, described on page 141, a border appears both between each cell and around the table itself. HTML 4 lets you choose which external sides of the table should have a border as well as which internal borders should be displayed.

To choose which external sides should have a border:

In the TABLE tag, after the required BORDER attribute, type **FRAME=location**, where *location* is one of the values listed below:

- *void*, for no external borders

- *above*, for a single border on top

- *below*, for a single border on bottom

- *hsides*, for a border on both the top and bottom sides

- *vsides*, for a border on both the right and left sides

- *rhs*, for a single border on the right side

- *lhs*, for a single border on the left side

- *box* or *border*, for a border on all sides (default)

```
<HTML><HEAD><TITLE>Choosing which exterior
borders to display</TITLE></HEAD>
<BODY>
<TABLE BORDER FRAME=vsides>
<CAPTION ALIGN=top>Bear sightings in Western
Massachusetts</CAPTION>
<COLGROUP ALIGN=LEFT STYLE="font: 10pt
Lithos Regular">
<COLGROUP SPAN=3 ALIGN=CENTER>
    <COL SPAN=2>
    <COL STYLE="font-weight:900">
<THEAD STYLE="font: 10pt Lithos Regular">
<TR>
    <TD><BR>
    <TH>Babies
    <TH>Adults
    <TH>Total
<TBODY>
<TR>
    <TH>Northampton
    <TD>2
    <TD>4
    <TD>6
```

Figure 9.24 *Add the FRAME attribute just after the BORDER attribute within the TABLE tag.*

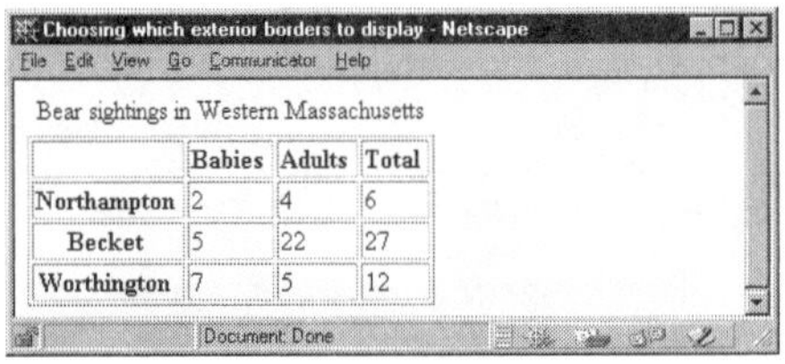

Figure 9.25 *The FRAME attribute has no effect in Netscape; the table appears with the complete border as usual.*

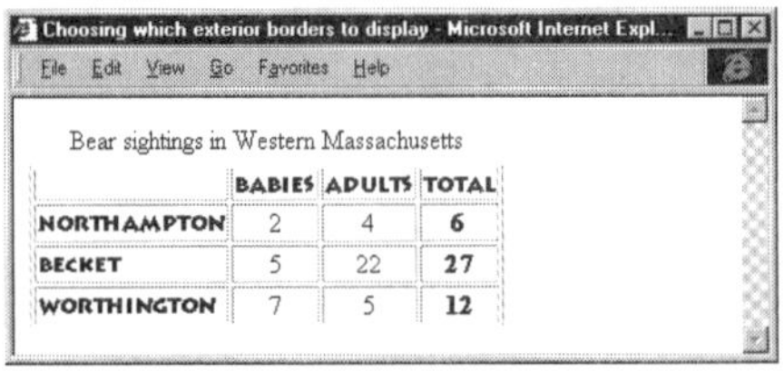

Figure 9.26 *In Internet Explorer, with a FRAME value of* vsides, *the external border appears only on the right and left sides of the table. The internal border appears as usual (and if you ask me, it looks kind of funny). To control the internal borders, use the RULES attribute described on page 143.*

```
                    code.html
<HTML><HEAD><TITLE>Choosing which interior
borders to display</TITLE></HEAD>
<BODY>
<TABLE BORDER RULES=cols>
<CAPTION ALIGN=top>Bear sightings in Western
Massachusetts</CAPTION>
<COLGROUP ALIGN=LEFT STYLE="font: 10pt
Lithos Regular">
<COLGROUP SPAN=3 ALIGN=CENTER>
    <COL SPAN=2>
    <COL STYLE="font-weight:900">
<THEAD STYLE="font: 10pt Lithos Regular">
<TR>
    <TD><BR>
```

Figure 9.27 *The RULES attribute goes in the TABLE tag, after the BORDER attribute, which is required for the RULES attribute to have an effect.*

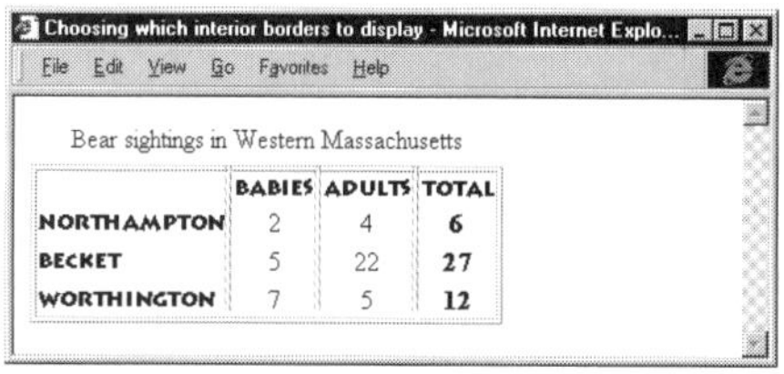

Figure 9.28 *With* RULES=cols, *only the vertical rules are displayed. Notice that the line around the perimeter of the table is part of the external border and is not affected by RULES.*

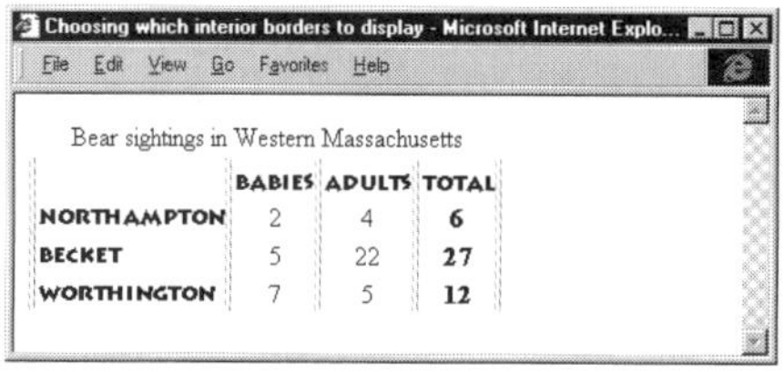

Figure 9.29 *To display only the vertical borders, combine* FRAME=vsides *with* RULES=cols.

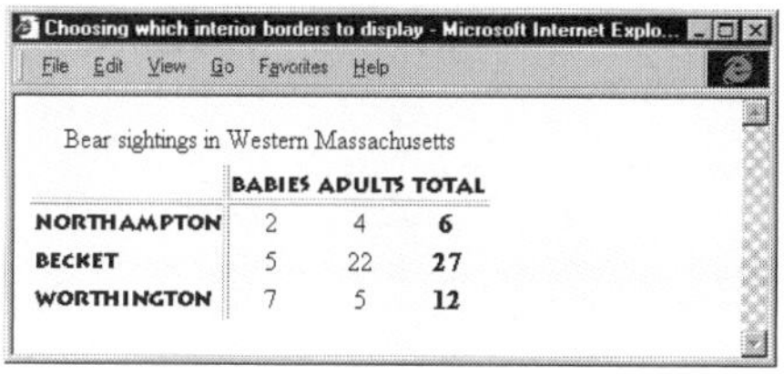

Figure 9.30 *The attribute* RULES=groups *is particularly useful when you've divided the table into column and row groups (see pages 138–140). Instead of rules between each column, rules are only displayed between* groups. *(I've also set* FRAME=void *in this example, to get rid of the external borders.)*

To choose which internal borders should be displayed:

In the TABLE tag, after the required BORDER attribute, type **RULES=area**, where *area* is one of the following values:

- *none*, for no internal rules

- *rows*, for horizontal rules between each row in the table

- *cols*, for vertical rules between each column in the table **(Figures 9.28 and 9.29)**

- *groups*, for rules between column groups and horizontal sections as defined by the tags described on pages 138–140 **(Figure 9.30)**

- *all*, for rules between each row and column in the table (default)

✔ Tips

■ You must use the BORDER tag in order for any of the FRAME or RULES attributes to have effect.

■ The *Void* value for FRAME seems rather pointless (you could just skip the BORDER attribute if you didn't want a border) until you pair it up with a value for RULES. The same goes for the *None* value for RULES, which makes most sense when you pair it with a positive value for FRAME.

■ The default values, *box* and *border* for FRAME and *all* for RULES, *are* pretty superfluous. If you want all the external borders, skip the FRAME attribute altogether. If you want all the internal borders, skip the RULES attribute. Don't forget to use the BORDER tag, of course. Without it, no borders will be drawn, no matter what you use for FRAME and RULES.

Spanning a cell across two or more columns

If you need to convey a lot of information in a table, one strategy is to divide a table header into categories by spanning it over several columns and adding more specific headers in the row below.

To span a cell across two columns:

1. When you get to the point in which you need to define the cell that spans more than one column, *either* type **<TH** *or* type **<TD**, depending on whether the cell should be a header cell or a regular cell, respectively.

2. Type **COLSPAN=n>**, where *n* equals the number of columns the cell should span.

3. Type the cell's contents.

4. Complete the rest of the table. If you create a cell that spans 2 columns, you will need to define one less cell in that row. If you create a cell that spans 3 columns, you will define two less cells for the row. And so on.

✔ Tip

■ Writing the HTML code for a table from scratch is, uh, challenging— especially when you start spanning columns and rows. It helps to sketch it out on paper first, as described on page 155, to get a handle on which information goes in which row and column. Or you can cheat and use a Web page editing program like FrontPage or PageMill (or the tip on page 286) to get started. You can always open the file and edit the HTML by hand later.

```
code.html
<COLGROUP ALIGN=LEFT STYLE="font: 9pt Lithos
Regular">
<COLGROUP SPAN=3 ALIGN=CENTER>
    <COL SPAN=2>
    <COL STYLE="font-weight:900">
<COLGROUP SPAN=3 ALIGN=CENTER>
    <COL SPAN=2>
    <COL STYLE="font-weight:900">
<THEAD STYLE="font: 9pt Lithos Regular">
<TR>
    <TD><BR>
    <TH COLSPAN=3>Black Bears
    <TH COLSPAN=3>Grizzlies
<TR>
    <TH><BR>
    <TD>Babies
    <TD>Adults
    <TD>Total
    <TD>Babies
    <TD>Adults
    <TD>Total
<TBODY>
<TR>
```

Figure 9.31 *In each row I've defined seven column positions. In the first row there is 1 empty cell and two headers of 3 columns each (1+3+3=7). In the following rows, there is one empty or header cell and six individual cells (1+6=7). (I've taken out the FRAME and RULES attributes so that you can see the cell borders clearly.)*

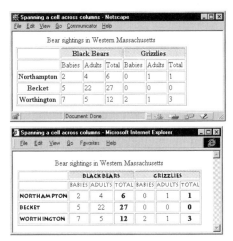

Figure 9.32 *The* Black Bears *and* Grizzlies *labels now span 3 columns each, both in Netscape (above) and Internet Explorer. (No, there aren't really grizzly bears in Western Massachusetts. Black bears, on the other hand, we have thousands of.)*

Spanning a cell across two or more columns

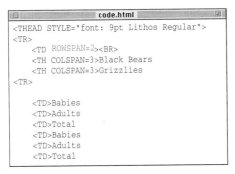

```
              code.html
<THEAD STYLE="font: 9pt Lithos Regular">
<TR>
    <TD ROWSPAN=2><BR>
    <TH COLSPAN=3>Black Bears
    <TH COLSPAN=3>Grizzlies
<TR>

    <TD>Babies
    <TD>Adults
    <TD>Total
    <TD>Babies
    <TD>Adults
    <TD>Total
```

Figure 9.33 *There are just two differences between this document and the one on the preceding page (Figure 9.31). First, the blank cell in the first row now spans two rows. Second, because the blank cell spans two rows, the first cell in the second row is already defined, and the original code is thus eliminated from the HTML.*

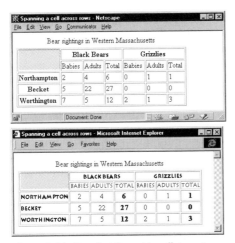

Figure 9.34 *Now that the empty cell spans two rows, the ugly line that separated the two rows disappears and the table looks much better.*

Figure 9.35 *Here's the table in Internet Explorer with RULES=groups and FRAME=void. You don't have to worry about spanning cells at all.*

Spanning a cell across two or more rows

Creating a cell that spans more than one row is essentially identical to spanning cells over more than one column—just from another angle. It is perfect for dividing the headers on the left side of the table into subcategories.

To span a cell across two or more rows:

1. When you get to the point in which you need to define the cell that spans more than one row, *either* type **<TH** *or* type **<TD**, depending on whether the cell should be a header cell or a regular cell, respectively.

2. Type **ROWSPAN=n>**, where *n* equals the number of rows the cell should span.

3. Type the cell's contents.

4. Complete the rest of the table. If you define a cell with a rowspan of 2, you will not need to define the corresponding cell in the next row. If you define a cell with a rowspan of 3, you will not need to define the corresponding cells in the next two rows.

Spanning a cell across two or more rows

Changing a table's width and height

You can use the WIDTH and HEIGHT attributes to resize the whole table, or to define the dimensions of particular cells.

To change a table's size:

Within the initial TABLE tag, type **WIDTH=x HEIGHT=y**, where *x* and *y* are either absolute values in pixels for the height and width of the table or percentages that indicate how big the table should be with respect to the full window size.

✔ Tips

■ You can't make the table too small for its contents; the browser will just ignore you.

■ WIDTH is standard HTML 4, HEIGHT is not. Nevertheless, the major browsers recognize both attributes.

■ If the table is narrower than the window, you can center it by adding **ALIGN=center** to the TABLE tag.

```
                      code.html
<HTML><HEAD><TITLE>Changing the table's
size</TITLE></HEAD>
<BODY>
<TABLE BORDER FRAME=void RULES=groups
WIDTH=50% HEIGHT=90%>
<CAPTION ALIGN=top>Bear sightings in Western
Massachusetts</CAPTION>
<COLGROUP ALIGN=LEFT STYLE="font: 9pt Lithos
Regular">
<COLGROUP SPAN=3 ALIGN=CENTER>
    <COL SPAN=2>
    <COL STYLE="font-weight:900">
<COLGROUP SPAN=3 ALIGN=CENTER>
    <COL SPAN=2>
    <COL STYLE="font-weight:900">
<THEAD STYLE="font: 9pt Lithos Regular">
<TR>
    <TD ROWSPAN=2><BR>
    <TH COLSPAN=3>Black Bears
    <TH COLSPAN=3>Grizzlies
<TR>

    <TD>Babies
    <TD>Adults
    <TD>Total
    <TD>Babies
    <TD>Adults
    <TD>Total
```

Figure 9.36 *Add the WIDTH and HEIGHT attributes to the initial TABLE tag.*

Both tables are generated from identical HTML

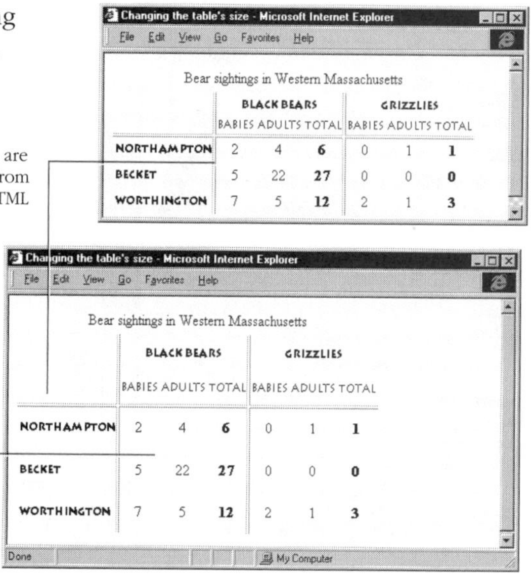

Figure 9.37 *If you use a percentage for HEIGHT and WIDTH, the size of the table changes as your visitor adjusts the size of the window—although it will never get too small to hold the table's contents.*

```
code.html
<THEAD STYLE="font: 9pt Lithos Regular">
<TR>
    <TD ROWSPAN=2><BR>
    <TH COLSPAN=3>Black Bears
    <TH COLSPAN=3>Grizzlies
<TR>

    <TD>Babies
    <TD>Adults
    <TD>Total
    <TD>Babies
    <TD>Adults
    <TD>Total
<TBODY>
<TR>
    <TH WIDTH=200 HEIGHT=100>Northampton
    <TD>2
    <TD>4
    <TD>6
    <TD>0
```

Figure 9.38 *Specify the dimensions of your cell by using the HEIGHT and WIDTH tags inside the cell definition tag (in this case, TH).*

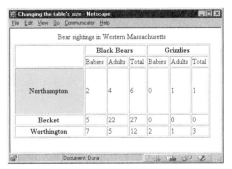

Figure 9.39 *I have had varying results— though consistent from browser to browser— with WIDTH and HEIGHT when used on cells. But, to tell the truth, I think they are usually more trouble than they are worth.*

Changing a cell's size

You can change the width and height of individual cells to emphasize important information.

To change the size of individual cells:

1. Place the cursor inside the cell tag (either TH or TD).

2. Type **WIDTH=x HEIGHT=y**, where x and y are either absolute values in pixels for the width and height of the cell or percentages that indicate how big the cell should be with respect to the full table size.

✔ Tips

- Changing one cell's size can affect the size of the entire row or column. You can use this fact to your advantage: you only need to adjust the width of the cells in the first row and the height of the cells in the first column (which is the first cell in each row definition).

- You can change the size of all of the cells in one or more rows or columns by placing the WIDTH attribute in the THEAD, TBODY, or TFOOT tags *(see page 140)*, or in the COLGROUP, or COL tags *(see page 138)*.

- The HEIGHT tag is not standard HTML 4. Perhaps this is the reason that it generally cannot be used in as many places as the WIDTH tag *(see previous tip)*.

- Browsers will attempt to follow your sizing instructions until you make it impossible to display the entire contents of the table (say, by making one cell or column too big). At that point, they'll just ignore you.

Aligning the contents of cells

Each browser shows the contents of the different cells in a table in its own way, by default, which may or may not be how you think the data looks best. To gain a little more control over the alignment of a cell's contents, use the ALIGN and VALIGN tags.

To align the contents of cells horizontally:

1. Place the cursor in the initial tag for the cell, row, or section, after the name of the tag but before the final >.

2. Type **ALIGN=direction**, where *direction* is left, center, right, justify (flush on both sides), or char (aligned with a given character).

3. If you've used char in step 2, type **CHAR="a"**, where *a* is the character to be used for alignment (like a decimal point or decimal comma).

✔ Tips

■ You can align all of the cells in one or more rows or columns by inserting the ALIGN attribute in the appropriate tag (TR, THEAD, TFOOT, TBODY, COLGROUP, or COL).

■ The default value for ALIGN in TD tags is *left*. In TH tags it's *center*.

■ If you use ALIGN in the TABLE tag, however, you align not the contents of the table's cells, but rather the table itself.

■ Neither of the major browsers supports justified text (ALIGN=justify) or text aligned by a given character (ALIGN=char CHAR="a").

```
                    code.html
<TBODY>
<TR ALIGN=CENTER>
    <TH ALIGN=LEFT>Northampton
    <TD>2
    <TD>4
    <TD>6
    <TD>0
    <TD>1
    <TD>1
<TR ALIGN=CENTER>
    <TH ALIGN=LEFT>Becket
    <TD>5
    <TD>22
    <TD>27
    <TD>0
    <TD>0
    <TD>0
<TR ALIGN=CENTER>
    <TH ALIGN=LEFT>Worthington
    <TD>7
```

Figure 9.40 *In the same table we've been working with for the last few pages, I've aligned the left-hand headers (the city names) to the left, and centered the numerical data. Notice that each row is aligned to center, but the individual cells' alignment attribute (left) overrides the row alignment. I could type an individual alignment for each cell, but I don't like typing that much.*

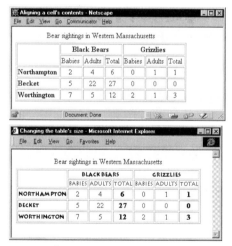

Figure 9.41 *The result is a clearer, more legible table, both in Netscape (above) and Internet Explorer. (Of course, we had already used the column and row groupings to align the cells' contents with Internet Explorer. Doing it manually makes the table appear almost the same way in both browsers.)*

```
                  code.html
<HTML><HEAD><TITLE>All the alignment
options</TITLE></HEAD>
<BODY>
<TABLE BORDER WIDTH=100% HEIGHT=100%>
<CAPTION>Aligning every which way</CAPTION>
<TR>
   <TD COLSPAN=2 ROWSPAN=2 HEIGHT=10><BR>
   <TH COLSPAN=3 HEIGHT=10>HORIZONTAL
<TR>
   <TH HEIGHT=10>Left
   <TH HEIGHT=10>Center
   <TH HEIGHT=10>Right
<TR>
   <TH ROWSPAN=4>V
   <TH>TOP
   <TD VALIGN=top ALIGN=left>Top Left
   <TD VALIGN=top ALIGN=center>Top Center
   <TD VALIGN=top ALIGN=right>Top Right
<TR>
   <TH>Middle
   <TD VALIGN=middle ALIGN=left>Middle Left
   <TD VALIGN=middle ALIGN=center>Middle
Center
   <TD VALIGN=middle ALIGN=right>Middle Right
<TR>
   <TH>Bottom
   <TD VALIGN=bottom ALIGN=left>Bottom Left
   <TD VALIGN=bottom ALIGN=center>Bottom
Center
   <TD VALIGN=bottom ALIGN=right>Bottom Right
<TR>
   <TH>Baseline
   <TD VALIGN=baseline ALIGN=left>Baseline
Left
   <TD VALIGN=baseline ALIGN=center>Baseline
Center
   <TD VALIGN=baseline ALIGN=right>Baseline
Right
</TABLE>
```

Figure 9.42 *This table illustrates each of the twelve alignment combinations.*

You can use the VALIGN attribute to align the cell's contents vertically.

To align a cell's contents vertically:

1. Place the cursor in the initial tag for the cell, after <TD or <TH but before the final >.

2. Type **VALIGN=direction**, where *direction* is either top, middle, bottom, or baseline.

✔ Tips

■ The default value for VALIGN is *middle*.

■ The baseline value aligns the contents of each cell with the baseline of the first line of text that it contains. *Baseline* is the same as *top* when there are several lines of text and no images. *Baseline* is the same as *bottom* when the cells contain both images and text.

■ You can align all of the cells in one or more rows or columns by inserting the VALIGN attribute in the appropriate tag (TR, THEAD, TFOOT, TBODY, COLGROUP, or COL), as in **<TR ALIGN=left VALIGN=bottom>**.

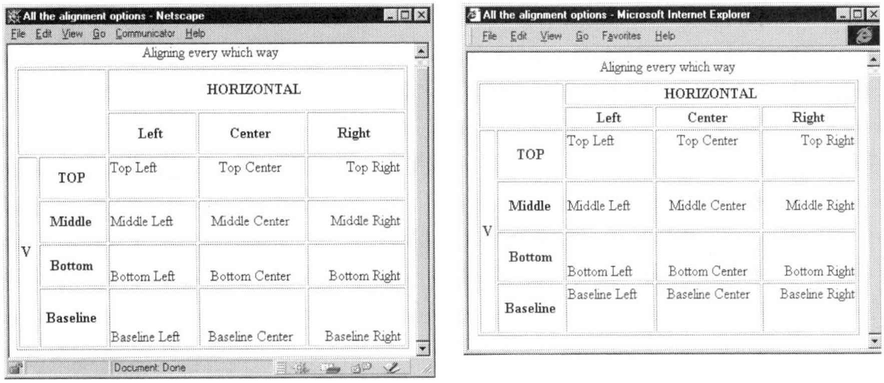

Aligning the contents of cells

Figure 9.43 *Both Netscape (left) and Internet Explorer can align the contents of cells in each of the first nine possible positions. Netscape also recognizes the baseline attribute, whose behavior depends on how many lines and graphics are in the cell.*

Changing a cell's color

Changing the color of one or more cells is a great way to set off important information such as the column of totals in a table.

To change a cell's color:

1. Within the TH or TD tag, type **BGCOLOR=**.

2. Type **"#rrggbb"**, where *rrggbb* is the hexadecimal representation of the desired color.

Or type **color**, where *color* is one of the sixteen predefined color names *(see inside back cover)*.

✔ Tips

■ You can change the color of the cells in one or more rows or columns by adding the BGCOLOR attribute to the appropriate tag (TR, THEAD, TFOOT, TBODY, COLGROUP, or COL).

■ Explorer supports using BGCOLOR in the TABLE tag for changing the background of the whole table.

■ The BGCOLOR in an individual cell (TH or TD) overrides the color specified in a row (in a TR tag), which in turn overrides the color specified for a group of rows or columns (in THEAD, COLGROUP, etc.), which, as you might expect, overrides the color specified for the entire table (in the TABLE tag).

■ Consult *Colors in Hex* on page 311 and the inside back cover for help choosing colors.

■ The BGCOLOR has been deprecated in HTML 4. The W3C recommends the use of styles to change the background color *(see page 262)*

```
                    code.html
<TR>
     <TD>Babies
     <TD>Adults
     <TD BGCOLOR=yellow>Total
     <TD>Babies
     <TD>Adults
     <TD BGCOLOR=yellow>Total
<TBODY>
<TR ALIGN=CENTER>
     <TH ALIGN=LEFT>Northampton
     <TD>2
     <TD>4
     <TD BGCOLOR=yellow>6
     <TD>0
     <TD>1
     <TD BGCOLOR=yellow>1
<TR ALIGN=CENTER>
     <TH ALIGN=LEFT>Becket
     <TD>5
     <TD>22
     <TD BGCOLOR=yellow>27
     <TD>0
     <TD>0
     <TD BGCOLOR=yellow>0
```

Figure 9.44 *You can add the BGCOLOR attribute to TD or TH tags as shown here to modify individual cells, or you can use it with larger elements (TR, THEAD, COLGROUP, TABLE, etc.) to change a group of cells all at once.*

Figure 9.45 *Add the BGCOLOR attribute to all of the TD or TH cells in a particular column or columns (here, I've colored the Total columns) to make certain data stand out. (If you're certain your visitors use IE—or if Netscape updates its browser—add the BGCOLOR attribute to the appropriate COLGROUP or COL tag.)*

```
┌─────────── code.html ───────────┐
<HTML><HEAD><TITLE>Changing the background
image</TITLE></HEAD>
<BODY>
<TABLE BORDER BACKGROUND="bears4.jpg">
<CAPTION ALIGN=top>Bear sightings in Western
Massachusetts</CAPTION>
<COLGROUP ALIGN=LEFT STYLE="font: 9pt Lithos
Regular">
<COLGROUP SPAN=3 ALIGN=CENTER>
    <COL SPAN=2>
    <COL STYLE="font-weight:900">
<COLGROUP SPAN=3 ALIGN=CENTER>
    <COL SPAN=2>
    <COL STYLE="font-weight:900">
<THEAD STYLE="font: 9pt Lithos Regular">
<TR>
    <TD ROWSPAN=2><BR>
    <TH COLSPAN=3>Black Bears
    <TH COLSPAN=3>Grizzlies
```

Figure 9.46 *Use a background image for your table by adding BACKGROUND="image.gif" to the TABLE tag.*

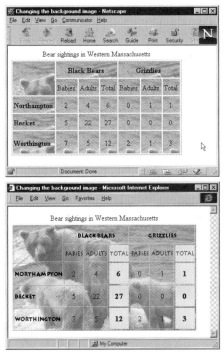

Figure 9.47 *Both browsers recognize the BACKGROUND attribute, so why such different results? Netscape (top) uses the upper left corner of the image in each cell (lots of water in this example). Explorer centers the image behind the entire table. Notice how the background color (in the Total columns) is lost in Netscape but covers over the background image in Explorer.*

Using a background image

If you want to make it really hard for people to read the text in your table, you can use an image as the background. OK, maybe you can make it look good—send me the URL.

To use a background image for a cell:

Within the TH or TD tag, type **BACKGROUND="image.gif"** where *image.gif* is the URL of the image that you wish to use as the backdrop for your cell.

To use a background image for the entire table:

Within the TABLE tag, type **BACKGROUND="image.gif"** where *image.gif* is the URL of the image that you wish to use as the backdrop for your table.

✔ Tips

■ If you set a background image for the whole table, Explorer uses one image for the background while Netscape copies the whole image into each cell individually **(Figure 9.47)**.

■ In Explorer, the BGCOLOR attribute overrides the background image—except in the cell spacing area *(see page 152)*. If you view the same page with Netscape, you'll find that background colors disappear completely if you specify a background image. Can we say "consensus" please?

■ For some reason, you can't use BACKGROUND in the THEAD, TBODY, TFOOT, COL, or COLGROUP tags with either browser. Explorer won't accept the BACKGROUND attribute in TR either, but Netscape will.

Using a background image

Spacing and padding the cells

Cell spacing adds space between cells, making the table bigger without changing the size of individual cells.

To add cell spacing:

Within the initial TABLE tag, type **CELL-SPACING=n**, where *n* is the number of pixels desired between each cell. (The attribute *cellspacing* is one word.)

Cell padding adds space around the contents of a cell, in effect, pushing the walls of the cell outward.

To add cell padding:

Within the initial TABLE tag, type **CELL-PADDING=n**, where *n* is the number of pixels desired between the contents and the walls of the cell. (The attribute *cellpadding* is one word.)

✔ Tips

■ The default for cell spacing is 2 pixels. The default for cell padding is 1 pixel.

■ The alignment options *(see page 148)* consider the cell padding as the actual cell limits, and thus, may give unexpected results.

■ Both Netscape and Internet Explorer understand the CELLSPACING and CELLPADDING tags. There just isn't enough room to display both here.

Figure 9.48 *I've added a white background color to every cell except the upper left one. The default cell spacing is the part of the image you see between the cells—not very much!*

```
<HTML><HEAD><TITLE>Changing the cell spacing
and padding</TITLE></HEAD>
<BODY>
<TABLE BORDER BACKGROUND="bears4.jpg"
CELLSPACING=15>
<CAPTION ALIGN=top>Bear sightings in Western
Massachusetts</CAPTION>
```

Figure 9.49 *A large value of cell spacing increases the space between the cells (where you see the image).*

```
<HTML><HEAD><TITLE>Changing the cell spacing
and padding</TITLE></HEAD>
<BODY>
<TABLE BORDER BACKGROUND="bears4.jpg"
CELLPADDING=8>
<CAPTION ALIGN=top>Bear sightings in Western
Massachusetts</CAPTION>
```

Figure 9.50 *Adding cell padding makes the cells larger, with more space around the contents.*

Spacing and padding the cells

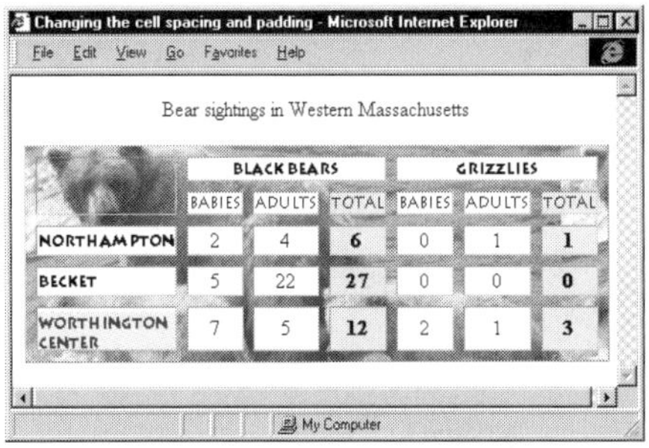

Figure 9.51 *Imagine if the name of the third city were longer than would fit on one line.*

```
                        code.html
    <TD BGCOLOR=yellow>27
    <TD>0
    <TD>0
    <TD BGCOLOR=yellow>0
<TR ALIGN=CENTER>
    <TH ALIGN=LEFT NOWRAP>Worthington Center
    <TD>7
    <TD>5
    <TD BGCOLOR=yellow>12
    <TD>2
    <TD>1
    <TD BGCOLOR=yellow>3
</TABLE>
</BODY></HTML>
```

Figure 9.52 *Simply add NOWRAP to the TD or TH tag of the offending cell.*

Figure 9.53 *Now the entire city name fits on one line. Note that the whole table is a bit bigger—I've reduced it here to fit in the margin.*

Controlling line breaks in a cell

Unless you specify otherwise, a browser will divide the lines of text in a cell as it decides on the height and width of each column and row. The NOWRAP attribute forces the browser to keep all the text in a cell on one line.

To keep text in a cell on one single line:

1. Place the cursor in the initial tag for the cell, after <TD or <TH but before the final >.

2. Type **NOWRAP**.

✔ Tips

■ Netscape will make the cell (and the table that contains it) as wide as it needs to accommodate the single line of text—even if it looks really ugly.

■ You can use regular line breaks (BR) between words to mark where you *do* want the text to break.

■ You can also type ** ** instead of a regular space to connect pairs of words or other elements with non-breaking spaces.

■ For more information on line breaks, consult *Controlling line breaks* on page 106.

Speeding up table display

Although tables are extremely powerful, they can be very slow to appear in your visitor's browser. The major factor is that the browser must calculate the width and height of the table before it can begin to display the cells. So, if you can keep the browser's calculations to a minimum, the table will appear more quickly and your visitors may actually wait to see it.

To speed up table display:

■ Use absolute values (in pixels) or percentages for determining cell width.

■ Only specify proportional widths for cells, columns, and horizontal sections when you've already set a fixed width in pixels for the entire table.

■ Divide your table into column groups.

Speeding up table display

Figure 9.54 *First, draw out your table as simply as possible, including all your headers, but no data.*

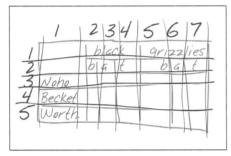

Figure 9.55 *To separate the table into rows and columns, draw a line from one end to another (either top to bottom or right to left) everywhere there is a division in the table. In this table, we find five rows and seven columns.*

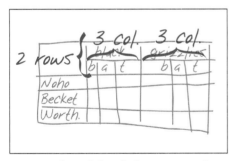

Figure 9.56 *Mark the cells that span more than one column or row. In this example, there is the top left blank row that spans 2 rows (but just 1 column), and the "black" and "grizzlies" headers that span 3 columns each (but just one row). Every other cell spans exactly one column and one row.*

Mapping out a table

Setting up complicated tables in HTML can be really confusing. All you need are a couple of column spans to throw the whole thing off. The trick is to draw a map of your table before you start.

To map out your table:

1. Sketch your table quickly on a piece of paper (yes, with a pen) **(Fig. 9.54)**.

2. Divide the table into rows and columns. Number each row and column **(Figure 9.55)**.

3. Mark the cells that will span more than one column or row **(Fig. 9.56)**.

4. Count the number of cells in each row (1 point for single cells, 2 points for cells that span two columns, 3 for cells that span three columns, etc.). There should be as many cell definitions in each row as there are columns in the table. (See step 2.)

5. Once you have your table straight on paper, write the HTML code, row by row.

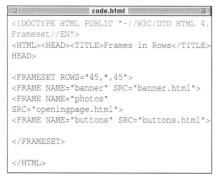

```
            code.html
<!DOCTYPE HTML PUBLIC "-//W3C/DTD HTML 4.
Frameset//EN">
<HTML><HEAD><TITLE>Frames in Rows</TITLE>
HEAD>

<FRAMESET ROWS="45,*,45">
<FRAME NAME="banner" SRC="banner.html">
<FRAME NAME="photos"
SRC="openingpage.html">
<FRAME NAME="buttons" SRC="buttons.html">

</FRAMESET>

</HTML>
```

Figure 10.1 *Web pages with frames should be identified by using the !DOCTYPE tag and the proper version information. For details, consult* Starting your Web page *on page 37.*

One of the trickier parts of creating a Web site is giving your visitors an idea of the scope of information contained in your site and then making that information easily accessible without confusing or overwhelming them. Frames can be the key to organizing your site and making it easy to navigate.

By dividing a page, called a *frameset*, into frames, you can allow the visitor to see more than one page at a time, without completely cluttering up their screen. Each frame contains its own Web page, and theoretically could be viewed independently in a separate window.

The beauty of having several Web pages open on a screen at a time, however, lies in the ability to interrelate the information in each of the pages. For example, you can have a stationary banner frame across the top of the window that includes your company name and logo. Meanwhile, a dynamic frame on the left side of the window can include a table of contents. Finally, the main area of the window will be devoted to the *contents frame*, whose data changes each time your visitor clicks on a new topic in the table of contents.

As of version 4, frames are finally part of standard HTML. However, you're supposed to label your Web pages that include frames to help browsers recognize them **(Figure 10.1)**. For more information, consult *Starting your Web page* on page 37.

Creating a simple frameset

Think of a frameset as a window with individual panes. Each pane shows different information. You decide how many panes your window will have, what size each pane will be, how its borders should look and if it should have scroll bars or not. Once you've built the window, you create the initial landscape behind the window by assigning individual URLs to each pane, that is, frame.

First, you'll learn to create a simple frameset with three horizontal rows all in the same column.

To create a simple frameset:

1. Type **<FRAMESET** after the </HEAD> tag on the frameset page.

2. Type **ROWS="a** where *a* is the height of the first row. The value may either be a percentage (40%), an exact number of pixels (35), or completely variable (with an asterisk *), depending on the size of the other rows.

3. Type **, b** where *b* is the height of the second row, again expressed as a percentage, an absolute value in pixels, or a variable (with an asterisk: *).

4. Repeat step 3 for each additional row.

5. Type **">** to complete the row definition.

6. Type **<FRAME** to assign a URL and other attributes to the top row/pane.

7. Type **NAME="name"** where *name* is a word that identifies this particular frame's use, like *banner*, *index*, or *contents*. (The name is used when you're targeting links to this frame. For more details, see page 172.)

```
code.html
<!DOCTYPE HTML PUBLIC "-//W3C/DTD HTML 4.0
Frameset//EN"><HTML><HEAD><TITLE>Frames in
Rows</TITLE></HEAD>

<FRAMESET ROWS="45,*,45">
<FRAME NAME="banner" SRC="banner.html">
<FRAME NAME="photos"
SRC="openingpage.html">
<FRAME NAME="buttons" SRC="buttons.html">

</FRAMESET>
```

Figure 10.2 *The frameset page has no actual content. Instead, it defines the frames and links them with the pages that hold the content.*

Figure 10.3 *Once you've created a frameset, the next step is to create the pages that will appear within the frames.*

Figure 10.4 *Viewed individually, the pages shown in Figure 10.3 appear just as any other Web page.*

Figure 10.5 *By default, Netscape displays the frames with rather thick borders and scroll bars.*

Figure 10.6 *Internet Explorer's frames have thinner default borders, but also include scroll bars.*

8. Type **SRC="content.html">** where *content.html* is the URL for the page that will be initially displayed in this frame when the visitor first navigates to this frameset.

9. Repeat steps 6–8 for each row you defined in steps 2–4.

10. Type **</FRAMESET>** to complete the frameset and the construction of your "window".

11. Create the pages that will be displayed initially in the frames, that is, those referenced by the SRC tag in step 8 **(Figures 10.3 and 10.4)**. This is the "landscape" behind the window.

✔ Tips

- Use the asterisk (*) to allocate to a frame whatever leftover space there is available in the window. That is, if the first two frames occupy 40 and 60 pixels respectively, and the window size is 250 pixels, the frame with the asterisk will occupy 150 pixels.

- You can use more than one asterisk at a time. The remaining space will be divided equally among the frames marked with an asterisk. To divide the remaining space unequally, add a number to the asterisk, e.g., **2***. In this case, two thirds of the remaining space will go to the frame marked 2* and the last third will go to the frame marked with just a plain asterisk.

- The BODY tag is not used at all in frameset pages.

- To provide information for visitors whose browsers don't support frames, see page 176.

Creating a simple frameset

Creating frames in columns

Another simple way to divide a frameset is into columns instead of rows.

To create frames in columns:

1. Type **<FRAMESET** after the </HEAD> tag in the frameset page.

2. Type **COLS="a,b">** where *a* and *b* (and any others) represent the width of the corresponding column, as a percentage, number of pixels, or variable (*).

3. Type **<FRAME** to define the leftmost frame/column.

4. Type **NAME="name"** where *name* is a word that identifies this particular frame's use, like *banner*, *index*, or *contents*.

5. Type **SRC="content.html">** where *content.html* is the URL of the page that you want to be displayed in this frame when the visitor initially navigates to this frameset.

6. Repeat steps 3–5 for each frame/column.

7. Type **</FRAMESET>**.

8. Create the Web pages that will be shown initially in the frameset page.

✔ Tips

■ Consult the tips on page 159 for details on allocating the space among frames with variables (*).

■ A frame's name is used when you're targeting links to appear in the frame. For details, consult *Targeting links to particular frames* on page 172.

```
                code.html
<HTML><HEAD><TITLE>Frames in COLUMNS</
TITLE></HEAD>

<FRAMESET COLS="110,*,100">
<FRAME NAME="banner" SRC="bannerCOLS.html">
<FRAME NAME="photos"
SRC="openingpageCOLS.html">
<FRAME NAME="buttons"
SRC="buttonsCOLS.html">

</FRAMESET>
```

Figure 10.7 *To create a page with frames in columns, use the COLS attribute instead of ROWS.*

Figure 10.8 *Don't forget to create the content for the frames. Although these pages are very similar to the ones shown in Figure 10.3, they have been adjusted slightly to fit better vertically.*

Figure 10.9 *Both Netscape (shown here) and Internet Explorer show the columns of frames in very much the same way as they show frames in rows.*

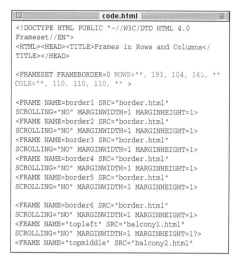

```
┌─────────────────── code.html ───────────────┐
<!DOCTYPE HTML PUBLIC "-//W3C/DTD HTML 4.0
Frameset//EN">
<HTML><HEAD><TITLE>Frames in Rows and Columns</
TITLE></HEAD>

<FRAMESET FRAMEBORDER=0 ROWS="*", 193, 104, 165, *"
COLS="*", 110, 110, 110, *" >

<FRAME NAME=border1 SRC="border.html"
SCROLLING="NO" MARGINWIDTH=1 MARGINHEIGHT=1>
<FRAME NAME=border2 SRC="border.html"
SCROLLING="NO" MARGINWIDTH=1 MARGINHEIGHT=1>
<FRAME NAME=border3 SRC="border.html"
SCROLLING="NO" MARGINWIDTH=1 MARGINHEIGHT=1>
<FRAME NAME=border4 SRC="border.html"
SCROLLING="NO" MARGINWIDTH=1 MARGINHEIGHT=1>
<FRAME NAME=border5 SRC="border.html"
SCROLLING="NO" MARGINWIDTH=1 MARGINHEIGHT=1>

<FRAME NAME=border6 SRC="border.html"
SCROLLING="NO" MARGINWIDTH=1 MARGINHEIGHT=1>
<FRAME NAME="topleft" SRC="balcony1.html"
SCROLLING="NO" MARGINWIDTH=1 MARGINHEIGHT=1?>
<FRAME NAME="topmiddle" SRC="balcony2.html">
```

Figure 10.10 *You set the size of rows and columns in the FRAMESET tag. Then define each row from left to right, and from top to bottom.*

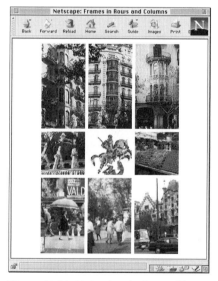

Figure 10.11 *Notice that the first and last rows and first and last columns of frames are set to take up all the leftover space not used up by the photos. Then I set each of those frames to display an empty page with a white background. No matter what size window my visitors look at this page with, the outside frames will expand or contract, but the photo filled frames will stay the same size.*

Creating frames in rows and columns

Some information is best displayed horizontally while some looks better vertically. You can create both rows and columns in the same frameset to accommodate different kinds of information.

To create a frameset with both rows and columns:

1. Type **<FRAMESET** to begin.

2. Type **ROWS "a, b"** where *a* and *b* (and any others) represent the height of the corresponding rows.

3. Type **COLS="x, y"** where *x* and *y* (and any others) represent the width of the corresponding columns.

4. Type **>**.

5. Define the first frame in the first row by typing **<FRAME NAME="name" SRC="initialurl.html">**.

6. Define the rest of the frames in the first row from left to right.

7. Repeat steps 4 and 5 for each row, from top to bottom.

8. Type **</FRAMESET>** to complete the frameset.

✔ Tips

- Defining rows and columns in this way limits you to the same number of frames in each row or column. To create one row with two frames and another row with three, you'll have to combine multiple framesets *(see page 162)*.

- There is more about this technique (and this particular example) on the Web site *(see page 21)*.

Creating frames in rows and columns

Combining framesets

One of the most common layouts for frames you'll see on the Web is to have one row at the top that spans the width of the browser, and then a second row divided into two frames. This effect is achieved by inserting a frameset in the second row.

To combine framesets:

1. Make a sketch of your frameset and determine how many rows and columns you will need.

2. Type **<FRAMESET** to begin.

3. Type **ROWS="a, b">** where *a* and *b* (and any others) represent the height of the corresponding rows.

4. In the example in Figure 10.12, the first and third rows are a single frame while the second row is divided into columns. For a row with just a single frame, type **<FRAME NAME="name" SRC="contents.html">** in the usual way.

5. For the second row, which is divided into columns in this example, type **<FRAMESET COLS="a, b">** where *a* and *b* (and any others) represent the width of each column in the row.

6. Type **<FRAME NAME="name" SRC="contents.html">** where *name* is the reference for the frame and *contents.html* is the page that will be initially shown in that frame.

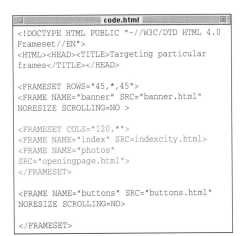

```
code.html
<!DOCTYPE HTML PUBLIC "-//W3C/DTD HTML 4.0
Frameset//EN">
<HTML><HEAD><TITLE>Targeting particular
frames</TITLE></HEAD>

<FRAMESET ROWS="45,*,45">
<FRAME NAME="banner" SRC="banner.html"
NORESIZE SCROLLING=NO >

<FRAMESET COLS="120,*">
<FRAME NAME="index" SRC=indexcity.html>
<FRAME NAME="photos"
SRC="openingpage.html">
</FRAMESET>

<FRAME NAME="buttons" SRC="buttons.html"
NORESIZE SCROLLING=NO>

</FRAMESET>
```

Figure 10.12 *First create the outer frameset. Then define each row from top to bottom. For rows that will be divided, use an inner frameset. The highlighted area here corresponds to just the second row of the Web page.*

Figure 10.13 *In this example, the first and third rows are simple frames while the second row is a frameset divided into two columns.*

Combining framesets

7. Repeat step 6 for each frame in the column. (In this example, there are two columns, so you'll have to define two frames in the inner frameset.)

8. When you've finished defining the frames/columns in the divided row, type **</FRAMESET>**.

9. Continue defining each row individually. For a row with just one frame (i.e., just one column), just use a FRAME tag. For rows divided into multiple columns, repeat steps 5–8.

10. Type **</FRAMESET>** to complete the outer frameset.

✔ Tips

■ Although I've defined the rows first and then the columns in this example, you can define the columns first if it works better for your particular layout. In fact, when adjusting the borders, both methods have distinct advantages (see the tips on page 169). The only thing to watch is that each frameset have opening and closing <FRAMESET> tags, and that each frameset is contained completely with no overlapping *(see page 24)*.

■ It is important to stress that not every row need be divided into columns. For rows with a single frame (i.e., that span the entire window from left to right), just use a FRAME tag. For rows divided into columns, use an inner frameset.

■ If you want to create the *same number* of frames in each row and each column, you don't need to combine multiple framesets. For more information, consult *Creating frames in rows and columns* on page 161.

Combining framesets

Creating an inline frame

If you want to mix text, graphics, and a frame all on one page, you'll need to create a floating or *inline* frame—and hope that your visitors view the page with Explorer (although it *is* standard HTML 4).

To create an inline frame:

1. In the container page, type **<IFRAME SRC="frame.url"**, where *frame.url* is the page that should be initially displayed in the inline frame.

2. Type **NAME="name"**, where *name* is a word that identifies this inline frame's use.

3. Type **WIDTH=x HEIGHT=y** where *x* and *y* represent the width and height, respectively, of the inline frame as a percentage or as an absolute value in pixels.

4. If desired, type **ALIGN=LEFT** or **ALIGN=RIGHT** to wrap the text that comes after the frame around the frame.

5. Type **>**.

6. Type the text that should appear if the browser doesn't support inline frames.

7. Type **</IFRAME>** to complete the inline frame.

✔ Tips

- You can also use the FRAMEBORDER *(see page 169)*, HSPACE/VSPACE *(see page 86)*, SCROLLING *(see page 166)*, and MARGINWIDTH/MARGINHEIGHT *(see page 165)* tags with inline frames.

- Netscape (as of version 4) does not support inline frames.

```
code.html
<!DOCTYPE HTML PUBLIC "-//W3C/DTD HTML 4.0
Frameset//EN"><HTML><HEAD><TITLE>Floating
Frames</TITLE></HEAD>
<BODY BGCOLOR="#FFFFFF">

<H1>Barcelona Tours</H1>
Here's an idea of what the Barcelona Tours
home page looks like:
<HR>

<P><CENTER>
<IFRAME WIDTH=90% HEIGHT=70%
SRC="BCNtourRC.html">
The <A HREF="BCNtourRC.html">Barcelona
Tours</A> page contains great photos and
essential tips for making your vacation a
success.
</IFRAME>
<CENTER>
```

Figure 10.14 *Because many Web surfers use Netscape, and Netscape doesn't support inline frames, it's important to add alternate text between the opening and closing IFRAME tags.*

Figure 10.15 *Floating frames won't appear in Netscape but the alternate text (here with a link to the frameset) will.*

Figure 10.16 *Floating frames function similarly to images, flowing with the rest of the content on the page.*

Creating an inline frame

Figure 10.17 *In this illustration you can see the default margins. Note how the contents of each frame begins slightly down and to the right.*

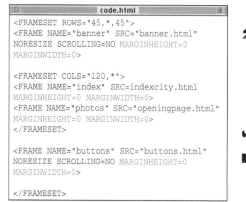

```
code.html
<FRAMESET ROWS="45,*,45">
<FRAME NAME="banner" SRC="banner.html"
NORESIZE SCROLLING=NO MARGINHEIGHT=0
MARGINWIDTH=0>

<FRAMESET COLS="120,*">
<FRAME NAME="index" SRC=indexcity.html
MARGINHEIGHT=0 MARGINWIDTH=0>
<FRAME NAME="photos" SRC="openingpage.html"
MARGINHEIGHT=0 MARGINWIDTH=0>
</FRAMESET>

<FRAME NAME="buttons" SRC="buttons.html"
NORESIZE SCROLLING=NO MARGINHEIGHT=0
MARGINWIDTH=0>

</FRAMESET>
```

Figure 10.18 *Adjust the margins of each frame by adding a MARGINWIDTH and/or MARGIN-HEIGHT tag to the desired FRAME tags. In this case, all the margins have been set to 0.*

Figure 10.19 *With the margins set at 0, each frame's contents start right up in the top left corner of each frame.*

Adjusting a frame's margins

By default, both Netscape and Explorer display a frame's contents with a margin of 8 pixels on each side **(Figure 10.17)**. You can adjust the margin so that there is more space, or, if you prefer, so that the frame's contents begin in the top left corner.

To adjust a frame's margins:

1. In the desired FRAME tag, before the final >, type **MARGINWIDTH=w** where *w* is the desired amount of space, in pixels, between the left and right edges of the frame and the frame's contents **(Figure 10.18)**.

2. Type **MARGINHEIGHT=h** where *h* is the desired amount of space, in pixels, between the top and bottom edges of the frame and the frame's contents.

✔ Tip

■ The margin is transparent and thus always appears to be the same color as the background of the page displayed in the frame.

Adjusting a frame's margins

Showing or hiding scroll bars

You can decide whether each individual frame should have a scroll bar all the time, never, or only when needed. *Only when needed* means that the scroll bars will appear only when there is more information than can be shown at one time in the frame. If the visitor makes the window big enough, these scroll bars will eventually disappear.

To show scroll bars all the time:

In the FRAME tag of the particular frame for which you wish to show the scroll bar, type **SCROLLING="YES"**.

To hide scroll bars all the time:

In the FRAME tag of the particular frame for which you wish to hide the scroll bar, type **SCROLLING="NO"**.

✔ Tips

- The default is for scroll bars to appear only when necessary, that is, when there is more information than can fit in the frame. To use the default, type **SCROLLING="AUTO"** or, more simply, don't type any SCROLLING tag at all.

- There are few things more frustrating than jumping to a frameset page with tiny little frames that make it impossible to view the entire contents. Even worse is when you cannot scroll around (or make the frame bigger—see page 170) to make the hidden information visible. To avoid frustrating *your* visitors, make sure you test your frameset page in a small window and ensure that all the frames without scroll bars are big enough to display their entire contents.

```
                  code.html
<HTML><HEAD><TITLE>Frames without Scroll
bars</TITLE></HEAD>

<FRAMESET ROWS="45,*,45">
<FRAME NAME="banner" SRC="banner.html"
SCROLLING="NO">

<FRAMESET COLS="120,*">
<FRAME NAME="index" SRC=indexcity.html>
<FRAME NAME="photos"
SRC="openingpage.html">
</FRAMESET>

<FRAME NAME="buttons" SRC="buttons.html"
SCROLLING="NO">

</FRAMESET>
```

Figure 10.20 *So that the top and bottom frames never display scroll bars, add SCROLLING=NO to their FRAME tags.*

Figure 10.21 *Eliminating scroll bars from certain areas makes the information much clearer and more attractive. But be careful not to take away scroll bars from areas that need them. Remember, you can't control the size of your visitor's window.*

```
┌─────────────────────────────────┐
│          code.html              │
├─────────────────────────────────┤
│<FRAMESET BORDERCOLOR="#000000"  │
│ROWS="45,*,45">                  │
│<FRAME NAME="banner" SRC="banner.html"│
│SCROLLING=NO>                    │
│                                 │
│<FRAMESET COLS="120,*">          │
│<FRAME NAME="index" SRC=indexcity.html>│
│<FRAME NAME="photos"             │
│SRC="openingpage.html">          │
│</FRAMESET>                      │
└─────────────────────────────────┘
```

Figure 10.22 *You can add the BORDERCOLOR tag to any frameset or frame tag. Here it's been added to the topmost frameset tag so that it will affect all the frames contained within.*

Figure 10.23 *Only Netscape can show colored borders.*

Figure 10.24 *Internet Explorer keeps on displaying the same, boring, gray frame borders.*

Adjusting the color of the borders

 In theory, you can change the color of each frame (viewed with Netscape) individually. In practice, however, since the borders are shared between frames, the possibilities are more limited.

To adjust the color of all the borders in the frameset:

Inside the topmost FRAMESET tag before the final >, type **BORDERCOLOR=color**, where *color* is one of the sixteen pre-defined colors *(see page 311)*.

To change the color of rows, columns, or individual frames:

In the appropriate FRAMESET or FRAME tag, type **BORDERCOLOR=color**.

✔ Tips

- You can also type **BORDERCOLOR= "#rrggbb"**. Consult *Colors in Hex* starting on page 311 for more details.

- A BORDERCOLOR tag in an individual frame overrides a BORDERCOLOR tag in a row or column, which in turn overrides the tag defined in the topmost FRAMESET. If two BORDER-COLOR tags at the same level conflict, the one that comes first in your HTML file takes precedence.

- When you change the border of an individual frame, other frames that share its borders are also affected.

- For simulating colored borders in Explorer, see the last tip on page 171.

Adjusting the color of the borders

Adjusting the borders' thickness

```
<FRAMESET BORDERCOLOR="#000000" BORDER=10
ROWS="45,*,45">
<FRAME NAME="banner" SRC="banner.html"
SCROLLING=NO>

<FRAMESET COLS="120,*">
<FRAME NAME="index" SRC="indexcity.html>
<FRAME NAME="photos"
SRC="openingpage.html">
</FRAMESET>
```

Figure 10.25 *Add the BORDER tag to any frameset or frame tag to adjust its borders' thickness. Here, I've added the tag to the topmost frameset tag so that all the frames are affected.*

You can change the thickness of the frames' borders to suit your design— as long as your public uses Netscape, and not Internet Explorer, to view them.

To make the borders thicker or thinner:

Inside the topmost FRAMESET tag, before the final >, type **BORDER=n** where *n* is the desired width of the border in pixels.

✔ Tips

■ You can set the border width to 0 (BORDER=0) to make the borders disappear, but only Netscape will get it. Explorer will continue to display the borders.

■ In fact, if you want the frames to jut right up next to each other, you should use the BORDER tag, set to 0, (for viewing in Netscape) *as well as* the FRAMEBORDER tag described on page 169 (for viewing with Internet Explorer and Netscape).

■ The default border width is 5 pixels.

■ You cannot set the thickness for individual frames.

■ To approximate this effect in Internet Explorer, hide the borders altogether *(see page 169)* and use frame spacing *(see page 171).*

Figure 10.26 *Thick, colored borders can help divide information into understandable chunks.*

Figure 10.27 *A value of 1 for BORDER produces thinner, more discreet borders.*

```
code.html
<FRAMESET BORDERCOLOR="#000000" BORDER=0
FRAMEBORDER=0 ROWS="45,*,45">
<FRAME NAME="banner" SRC="banner.html"
SCROLLING=NO>

<FRAMESET COLS="120,*">
<FRAME NAME="index" SRC=indexcity.html>
<FRAME NAME="photos"
SRC="openingpage.html">
</FRAMESET>
```

Figure 10.28 *If you want to be sure that your page has no borders, whether it is viewed in Netscape or with Internet Explorer, set both the BORDER and FRAMEBORDER tags to 0.*

Figure 10.29 *Netscape will only show the frames right next to each other if you use both the BOR-DER and FRAMEBORDER tags. FRAMEBORDER by itself merely makes the border the same color as the background. BORDER=0 makes it invisible.*

Figure 10.30 *Internet Explorer's borders don't completely disappear if your individual frames have different background colors. The only solution is to use the same background color for each frame, as well as for the frameset itself.*

Hiding or showing the borders

Depending on the content of your frames, you may not want to have any visible division between them at all. In that case, you can make the borders disappear.

To make all the borders disappear:

Type **FRAMEBORDER=0** inside the topmost FRAMESET tag, before the final >.

To make *only* the vertical borders disappear:

Within each FRAME tag in the desired row, type **FRAMEBORDER=0**.

✔ Tips

- Both Netscape and IE understand a value of 0 for the FRAMEBORDER tag. Netscape also understands "No".

- To view *some* borders when the topmost frameset is set for none, type **FRAMEBORDER=1** (or for Netscape only, use **FRAMEBORDER=Yes**) in the desired FRAME or FRAMESET tag.

- To make the horizontal borders disappear, define the columns in the outer frameset and the rows in the inner frameset and then type **FRAMEBOR-DER=0** within each of the FRAME tags in the desired column.

- You can use the FRAMEBORDER tag with individual frames but since each frame shares its borders with other frames, the results can be unexpected.

- FRAMEBORDER makes the borders blend with the background in Netscape, but to make adjacent frames actually touch, see page 168.

Keeping visitors from resizing frames

Frames with relative or variable sizes are always resized when the visitor changes the size of the browser window. However, you can also choose whether to let the visitor resize individual frames.

To keep visitors from resizing your frames:

Type **NORESIZE** in the FRAME tag for the desired frame.

✔ Tips

- Netscape displays resizable frames with a small hash mark in the middle of the border. The mark disappears if you've used the NORESIZE attribute.

- If you use very small pixel values for your frames and the visitor views the frameset page in a very large window, the width of the frames will probably not be quite as you wished. The entire frameset is always stretched to fill the window.

- If you set the border width to 0 with the BORDER tag *(see page 168)*, visitors who view the page in Netscape won't be able to resize the frames at all. The borders will remain flexible in Internet Explorer, since Explorer doesn't recognize the BORDER tag.

Figure 10.31 *Normally when the visitor places the pointer over a border, it changes into a double-headed arrow with which she can change the size of the frame. Also notice the hash mark which indicates the frame can be resized.*

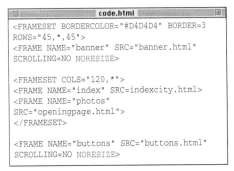

```
<FRAMESET BORDERCOLOR="#D4D4D4" BORDER=3
ROWS="45,*,45">
<FRAME NAME="banner" SRC="banner.html"
SCROLLING=NO NORESIZE>

<FRAMESET COLS="120,*">
<FRAME NAME="index" SRC=indexcity.html>
<FRAME NAME="photos"
SRC="openingpage.html">
</FRAMESET>

<FRAME NAME="buttons" SRC="buttons.html"
SCROLLING=NO NORESIZE>
```

Figure 10.32 *Add the NORESIZE tag to any frames that you don't want the visitor to be able to resize. Here, I've modified the top and bottom frames and left the middle frames flexible.*

Figure 10.33 *Once you've restricted the resizability, the pointer will not turn into a double-pointed arrow and the visitor will not be able to change the size of the frame. (In Netscape, the hash mark disappears as well.)*

```
code.html
<FRAMESET FRAMESPACING=10 ROWS="45,*,45">
<FRAME NAME="banner" SRC="banner.html"
SCROLLING=NO NORESIZE>

<FRAMESET COLS="120,*">
<FRAME NAME="index" SRC=indexcity.html>
<FRAME NAME="photos"
SRC="openingpage.html">
</FRAMESET>

<FRAME NAME="buttons" SRC="buttons.html"
SCROLLING=NO NORESIZE>
```

Figure 10.34 *To add spacing between the frames in Explorer, use the FRAMESPACING tag and a value in pixels.*

Figure 10.35 *The FRAMESPACING tag has no effect on frames viewed with Netscape.*

Figure 10.36 *In Internet Explorer, however, the spacing is very effective and is somewhat similar to colored borders with Netscape. However, the color used is the background color (or image) specified on the frameset page.*

Adjusting the spacing between frames

Adding spacing between frames is very similar to adding space between cells, rows, and columns in a table *(see page 152)*. The space goes between the contents and the border. Unfortunately, Netscape doesn't support frame spacing.

To adjust the spacing of all the frames at the same time:

Within the topmost FRAMESET tag, type **FRAMESPACING=n** where *n* is the width in pixels of the desired spacing.

To adjust the spacing of the vertical borders between frames:

Within the FRAME tag of the desired row, type **FRAMESPACING=n** where *n* is the width in pixels of the desired spacing.

✔ Tips

■ You can use different FRAMESPAC-ING values for each frameset on your page. The innermost tags override the outer ones.

■ You can adjust the spacing of the horizontal borders between frames by defining first the columns and then the rows, and then setting the FRAMESPACING tag for the desired column.

■ You can use the FRAMESPACING tag to simulate colored borders for Internet Explorer users. Simply give the frameset page a background color (or image) and set the spacing so that the color (or image) shows through. Hide the frame borders for maximum effect *(see page 169)*.

Targeting links to particular frames

The initial contents of a given frame is specified in the frameset page with the SRC tag. However, you can have other pages appear in that same frame. The trick is to add a pointer, called a *target*, to the links to those pages. The target says "open this link in frame xyz".

To target a link to a particular frame:

1. Make sure the target frame has a name **(Figure 10.37)**. For more information, consult *Creating a simple frameset* on page 158.

2. On the page where the link should appear, type **<A HREF="page.html"** where *page.html* is the file that should be displayed in the target frame.

3. Type **TARGET="name"** where *name* is the reference given to the target frame within the FRAME tag **(Figure 10.38)**.

4. Add any other attributes as desired to the link and then type the final **>**. For more information on creating links, see Chapter 7, *Links*.

✔ Tips

■ The frame must have a name to be targeted. For more information on naming frames, consult *Creating a simple frameset* on page 158.

■ Frame names must begin with an alphanumeric character (except the special names described on page 173).

■ If you don't specify a target, the link will open in the frame that contains the link.

Figure 10.37 *Targets will only work if the frame in which you want the page to appear has a name.*

```
code.html
<TR><TD BGCOLOR="#F3D7E3">
<A HREF="openingpage.html" TARGET=photos>
Beginning</A>
<TR><TD BGCOLOR="#F6D5C3">
<A HREF="rambles.html" TARGET=photos>Les
Rambles Boulevard</A>
<TR><TD BGCOLOR="#D8E9D6"><A
HREF="plcat.html" TARGET=photos>Pla&#231;a
```

Figure 10.38 *Within the link, type* **TARGET=name** *where name matches the frame name in Figure 10.37.*

Figure 10.39 *The original contents of the* photos *frame is the* Welcome *page. But when the visitor clicks the* Les Rambles *link (which is targeted to appear in the* photos *frame)...*

Figure 10.40 *...the* Les Rambles *page replaces the* Welcome *page in the* photos *frame.*

```
======== code.html ========
boulevard, carving it out sort of like a
Catalan Colorado River...
<P>One of the wonderful things about the
Rambles is that it is filled with all
<em>different</em> kinds of people. On a
Saturday afternoon, at its most crowded,
you'll see older couples checking out the
bird and flower stalls, younger people
arguing at the political booths, mimes and
bands, beggars and pickpockets (well, maybe
you won't <em>see</em> them). If I were
there, I'd be drinking an orxata at the
Caf&#233; de l'&#211;pera watching all the
people go by.
<BR>
<A HREF="rambles2.html" TARGET=_self>More
about Les Rambles</A>
```

Figure 10.41 *In this example, the link accesses a second page of information. It makes sense to display this second page in the same frame.*

Figure 10.42 *When the visitor clicks a link that is targeted to the same frame that contains the link...*

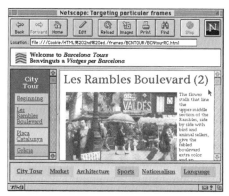

Figure 10.43 *...the frame's contents are replaced with the new contents from the link.*

Targeting links to special spots

Although many times you'll be happy with targeting a link to a particular frame, as described on page 172, other times you will want to make more general instructions, like having the link open in a new window, or opening the link in the same window that contained the link.

To target a link to a special spot:

1. Type **<A HREF="contents.html"** where *contents.html* is the page that you wish to be displayed in the special spot.

2. Type **TARGET=_blank** to have the link open in a new, blank window. This is the ideal targeting for external links which may not fit very well inside your frames.

   Or type **TARGET=_self** to open the link in the same frame that contains the link **(Figure 10.41)**. The information in the frame (including the link itself) will be replaced by the *contents.html* file specified in step 1.

   Or type **TARGET=_top** to open the link in the current browser window but independently of the rest of the frameset to which it currently belongs.

   Or type **TARGET=_parent** to open the link in the frame that contains the current frameset. This will only be different from _top when you are using nested framesets. For more information on nested framesets, consult *Nesting framesets* on page 175.

Changing the default target

If a frame contains a link, the link will open up in that same frame, by default, unless you change the target as described on pages 172–173. You can change the default target for all of the links on a page by using the BASE tag.

To change the default target:

1. In the HEAD section of the page that contains the links, type **<BASE**.

2. Type **TARGET="name"**, where *name* is the word that identifies the frame or window in which you want the links to appear, by default.

3. Type **>** to complete the BASE tag.

✔ Tip

■ You can override the target specified in the BASE tag by choosing a target in the link itself *(see page 172).*

```
code.html
<HTML><HEAD><TITLE>Buttons</TITLE></HEAD>
<BODY BGCOLOR=#FF0000>

<TABLE CELLPADDING=5 CELLSPACING=0 WIDTH=100%>
<TR><TH><FONT COLOR="#FFFFFF" SIZE=+1>City
Tour</FONT></A>
<TR><TD BGCOLOR="#F3D7E3"><A
HREF="openingpage.html"
TARGET=photos>Beginning</A>
<TR><TD BGCOLOR="#F6D5C3"><A
HREF="rambles.html" TARGET=photos>Les Rambles
Boulevard</A>
<TR><TD BGCOLOR="#D8E9D6"><A HREF="plcat.html"
TARGET=photos>Pla&#231;a Catalunya</A>
<TR><TD BGCOLOR="#D1C9DF"><A HREF="gracia.html"
TARGET=photos>Gr&#224;cia</A>
<TR><TD BGCOLOR="#D4EBF9"><A HREF="port.html"
TARGET=photos>The Port</A>
<TR><TD BGCOLOR="#CECDB4"><A
HREF="laberint.html" TARGET=photos>The
Labyrinth in Horta</A>
<TR><TD BGCOLOR="#C5D300"><A HREF="sagfam.html"
TARGET=photos>The Sagrada Fam&#237;lia Church</
A>
<TR><TD BGCOLOR="#F7BD00"><A HREF="fonts.html"
TARGET=photos>The Magical Fountains of
Montjuich</A>
<TR><TD BGCOLOR="#148DC6"><A
HREF="barrigotic.html" TARGET=photos>The Gothic
Quarter</A>
```

Figure 10.44 *In the original document, I've set the target for each link individually.*

```
code.html
<HTML><HEAD><TITLE>Buttons</TITLE>
<BASE TARGET=photos></HEAD>
<BODY BGCOLOR=#FF0000>

<TABLE CELLPADDING=5 CELLSPACING=0 WIDTH=100%>
<TR><TH><FONT COLOR="#FFFFFF" SIZE=+1>City
Tour</FONT></A>
<TR><TD BGCOLOR="#F3D7E3"><A
HREF="openingpage.html">Beginning</A>
<TR><TD BGCOLOR="#F6D5C3"><A
HREF="rambles.html">Les Rambles Boulevard</A>
<TR><TD BGCOLOR="#D8E9D6"><A
HREF="plcat.html">Pla&#231;a Catalunya</A>
<TR><TD BGCOLOR="#D1C9DF"><A
HREF="gracia.html">Gr&#224;cia</A>
<TR><TD BGCOLOR="#D4EBF9"><A
HREF="port.html">The Port</A>
<TR><TD BGCOLOR="#CECDB4"><A
HREF="laberint.html">The Labyrinth in Horta</A>
<TR><TD BGCOLOR="#C5D300"><A
HREF="sagfam.html">The Sagrada Fam&#237;lia
Church</A>
<TR><TD BGCOLOR="#F7BD00"><A
HREF="fonts.html">The Magical Fountains of
Montjuich</A>
<TR><TD BGCOLOR="#148DC6"><A
HREF="barrigotic.html">The Gothic Quarter</A>
```

Figure 10.45 *You can save a lot of typing by using the BASE tag to set the default target for every link on the page. This document is equivalent to the one shown in Figure 10.44.*

```
                  code.html
<!DOCTYPE HTML PUBLIC "-//W3C/DTD HTML 4.0
Frameset//EN">
<HTML><HEAD><TITLE>Nesting Frames</TITLE></
HEAD>

<FRAMESET COLS="*,4*">
<FRAME SRC="bigindex.html">
<FRAME NAME="main" SRC="BCNtourRC.html">

</FRAMESET>

</HTML>
```

Figure 10.46 *The frameset shown has two columns. The first column will contain a simple index page, while the second column will contain a distinct frameset (in fact, the one used in most of the previous examples in this chapter).*

Figure 10.47 *In this example, the Barcelona tour is easily integrated into a larger group of topics just by nesting its frameset into the larger one.*

Nesting framesets

As if frames and framesets weren't complicated enough, you can nest framesets inside of frames to achieve special effects.

To nest framesets:

1. Build the child, or inner, frameset *(see page 158)*.

2. Build the parent, or outer, frameset **(Figure 10.46)**. When you reach the frame in which you wish to nest the child frameset, type **SRC="child.html"** in the FRAME tag, where *child.html* is the file that you built in step 1.

✔ Tips

- You can target a link to open in the parent frame of a frameset (in this example, the right column is the parent frame of the Barcelona tour frameset). For more information, consult *Targeting links to special spots* on page 173.

- You can't nest a frameset inside a frame that is in that same frameset. Hey, and why would you want to?

Creating alternatives to frames

Although Netscape and Internet Explorer have been able to display frames since version 2, and frames have been added to the official HTML specifications with version 4, some browsers (OK, not many) still do not support them. You can create alternate content that will appear if your visitor's browser doesn't support frames.

To create alternatives to frames:

1. Type **<NOFRAMES>** after the last </FRAMESET> tag **(Figure 10.48)**.

2. Create the content that you want to appear if the frames do not.

3. When you've finished creating the alternate content, type **</NOFRAMES>**.

✔ Tips

■ The information found within the NOFRAMES tags will not be shown in browsers that can interpret frames, like Netscape **(Figure 10.49)** and Internet Explorer. Instead, the frames will be shown.

■ Some people set up Internet Explorer so that it doesn't view frames (by unchecking Frames in the Web Content preferences). They will see the NOFRAMES content.

■ If you don't create a NOFRAMES section, beware! When visitors jump to your page with a browser that can't read frames, instead of an error message, they simply won't see anything! If nothing else, the NOFRAMES section can be used to explain what the problem is **(Figure 10.50)**.

```
<FRAMESET ROWS="45,*,45">
<FRAME NAME="banner" SRC="banner.html"
NORESIZE SCROLLING=NO >

<FRAMESET COLS="120,*">
<FRAME NAME="index" SRC=indexcity.html>
<FRAME NAME="photos"
SRC="openingpage.html">
</FRAMESET>

<FRAME NAME="buttons" SRC="buttons.html"
NORESIZE SCROLLING=NO>

</FRAMESET>

<NOFRAMES>
<BODY>
The information on this page is displayed in
frames. Your browser can't view frames (or
if you're using Internet Explorer, you've
turned frame viewing off--go to Preferences
under Edit and then Web Content and check
Show Frames). Sorry!
</BODY></NOFRAMES>
```

Figure 10.48 *The NOFRAMES tags come after all of the framesets and frames have been defined.*

Figure 10.49 *Netscape always displays frames, and therefore never displays the information between the NOFRAMES tags.*

Figure 10.50 *When you turn frames off in Internet Explorer, you can see the alternate information. This is a good way to test how this information will appear. Although this example is rather simple, don't be misled: you can put practically anything in the NOFRAMES section.*

Forms

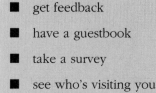

✔ What you can do with forms:

- get feedback
- have a guestbook
- take a survey
- see who's visiting you
- sell stuff
- and much more!

Up to now, all the HTML you have learned has helped you communicate *your* ideas with your visitors. In this chapter, you'll learn how to create forms which enable your visitors to communicate with you.

There are two basic parts of a form: the structure or shell, that consists of fields, labels, and buttons that the visitor sees on a page and hopefully fills out, and the processing script that takes that information and converts it into a format that you can read or tally.

Constructing a form's shell is quite straightforward and is similar to creating any other part of the Web page. You can create text boxes, special password boxes, radio buttons, check boxes, drop-down menus, larger text areas, and even clickable images. You will give each element a name that will serve as a label to identify the data once it is processed. Constructing forms is discussed on pages 182–196.

Processing the data from a form is a bit more complicated. The principal tool, the *CGI script*, is typically written in Perl or some other programming language. However, Perl programming is beyond the scope of this book, and even explaining how to use existing Perl scripts stretches its limits a bit. Nevertheless, I'll start off the chapter with enough information to get you pointed in the right direction.

If this all seems a bit daunting, or if your ISP doesn't allow you to run CGI scripts, you might decide to use a public form host. These are described on page 203.

Forms

About CGI scripts

In earlier editions of this book, I left the discussion of CGI scripts until the end of the Forms chapter. I've come to believe that was a bit of a tease. I've gotten more than one letter from readers saying "I've got my form set up. Now how do I make it run?" So this time, I'll be brutally honest from the outset: You can't use a form without a CGI script. Hey, but don't worry, it's not *that* hard.

What is a CGI script?

If you're a non-programmer, the phrase *CGI script* may make you want to quickly close this book and forget about forms altogether. Hold on. What's CGI? What's a script? It's not as impossible as it sounds. First, a script is another word for a program, just like Microsoft Word or Adobe Photoshop. Of course, the scripts you'll use to process forms are a good deal simpler than commercial applications that cost hundreds of dollars. But they work in a similar way.

CGI, which stands for *Common Gateway Interface*, is simply a standardized way for sending information between the server and the script. So, to resume, a CGI script is a program (usually written in a programming language called Perl) that communicates with the server in a standard (CGI-like) way.

What does the CGI script do?

Each element on your form will have a *name* and a *value* associated with it. The name identifies the data that is being sent. It might be something like *visitor_name*. The value is the data (say, *Castro*), and can either come from you, the Web page designer, or from the visitor who types it in a field **(Figures 11.1 and 11.2)**.

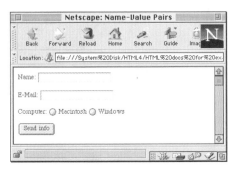

Figure 11.1 *Here's your basic form. There are two text fields, one set of radio buttons and a submit button. The words Name, E-Mail, Computer, Macintosh, and Windows are all labels. They do not affect the data that is collected in any way.*

```
<HTML><HEAD><TITLE>Name-Value Pairs</TITLE></HEAD>
<BODY>
<FORM METHOD=GET ACTION="cgi.script.url">
<P>Name: <INPUT TYPE="text" NAME="visitor_name">
<P>E-Mail: <INPUT TYPE="text" NAME="visitor_email">
<P>Computer:
<INPUT TYPE="radio" NAME="computer" VALUE="Mac">Macintosh
<INPUT TYPE="radio" NAME="computer" VALUE="PC">Windows
<P><INPUT TYPE="submit" NAME="submit" VALUE="Send info">
</FORM>
</HTML>
```

Figure 11.2 *Here's the HTML code that is behind the table in Figure 11.1. Just focus on the NAME and VALUE attributes for now. (You'll learn how to create form elements later on in the chapter.) First, notice how each form element has a NAME attribute, but only some have a VALUE. The VALUE attribute determines the data that is sent to the server for that element. Some form elements allow the visitor to type in any value (like text boxes) while others do not (like radio buttons). Form elements that work by checking or selecting must have the value specified in the VALUE attribute.*

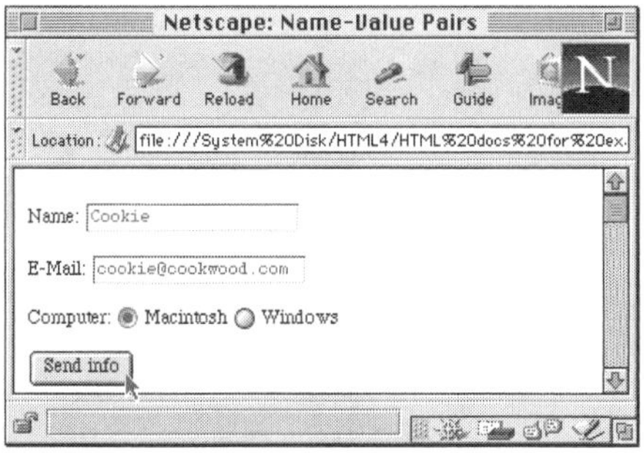

Figure 11.3 *When the visitor enters information in the text fields and chooses a radio button, the name-value pairs are set. Clicking the submit button (labeled here "Send info") will send the name-value pairs to the CGI-script on the server.*

Label	Name	Value
Name	visitor_name	Cookie
E-Mail	visitor_email	cookie@cookwood.com
Computer	computer	Mac
Submit	submit	Send info

Figure 11.4 *These are the actual name-value pairs that will be sent when the visitor clicks the submit button in Figure 11.3. Be sure not to confuse* label *with* name. *Also, notice that the values for the first two fields correspond to what the visitor has typed. The value for the radio button—Mac, not Macintosh (which is the label)—was set by me, the author of this Web page (see Figure 11.2) since the visitor can only click the button (and not type).*

http://www.cookwood.com/cgi-bin/cgi.script.url?visitor_name=Cookie&visitor_email=cookie@cookwood.com&computer=Mac&submit=Send+info

Figure 11.5 *If you use the GET method, this is what the data that is sent to the CGI script looks like. Notice that the string is separated from the URL for the CGI script by a question mark (?). Then each name is linked with its value with an equals sign (=). Finally, an ampersand (&) separates each name-value pair.*

When a visitor clicks the submit button (or an active image—see page 196), the name-value pair of each form element (it might look like *visitor_name=Castro*) is sent to the server. The CGI script takes all the name-value pairs and separates them out into something a real human (or a database) can read and understand.

GET vs. POST

There are two ways to send information to the server: *GET* and *POST*. It's important to know the difference because you'll have to decide which one is used when you set up your form *(see page 182)*.

The GET method appends the name-value pairs to the end of the URL. This information is then passed to the QUERY_STRING variable. The CGI script must then break down the QUERY_STRING environment variable to analyze the incoming data. The principal disadvantage of the GET method is that the amount of data you can retrieve is limited. Its chief advantage is that you can create a link that accesses a CGI script.

The POST method sends a data file with the name-value pairs to the server's standard input, together with the Content-Type and the Content Length in bytes. The CGI script then takes the data from standard input and analyzes it. The principal advantage? No size limit.

Which one should you use? If you want to make a link to a CGI script, use GET. If you're worried that the data will be truncated, use POST. The most important thing is that the CGI script that you use knows how to parse information gathered with the method that you choose.

About CGI scripts

Security

Before you get too excited, you should know that CGI scripts can leave your server wide open to invaders. That's one reason many ISPs do not allow their users to use CGI scripts. If this is your case, one alternative is to use a form hosting service, as described on page 203.

If your ISP does allow you to run CGI-scripts, you should still read up on security issues. You might start with *http://www.go2net.com/people/paulp/cgi-security/* for more information on what CGI scripts can make you vulnerable to.

Getting a script

If your ISP okays your use of CGI scripts, your next step is to get your hands on one. If you're a programmer, you can write your own. If not, you can find scripts on the Web and adapt them for your own use.

Perl is the most common language used for CGI scripts, partly because it's easily ported from one platform to another, partly because it's great for massaging data into understandable information, and partly because it has this reputation as a cool language—really! Perl programmers love to brag about how they can do anything with Perl, on one line, in a million different ways.

You can use other programming languages, like C++, tcl, Visual Basic, or even AppleScript to create CGI scripts. My advice is that if you know one of these languages, you should use it; otherwise, use Perl **(Figure 11.6)**.

One extra nice thing about Perl programmers is that they like to share. You can find tons of ready-to-use CGI scripts written in Perl all over the Web **(Figure 11.7)**.

Figure 11.6 *On your next holiday, you might like to visit the Programming Republic of Perl. You'll find it at www.perl.com.*

Figure 11.7 *Selena Sol's Public Domain CGI Script Archive is one of the nicer places you can visit to find CGI scripts to use with your own page.*

Getting a script ready

Whether you've written your own script or are using someone else's, you'll have to do a couple of things to get it ready for use with your form.

Adapting scripts for your use

If you're using a Perl script that you've downloaded from someone else, you'll have to open it up and see what variables and path names it uses. You will have to change these to reflect your particular situation.

Transferring the script to the server

The next step is to copy the script to the server, generally with an FTP program like Fetch or WS_FTP *(see page 296)*. Some servers require that all CGI scripts be located in the cgi-bin directory. Others provide a personal cgi-bin directory for each user. Still others let you store CGI scripts wherever you want, as long as you add a particular extension to them for identification. You'll have to ask your ISP.

Permissions

If your page is on a Unix server, you will have to use chmod to make the CGI script accessible and executable. For more information, consult *Changing permissions* on page 301.

Add it to your form!

So you've got your CGI script on your server, ready to go. The only thing left is to add it to your form *(see page 182)*.

Getting a script ready

Creating a form

A form has three important parts: the FORM tag, which includes the URL of the CGI script that will process the form; the form elements, like fields and menus; and the submit button which sends the data to the CGI script on the server.

To create a form:

1. Type **<FORM**.

2. Type **METHOD=method**, where *method* is either GET or POST *(see page 179)*.

3. Type **ACTION="script.url">** where *script.url* is the location on the server of the CGI script that will run when the form is submitted *(see pages 178–181)*.

4. Create the form's contents, as described on pages 183–196.

5. Type **</FORM>** to complete the form.

✔ Tips

■ In order for your visitor to send you the information on the form, you'll need either a submit button (if your form contains fields, buttons, and other elements that your visitors will fill in) or an active image. For details about submit buttons, consult *Creating the submit button* on page 192. For information on active images, consult *Active images* on page 196.

■ You can use tables to lay out your form elements more precisely. For more information, consult Chapter 9, *Tables*.

```
☐☐☐☐☐☐☐☐☐☐  code.html  ☐☐☐☐☐☐
<HTML><HEAD>
<TITLE>VQS Guide to HTML - Forms</TITLE>
</HEAD><BODY>

<H1>Using forms </H1>
<FORM METHOD=POST ACTION="http://site.com/
cgi-bin/gather_info">

<HR>
<H2>Please fill in your name and address: </
h2>
<P>Name: <INPUT TYPE="text" NAME="userid"
SIZE="20">
<P>Street: <INPUT TYPE="text" NAME="address"
SIZE="30">
<P> City: <INPUT TYPE="text" NAME="city"
SIZE="15">
State: <INPUT TYPE="text" NAME="state"
SIZE="2">
Zip code: <INPUT TYPE="text" NAME="zip code"
SIZE="5">

<HR>
<INPUT TYPE="submit" VALUE="Send info">
<INPUT TYPE="reset">
</FORM>
</BODY></HTML>
```

Figure 11.8 *Every form has three parts: the FORM tag, the actual form elements where the visitor enters information, and the SUBMIT tag which creates the button that sends the collected information to the server (or an active image).*

Figure 11.9 *This form contains only text boxes. It could also contain check boxes, radio buttons, menus, larger text entry areas, and an active image.*

Creating a form

```
code.html
<HTML><HEAD><TITLE>Visual QuickStart Guide
to HTML-Forms</TITLE></HEAD><BODY>
<H1>Creating text boxes for forms </H1>
<P>Text boxes are perfect for gathering a
single line of information, like a name or
product code.
<FORM METHOD=POST ACTION="http://site.com/
cgi-bin/gather_textboxes">
<H2>Please fill in your name and address: </
h2>
<P>Name: <INPUT TYPE="text" NAME="userid"
SIZE="20">
<P>Street: <INPUT TYPE="text" NAME="address"
SIZE="30">
<P> City: <INPUT TYPE="text" NAME="city"
SIZE="15">
State: <INPUT TYPE="text" NAME="state"
SIZE="2">
Zip code: <INPUT TYPE="text" NAME="zip code"
SIZE="5">
<H2>Please enter the product code of the item
that you wish to order:
<INPUT TYPE="text" NAME="productID">
<P>
<HR>
<INPUT TYPE="submit" VALUE="Send info">
<INPUT TYPE="reset">
</FORM>
</BODY></HTML>
```

Figure 11.10 *Each text box is defined with its own INPUT line.*

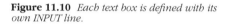

Figure 11.11 *Place text boxes on separate lines by adding a <P> between them.*

Creating text boxes

Text boxes contain one line of text and are typically used for names, addresses, and the like.

To create a text box:

1. Inside the FORM area of your HTML document, type the title of the text box (for example, **Name:**), if desired.

2. Type **<INPUT TYPE="text"**.

3. Type **NAME="title"**, where *title* is the word that identifies the data entered in the text box when it is collected by the server.

4. If desired, define the size of the box on your form by typing **SIZE="n"**, replacing *n* with the desired width of the box, measured in characters.

5. If desired, define the maximum number of characters that can be entered in the box by typing **MAXLENGTH="n"**, replacing *n* with the desired maximum length in characters.

6. Finish the text box by typing a final **>**.

✔ Tip

■ The default value for the SIZE attribute is 20. Visitors can add more text than fits in the text box, up to the value defined for MAXLENGTH.

Creating password boxes

A password box is similar to a text box, but when the visitor types in it, the letters are hidden by bullets or asterisks.

To create password entry boxes:

1. Inside the FORM area of your HTML document, type the title of the password box, if desired. Something like **Enter password** will do fine.

2. Type **<INPUT TYPE="password"**.

3. Give the password box a name by typing **NAME="title"**, where *title* is the word that identifies the data entered in the password box when it is collected by the server.

4. If desired, define the size of the box on your form by typing **SIZE="n"**, replacing *n* with the desired width of the box, measured in characters.

5. If desired, define the maximum number of characters that can be entered in the box by typing **MAXLENGTH="n"**, replacing *n* with the desired value.

6. Finish the text box by typing a final **>**.

✔ Tip

■ The only kind of protection the password box offers is from folks peering over the shoulder of your visitor as he types in his password. Since the data is not encrypted when the information is sent to the server, moderately experienced crackers can discover the password without much trouble.

```
code.html
<HTML><HEAD><TITLE>Visual QuickStart Guide
to HTML-Forms</TITLE>
</HEAD><BODY>
<H1>Creating passwords for forms </H1>
<P>Password style input items hide the text
with asterisks or bullets as it is entered.
<FORM METHOD=POST ACTION="http://site.com/
cgi-bin/gather_textboxes">
<H2>Please fill in your name and password:
</h2>
<P>Name: <INPUT TYPE="text" NAME="userid"
SIZE="20">
Password: <INPUT TYPE="password"
NAME="password" SIZE="8">

<HR>
<INPUT TYPE="submit" VALUE="Send info">
<INPUT TYPE="reset">
</FORM>
</BODY></HTML>
```

Figure 11.12 *The word Password, before the actual HTML tag labels the password box so that visitors know what to type there.*

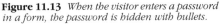

Figure 11.13 *When the visitor enters a password in a form, the password is hidden with bullets.*

```
                 code.html
<HTML><HEAD><TITLE>VQS Guide to HTML - Forms
- check boxes</TITLE></HEAD><BODY>
<H1>Creating check boxes </H1>
<P>Check boxes let the user select as many
of the options as they want.
<FORM METHOD=POST ACTION="http://site.com/
cgi-bin/gather_boxes">

<HR><H2>Check as many as you wish: </H2>
<INPUT TYPE="checkbox" NAME="mate"
VALUE="tall">Tall
<INPUT TYPE="checkbox" NAME="mate"
VALUE="dark">Dark
<INPUT TYPE="checkbox" NAME="mate"
VALUE="handsome">Handsome
<INPUT TYPE="checkbox" NAME="mate"
VALUE="smart">Smart
<INPUT TYPE="checkbox" NAME="mate"
VALUE="rich">Rich
<INPUT TYPE="checkbox" NAME="mate"
VALUE="famous">Famous
<HR>
<INPUT TYPE="submit" VALUE="Send info">
<INPUT TYPE="reset">
</FORM>
</BODY></HTML>
```

Figure 11.18 *Check boxes are linked by a common NAME.*

Figure 11.19 *Visitors can check as many of the options in a set of check boxes as they wish.*

Creating check boxes

While radio buttons can accept only one answer per set, a visitor can check as many check boxes in a set as they like. Like radio buttons, check boxes are linked by the value of the NAME attribute.

To create check boxes:

1. In the FORM area of your HTML document, type the introductory text (something like **Select one or more of the following**) for your check boxes.

2. Type **<INPUT TYPE="checkbox"**. (Notice there is no space in the word *checkbox.*)

3. Type **NAME="title"**, where *title* is the word that identifies all of the check boxes in a particular set.

4. Type **VALUE="value"** to define a value for each check box. The value will be sent to the server if the check box is checked (either by the visitor, or by you as described in step 4).

5. Type **CHECKED** to make the check box checked by default when the page is opened. You (or the visitor) may check as many check boxes as desired.

6. Type **>** to complete the check box.

7. Type the text that identifies the check box to the user. This is often the same as the VALUE, but doesn't have to be.

8. Repeat steps 2-7 for each check box in the set.

✔ Tip

■ You can create a separate keyboard shortcut for each check box in a set. For more information, consult *Adding keyboard shortcuts* on page 200.

Creating menus

Creating menus for your visitors makes it easy for them to enter information or provide criteria for a search.

To create menus:

1. In the FORM area of your HTML document, type the introductory text for your menu, if desired.

2. Type **<SELECT**.

3. Type **NAME="name"**, where *name* will identify the data collected from the menu when it is sent to the server.

4. Type **SIZE="n"**, where *n* represents the number of options that should be initially visible in the menu.

5. If desired, type **MULTIPLE** to allow your visitor to select more than one menu option.

6. Type **>**.

7. Type **<OPTION**.

8. Type **SELECTED** if you want the option to be selected by default.

9. Type **VALUE="value"**, where *value* specifies the data that will be sent to the server when the option is selected.

10. Type **>**.

11. Type the option name as you wish it to appear in the menu.

12. Repeat steps 7-11 for each option.

13. Type **</SELECT>**.

```
┌─────────── code.html ───────────┐
<HTML><HEAD><TITLE>VQS Guide to HTML - Forms
- menus</TITLE></HEAD><BODY>
<H1>Creating menus </H1>
<P>Menus let users choose one or more options
from a set.
<FORM METHOD=POST ACTION="http://site.com/
cgi-bin/gather_menu">

<HR>
<STRONG>How old are you?</STRONG><BR>
<SELECT NAME="age" Size="5">
<OPTION VALUE="youth">10-19
<OPTION SELECTED VALUE="genx">20-29
<OPTION VALUE="nolabel">30-39
<OPTION VALUE="boomers">40-49
</SELECT>
<HR>
<INPUT TYPE="submit" VALUE="Send info">
<INPUT TYPE="reset">
</FORM>
</BODY></HTML>
```

Figure 11.20 *Notice that the option values don't have to match what the visitor sees (e.g., youth vs. 10-19). You can use whatever variable name that makes analyzing the information easier.*

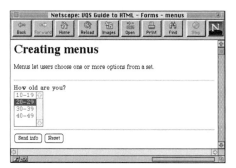

Figure 11.21 *The option with the SELECTED tag is automatically checked when the visitor jumps to this page. When you choose a value for SIZE that is greater than the number of options defined, an empty option appears which allows the visitor to deselect whatever option(s) were previously selected.*

Creating menus

```
                code.html
<HTML><HEAD><TITLE>VQS Guide to HTML - Forms
- menus</TITLE></HEAD><BODY>
<H1>Creating menus </H1>
<P>Menus let users choose one or more options
from a set.
<FORM METHOD=POST ACTION="http://site.com/
cgi-bin/processform.cgi">

How old are you?
<SELECT NAME=menu SIZE=5 MULTPLE>
<OPTGROUP LABEL="10-19">
<OPTION VALUE="10">10
<OPTION VALUE="11">11
<OPTION VALUE="12">12
<OPTION VALUE="13">13
<OPTION VALUE="14">14
<OPTION VALUE="15">15
<OPTION VALUE="16">16
<OPTION VALUE="17">17
<OPTION VALUE="18">18
<OPTION VALUE="19">19
</OPTGROUP>
<OPTGROUP LABEL="20-29">
<OPTION VALUE="20">20
```

Figure 11.22 *Each submenu has a title, speci-fied in the LABEL attribute of the OPTGROUP tag, and a series of options (defined with OPTION tags and regular text).*

If you have a particularly large menu with many options, you may want to group the options into categories and place them in submenus.

To create a menu with submenus:

1. Create a menu as described on page 188.

2. Before the first <OPTION> tag in the first group that you wish to place together in a submenu, type **<OPTGROUP.**

3. Type **LABEL="submenutitle">,** where *submenutitle* is the header for the submenu.

4. After the last <OPTION> tag in the group, type **</OPTGROUP>.**

5. Repeat steps 2–4 for each submenu.

✔ Tips

■ You can add **LABEL="option_name"** to the OPTION tag to specify what the menu option should say. However, while this is standard HTML 4, neither Explorer nor Navigator uses this infor-mation properly. If there is no LABEL attribute, the browser automatically uses the text that follows the OPTION tag (as described in step 11 on page 188).

■ Submenus are not yet supported by Explorer or Netscape.

Creating menus

Allowing visitors to upload files

If the information you need from the folks filling out your form is complicated, you might want to have them upload an entire file to your server.

To allow visitors to upload files:

1. Make sure you have **METHOD=POST** in the FORM tag. You cannot use the GET method for a form that includes a file upload area.

2. In the FORM area, type the caption for the file upload area. Something like **What file would you like to upload?** will work well.

3. Type **<INPUT TYPE="file"** to create a file upload box and a Browse button.

4. Type **ENCTYPE="multipart/form-data"** so that the file is uploaded in the proper format.

5. Type **NAME="title"**, where *title* identifies to the server the files being uploaded.

6. If desired, type **SIZE="n"**, where *n* is the width (in characters) of the field in which the visitor will enter the path name to the file.

7. Type the final **>** to complete the file upload area.

✔ Tip

■ The SIZE attribute is optional, but since most paths and file names are pretty long, it's a good idea to set it at 40 or 50. The default is 21.

```
code.html
<HTML><HEAD><TITLE>VQS Guide to HTML - Forms
- menus</TITLE></HEAD><BODY>
<H1>Creating menus </H1>
<P>Menus let users choose one or more options
from a set.
<FORM METHOD=POST ACTION="http://site.com/
cgi-bin/processform.cgi">

Name: <INPUT TYPE="text" NAME="firstname"
SIZE=20>
<P><B>What files are you sending?</B>
<BR><INPUT TYPE="file" ENCTYPE="multipart/
form-data" NAME="files" SIZE=40>

<INPUT TYPE="submit" Name="Submit"
VALUE="Submit">
</FORM>
</BODY></HTML>
```

Figure 11.23 *There are two crucial steps in allowing visitors to upload files. First, make sure you use the POST method in the FORM tag. Second, don't forget to set the ENCTYPE in the INPUT tag.*

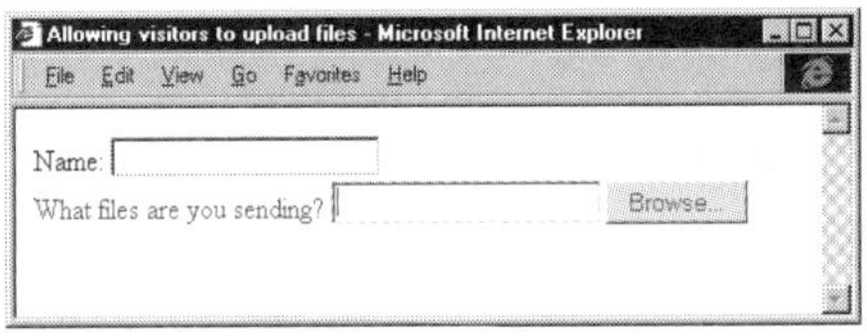

Figure 11.24 *When you create a file upload area, both a field where the visitor can type the path to the file and a Browse button (so the visitor can use an Open dialog box to choose the file) appear on your page.*

```
┌──────────────code.html──────────────┐
<HTML><HEAD>
<TITLE>VQS Guide to HTML - Forms - submit
buttons</TITLE>
</HEAD>
<BODY>
<P>Hidden form elements are invisible to the
user.
<FORM METHOD=POST ACTION="http://site.com/
cgi-bin/gather_buttons">

Sex <INPUT TYPE="radio" NAME="sex"
VALUE="woman">Woman
<INPUT TYPE="radio" NAME="sex"
VALUE="man">Man
<HR>
Age <SELECT NAME="age" Size="5">
<OPTION VALUE="youth">10-19
<OPTION SELECTED VALUE="genx">20-29
<OPTION VALUE="nolabel">30-39
<OPTION VALUE="boomers">40-49
</SELECT>
<INPUT TYPE="hidden" NAME="idnumber"
VALUE="id">
<HR>
<INPUT TYPE="submit" VALUE="Send info">
<INPUT TYPE="reset" VALUE="Start over">
</FORM>
</BODY></HTML>
```

Figure 11.25 *The Hidden element can be placed anywhere in the form element.*

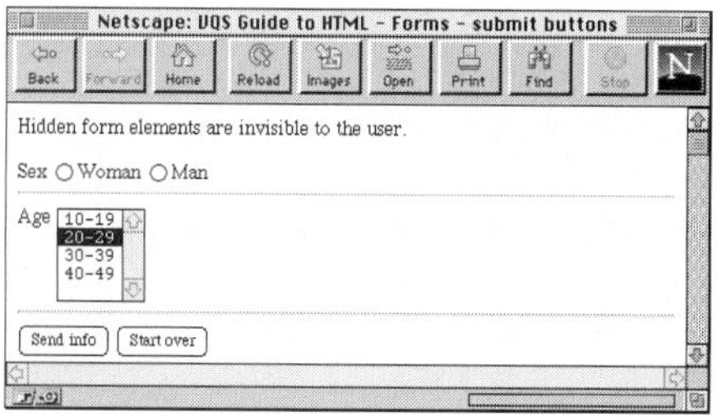

Figure 11.26 *Hidden elements are invisible to the visitor in all browsers.*

Creating hidden elements

At first glance, creating hidden elements in a form seems counterproductive. How can the visitor enter information if they can't see where to put it? Actually, they can't. However, hidden elements can be used by you to store information gathered from an *earlier* form so that it can be combined with the present form's data.

For example, if you ask for a visitor's name in an earlier form, you can save it in a variable and then add it to a new form as a hidden element so that the name is related to the new information gathered without having to bother the visitor to enter the name several times.

To create a hidden element:

1. Type **<INPUT TYPE="hidden"**.

2. Type **NAME="name"** where *name* is a short description of the information to be stored.

3. Type **VALUE="value"** where *value* is the information itself that is to be stored.

4. Type **>**.

✔ Tip

■ To create an element that will be submitted with the rest of the data when the visitor clicks the submit button but that is also visible to the visitor, create a regular form element and use the READONLY attribute *(see page 202)*.

Creating hidden elements

Creating the submit button

All the information that your visitors enter won't be any good to you unless they send it to the server. You should always create a submit button for your forms so that the visitor can deliver the information to you. You can create a submit button simply without an image or style information, or you can use new HTML 4 tags to make a button so gorgeous that your visitors won't be able to resist pressing it. (If you use images as active elements in a FORM area, see page 196.)

To create a submit button:

1. Type **<INPUT TYPE="submit"**.

2. If desired, type **VALUE="submit message"** where *submit message* is the text that will appear in the button. The default submit message is *Submit Query*.

3. Type the final **>**.

```
┌──────────────── code.html ──────────────────┐
<HTML><HEAD>
<TITLE>VQS Guide to HTML - Forms - submit
buttons</TITLE>
</HEAD>
<BODY>
<P>A Submit button sends the entered
information to the server.
<FORM METHOD=POST ACTION="http://site.com/
cgi-bin/gather_buttons">

Sex <INPUT TYPE="radio" NAME="sex"
VALUE="woman">Woman
<INPUT TYPE="radio" NAME="sex"
VALUE="man">Man
<HR>
Age <SELECT NAME="age" Size="5">
<OPTION VALUE="youth">10-19
<OPTION SELECTED VALUE="genx">20-29
<OPTION VALUE="nolabel">30-39
<OPTION VALUE="boomers">40-49
</SELECT>
<HR>
<INPUT TYPE="submit" VALUE="Send info">
<INPUT TYPE="reset" VALUE="Start over">
</FORM>
</BODY></HTML>
```

Figure 11.27 *You can use any text you wish for the submit button. Just make it clear that a click will send the information gathered to the server.*

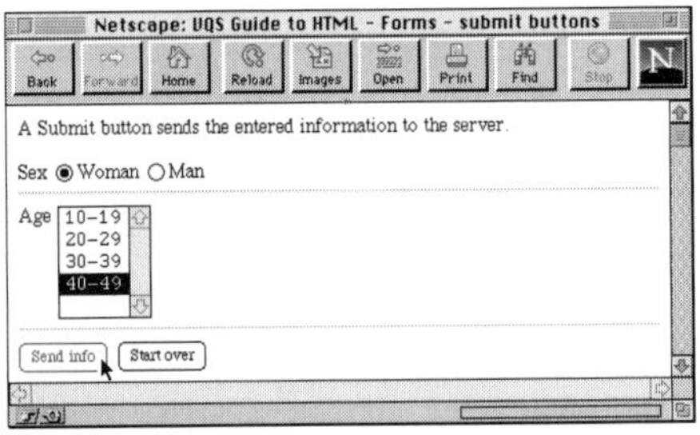

Figure 11.28 *Once the visitor has entered the appropriate information, they click on the submit button to send the information to the server.*

```
                code.html
<HTML><HEAD><TITLE>Creating graphic submit
buttons</TITLE></HEAD>
<BODY>
<H1>Ready to vote?</H1>
<FORM ACTION="processform.cgi" METHOD=POST>
<INPUT TYPE="radio" NAME="cats"
ACCESSKEY=w>Woody
<BR><INPUT TYPE="radio" NAME="cats"
ACCESSKEY=c>Cookie
<BR><INPUT TYPE="radio" NAME="cats"
ACCESSKEY=x>Xixona
<BR><INPUT TYPE="radio" NAME="cats"
ACCESSKEY=l>Llumeta
<BR><INPUT TYPE="radio" NAME="cats"
ACCESSKEY=a>All of them (Don't make me
choose!)
<P>
<BUTTON TYPE="submit" NAME="submit"
VALUE="submit" STYLE="font: 24pt Arial
Black; background:yellow">
<IMG SRC="check.gif" WIDTH=40
HEIGHT=40>Vote</BUTTON>
</FORM>
</BODY></HTML>
```

Figure 11.29 *The HTML code for a submit button with an image is a little more complicated, but it's so worth it!*

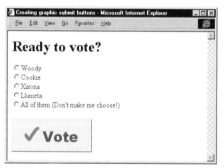

Figure 11.30 *If you want a submit button with an image, you'll have to create it with the BUTTON tag. It's probably a good idea to make the background transparent and save the image in GIF format so that it blends in with the button.*

HTML 4 adds several new tags that let you create prettier submit buttons. You can add an image, change the font, or even change the background color. That'll get them to submit that form!

To create a submit button with an image:

1. Type **<BUTTON NAME="submit" VALUE="submit" TYPE="submit"**

2. If desired, type **STYLE="font: 24pt Arial Black; background:yellow"** (or whatever) to change the appearance of the button text *(see page 233)*.

3. Type **>**.

4. Type the text, if any, that should appear on the left side of the image in the button.

5. Type **<IMG SRC="image.gif"** where *image.gif* is the name of the image that will appear on the button.

6. If desired, add any other image attributes.

7. Type **>** to complete the image.

8. Type the text, if any, that should appear on the right side of the image in the button.

9. Type **</BUTTON>**.

✔ Tips

- You can also use the BUTTON tag to create a submit button without an image. Just skip steps 5–7.

- For information on creating buttons with scripts, consult *Creating a button that executes a script* on page 272.

- Only Explorer 4 for Windows currently supports the BUTTON tag, despite the fact that it is a standard part of HTML 4.

Resetting the form

If humans could fill out forms perfectly on the first try, there would be no erasers on pencils and no backspace key on your computer keyboard. You can give your visitors a reset button so that they can start over with a fresh form (including all the default values you've set).

To create a reset button:

1. Type **<INPUT TYPE="reset"**.

2. If desired, type **VALUE="reset message"** where *reset message* is the text that appears in the button. The default reset message is *Reset*.

3. Type **>**.

```
                          code.html
<HTML><HEAD>
<TITLE>VQS Guide to HTML - Forms - submit
buttons</TITLE>
</HEAD>
<BODY>
<P>A Submit button sends the entered
information to the server.
<FORM METHOD=POST ACTION="http://site.com/
cgi-bin/gather_buttons">

Sex <INPUT TYPE="radio" NAME="sex"
VALUE="woman">Woman
<INPUT TYPE="radio" NAME="sex"
VALUE="man">Man
<HR>
Age <SELECT NAME="age" Size="5">
<OPTION VALUE="youth">10-19
<OPTION SELECTED VALUE="genx">20-29
<OPTION VALUE="nolabel">30-39
<OPTION VALUE="boomers">40-49
</SELECT>
<HR>
<INPUT TYPE="submit" VALUE="Send info">
<INPUT TYPE="reset" VALUE="Start over">
</FORM>
</BODY></HTML>
```

Figure 11.31 *You can use any text you wish for the reset button.*

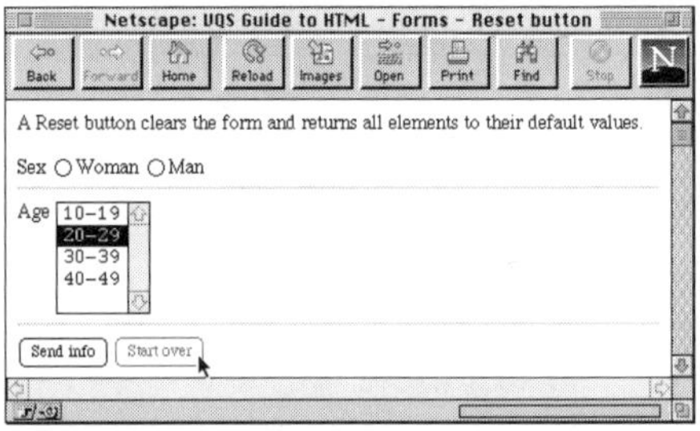

Figure 11.32 *A click on the reset button clears the form and returns all variables to their default values. In this case, there is no default for Sex and so it returns to its unchecked state. The default for Age was 20-29.*

```
code.html
<HTML><HEAD><TITLE>Creating graphic submit
buttons</TITLE></HEAD>
<BODY>
<H1>Ready to vote?</H1>
<FORM ACTION="processform.cgi" METHOD=POST>
<INPUT TYPE="radio" NAME="cats"
ACCESSKEY=w>Woody
<BR><INPUT TYPE="radio" NAME="cats"
ACCESSKEY=c>Cookie
<BR><INPUT TYPE="radio" NAME="cats"
ACCESSKEY=x>Xixona
<BR><INPUT TYPE="radio" NAME="cats"
ACCESSKEY=l>Llumeta
<BR><INPUT TYPE="radio" NAME="cats"
ACCESSKEY=a>All of them (Don't make me
choose!)
<P>
<BUTTON TYPE="submit" NAME="submit"
VALUE="Submit" STYLE="font: 24pt Arial
Black; background:yellow"><IMG
SRC="check.gif" WIDTH=40 HEIGHT=40
ALT="">Vote</BUTTON>
<BUTTON TYPE="reset" NAME="reset"
VALUE="reset" STYLE="font: 24pt Arial Black;
background:yellow"><IMG SRC="reset.gif"
WIDTH=40 HEIGHT=40 ALT="">Reset</BUTTON>
</FORM>
</BODY></HTML>
```

Figure 11.33 *Make sure you set the TYPE to* reset. *Otherwise, the button won't actually do anything at all.*

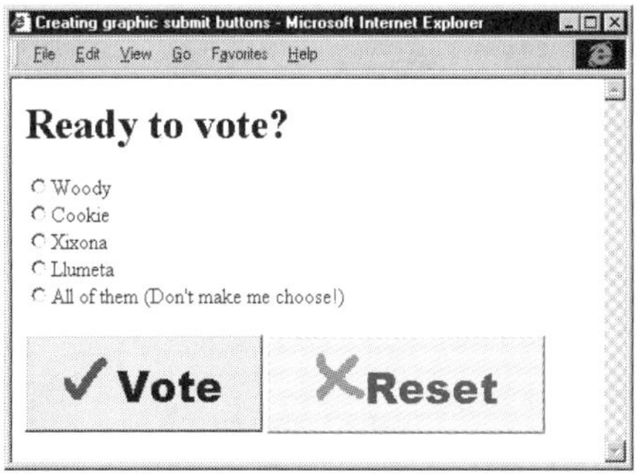

Figure 11.34 *You can also use the BUTTON tag to create a reset button with an image (and you can probably create a much prettier image than mine).*

With HTML 4 (and Explorer for the time being), you can add images, font choices, and even a background color to your reset button.

To create a reset button with an image:

1. Type **<BUTTON NAME="reset" VALUE="reset" TYPE="reset"**

2. If desired, type **STYLE="font: 24pt Arial Black; background:yellow"** (or whatever) to change the appearance of the button text *(see page 233)*.

3. Type **>**.

4. Type the text, if any, that should appear on the left side of the image in the button.

5. Type **<IMG SRC="image.gif"**, where *image.gif* is the name of the image that will appear on the button.

6. If desired, add any other image attributes.

7. Type **>** to complete the image.

8. Type the text, if any, that should appear on the right side of the image in the button.

9. Type **</BUTTON>**.

✔ Tips

■ You can also use the BUTTON tag to create a reset button without an image. Just skip steps 5–7.

■ For information on creating buttons with scripts, consult *Creating a button that executes a script* on page 272.

■ Only Explorer 4 for Windows currently supports the BUTTON tag, despite the fact that it is a standard part of HTML 4.

Active images

You may use images as active elements in a FORM area. A click on the image appends the current mouse coordinates (as measured from the top left corner) to the variable name and sends the data to the server.

To create an active image:

1. Create a GIF image and save it in your images directory on your server (*see page 62*).

2. Type **<INPUT TYPE="image"**.

3. Type **SRC="image_url"** where *image_url* is the location of the image on the server.

4. Type **NAME="name"**. When the visitor clicks on the image, the x and y coordinates of the mouse will be appended to the name defined here and sent to the server.

5. Type the final **>** to finish the active image definition for the FORM.

✔ Tips

- *All* the form data is sent automatically when the visitor clicks on the active image. Therefore, it's a good idea to give instructions on how to use the active image and to place the image at the end of the form so that the visitor completes the other form elements before clicking the image and sending the data.

- You can create an entire questionnaire out of pictures by making the next question (and active image) appear after the data is sent from the last question to the server.

```
code.html
<HTML><HEAD><TITLE>VQS Guide to HTML - Forms
- active image</TITLE></HEAD>
<BODY>
<P>You can use an active image to get info
from your user with the click of the mouse.
<HR>
<FORM METHOD=POST ACTION="http://site.com/
cgi-bin/gather_aimage">
<STRONG>Where are you from?</STRONG> (Click
on the map to answer.)<BR>
<INPUT TYPE="image" SRC="map.gif"
NAME="map">
</FORM>
</BODY></HTML>
```

Figure 11.35 *You don't need to include a submit button with an active image since a click will automatically submit the data.*

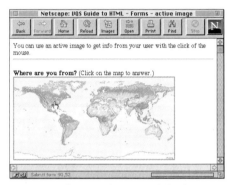

Figure 11.36 *When the visitor clicks the image, the present coordinates of the mouse are sent to the server.*

```
                code.html
<HTML><HEAD><TITLE>Organizing your forms</
TITLE></HEAD><BODY>
<FORM METHOD=POST ACTION="processform.cgi"
METHOD="POST">
<FIELDSET>
<LEGEND>Personal Information</LEGEND>
<P>Name: <INPUT TYPE="text" NAME="firstname"
SIZE=15><BR>
E-mail: <INPUT TYPE="text" NAME="email"
SIZE=25>
</FIELDSET>
<FIELDSET>
<LEGEND ALIGN="right">Comments</LEGEND>
Please let us know what you think:<BR>
<TEXTAREA COLS="40" ROWS="7" NAME="comments"
WRAP><B>I</B> think your cats are...
</TEXTAREA>
</FIELDSET>
<INPUT TYPE="submit" NAME="Submit"
VALUE="Send info">
</FORM>
</BODY></HTML>
```

Figure 11.37 *The FIELDSET tag is ideal for separating your form into smaller, more easily understood chunks.*

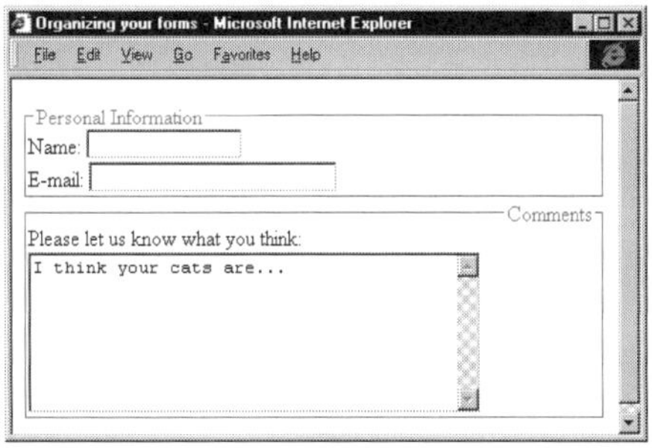

Figure 11.38 *The fieldsets are outlined with a thin line. The caption appears at the top right or top left.*

Organizing the form elements

If you have a lot of information to fill out on a form, you can group related elements together to make the form easier to follow. The easier it is for your visitors to understand the form, the more likely they are to fill it out correctly.

To organize the form elements:

1. Below the FORM tag but above any form elements that you wish to have contained in the first group, type **<FIELDSET>**.

2. Type **<LEGEND**.

3. If desired, type **ALIGN=direction** where *direction* is top, bottom, left, or right.

4. Type **>**.

5. Type the text for the legend.

6. Type **</LEGEND>** to complete the legend.

7. Create the form elements that should belong in the first group. For more information, see pages 183–196.

8. Type **</FIELDSET>** to complete the first group of form elements.

9. Repeat steps 1-8 for each group of form elements.

✔ Tips

■ You don't have to create a legend. To omit it, skip steps 2-6. In fact, you don't have to organize your form into groups at all. While it is a useful tool, it's completely optional.

■ At press time, only IE 4 for Windows recognized field set definitions. And it only aligns legends to the left or right.

Organizing the form elements

Formally labelling form parts

As you've seen, the explanatory information next to a form element is generally just plain text. For example, you might type "First name" before the Text field where the visitor should type her name. HTML 4 provides a method for marking up labels so that you can formally link them to the associated element and use them for scripting or other purposes.

To formally label form parts:

1. Type **<LABEL**.

2. Type **FOR="idname">**, where *idname* is the value of the ID attribute in the corresponding form element.

3. Type the contents of the label.

4. Type **</LABEL>**.

✔ Tips

■ You have to use the ID attribute in the form element's tag in order to mark it with a LABEL. For example, you might have <INPUT TYPE=text SIZE=15 ID=firstname>. For more details about the ID attribute, consult *Identifying particular tags* on page 229.

■ Labels are part of HTML 4, but at press time, neither Explorer nor Communicator supports them. And frankly, they're rather a pain for what they're worth. Personally, I'd leave them out.

```
code.html
<HTML><HEAD><TITLE>Formally labelling form
parts</TITLE></HEAD>
<BODY>
<FORM METHOD=POST ACTION="processform.cgi">
<LABEL for="firstname">Name: </LABEL>
<INPUT TYPE="text" NAME="firstname"
ID="firstname" SIZE=20><BR>
<LABEL for="email">E-mail address:</LABEL>
<INPUT TYPE="text" NAME="email" ID="email">
</FORM>
</BODY></HTML>
```

Figure 11.39 *You link a label to its form element with the FOR and ID attributes.*

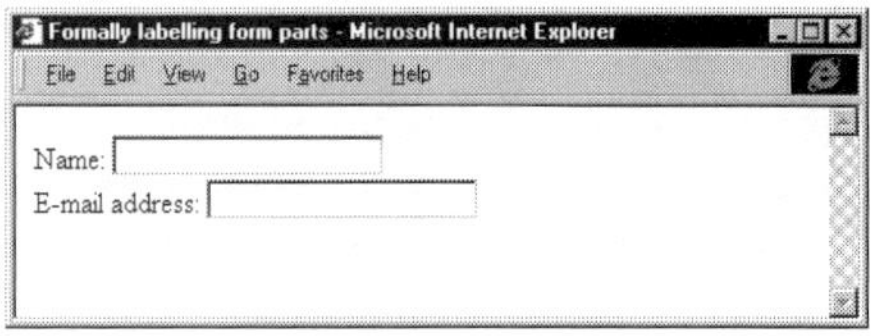

Figure 11.40 *There's no outward difference in appearance when you use labels—at least not yet.*

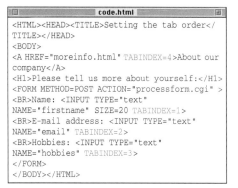

```
code.html
<HTML><HEAD><TITLE>Setting the tab order</
TITLE></HEAD>
<BODY>
<A HREF="moreinfo.html" TABINDEX=4>About our
company</A>
<H1>Please tell us more about yourself:</H1>
<FORM METHOD=POST ACTION="processform.cgi" >
<BR>Name: <INPUT TYPE="text"
NAME="firstname" SIZE=20 TABINDEX=1>
<BR>E-mail address: <INPUT TYPE="text"
NAME="email" TABINDEX=2>
<BR>Hobbies: <INPUT TYPE="text"
NAME="hobbies" TABINDEX=3>
</FORM>
</BODY></HTML>
```

Figure 11.41 *You can add the TABINDEX attribute to links, form elements, and client-side image maps.*

Figure 11.42 *With forms on a page that begins with a link, you may want to change the tab order so that the first tab takes you to the first field, not the first link.*

Setting the tab order

By pressing the Tab key, visitors can move through the fields in your form from top to bottom. Depending on your form's layout, you may prefer to set the tab order yourself so that the visitor fills out all the fields in a particular group before going on to the next group.

To set the tab order:

In the form element's tag, type **TABINDEX="n"** where *n* is the number that indicates the tab order.

✔ Tips

- The value for TABINDEX can be any number between 0 and 32767.

- By default, the tab order depends on the order of the elements in the HTML code. When you change the tab order, the lower numbered elements are activated first, followed by higher numbered elements.

- In a form, you can assign tab order to text fields, password fields, check boxes, radio buttons, text blocks, menus, and buttons.

- You can also assign tab order to links and client-side image maps. For more information, consult *Setting the tab order for links* on page 117 or *Creating a client-side image map* on page 120, respectively.

- OK, I cannot tell a lie. The first time your visitor hits the Tab key, the Address field (where the current URL is displayed) is activated (even if its toolbar is hidden). Then, the next tab brings the visitor where *you* say.

Setting the tab order

Adding keyboard shortcuts

One great new feature of HTML 4 is the ability to add keyboard shortcuts to different parts of your page, including form elements. When the visitor types the keyboard shortcut, the form element is made active for further input (in the case of a text field) or selected (like a radio button).

To add a keyboard shortcut to a form element:

1. Inside the form element's tag, type **ACCESSKEY="**.

2. Type the keyboard shortcut (any letter or number).

3. Type the final **"**.

4. If desired, add information about the keyboard shortcut to the text so that the visitor knows that it exists.

✔ Tips

- On Windows systems, to invoke the keyboard shortcut, visitors use the Alt key plus the letter you've assigned. On Macs, visitors will probably use the Command key (although it doesn't work yet).

- Keyboard shortcuts that you choose may override the browser's shortcuts. If you assign a popular shortcut used in a browser to some part of your form (like S for Save), you may annoy your visitors. Keep in mind though, that at least on Windows machines, the important browser keyboard shortcuts go with the Ctrl key, not Alt.

```
code.html
<HTML><HEAD><TITLE>Setting the tab order</
TITLE></HEAD>
<BODY>
<H1>Vote for the cutest cat:</H1>
<FORM ACTION="processform.cgi"
METHOD="POST">
<BR><INPUT TYPE="radio" NAME="cats"
ACCESSKEY=w>Woody (Alt-W)
<BR><INPUT TYPE="radio" NAME="cats"
ACCESSKEY=c>Cookie (Alt-C)
<BR><INPUT TYPE="radio" NAME="cats"
ACCESSKEY=x>Xixona (Alt-X)
<BR><INPUT TYPE="radio" NAME="cats"
ACCESSKEY=l>Llumeta (Alt-L)
<BR><INPUT TYPE="radio" NAME="cats"
ACCESSKEY=a>All of them (Don't make me
choose!) (Alt-A)<BR><INPUT TYPE="submit"
NAME="submit" VALUE="Vote">
</FORM>
</BODY></HTML>
```

Figure 11.43 *Add keyboard shortcuts to your form elements with the ACCESSKEY attribute.*

Figure 11.44 *When the visitor views the page, no item is selected. It's a good idea to show the keyboard shortcuts so that the visitor knows they're available.*

Figure 11.45 *Once the visitor uses the keyboard shortcut (Alt-A in this case), the radio button is activated and actually selected. In the case of a text box or text area, the cursor would be placed in the field, and the visitor could proceed to type in the information.*

```
                code.html
<HTML><HEAD><TITLE>Setting the tab order</
TITLE></HEAD>
<BODY>
<H1>Vote for the cutest cat:</H1>
<FORM ACTION="processform.cgi"
METHOD="POST">
<BR><INPUT TYPE="radio" NAME="cats"
ACCESSKEY=w>Woody
<BR><INPUT TYPE="radio" NAME="cats"
ACCESSKEY=c>Cookie
<BR><INPUT TYPE="radio" NAME="cats"
ACCESSKEY=x>Xixona
<BR><INPUT TYPE="radio" NAME="cats"
ACCESSKEY=l>Llumeta
<BR><INPUT TYPE="radio" NAME="cats"
ACCESSKEY=a>All of them (Don't make me
choose!)
<BR><INPUT TYPE="submit" NAME="submit"
VALUE="Vote" DISABLED>
</FORM>
</BODY></HTML>
```

Figure 11.46 *You can add the DISABLED attribute to any form element, but it probably makes most sense in the INPUT tag for a submit button.*

Figure 11.47 *In this example, the Vote button is grayed out because the visitor has not yet chosen any of the radio buttons. A script will be necessary to enable the submit button once a choice is made.*

Disabling form elements

In some cases, you may not want visitors to use certain parts of your form. For example, you might want to disable a submit button until all the required fields have been filled out.

To disable a form element:

In the form element's tag, type **DISABLED**.

✔ Tips

- The only way you can change the contents of a disabled form element is with a script. For more information on scripting, consult Chapter 16, *Scripts*.

- If you disable a form element, its keyboard shortcut is also disabled. For more information on keyboard shortcuts, consult *Adding keyboard shortcuts* on page 200.

Keeping elements from being changed

Sometimes it may be necessary to automatically set the contents of a form element and keep the visitor from changing it. For example, you could have the visitor confirm information, or you could show a past history of transactions and then submit that information again with the new data collected. You can do this by making the element "read-only".

To keep elements from being changed:

Type **READONLY** in the form element's tag.

✔ Tips

■ You can use the READONLY attribute in text boxes, password boxes, check boxes, radio buttons, and text areas.

■ Setting the READONLY attribute is something like using a hidden field without making it hidden. For more information on hidden fields, consult *Creating hidden elements* on page 191.

```
code.html
<HTML><HEAD><TITLE>Setting the tab order</
TITLE></HEAD>
<BODY>
<H1>Vote again:</H1>
<FORM METHOD=POST ACTION="processform.cgi">
<BR>So far you've voted for
<TEXTAREA NAME="votehistory" COLS=25 ROWS=3
READONLY>Woody on Monday, Cookie on Tuesday,
Xixona on Thursday, and Llumeta on
Wednesday</TEXTAREA>
<BR><INPUT TYPE="radio" NAME="cats"
ACCESSKEY=w>Woody
<BR><INPUT TYPE="radio" NAME="cats"
ACCESSKEY=c>Cookie
<BR><INPUT TYPE="radio" NAME="cats"
ACCESSKEY=x>Xixona
<BR><INPUT TYPE="radio" NAME="cats"
ACCESSKEY=l>Llumeta
<BR><INPUT TYPE="radio" NAME="cats"
ACCESSKEY=a>All of them (Don't make me
choose!)
<BR><INPUT TYPE="submit" NAME="submit"
VALUE="Vote" DISABLED>
</FORM>
</BODY></HTML>
```

Figure 11.48 *Add the READONLY attribute to any form element that you want to show to visitors but that you don't want them to change.*

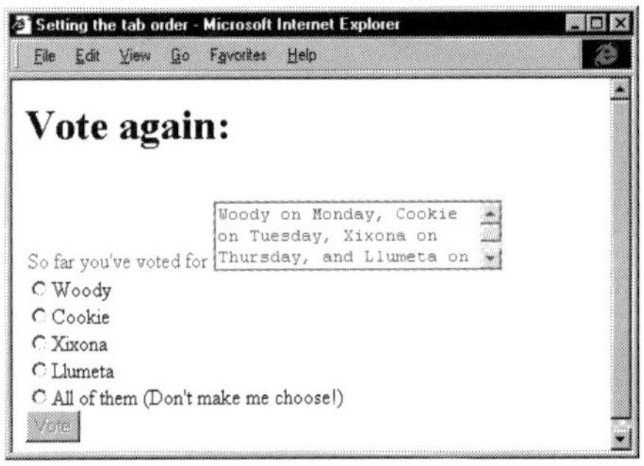

Figure 11.49 *In this example, the visitor's prior votes are displayed in the read-only text area. They can be viewed by the visitor and then submitted with the new vote.*

Figure 11.50 *This is Response-O-Matic's home page (www.response-o-matic.com). They're one of the better form hosting services I've seen.*

Figure 11.51 *Response-O-Matic gets you started by asking you a few questions and then creating a template, as shown in Figure 11.52.*

Figure 11.52 *Save the template to your hard disk and edit it as necessary. (Just don't change the hidden fields.)*

Using a form hosting service

Even if you're wary of CGI scripts or if your ISP doesn't allow you to use them, you can still have forms on your Web page. Several companies create forms for you, give you access to CGI scripts that process the forms, or process the forms directly and send you the results via e-mail. You generally "pay" for the form by including some sort of advertisement on your page.

To use a form hosting service:

1. Connect to a form hosting service.

2. Read their site to answer the following questions:

Who creates the form: you or them?

What do you have to do in exchange for them processing your forms?

Is it OK to use their processing for commercial forms, or just personal ones?

3. Follow their instructions for setting up your form. Consult the earlier sections of this chapter for more information about creating form elements.

✔ Tips

■ Most form hosting services send you the gathered information in an e-mail message.

■ There is a lot of variety from one form hosting service to another. Do a search on Yahoo or AltaVista for the one you like best. They generally all do it in exchange for advertising, but some ads are not as intrusive as others. For example, Response-o-Matic (shown here) only shows their ad in the Thank You page, not on the form itself.

Multimedia

One of the things that has made the Web so popular is the idea that you can add graphics, sound, and movies to your Web pages. The truth is that today's browsers can only show a few kinds of graphic images inline and that they rely on external applications called *helpers* to open other types of multimedia files. (Of course, the technology is moving so fast that tomorrow's browsers, or perhaps even this afternoon's browsers, may in fact be able to handle more complicated multimedia files without helpers.)

The main problem with multimedia is that the files are generally very large. Ten seconds of average quality sound take up more than 200K, which will take your visitor three and a half minutes to download before they can hear it with the helper program. A ten second file of a movie displayed in a tiny 2" x 3" window would be considerably larger. Similarly, large still images (even if they are JPEG or GIF format) can really try your visitor's patience.

Finally, since the Web population is diverse, and uses many different kinds of computers, you have to make sure that the files you provide can be read (viewed, heard, etc.) by your visitors (or the largest number possible of them). This is probably the trickiest part of all.

Helper applications

If a browser cannot handle a certain type of file, it calls up a "helper application" to view the file. A helper application can be any program that is capable of opening the particular format of the file.

For example, a Web surfer could conceivably use Adobe Photoshop as a helper application to view TIFF images. But since Photoshop is such a complete program, it takes several seconds to load and view the image—not to mention the fact that it costs $900. A better solution is a small, fast, free, helper application that is good at just one thing: viewing or playing specific file formats. See Table 12.2 for a list of common helper applications.

A browser can only call a helper application if two conditions are met. First, the user must already have the helper application on the computer (*and* have specified which helper application to use for which types of files).

Although helper applications are easily acquired through many FTP servers, not all users have taken the time to download them. If your users don't have the proper helper application, they won't be able to view your files.

Second, you, the page designer, must use the proper extension for the file so that the browser knows which helper application will be necessary to access the file. The system of standardized extensions is known as MIME—Multipurpose Internet Mail Extensions *(see Table 12.1).*

MIME type	Extension(s)
image/gif	.gif
image/jpeg	.jpeg .jpg .jpe
image/pict	.pic .pict
image/tiff	.tif .tiff
image/x-xbitmap	.xbm
audio/basic	.au snd
audio/aiff	.aiff .aif
audio/x-wav	.wav
video/quicktime	.qt .mov
video/mpeg	.mpg .mpeg .mpe
video/x-msvideo	.avi
application/mac-binhex40	.hqx
application/x-stuffit	.sit
application/x-macbinary	.bin
application/octet-stream	.exe
application/postscript	.ai .eps .ps
application/rtf	.rtf
application/x-compressed	.zip .z .gz .tgz
application/x-tar	.tar

Table 12.1: *It is extremely important to use the proper extension to identify your external files. If there is more than one possible extension, you can generally use whichever you prefer, as long as you follow the naming limitations of the server (e.g., DOS servers insist on three letter extensions).*

	Mac	Windows	Unix
Graphics	JPEGView GraphicConverter	LView Pro PaintShop Pro	xv
Sound	SoundMachine SoundApp	Wham Wplany	audiotool audioplayer
Video	Sparkle Fast Player	Media Player mpegplay	mpeg_play xplaygizmo
PostScript	(built-in)	ghostscript ghostview	ghostscript ghostview

Table 12.2: *Some common helper applications.*

Helper applications

```
code.html
<HTML>
<HEAD>
<TITLE>Opening TIFFs</TITLE>
</HEAD>
<BODY>
Woody went through his own particular
psychedelic stage:<BR>
<A HREF="woodycolor.tiff"><IMG
SRC=woodycolor.icon.gif> 225K Tiff image</A>
</BODY>
</HTML>
```

Figure 12.3 *Since a visitor has to take the time to download large images like the one referenced here, you should at least give them an idea of how big the image is.*

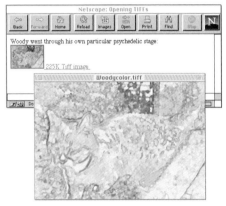

Figure 12.4 *Once the visitor clicks on the icon, the browser launches the helper application (in this case JPEGView) and the helper application shows the TIFF file.*

Non-supported images

In the current race to be the best browser, both Netscape and Internet Explorer are adding capabilities to view as many types of images as possible internally. If you need to create a link to an image in an as-yet unrecognized format, you'll need to use the proper extension and the visitor will have to have a helper application that can view the image.

To create a link to a non-supported image:

1. Create an image and save it in the desired format with the proper extension. *(See Table 12.1 on page 206.)*

2. In your HTML document where you want the image to appear, type **<A HREF="image.ext">** where *image.ext* is the name of the image file on the server with the appropriate extension.

3. If desired, use an icon to indicate the external image by typing **<IMG SRC="icon.gif">** where *icon.gif* is the location on the server of the icon.

4. Give a description of the image, including its size and format.

5. Complete the link by typing **</A>**.

✔ Tips

■ Why bother with other formats besides GIF or JPEG? Perhaps you want to provide non-expert visitors with a certain type of graphic image (TIFF, say) and you don't want them to have to bother with converting it.

■ Since non-GIF/JPEG images generally will not appear inline, there is little advantage to using additional image formatting, like ALIGN or LOWSRC.

Non-supported images

Sound

As with images, one of the main factors to consider when adding sound to your page is the format. Use a format that few computers can recognize and few visitors will hear your sound. The most common sound format is the AU format developed by Sun Microsystems. It can be used on Mac, Windows, Unix, and other systems. Unfortunately, the AU format only allows for 8-bit sampling, which is certainly at the low end of the quality scale.

The standard format for Macintosh sound is AIFF while Windows machines read sound in the WAV format. You can add sound files to your Web pages in any of these formats, but only those visitors with the corresponding computer system will be able to download and listen to the sounds right away.

One alternative is to use a conversion program to create several different versions of your sound files and then give your visitors access to all of them. Then they can download and listen to the one that corresponds to their system.

If your computer has a sound card and microphone (like most Macs and many PCs), and you have a sound editing program, you can create your own sound files.

To create a sound on the Mac:

1. Open the Sound control panel **(Figure 12.5)**.

2. Click Add.

3. Click Record in the dialog box that appears **(Figure 12.6)**.

4. Record your sound.

5. Click Stop and then Save.

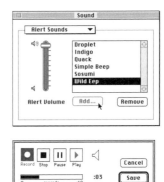

Figure 12.5
To create a sound with the Macintosh's Sound control panel, click Add.

Figure 12.6 *Click Record to start recording your sound and Stop when you are finished. Then click Save to save your sound.*

Figure 12.7 *Finally, give your sound a name.*

Figure 12.8 *Once you have created the sound, you can find it in the System file icon inside the System folder. Drag it out and place it in the folder with the rest of your HTML files.*

Sound

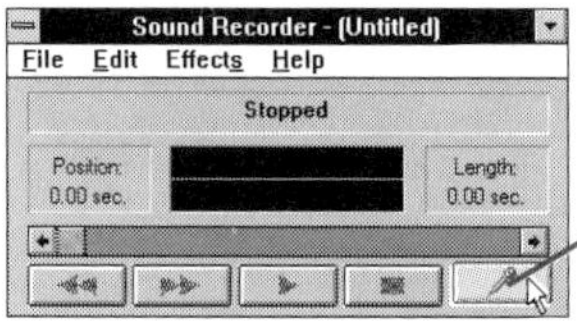

Click here to start recording.

Figure 12.9 *The Sound Recorder main window in Windows.*

Figure 12.10 *Be sure and choose the appropriate format in the pop-up menu when you save your sound.*

6. Give the sound a name and click OK **(Figure 12.7)**.

7. Close the Sound control panel.

8. Open the System Folder and then double click the System icon. You'll find the new sound here **(Figure 12.8)**. Drag it to the same folder that contains your other HTML files.

To create a sound in Windows:

1. Open Sound Recorder **(Figure 12.9)**.

2. Click on the microphone icon at the far right.

3. Start recording your sound.

4. Click Stop (the button with the square) to finish recording.

5. Choose File > Save As to save your sound file.

6. Choose the appropriate format for the file in the Save As dialog box, and make sure the appropriate extension (.au for AU files, .aif for AIFF files, and .wav for WAV files) is added to the file name **(Figure 12.10)**.

✔ Tips

■ Creating sounds for other systems is essentially the same process as outlined here, using the sound editor appropriate to that system.

■ One of the most exciting sound-related improvements to the Web is RealAudio and its ability to download part of a sound, play it, download another piece, play it, and so on, approximating live audio. For more information, check out RealAudio's Web site at *www.realaudio.com.*

Sound

Converting sound formats

Once you have a sound, you need to convert it to the proper format for publication on the Web. Although the AU format can be understood by many different kinds of computers, the quality is not that great. Therefore, you may want to provide several versions of your sound file: one in AU, one in AIFF for Macintosh, and one in WAV for Windows.

To convert a sound from one format to another:

1. Open SoundApp (for Macintosh) or some other sound conversion program (like Wham for Windows).

2. Choose Convert in the File menu **(Figure 12.11)**.

3. Choose the desired sound document in the dialog box that appears. Select a format in the Convert To pop-up menu **(Figure 12.12)**.

4. Click Open. A progress report appears **(Figure 12.13)**.

5. SoundApp places the converted file in a new folder inside the current folder **(Figure 12.14)**.

6. Add the correct extension to the end of the name (even for Macintosh files). Use .au for AU files, .aif for AIFF files and .wav for WAV files.

✔ Tip

■ You can convert files from the Finder with SoundApp. Select the files, hold down the Shift key and drag them onto the SoundApp application. You can change the default destination format (and keyboard shortcut) in the Preferences dialog box.

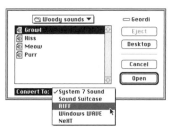

Figure 12.11 *In SoundApp (for Macintosh), choose Convert in the File menu.*

Figure 12.12 *Choose the desired file and the appropriate format in the Convert To menu.*

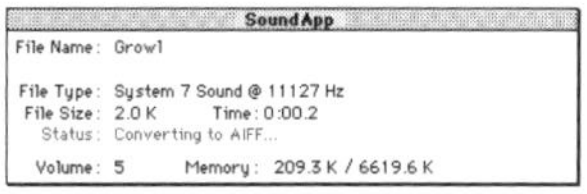

Figure 12.13 *SoundApp shows you the progress of the file conversion.*

Figure 12.14 *When SoundApp has finished converting the files, it places them in a folder called SoundApp Converted f inside the current folder.*

```
┌─────────────────────────────────┐
│▒▒▒▒▒▒▒  code.html  ▒▒▒▒▒▒▒▒      │
├─────────────────────────────────┤
│<HTML>                           │
│<HEAD>                           │
│<TITLE>Listening to sounds</TITLE>│
│</HEAD>                          │
│<BODY>                           │
│At night, Woody serenades the neighborhood│
│with his latest hit caterwaul:<P>│
│<A HREF="sound.woody.aif"><IMG   │
│SRC=victrola.gif WIDTH=52 HEIGHT=73> 40K│
│Sound @ 22.3kHz</A>              │
│<P>OK, I admit it. That's not Woody. It's me.│
│Makes the cats come investigate, just the│
│same, though.                    │
│</BODY>                          │
│</HTML>                          │
└─────────────────────────────────┘
```

Figure 12.15 *Always include information on your page about the size and recording quality of your sound.*

Figure 12.16 *When the visitor clicks the sound icon (the victrola) or the clickable text description of the sound, the browser downloads the sound and launches the helper application (in this case SoundMachine) which plays the sound.*

Adding external sound to a Web page

Currently there are three main ways to add sound to a page. For Netscape, you can create a sound that can be played from within the page *(see page 212)*. For browsing in Internet Explorer, you can add a background sound that loads automatically when the visitor jumps to the page *(see page 213)*. Finally, you can create a link to a sound that can be played with a helper application, regardless of the browser the page is viewed with.

To add a sound to your page:

1. If desired, create a small icon that you can use to indicate the link to the sound and call it *soundicon.gif.*

2. Make sure the sound file has the correct extension. Use .au for AU files, .aif for AIFF files and .wav for WAV files.

3. In your HTML document where you wish to place the link to the sound file, type **<A HREF="sound.ext">** where *sound.ext* is the location of the sound file, including the correct extension, on the server.

4. Type **<IMG SRC="soundicon.gif">** where *soundicon.gif* is the icon that will indicate the link to the sound that you created in step 1.

5. Type the description, size, and format of the audio file.

6. Type **</A>** to complete the link.

✔ Tip

■ Give extra information to your visitors, including the format and size of the audio file, so that they can decide whether or not to download the sound.

Adding internal sound for Netscape users

 Netscape includes the LiveAudio plug-in that lets the browser play sound right in the Web page itself, without having to resort to an external helper application. The plug-in recognizes AIFF, WAV, AU, and MIDI formats.

To add internal sound for Netscape visitors:

1. In your HTML document, type **<EMBED SRC="sound.url"**, where *sound.url* is the complete file name and extension for the sound file.

2. If desired, type **CONTROLS=form** where *form* determines how the sound controls should appear. The available options are *console, smallconsole, playbutton, pausebutton, stopbutton,* and *volumelever.*

   If you choose a kind of control, type **WIDTH=w HEIGHT=h** where *w* and *h* represent the width and height, respectively, of the type of control.

3. If desired, type **AUTOSTART=true** to make the sound play automatically when the visitor jumps to the page.

4. If desired, type **LOOP=n** to repeat the sound automatically *n* number of times. Or type **LOOP=true** to repeat the sound until the visitor clicks the Stop button (if you've provided one) or jumps to another page.

5. If desired, type **ALIGN=direction** to align the controls on the page. The ALIGN tag works the same for LiveAudio as it does for images. For more information, see page 88.

6. Type the final **>**.

```
code.html
<HTML><HEAD><TITLE>Adding internal sound for
Netscape users</TITLE></HEAD>
<BODY>
<H1>Dakota</H1>

<EMBED SRC="dakota.aif" AUTOSTART=true
LOOP=3 CONTROLS=smallconsole WIDTH=144
HEIGHT=15 ALIGN=right>

Dakota is Kevin's lovable golden lab. I
haven't actually met him, though I'm looking
forward to it. But I know he sounds something
like this.
<P>
<EMBED SRC="dakota2.aif"
CONTROLS=playbutton WIDTH=37 HEIGHT=22
ALIGN=left HSPACE=10>

Click on the playbutton at left to hear
Dakota when he sees a squirrel outside.

</BODY></HTML>
```

Figure 12.17 *In the top sound, there will be a small console (note the default width and height values). In the bottom sound, I've only included a play button. Notice that although the HSPACE (and VSPACE) attributes are not documented, they work correctly.*

Figure 12.18 *The small console (right) contains, from right to left, a play button, stop button, and progress indicator. The independent play button is shown at bottom left.*

```
                    code.html
<HTML><HEAD><TITLE>Inserting a background
sound for IE</TITLE></HEAD>
<BODY>
<H1>Dakota</H1>

<BGSOUND SRC=dakota.aif LOOP=2>

Dakota is Kevin's lovable golden lab. I
haven't actually met him, though I'm looking
forward to it. But I know he sounds something
like this.

</BODY></HTML>
```

Figure 12.19 *The BGSOUND tag can be placed anywhere on the page. However, since Internet Explorer will play the sound as soon as it encounters the tag you may want to place the tag at the end of the page so that the visitor sees the page before hearing the sound.*

```
                Inserting a background sound for IE

  Back  Forward  Stop  Refresh  Home  Search  Mail  News  Favorites  Larger  Smaller

Dakota

Dakota is Kevin's lovable golden lab. I haven't actually met him, though I'm
looking forward to it. But I know he sounds something like this.
```

Figure 12.20 *Woof, Woof. You can't see sound, but trust me, if you play it loud enough, your cats will disappear. (I scared mine so much they wouldn't come in the office for a week!)*

Adding background sound for Explorer users

Internet Explorer has a special tag that lets you link a sound to a page and have the sound play automatically whenever a visitor jumps to the page.

To add background sound:

1. In the HTML document, type **<BGSOUND SRC="sound.url"** where *sound.url* is the complete file name, including the extension of the sound.

2. If desired, type **LOOP=n** where *n* is the number of times you wish the sound to be played. Use **LOOP=-1** or **LOOP=infinite** to play the sound over and over.

3. Type the final **>**.

✔ Tips

■ You can create a background sound for pages that will be viewed in Netscape by following the instructions on page 212. Omit the CONTROLS, HEIGHT and WIDTH attributes and the sound will be hidden. Then add **AUTOSTART=true** so that the sound plays automatically when the visitor jumps to the page.

■ Don't use a really obnoxious, annoying, or long sound (or even a particularly loud one) if you want people to come back to your page with any regularity.

■ The BGSOUND tag recognizes WAV, AU, or MIDI formatted sounds.

Adding background sound for Explorer users

Video

If you listen to the Web hype long enough, you'll believe you can tune into Paramount's home page and watch previews to their new movies. Unfortunately, thanks to the huge size of video files and the relative minuscule speed of most home modems, although you might be *able* to do this, you might be gray before the opening credits finish rolling.

Nevertheless, it is possible to add links to video on your Web pages. As with sound files, you have to be especially careful to provide video in a format that your visitors will be able to use: QuickTime and MPEG for Mac and Windows, AVI just for Windows.

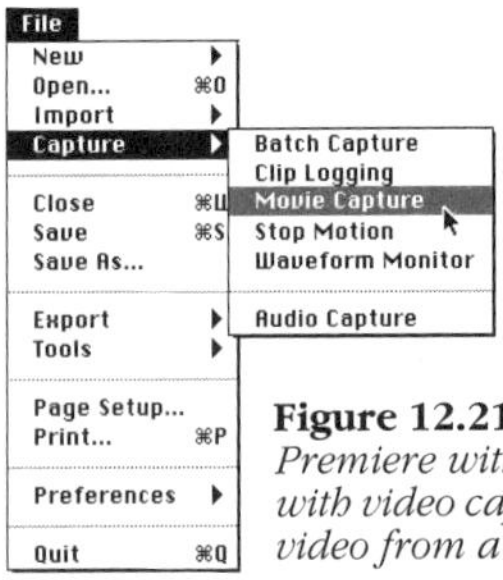

Capturing video

If you have an AV Mac or PowerMac or a video capture card for your PC, you can create video files by copying clips from your VCR to your computer. Along with the video-specific hardware, you will need a fast computer and a big, fast, hard disk.

The actual process, although not difficult, is a bit beyond the scope of this book. Your AV Mac or Video card should have instructions on how to digitize video. In my experience, the hardest part is figuring out where to connect all the cables.

Once again, you have to be careful about just what you copy. Most broadcast television is copyrighted and may not be published without permission. Of course, you are welcome to insert videos on your page that you've filmed yourself.

You may also find video files online or in a commercial library on CD-ROM.

Figure 12.21 *You can use Adobe Premiere with an AV Mac or a PC with video capture card to capture video from a VCR.*

Figure 12.22 *If you don't have your own home movies, you can use copyright free clips included in CD-ROM collections, like this short movie, which is included in the Adobe Premiere Deluxe CD-ROM.*

Figure 12.23 *These tiny menus reveal the simplicity of many video conversion programs. FastPlayer (left) flattens Macintosh QuickTime movies for viewing on Windows machines. AVI->QT (right) converts AVI format movies to QuickTime format.*

Converting video to the proper format

Your visitors will only be able to download and view your video files if you have saved them in the proper format, with the proper extension.

To convert video to the proper format:

1. Open a video conversion program.

2. Open the video file.

3. Choose File > Save As **(Figure 12.23)**.

4. In the Format submenu, choose QuickTime, AVI, or MPEG. QuickTime and MPEG movies can be viewed on both Macintosh and Windows machines. AVI movies are only for Windows.

5. Give the new movie file a distinct name and the proper extension (.qt or .mov for QuickTime, .avi for AVI, and .mpeg or .mpg for MPEG).

6. Click Save.

✔ Tip

■ In addition, QuickTime movies need to be *flattened* before they can be viewed on other types of computers besides Macintosh. Use a tool like FastPlayer (for Macintosh) or Qflat (for Windows).

Converting video to the proper format

Adding external video to your page

Although both Internet Explorer and Netscape can display video within a Web page *(see pages 217 and 218)*, they do it in two different ways. To make video accessible to your visitors regardless of their browser, you might consider using, or at least adding, a link to an external video file. When the visitor clicks the link, the browser downloads the video file and opens the appropriate helper program which then views the video.

To add a link to external video:

1. Create a small icon that you can use as an inline image on your page to indicate the link to the video and call it *video.gif.*

2. Make sure the video file has the correct extension (even for Macintosh files). Otherwise, the visitor's browser will not know what kind of file it is and may be unable to open it. (Use .qt or .mov for QuickTime files, .avi for AVI files, and .mpeg or .mpg for MPEG files.)

3. In your HTML document, where you wish to place the link to the video file, type **<A HREF="video.ext">** where *video.ext* is the location of the video file, including the correct extension, on the server.

4. Type **<IMG SRC="video.gif">** where *video.gif* is the location of the icon that will indicate the link to the video.

5. Type the size and format of the video file, for example, **5.2 Mb QuickTime movie**.

6. Type **</A>** to complete the link to the video file.

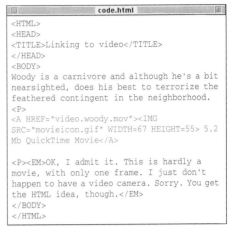

```
<HTML>
<HEAD>
<TITLE>Linking to video</TITLE>
</HEAD>
<BODY>
Woody is a carnivore and although he's a bit
nearsighted, does his best to terrorize the
feathered contingent in the neighborhood.
<P>
<A HREF="video.woody.mov"><IMG
SRC="movieicon.gif" WIDTH=67 HEIGHT=55> 5.2
Mb QuickTime Movie</A>

<P><EM>OK, I admit it. This is hardly a
movie, with only one frame. I just don't
happen to have a video camera. Sorry. You get
the HTML idea, though.</EM>
</BODY>
</HTML>
```

Figure 12.24 *It's a good idea to tell your visitors how big the video file is so that they know how long it will take to download.*

Figure 12.25 *A click by the visitor on the icon or text downloads the video file, launches the video player, and then plays the video.*

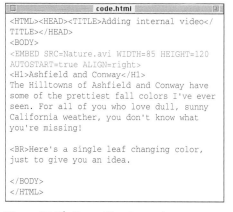

```
code.html

<HTML><HEAD><TITLE>Adding internal video</
TITLE></HEAD>
<BODY>
<EMBED SRC=Nature.avi WIDTH=85 HEIGHT=120
AUTOSTART=true ALIGN=right>
<H1>Ashfield and Conway</H1>
The Hilltowns of Ashfield and Conway have
some of the prettiest fall colors I've ever
seen. For all of you who love dull, sunny
California weather, you don't know what
you're missing!

<BR>Here's a single leaf changing color,
just to give you an idea.

</BODY>
</HTML>
```

Figure 12.26 *Since videos inserted on a page with the EMBED tag do not always have controls, you might want to add the AUTOSTART attribute so that they project automatically. Otherwise, instruct your visitors to click the video to play it.*

Figure 12.27 *To play a movie that is inserted with the EMBED tag, just click it.*

Figure 12.28 *Internet Explorer can also view videos inserted with the EMBED tag, although it offers more flexibility with the DYNSRC tag described on page 218.*

Adding internal video

Miracle of miracles, there is a way to insert video on a page in way that both Netscape and Explorer recognize, as long as you use AVI format movies.

To add internal video:

1. Create a movie in AVI format. You can also convert an existing movie.

2. In your HTML document, type **<EMBED SRC="movie.avi"**, where *movie.avi* is the URL for the desired movie file, including the extension.

3. Type **WIDTH=w HEIGHT=h** where *w* and *h* are the width and height, respectively, in pixels, of the movie.

4. If desired, type **AUTOSTART=true** to have the movie play automatically when the visitor jumps to the page.

5. If desired, type **LOOP=true** to have the movie play continuously until the visitor clicks on the movie or jumps to a different page.

6. If desired, type **ALIGN=direction**. The ALIGN tag works the same for video as it does for images. For more information, see page 88.

7. Type **>**.

✔ Tips

■ Explorer 4 for Macintosh doesn't support this technique. For information on adding links to movies that can be seen on any platform with practically any browser (albeit externally), see page 216.

■ You have to make sure the HEIGHT and WIDTH attributes are specified correctly in order for the controls in a QuickTime movie to appear.

Adding internal video for Internet Explorer

Internet Explorer recognizes a special attribute of the IMG tag that allows you to insert video on a page.

To add video for Internet Explorer:

1. Create an AVI movie. Create a static image, perhaps of the first frame of the movie.

2. In your HTML document, type **<IMG SRC="image.gif"** where *image.gif* is the static image that will be displayed before and after the movie is played.

3. Type **DYNSRC="movie.avi"** where *movie.avi* is the URL of the desired movie.

4. If desired, type **LOOP=n** where *n* is the number of times the movie should be projected. Use **LOOP=-1** or **LOOP=infinite** to project the movie continuously.

5. If desired, type **CONTROLS** to show the play, pause, and stop buttons under the movie.

6. If desired, type **START=event**, where *event* is either **FILEOPEN** to project the movie when the visitor jumps to the page, or **MOUSEOVER**, to project the movie when the visitor points at the link with the mouse.

7. Type the final **>**.

✔ Tip

- To add video that can be accessed by most browsers (although not internally), consult *Adding external video to your page* on page 216.

```
code.html
<HTML><HEAD><TITLE>Inserting video on your
pages for IE</TITLE></HEAD>
<BODY>
<IMG SRC=leaf.gif DYNSRC=Nature.avi CONTROLS
ALIGN=right>
<H1>Ashfield and Conway</H1>
The Hilltowns of Ashfield and Conway have
some of the prettiest fall colors I've ever
seen. For all of you who love dull, sunny
California weather, you don't know what
you're missing!

<BR>Here's a single leaf changing color,
just to give you an idea.

</BODY>
</HTML>
```

Figure 12.29 *You can specify a regular image with the SRC attribute as usual. It will be displayed as the movie is loading, as well as in browsers (like Netscape) that don't recognize the DYNSRC attribute.*

Figure 12.30 *Since Netscape can't view the video, it just shows the static image.*

Figure 12.31 *If you use the CONTROLS attribute (see step 5), a play button and progress bar appear below the video.*

Adding internal video for Internet Explorer

```
                code.html
<HTML><HEAD><TITLE>Using a marquee</
TITLE></HEAD><BODY>

<H1>The Quabbin Reservoir</H1>
They had to flood four towns and three
villages to create the incredible Quabbin
Reservoir. They pipe the water some 75 miles
East so that the folks in Boston have
something to put their tea bags in.

<MARQUEE WIDTH=75% HEIGHT=15 BEHAVIOR=scroll
DIRECTION=left LOOP=infinite
BGCOLOR=yellow>
Attention: Quabbin Enthusiasts General
Meeting Dec 9 at 7pm
</MARQUEE>
```

Figure 12.32 *A marquee begins with an opening tag that contains the attributes. It is followed by the text that will scroll and then the closing tag.*

Figure 12.33 *Netscape does not recognize the MARQUEE tag and instead displays plain text.*

Figure 12.34 *With the attributes BEHAVIOR=scroll and DIRECTION=left, the text begins at the left and then disappears off the right. You can also use the CENTER and FONT tags to change the appearance of the marquee.*

Creating a marquee

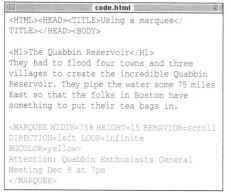 A marquee is text that starts at one part of the screen and floats across to the left, rather like the messages that advertise sales in the window of a 24-hour gas station. Internet Explorer lets you put marquees on your Web page.

To create a marquee:

1. Type **<MARQUEE**.

2. If desired, type **BEHAVIOR=type** where *type* is **scroll**, for text that starts at one side of the screen and disappears off the other, **slide** for text that starts at one side of the screen and stops when it reaches the other, or **alternate** for text that starts at one side of the screen and bounces back when it reaches the other side.

3. To determine which direction the text starts from, type **DIRECTION=left** or **DIRECTION=right**.

4. If desired, type **LOOP=n**, where *n* is the number of times the text will pass across the screen. Use **LOOP=infinite** to have the text appear continuously.

5. Type **SCROLLAMOUNT=n** to determine how much space, in pixels, is left between each pass of the text.

6. Type **SCROLLDELAY=n** to determine how much time, in milliseconds, passes before the text scrolls again.

7. Use the **HEIGHT**, **WIDTH**, **HSPACE**, **VSPACE**, **ALIGN**, and **BGCOLOR** attributes as usual, if desired.

8. Type the final **>**.

9. Type the scrolling text.

10. Type **</MARQUEE>**.

Creating a marquee

Inserting applets

Java applets are little applications (hence the term *applets*) that can be run in your browser to create special effects on your page, like clocks, calculators, and interactive events. There are whole books devoted to Java; here we'll restrict the topic to how to insert applets on your page once you've written or copied them from another source.

Figure 12.35 *The most important attribute in the APPLET tag is CODE. Make sure that it points to the proper Java compiled applet (not the source).*

To insert an applet:

1. Type **<APPLET CODE="applet.class"** where *applet.class* is the name of the compiled applet.

2. If desired, type **WIDTH=w HEIGHT=h** to specify the applet size in pixels.

3. Type **></APPLET>**.

Figure 12.36 *Applets let you create interactive, multimedia effects on your page without having to know how to program or script. (For information about JavaScript, see Chapter 16, Scripts.)*

✔ Tips

- If you don't know how to write your own applets, you can download freeware applets from many sources on the Web. For starters, try *http://www.gamelan.com*.

- You can also download the Java Development Kit (for Mac and Windows, among others) from Sun, its developer *(http://java.sun.com)*.

- Even if you don't know how to write Java applets from scratch, you can use the JDK for making minor changes to existing applets. Simply download the source (if it is available), make the desired changes, and then compile the new class file with the Java Compiler that comes with the JDK.

- The APPLET tag has been deprecated in HTML 4 in favor of the more generic OBJECT, but is still supported.

```
code.html
<!DOCTYPE HTML PUBLIC "-//W3C//DTD HTML 4 Transitional//
EN"><HTML><HEAD><TITLE>Why bother with styles?</TITLE>
</HEAD>
<BODY>
<P><FONT FACE="Myriad Roman, Verdana" SIZE=-1><EM><B>On
this page, you'll learn a little about each of our cats,
and how they have created </EM>their own<EM> style</EM></
B></FONT>.
<H1><FONT FACE="Nueva Roman, Lithos Regular"
SIZE=+2>Llumi, the Huntress</FONT></H1>
<P><FONT FACE="Myriad Roman, Verdana" SIZE=-1>Llumi is our
sweet, but <EM>ferocious</EM> hunter-kitty. Maybe it's
because she was born out in the wild (OK, the parking lot
of the <A HREF="commonwealth.htm">place my brother-in-law
works</A>) or maybe because she was an orphan (he found
her when she and her six brothers and sisters were just
two days old.) Then again, maybe it's because we brought
her home to a rather hostile environment: a fiercely
territorial <A HREF="cookie.html">Catalan cat</A> who had
just had a baby of her own, who didn't see any reason why
she should share her bed (that is, <EM>our</EM> bed), with
this outsider, an American, no less.</FONT>
<H1><FONT FACE="Nueva Roman, Lithos Regular"
SIZE=+2>Xixona, the Hungry </FONT></H1>
<P><FONT FACE="Myriad Roman, Verdana" SIZE=-1>Xixona, we
call her Xixo (pronounced Shi-shoe) for short, looks like
a carbon-copy of her mother, <A
HREF="cookie.html">Cookie</A>, if a bit darker. It's very
easy to tell them apart, though, all you have to do is
```

Figure 13.1 *When you format text with HTML tags, apart from invoking the wrath of the W3C—which has deprecated those tags—you spend an inordinate amount of time typing while being limited to very basic styles.*

```
code.html
<!DOCTYPE HTML PUBLIC "-//W3C//DTD HTML 4 Transitional//
EN"><HTML><HEAD><TITLE>Setting all font values at once</
TITLE>
<STYLE>
H1 {font: normal 20pt "Nueva Roman", "Lithos Regular"}
P {font: 10pt/15pt "Myriad Roman", "Verdana"}

P.intro {font: italic bold}
P.intro EM {font-style:normal}
</STYLE>
</HEAD>
<BODY>
<P class=intro>On this page, you'll learn a little about
each of our cats, and how they have created <EM>their own</
EM> style.
<H1>Llumi, the Huntress</H1>
<P>Llumi is our sweet, but <EM>ferocious</EM> hunter-
kitty. Maybe it's because she was born out in the wild (OK,
the parking lot of the <A HREF="commonwealth.htm">place my
brother-in-law works</A>) or maybe because she was an
orphan (he found her when she and her six brothers and
sisters were just two days old.) Then again, maybe it's
because we brought her home to a rather hostile
environment: a fiercely territorial <A
HREF="cookie.html">Catalan cat</A> who had just had a baby
of her own, who didn't see any reason why she should share
her bed (that is, <EM>our</EM> bed), with this outsider,
an American, no less.
<H1>Xixona, the Hungry </H1>
<P>Xixona, we call her Xixo (pronounced Shi-shoe) for
```

Figure 13.2 *With styles, all the formatting information is centralized either at the top of the page or in a separate document. Changes are easy, fast, and global.*

Cascading Style Sheets, also known as *CSS*, or simply *styles*, let you assign several properties at once to all the elements on your page marked with a particular tag. For example, you can display all your H1 headers in a particular size, font, and color. Although you could conceivably use HTML tags to achieve at least some of this formatting (say with FONT or BIG), styles offer several advantages.

First, styles save time. Imagine setting the font for each header and each paragraph in a long Web page **(Figure 13.1)**. Don't forget the closing </FONT> tags! With styles, you type a single line for each element at the top of the page **(Figure 13.2)**.

Second, styles are easy to change. Go back to your page and change the font, size, and color of each paragraph by hand. With styles, you make edits quickly—in just one place.

Third, computers are better at applying styles consistently than you are. Really. Did you remember to format each and every paragraph? You can be sure that the computer did.

Next, styles let you control text in ways that are out of reach of HTML tags. You can set line spacing (leading), background color, and remove bold and italic formatting, among other things.

Finally, styles make it easy to create a common format for all your Web pages. And you still only have to define the styles once. Make changes in one centralized place and—voilà!—all the pages are updated right away.

The anatomy of a style

A style is made up of a tag name (H1, P, etc.) and one or more definitions* that determine how the elements marked with that tag should be displayed—perhaps in red, at 12 points, with Lithos Regular.

Each definition contains a property, a colon, and one or more values. For example, to change the color of text, you use the *color* property with a value of say, *red*. The definition would read **color: red**. The space after the colon is not required. Multiple definitions must be separated by semi-colons **(Figure 13.3)**.

Some properties can be grouped together with a special umbrella property (like, *font, background,* and *border,* among others). For example, **font: bold 12pt Tekton** is the same as writing **font-size: 12pt; font-weight: bold; font-family: Tekton**.

Definitions (and thus, the properties and values) always look the same, whether the style is applied locally *(see page 223),* internally *(see page 224),* or externally *(see page 226).* The only difference is in the punctuation surrounding them—curly brackets vs. quote marks **(Figure 13.4)**.

The available properties and corresponding values that you use in defining styles are described in detail on pages 233–265.

Some properties are automatically inherited from tag to tag. For example, if you define H1 tagged text as blue, any text marked with an EM tag that is inside the H1 tag will also be blue. Of course, EM tagged text inside a paragraph defined with P (or any other tag) will not be blue.

*(The W3C uses fancier words than I do: the tag name is called a *selector* and the definitions are called *declarations*.)

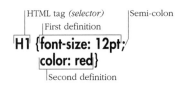

Figure 13.3 *A style is made up of a tag name (H1) and one or more definitions (font-size: 12pt and color: red) that specify how you want to display elements marked with that tag.*

Figure 13.4 *The outer parts of this style look a bit different from the one in Figure 13.3 because this style is being applied locally (see page 223). Note, more importantly, how the definition has exactly the same appearance: a property, a colon, and a value.*

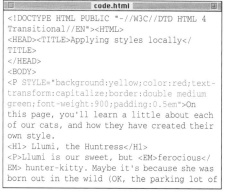

```
      code.html
<!DOCTYPE HTML PUBLIC "-//W3C//DTD HTML 4
Transitional//EN"><HTML>
<HEAD><TITLE>Applying styles locally</
TITLE>
</HEAD>
<BODY>
<P STYLE="background:yellow;color:red;text-
transform:capitalize;border:double medium
green;font-weight:900;padding:0.5em">On
this page, you'll learn a little about each
of our cats, and how they have created their
own style.
<H1> Llumi, the Huntress</H1>
<P>Llumi is our sweet, but <EM>ferocious</
EM> hunter-kitty. Maybe it's because she was
born out in the wild (OK, the parking lot of
```

Figure 13.5 *Except for coloring the text red, all the other styles applied here are not available through HTML tags. You need CSS!*

Figure 13.6 *The styles are applied to the paragraph. Hopefully, you'll have better taste.*

Applying styles locally

If you are new to style sheets and would like to experiment a bit before taking the plunge, applying styles locally is an easy, small-scale, and rather safe way to begin. Although it doesn't centralize all your formatting information for easy editing and global updating, it does open the door to the additional formatting that is impossible to create with conventional HTML tags.

To apply styles locally:

1. Within the HTML tag that you want to format, type **STYLE="**.

2. Type **property: value**, using the steps described on pages 233–265.

3. To create additional style definitions, type a semi-colon **;** and repeat step 2.

4. Type the final quote mark **"**.

✔ Tips

■ Be careful not to confuse the equals signs with the colon. Since they both assign values it's easy to interchange them without thinking.

■ Don't forget to separate multiple property definitions with a semi-colon.

■ Don't forget to enclose your style definitions in straight quote marks.

Applying styles locally

Creating an internal style sheet

Internal style sheets are ideal for individual pages with lots of text. They let you set the styles that should be used throughout an HTML document at the top of your page. If you plan to apply the style sheet to more than one page, you're better off using external style sheets *(see page 226)*.

To create an internal style sheet:

1. At the top of your HTML document, between the <HEAD> and </HEAD> tags, type **<STYLE>**.

2. Type the name of the tag whose properties you wish to define (**H1**, **P**, or whatever).

3. Type **{** to mark the beginning of this tag's properties.

4. Define as many properties as desired for this tag, using the steps described on pages 233–265. Separate each property with a semi-colon.

5. Type **}** to mark the end of this tag's properties.

6. Repeat steps 2–5 for each tag for which you wish to define properties.

7. Type **</STYLE>** to complete the style sheet.

```
code.html
<!DOCTYPE HTML PUBLIC "-//W3C//DTD HTML 4
Transitional//EN"><HTML><HEAD><TITLE>Creating an
internal style sheet</TITLE>
<STYLE>
H1 {text-align:center;
    letter-spacing:.5em;
    background:green;
    color:yellow;
    font: normal 20pt "Nueva Roman", "Lithos Regular"}

P  {text-align:justify;
    text-indent:8pt;
    font: 10pt/15pt "Myriad Roman", "Verdana"}

P.intro {text-indent:0;font: italic bold}
P.intro EM {font-style:normal}

A:link {background:yellow;color:green;
        text-decoration:none}
A:visited {background:orange; color:yellow;text-
decoration:none}
A:hover {background:red;color:white;text-
decoration:none}
A:active {background:white;color:black;text-
decoration:none}
</STYLE>
</HEAD>
<BODY>
<P class=intro>On this page, you'll learn a little
about each of our cats, and how they have created
<EM>their own</EM> style.
<H1>Llumi, the Huntress</H1>
<P>Llumi is our sweet, but <EM>ferocious</EM>
hunter-kitty. Maybe it's because she was born out
```

Figure 13.7 *An internal style sheet goes in the HEAD section of your HTML document.*

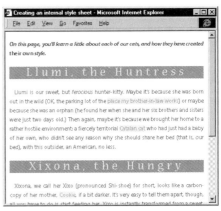

Figure 13.8 *Each element is displayed according to the styles defined at the top of the HTML page.*

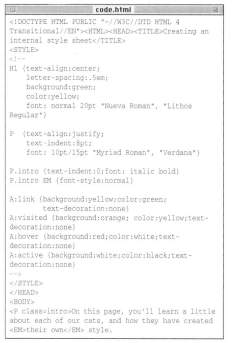

```
                    code.html
<!DOCTYPE HTML PUBLIC "-//W3C//DTD HTML 4
Transitional//EN"><HTML><HEAD><TITLE>Creating an
internal style sheet</TITLE>
<STYLE>
<!--
H1 {text-align:center;
    letter-spacing:.5em;
    background:green;
    color:yellow;
    font: normal 20pt "Nueva Roman", "Lithos
Regular"}

P  {text-align:justify;
    text-indent:8pt;
    font: 10pt/15pt "Myriad Roman", "Verdana"}

P.intro {text-indent:0;font: italic bold}
P.intro EM {font-style:normal}

A:link {background:yellow;color:green;
        text-decoration:none}
A:visited {background:orange; color:yellow;text-
decoration:none}
A:hover {background:red;color:white;text-
decoration:none}
A:active {background:white;color:black;text-
decoration:none}
-->
</STYLE>
</HEAD>
<BODY>
<P class=intro>On this page, you'll learn a little
about each of our cats, and how they have created
<EM>their own</EM> style.
```

Figure 13.9 *To hide styles from browsers that don't support them, add commenting just after the initial STYLE tag and before the final one.*

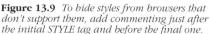

✔ **Tips**

■ Each set of properties must begin with an opening curly bracket "**{**" and end with a closing curly bracket "**}**". Each property and its values must be separated with a semi-colon "**;**".

■ You can define properties for several tags at once by separating each tag with a comma: **H1, H2, H3 {color:red}** will display the three levels of headers in red.

■ Define the properties for a tag that depends on another by typing the dependent tag after the parent one, separated by just a space: **H1 EM {color:red}** means that all text marked with the EM tag *that is found within the H1 tags* should be shown in red. EM tags found anywhere else (say, in a P tag) will not be red.

■ Add comment tags after (**<!--**) the initial <STYLE> tag and before (**-->**) the final </STYLE> tag to hide styles from browsers that don't yet understand them **(Figure 13.9)**. Otherwise, the errant browser may show the style definitions to your visitors. For more information on comments, consult *Hiding text (Adding comments)* on page 56.

■ You can also apply styles to individual HTML tags. For more details, consult *Applying styles locally* on page 223.

■ If you want to apply your styles to more than one Web page, you should use an external style sheet. For more information, consult *Creating an external style sheet* on page 226 and *Using an external style sheet* on page 227.

Creating an internal style sheet

Creating an external style sheet

External style sheets are ideal for giving all the pages on your Web site a common look. Instead of getting their styles from individual internal style sheets, you can set each page to consult the external sheet, thus ensuring that each will have the same settings.

To create an external style sheet:

1. Create a new text document.

2. Type the name of the tag whose properties you wish to define (**H1**, **P**, or whatever).

3. Type **{** to mark the beginning of this tag's properties.

4. Define as many properties as desired for this tag, using the steps described on pages 233–265. Separate each property with a semi-colon.

5. Type **}** to mark the end of this tag's properties.

6. Repeat steps 2–5 for each tag for which you wish to define properties.

7. Save the document in text-only format. Give the document the extension .css to designate the document as a cascading style sheet.

✔ Tip

■ All of the tips listed on page 225 also apply to external style sheets.

```
                    styles.css
H1 {text-align:center;
    letter-spacing:.5em;
    background:green;
    color:yellow;
    font: normal 20pt "Nueva Roman", "Lithos
Regular"}

P  {text-align:justify;
    text-indent:8pt;
    font: 10pt/15pt "Myriad Roman", "Verdana"}

P.intro {text-indent:0;font: italic bold}
P.intro EM {font-style:normal}

A:link {background:yellow;
        color:green;
        text-decoration:none}
A:visited {background:orange; color:yellow;text-
decoration:none}
A:hover {background:red;color:white;text-
decoration:none}
A:active {background:white;color:black;text-
decoration:none}
```

Figure 13.10 *The external style sheet contains precisely the same information as the internal one—but no HTML tags. Make sure you save it as text-only with the .css extension (even for a Mac).*

```
                    code.html
<!DOCTYPE HTML PUBLIC "-//W3C//DTD HTML 4
Transitional//EN"><HTML><HEAD><TITLE>Creating an
external style sheet</TITLE>
<LINK REL=stylesheet TYPE="text/css"
HREF=styles.css>
</HEAD>
<BODY>
<P class=intro>On this page, you'll learn a little
about each of our cats, and how they have created
<EM>their own</EM> style.
<H1>Llumi, the Huntress</H1>
<P>Llumi is our sweet, but <EM>ferocious</EM>
hunter-kitty. Maybe it's because she was born out
in the wild (OK, the parking lot of the <A
HREF="commonwealth.htm">place my brother-in-law
works</A>) or maybe because she was an orphan (he
```

Figure 13.11 *An external style sheet is linked to a particular Web page with the LINK tag.*

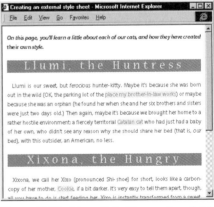

Figure 13.12 *A page linked to an external style sheet looks just as it would if the style sheet were right in the page itself (see Figure 13.8).*

```
code.html
<!DOCTYPE HTML PUBLIC "-//W3C//DTD HTML 4
Transitional//EN"><HTML><HEAD><TITLE>Creating an
external style sheet</TITLE>
<LINK REL=stylesheet TYPE="text/css"
HREF=styles.css>
</HEAD>
<BODY>
<P class=intro>On this page, you'll learn a little
about Cookie, our Catalan cat.
<H1>Cookie, the Invisible</H1>
<P>When we lived in Barcelona, people would come to
our house and rave about our big, American cat, <A
HREF="woody.htm">Woody</A>. Poor Cookie never got
even a mention. Of course, that was because as soon
as she heard the doorbell, she ran under the bed and
stayed there until the guests had long gone home.
I'm not sure why she was so shy with people. It might
have to do with the fact that she was born in a
planter on the busiest street in Barcelona, and I
abducted her from her mother all of a sudden one
Saturday morning to bring her home to our sixth
floor apartment, with the aforementioned big,
American cat.
```

Figure 13.13 *Here is a second page that I will link to the same external style sheet.*

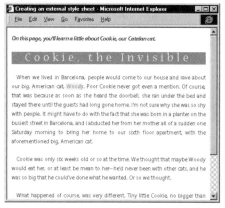

Figure 13.14 *The second page is displayed with the same styles as the first (see Figure 13.12).*

Using an external style sheet

Once you've created an external style sheet *(see page 226)*, you link it to each page it should format.

To use an external style sheet:

1. In the HEAD section of each HTML page in which you wish to use the style sheet, type **<LINK REL=stylesheet TYPE="text/css"**.

2. Type **HREF=url.css**, where *url.css* is the name you used in step 7 on page 226.

3. Type the final **>**.

✔ Tips

■ When you make a change to the style sheet, all the pages that reference it are automatically updated as well.

■ Theoretically, you can also import an external style sheet. However, I don't recommend it. It requires more typing than the method described above, and neither Netscape nor Explorer supports it.

■ You can link an external style sheet, include an internal style sheet, and apply local styles all in the same HTML document. Local styles override internal style sheets which, in turn, override external style sheets.

Defining styles for classes

You can divide your HTML elements into categories or *classes* in order to apply styles to them selectively. For example, you can create a class of introductory paragraphs that will have slightly different formatting than regular paragraphs.

To define styles for classes:

1. Mark the elements in your HTML page that belong to the class by adding **CLASS=classname** (where *classname* is the identifying word for the class) to the appropriate HTML tags.

2. In the STYLE section of your HTML page, type **parenttag.classname**, where *parenttag* is the tag that the class is a subset of, and *classname* is the same as in step 1. (Yes, that's a period between the parent tag and the class name.)

3. Type a curly bracket { to begin the definitions.

4. Type **property:value** to specify the additional properties that should be applied to elements of this class.

5. If desired, type a semi-colon ; and then specify additional properties and values *(see pages 233–265)*.

6. Type a right curly bracket } to complete the class definition.

✔ Tip

- You can only define styles for classes in internal or external style sheets. It doesn't make sense to define them locally since the whole point is to format a whole group of elements at once.

```
code.html
<!DOCTYPE HTML PUBLIC "-//W3C//DTD HTML 4
Transitional//
EN"><HTML><HEAD><TITLE>Applying styles to a
class</TITLE>
<STYLE>
H1 {text-align:center;
    letter-spacing:.5em;
    background:green;
    color:yellow;
    font: normal 20pt "Nueva Roman", "Lithos
Regular"}

P  {text-align:justify;
    text-indent:8pt;
    font: 10pt/15pt "Myriad Roman",
"Verdana"}

P.intro {text-indent:0;font: italic bold}
P.intro EM {font-style:normal}
</STYLE>
</HEAD>
<BODY>
<P CLASS=intro>On this page, you'll learn a
little about each of our cats, and how they
have created <EM>their own</EM> style.
<H1>Llumi, the Huntress</H1>
```

Figure 13.15 *In this example, regular P tags are indented. Those of class intro will not be indented, and will be displayed in italic bold.*

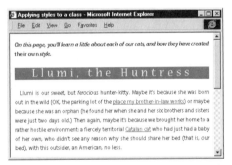

Figure 13.16 *Only the paragraph marked with the P tag as intro class will be formatted as intro. Paragraphs with the P tag without any class will be formatted as usual, as is the case with the last paragraph shown on this page.*

Defining styles for classes

```
                code.html
<!DOCTYPE HTML PUBLIC "-//W3C//DTD HTML 4
Transitional//
EN"><HTML><HEAD><TITLE>Applying styles to a
class</TITLE>
<STYLE>
H1 {text-align:center;
    letter-spacing:.5em;
    background:green;
    color:yellow;
    font: normal 20pt "Nueva Roman", "Lithos
Regular"}

P  {text-align:justify;
    text-indent:8pt;
    font: 10pt/15pt "Myriad Roman",
"Verdana"}

P#intro {text-indent:0;font: italic bold}
P.intro EM {font-style:normal}
</STYLE>
</HEAD>
<BODY>
<P ID=intro>On this page, you'll learn a
little about each of our cats, and how they
have created <EM>their own</EM> style.
<H1>Llumi, the Huntress</H1>
<P>Llumi is our sweet, but <EM>ferocious</
EM> hunter-kitty. Maybe it's because she was
born out in the wild (OK, the parking lot of
the <A HREF="commonwealth.htm">place my
brother-in-law works</A>) or maybe because
```

Figure 13.17 *In this example, regular P tags are indented. The one marked with ID intro will not be indented, and will be displayed in italic bold.*

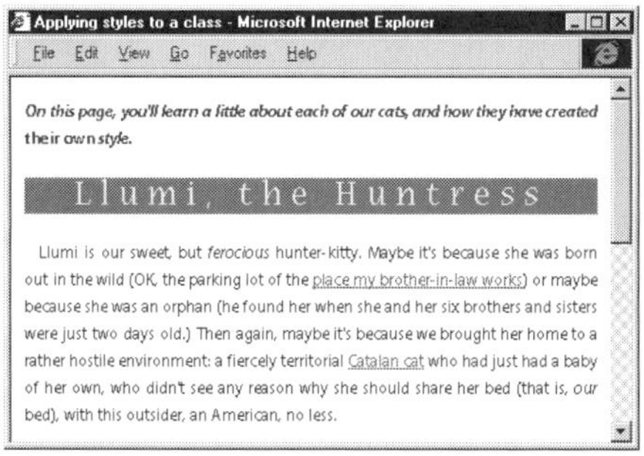

Figure 13.18 *Only the one paragraph with the unique ID of intro will be formatted.*

Identifying particular tags

Instead of creating a whole class of HTML tags, you can also identify individual tags, and then either apply style sheet information or JavaScript functions.

To identify particular tags:

1. Identify the element in your HTML page by adding **ID=idname** (where *idname* is the identifying word for the tag) to the appropriate HTML tag.

2. In the STYLE section of your HTML page, type **parenttag#idname**, where *parenttag* is the kind of HTML tag that is identified with the ID attribute, and *idname* is the same as in step 1. (Yes, that's a number sign between the parent tag and the ID name.)

3. Type a curly bracket **{** to begin the definitions.

4. Type **property:value** to specify the additional properties that should be applied to elements of this class.

5. If desired, type a semi-colon **;** and then specify additional properties and values *(see pages 233–265)*.

6. Type a right curly bracket **}** to complete the ID definition.

✔ Tips

■ Each ID in an HTML document must be unique.

■ IDs are particularly useful for applying JavaScript to particular parts of your Web page.

Special tags for styles

There are two tags that are particularly useful for applying styles. The first is DIV, which applies to one or more sections of your document. The second is SPAN, which can be applied to a few words of text. By themselves, they don't do much at all to the enclosed text. Coupled with a class *(see page 228)* or ID *(see page 229)* and a style, they let you create your own homegrown HTML tags.

To apply styles to the DIV tag:

1. In the STYLE section at the top of your HTML document or in an external style sheet, type **DIV.classname**, where *classname* is the identifying word for the class you're going to use.

Or type **DIV#IDname**, where *IDname* is the identifying word for this particular instance of the DIV tag.

2. Type **{property:value**, using the information on pages 233–265.

3. Create additional definitions, if desired, separating each with a **;**.

4. Add the final **}**.

To use the DIV tag:

1. At the beginning of the desired section of your document, type **<DIV**.

2. Type **CLASS="classname"**, where *classname* identifies the type of section.

Or type **ID="idname"**, where *idname* identifies this particular section.

3. Type the final **>**.

4. Create the contents of this section.

5. At the end of the desired section, type **</DIV>**.

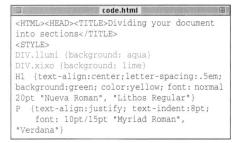

```
                code.html
<HTML><HEAD><TITLE>Dividing your document
into sections</TITLE>
<STYLE>
DIV.llumi {background: aqua}
DIV.xixo {background: lime}
H1  {text-align:center;letter-spacing:.5em;
background:green; color:yellow; font: normal
20pt "Nueva Roman", "Lithos Regular"}
P  {text-align:justify; text-indent:8pt;
    font: 10pt/15pt "Myriad Roman",
"Verdana"}
```

Figure 13.19 *Define the DIV styles in the STYLE section at the top of your HTML document.*

```
                code.html
<P class=intro>On this page, you'll learn a
little about each of our cats, and how they
have created <EM>their own</EM> style.
<DIV CLASS="llumi">
<H1>Llumi, the Huntress</H1>
<P>Llumi is our sweet, but <EM>ferocious</
EM> hunter-kitty. Maybe it's because she was
born out in the wild (OK, the parking lot of
the <A HREF="commonwealth.htm">place my
brother-in-law works</A>) or maybe because
she was an orphan (he found her when she and
her six brothers and sisters were just two
days old.) Then again, maybe it's because we
brought her home to a rather hostile
environment: a fiercely territorial <A
HREF="cookie.html">Catalan cat</A> who had
just had a baby of her own, who didn't see
any reason why she should share her bed (that
is, <EM>our</EM> bed), with this outsider,
an American, no less.
</DIV>
<DIV CLASS="xixo">
```

Figure 13.20 *Then mark the appropriate sections in your HTML page with DIV tags.*

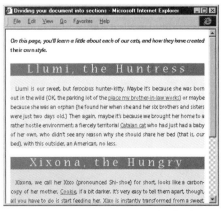

Figure 13.21 *DIV tags are great for dividing your document into thematic sections.*

```
┌─────────────────  code.html  ─────────────────┐
<STYLE>
DIV.llumi {background: aqua}
DIV.xixo {background: lime}
SPAN.initialcap {font-size:200%}
SPAN.allcaps {font-variant:small-caps}
H1 {text-align:center; letter-spacing:.5em;
background:green; color:yellow; font: normal
20pt "Nueva Roman", "Lithos Regular"}
P  {text-align:justify; text-indent:8pt;
font: 10pt/15pt "Myriad Roman", "Verdana"}
P.intro {text-indent:0;font: italic bold}
P.intro EM {font-style:normal}
</STYLE>
</HEAD><BODY>
<P class="intro">
<SPAN CLASS="initialcap">O</SPAN>
<SPAN CLASS="allcaps">n this page, you'll
</SPAN> learn a little about each of our
cats, and how they have created <EM>their
own</EM> style.
<DIV CLASS="llumi">
<H1>Llumi, the Huntress</H1>
<P>Llumi is our sweet, but <EM>ferocious</
EM> hunter-kitty. Maybe it's because she was
```

Figure 13.22 *Notice that the text affected by the SPAN tags here could not really be styled with any other tag without adding unwanted extra formatting.*

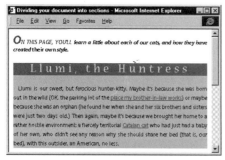

Figure 13.23 *SPAN tags are great for applying focused effects on individual letters or words.*

To apply styles to the SPAN tag:

1. In the STYLE section at the top of your HTML document or in an external style sheet, type **SPAN.classname**, where *classname* is the identifying word for the class you're going to use.

Or type **SPAN#idname**, where *idname* is the word that identifies this particular text.

2. Type **{property:value**, using the information on pages 233–265.

3. Create additional definitions, if desired, separating each with a **;**.

4. Add the final **}**.

To use the SPAN tag:

1. At the beginning of the desired words, type **<SPAN**.

2. Type **CLASS="classname"**, where *classname* identifies the type of text.

Or type **ID="idname"**, where *idname* identifies this particular text.

3. Type the final **>**.

4. Create the text you wish to affect.

5. Type **</SPAN>**.

✔ Tip

■ The DIV and SPAN tags let you create custom styles without co-opting any existing tags and their corresponding styles.

Defining styles for links

If you don't like underlined links, you can change the background and foreground color of your links to make them stand out with out looking so ugly. Link styles have a special syntax.

To define styles for links:

1. Type **A:**.

2. Type **link** to change the appearance of links that haven't yet been or currently aren't being clicked or pointed at.

Or type **visited** to change the appearance of links that the visitor has already clicked.

Or type **active** to change the appearance of links when clicked.

Or type **hover** to change the appearance of links when pointed to.

3. Type a curly bracket **{** to begin the definitions.

4. Type **property:value** to specify the how the links should look. You might try changing the color *(see page 241)*, the background color *(see page 242)*, and the underlining *(see page 246)*.

5. If desired, type a semi-colon **;** and then specify additional properties and values.

6. Type a right curly bracket **}** to complete the link definition.

✔ Tip

■ To change the appearance of all the links (in all states) at once, just type **A {property:value}**.

```
code.html
P  {text-align:justify;
    text-indent:8pt;
    font: 10pt/15pt "Myriad Roman",
"Verdana"}

P.intro {text-indent:0;font: italic bold}
P.intro EM {font-style:normal}

A:link {background:yellow;
        color:green;
        text-decoration:none}
A:visited {background:orange;
color:yellow;text-decoration:none}
A:hover {background:red;color:white;text-
decoration:none}
A:active
{background:white;color:black;text-
decoration:none}
</STYLE>
</HEAD>
<BODY>
<P class=intro>On this page, you'll learn a
little about each of our cats, and how they
have created <EM>their own</EM> style.
```

Figure 13.24 *You can create a different style for each state of a link.*

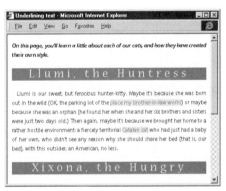

Figure 13.25 *In this example, I've created a background for links so they're visible, but gotten rid of the underlining so they're not so ugly.*

Formatting Text with Styles

Many tags deprecated

The W3 Consortium wants you to stop using the FONT tag. And about 20 other tags and attributes that add formatting to text, lists, tables, and the rest of your Web page. Instead, they think you should consolidate all that formatting information in one step: the style. And while leaving your familiar tags behind may take some practice, you'll soon find that styles save you time and typing.

HTML wasn't designed to be beautiful—it was designed to be universal. Thanks to pioneers like Netscape Corporation, a whole slew of tags were added to HTML (with version 3.2) that attempted to give designers much more control over the appearance of text on their Web pages. And while Web pages got a lot snazzier, they also got a lot more unwieldy. It is no fun formatting text word by word with a million tags before and after each change.

So, local formatting is on its way out, to be replaced by styles. Styles let you apply a whole set of formatting characteristics at once. For example, you can create a style for "body text" with red, 12 pt text set in Garamond. Then create a "header1" style in dark green, 26pt Arial Black. The great thing about styles is that you only have to define a paragraph as "body text" or "header1". You don't have to apply each size, color, font, or whatever, individually.

Styles also offer many more possibilities than HTML tags and extensions ever did. Now you can change the size, weight, slant, line height, foreground and background color, spacing, and alignment of text, decide whether it should be underlined, overlined, struck through, or blinking, and convert it to all uppercase, all lowercase, or small-caps.

Note: This chapter explains how to create individual styles. You can use these styles locally *(see page 223)*, in an internal style sheet *(see page 224)*, or in an external style sheet *(see page 226)*.

Choosing a font family

Because not everyone has the same set of fonts, the font-family marker has a special characteristic: you can specify more than one font, in case the first is not available in the user's system. You can also have a last ditch attempt at controlling the display in the user's system by specifying a generic font style like *serif* or *monospace*.

To set the font family:

1. Type **font-family: familyname**, where *familyname* is your first choice of font.

2. If desired, type **, familyname2**, where *familyname2* is your second font choice. Separate each choice with a comma and a space.

3. Repeat step 2 as desired.

✔ Tips

■ It's a good idea to specify at least two font choices, one of them a common font, so that you maintain some control over how the document is displayed. Common fonts in Macintosh systems are Times and Palatino for serif fonts and Helvetica for sans-serif. Most Windows systems contain Times as well, but Arial is more prevalent as a sans-serif choice.

■ You can use the following generic font names—**serif**, **sans-serif**, **cursive**, **fantasy**, and **monospace**—as a last attempt to influence which font is used for display.

■ You can set the font family, font size, and line height all at once, using the general font style *(see page 240)*.

■ You can use very specific font names, like *Futura Condensed Bold Italic*.

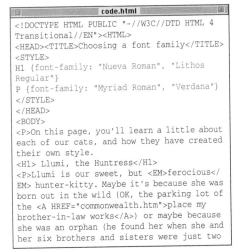

```
<!DOCTYPE HTML PUBLIC "-//W3C//DTD HTML 4
Transitional//EN"><HTML>
<HEAD><TITLE>Choosing a font family</TITLE>
<STYLE>
H1 {font-family: "Nueva Roman", "Lithos
Regular"}
P {font-family: "Myriad Roman", "Verdana"}
</STYLE>
</HEAD>
<BODY>
<P>On this page, you'll learn a little about
each of our cats, and how they have created
their own style.
<H1> Llumi, the Huntress</H1>
<P>Llumi is our sweet, but <EM>ferocious</
EM> hunter-kitty. Maybe it's because she was
born out in the wild (OK, the parking lot of
the <A HREF="commonwealth.htm">place my
brother-in-law works</A>) or maybe because
she was an orphan (he found her when she and
her six brothers and sisters were just two
```

Figure 14.1 *For the header, Nueva Roman is the first choice. If the user doesn't have Nueva Roman, Lithos Regular will be used. Similarly for P paragraphs, Myriad Roman is the first choice and Verdana is the second choice.*

Figure 14.2 *On this system, both first choices were available: Nueva Roman for headers and Myriad Roman for the P paragraphs.*

```
                  code.html
<!DOCTYPE HTML PUBLIC "-//W3C//DTD HTML 4
Transitional//
EN"><HTML><HEAD><TITLE>Embedding a font
family</TITLE>
<STYLE>
@font-face {font-family: "Nueva Roman";
        src: url(NUEVAR1.eot)}
H1 {font-family: "Nueva Roman", "Lithos
Regular"}
P {font-family: "Myriad Roman", "Verdana"}
</STYLE>
</HEAD>
<BODY>
<P>On this page, you'll learn a little about
each of our cats, and how they have created
their own style.
<H1> Llumi, the Huntress</H1>
<P>Llumi is our sweet, but <EM>ferocious</
EM> hunter-kitty. Maybe it's because she was
born out in the wild (OK, the parking lot of
the <A HREF="commonwealth.htm">place my
```

Figure 14.3 *To embed a font for Explorer users, insert the @font-face line within the STYLE tags in the HEAD of your Web page. The src URL points to a special version of the font that can be downloaded to your visitor's system.*

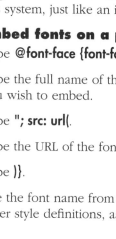

Figure 14.4 *The result looks exactly the same as Figure 14.2—even if your visitor doesn't have the fonts installed on their system.*

Embedding fonts on a page

You can choose whatever font you want, but if your visitor doesn't have it installed on their system, how will they view it? One of the latest features to be added to style sheets is the ability to embed a font in a page and have it downloaded to the visitor's system, just like an image.

To embed fonts on a page:

1. Type **@font-face {font-family: "**.

2. Type the full name of the font that you wish to embed.

3. Type **"; src: url(**.

4. Type the URL of the font.

5. Type **)}**.

6. Use the font name from step 2 in other style definitions, as desired.

✔ Tips

- You can't just choose any font file as the source for an embedded font (in step 4). You have to use a special format of the font. Internet Explorer requires fonts to be in the .eot format. You can convert your installed fonts into .eot with a program called WEFT. For more information, see *www.microsoft.com/typography/web/embedding/weft/*.

- Netscape Corporation is working on technology with Bitstream that uses a font embedding system developed by HexMac, that at press time, was also supported by Explorer. Check out *http://www.hexmac.com* or Netscape's developer's site at *http://devedge.netscape.com* for more details.

Creating italics

There are two ways to apply italic formatting. Either choose Garamond Italic or Palatino Italic (or whatever) for the font *(see page 234)*, or first choose the font (Garamond or Palatino) and then choose Italics. If all of your text in a given font should be in italics, the first method is simpler. But if you want to use the font in both its roman and italic forms, the second method, described here, will prove more flexible.

To create italics:

1. Type **font-style:**.

2. Type **oblique** for oblique text, or **italic** for italic text.

To remove italics:

1. Type **font-style:**.

2. Type **normal**.

✔ Tips

■ It used to be that the italic version of a font was created by a font designer from scratch, while the oblique version was created by the computer, on the fly. This distinction has blurred somewhat, but generally holds.

■ If you set the font style as italic and there is no italic style available, the browser should try to display the text in oblique style.

■ One reason you might want to remove italics is to emphasize some text in a paragraph that has inherited italic formatting from a parent tag. For information on inherited styles, see page 222.

```
code.html
<!DOCTYPE HTML PUBLIC "-//W3C//DTD HTML 4
Transitional//
EN"><HTML><HEAD><TITLE>Creating italics</
TITLE>
<STYLE>
H1 {font-family: "Nueva Roman", "Lithos
Regular"}

P {font-family: "Myriad Roman", "Verdana"}

P.intro {font-style:italic}
P.intro EM {font-style:normal}
</STYLE>
</HEAD>
<BODY>
<P class=intro>On this page, you'll learn a
little about each of our cats, and how they
have created <EM>their own</EM> style.
<H1> Llumi, the Huntress</H1>
<P>Llumi is our sweet, but <EM>ferocious</
EM> hunter-kitty. Maybe it's because she was
```

Figure 14.5 *In this example, I've set all the P elements of class "intro" in italics. Then I eliminated the italics from EM elements within P.intro elements, so that they will continue to stand out.*

Figure 14.6 *Notice that the P paragraph marked with the intro class (the first paragraph) is in italics. The text in that paragraph marked with the EM tag ("their own") is in roman face.*

```
                code.html
<!DOCTYPE HTML PUBLIC "-//W3C//DTD HTML 4
Transitional//
EN"><HTML><HEAD><TITLE>Applying bold
formatting</TITLE>
<STYLE>
H1 {font-weight:normal;
    font-family: "Nueva Roman", "Lithos
Regular"}

P {font-family: "Myriad Roman", "Verdana"}

P.intro {font-style:italic;
    font-weight:bold}
P.intro EM {font-style:normal}
</STYLE>
</HEAD>
<BODY>
<P class=intro>On this page, you'll learn a
little about each of our cats, and how they
have created <EM>their own</EM> style.
<H1> Llumi, the Huntress</H1>
```

Figure 14.7 *The H1 elements are automatically bold faced, but if I'm not crazy about how they look, I can override the bold formatting by using a value of "normal". I've also added bold formatting to the P.intro elements.*

Figure 14.8 *The headers are now shown in normal weight. The P intro paragraph is now both bold and italic (see page 236).*

Applying bold formatting

Bold formatting is probably the most common and effective way to make text stand out. Cascading style sheets gives you much more flexibility with bold text, providing relative values and allowing you to get rid of it altogether.

To apply bold formatting:

1. Type **font-weight:**.

2. Type **bold** to give an average bold weight to the text.

3. Or type **bolder** or **lighter** to use a value relative to the current weight.

4. Or type a multiple of **100** between 100 and 900, where 400 represents book weight and 700 represents bold.

To remove bold formatting:

1. Type **font-weight**.

2. Type **normal**.

✔ Tips

■ Since the way weights are defined varies from font to font, the values may not be relative from font to font. They are designed to be relative *within* a given font family.

■ If the font family has fewer than nine weights, or if they are concentrated on one end of the scale, it is possible that some numeric values correspond to the same font weight.

■ What can you remove bold formatting from? Any tag where it's been applied automatically (B and H1 come to mind) and where it's been inherited from a parent tag *(see page 222)*.

Setting the font size

You can set the font size of text marked with a particular HTML tag (or class) by specifying an exact size in points or pixels, or with descriptive words, or by specifying a relative size, with respect to a parent element.

To set the font size:

1. Type **font-size:**.

2. Type an absolute font size: **xx-small**, **x-small**, **small**, **medium**, **large**, **x-large**, or **xx-large**.

   Or type a relative font size: **larger** or **smaller**.

   Or type an exact size: say, **12pt** or **15px**.

   Or type a percentage relative to any parent style: e.g., **150%**.

✔ Tips

- The relative values (larger, smaller, and the percentage) depend on the size of the parent style. For example, if we defined a value of 150% for the P tag's intro class, it would mean 150% of 14pt, the defined size for the P tag in general, or 21pt.

- You can set font size together with other font values *(see page 240)*.

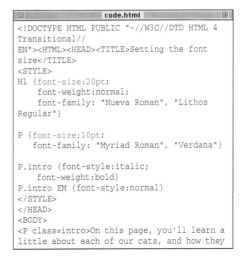

```
<!DOCTYPE HTML PUBLIC "-//W3C//DTD HTML 4
Transitional//
EN"><HTML><HEAD><TITLE>Setting the font
size</TITLE>
<STYLE>
H1 {font-size:20pt;
    font-weight:normal;
    font-family: "Nueva Roman", "Lithos
Regular"}

P {font-size:10pt;
    font-family: "Myriad Roman", "Verdana"}

P.intro {font-style:italic;
    font-weight:bold}
P.intro EM {font-style:normal}
</STYLE>
</HEAD>
<BODY>
<P class=intro>On this page, you'll learn a
little about each of our cats, and how they
```

Figure 14.9 *I'm going to make all the text a bit smaller in order to fit more on a page and reduce the amount of scrolling my visitors have to do. Don't forget the semi-colon at the end of each style.*

Figure 14.10 *You can start to get an idea of the power that styles give you. Just two lines change every marked paragraph on your page (compare with Figure 14.8).*

```
code.html
<!DOCTYPE HTML PUBLIC "-//W3C//DTD HTML 4
Transitional//
EN"><HTML><HEAD><TITLE>Setting the line
height</TITLE>
<STYLE>
H1 {font-size:20pt;
    font-weight:normal;
    font-family: "Nueva Roman", "Lithos
Regular"}

P {line-height:15pt;
    font-size:10pt;
    font-family: "Myriad Roman", "Verdana"}

P.intro {font-style:italic;font-
weight:bold}
P.intro EM {font-style:normal}
</STYLE>
</HEAD>
<BODY>
<P class=intro>On this page, you'll learn a
```

Figure 14.11 *The line-height determines the amount of leading, or space between lines.*

Figure 14.12 *Spacing out the lines makes them easier to read.*

Setting the line height

Line height refers to a paragraph's leading, that is, the amount of space between each line in a paragraph. Using a large line height can sometimes make your body text easier to read. A small line height for headers (with more than one line) often makes them look classier.

To set the line height:

1. Type **line-height:**.

2. Type **n**, where *n* is a number that will be multiplied by the font-size to obtain the desired line height.

   Or type **p%** where *p%* is a percentage of the font size.

   Or type **a**, where *a* is an absolute value in points, pixels, or whatever.

✔ Tips

■ You can specify the line height together with the font family, size, weight, style, and variant, as described on page 240.

■ If you use a number to determine the line height, this factor is inherited by all child items. If you use a percentage, only the resulting size is inherited, not the percentage factor.

Setting the line height

Setting all font values at once

You can set the font style, weight, variant, size, line height, and family all at once.

To set all font values at once:

1. Type **font:**.

2. Type **normal**, **oblique**, or **italic** to set the font-style *(see page 236)*.

3. Type **normal**, **bold**, **bolder**, **lighter**, or a multiple of **100** (between 100 and 900) to set the font-weight *(see page 236)*.

4. Type **small-caps** to use a small cap font variant *(see page 248)*.

5. Type the desired font size, using the values given in step 2 on page 238.

6. Type **/lineheight**, where *lineheight* is expressed in the same form as the font size *(see page 238)*.

7. Type a space followed by the desired font family or families, in order of preference, separated by commas, as described on page 234.

✔ Tips

■ You can also set each option separately. See the page referenced with that step.

■ You do not have to set every option at once. Any that you leave out will be set to its default value.

■ You can only set the line height if you have also set the font size. The line height must come directly after the font size and the slash.

■ If you want it to work in Netscape, use the order I've outlined above. Any order works with Explorer.

```
code.html
<!DOCTYPE HTML PUBLIC "-//W3C//DTD HTML 4
Transitional//
EN"><HTML><HEAD><TITLE>Setting all font
values at once</TITLE>
<STYLE>
H1 {font: normal 20pt "Nueva Roman", "Lithos
Regular"}
P {font: 10pt/15pt "Myriad Roman",
"Verdana"}

P.intro {font: italic bold}
P.intro EM {font-style:normal}
</STYLE>
</HEAD>
<BODY>
<P class=intro>On this page, you'll learn a
little about each of our cats, and how they
have created <EM>their own</EM> style.
<H1> Llumi, the Huntress</H1>
<P>Llumi is our sweet, but <EM>ferocious</
EM> hunter-kitty. Maybe it's because she was
```

Figure 14.13 *The styles defined for H1, P, and P.intro are exactly the same as on the preceding page (Figure 14.11). This method simply combines them all in one place.*

Figure 14.14 *The result is exactly the same as if you had defined each characteristic separately (cf. Figure 14.12).*

Setting all font values at once

```
┌─────────────────────────────────────┐
│ ▫          code.html          ▣ │
├─────────────────────────────────────┤
│ <!DOCTYPE HTML PUBLIC "-//W3C//DTD HTML 4
│ Transitional//
│ EN"><HTML><HEAD><TITLE>Setting the color</
│ TITLE>
│ <STYLE>
│ H1 {color:yellow;
│     font: normal 20pt "Nueva Roman", "Lithos
│ Regular"}
│ P {font: 10pt/15pt "Myriad Roman",
│ "Verdana"}
│
│ P.intro {font: italic bold}
│ P.intro EM {font-style:normal}
│ </STYLE>
│ </HEAD>
│ <BODY>
│ <P class=intro>On this page, you'll learn a
│ little about each of our cats, and how they
│ have created <EM>their own</EM> style.
│ <H1> Llumi, the Huntress</H1>
│ <P>Llumi is our sweet, but <EM>ferocious</
```

Figure 14.15 *You can use either color names, like* yellow, *in this example, or hexadecimal representations of colors.*

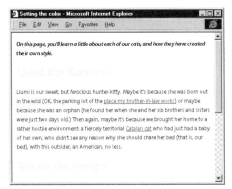

Figure 14.16 *These headers really are yellow! You can see it better on the Web (see page 21).*

Setting the text color

You can change the color of any tagged text, whether it be an entire paragraph, or just a few words.

To set the text color:

1. Type **color:**.

2. Type **colorname**, where *colorname* is one of the 16 predefined colors.

Or type **#rrggbb**, where *rrggbb* is the hexadecimal representation of the desired color.

Or type **rgb(r, g, b)** where *r*, *g*, and *b* are integers from 0–255 that specify the amount of red, green, or blue, respectively, in the desired color.

Or type **rgb(r%, g%, b%)** where *r*, *g*, and *b* specify the percentage of red, green, and blue, respectively, in the desired color.

✔ Tips

■ If you type a value for r, g, or b higher than 255 it will be replaced with 255. Similarly a percentage higher than 100% will be replaced with 100%.

■ You can use the color property to change the color of any HTML element. For more information, consult *Changing the foreground color* on page 261.

Changing the text's background

The background refers not to the background of the entire page, but to the background of the specified tag. In other words, you can change the background of just a few paragraphs or words, by setting the background of those words to a different color.

To change the text's background:

1. Type **background:**.

2. Type **transparent** or **color**, where *color* is a color name or hex color.

3. If desired, type **url(image.gif)**, to use an image for the background.

   If desired, type **repeat** to tile the image both horizontally and vertically, **repeat-x** to tile the image only horizontally, **repeat-y** to tile the image only vertically, and **no-repeat** to not tile the image.

   If desired, type **fixed** or **scroll** to determine whether the background should scroll along with the canvas.

   If desired, type **x y** to set the position of the background image, where *x* and *y* can be expressed as a percentage or an absolute distance from the top left corner. Or use values of *top*, *center*, or *bottom* for *x* and *left*, *center*, and *right* for *y*.

✔ Tip

■ You can specify both a color and a GIF image's URL for the background. The color will be used until the URL is loaded, and will be seen through any transparent portions of the image.

```
code.html
<!DOCTYPE HTML PUBLIC "-//W3C//DTD HTML 4
Transitional//
EN"><HTML><HEAD><TITLE>Changing the text's
background color or image</TITLE>
<STYLE>
H1 {background:green;
    color:yellow;
    font: normal 20pt "Nueva Roman", "Lithos
Regular"}
P {font: 10pt/15pt "Myriad Roman",
"Verdana"}

P.intro {font: italic bold}
P.intro EM {font-style:normal}
</STYLE>
</HEAD>
<BODY>
<P class=intro>On this page, you'll learn a
little about each of our cats, and how they
have created <EM>their own</EM> style.
<H1> Llumi, the Huntress</H1>
```

Figure 14.17 *In this example, the background of just the headers is set to green to offset the yellow text.*

Figure 14.18 *Be sure to use a background color that contrasts enough with the color of the text and the background of the page itself.*

```
code.html
<!DOCTYPE HTML PUBLIC "-//W3C//DTD HTML 4
Transitional//
EN"><HTML><HEAD><TITLE>Controlling
spacing</TITLE>
<STYLE>
H1 {letter-spacing:.5em;
    background:green;
    color:yellow;
    font: normal 20pt "Nueva Roman", "Lithos
Regular"}

P  {text-indent:8pt;
     font: 10pt/15pt "Myriad Roman",
"Verdana"}

P.intro {text-indent:0;font: italic bold}
P.intro EM {font-style:normal}
</STYLE>
</HEAD>
<BODY>
<P class=intro>On this page, you'll learn a
```

Figure 14.19 *You can specify tracking and kerning by using the letter-spacing and word-spacing tags, respectively. Indenting is defined with the text-indent marker.*

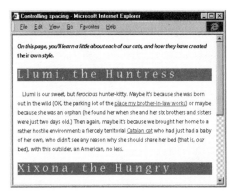

Figure 14.20 *Explorer currently supports text indents (notice the body text) and letter spacing (in the headers), but not word spacing. Netscape only supports text-indent.*

Controlling spacing

You can add more space between words (tracking) or between letters (kerning). You can also add a chunk of space, or an indent, before particular paragraphs.

To specify tracking:

1. Type **word-spacing:**.

2. Type **length**, where *length* is a numerical value in pixels, points, ems, etc.

To specify kerning:

1. Type **letter-spacing:**.

2. Type **length**, where *length* is a numerical value in pixels, points, ems, etc.

To add indents:

1. Type **text-indent:**.

2. Type a value for the text indent, either as an absolute value (either positive or negative) or as a percentage.

✔ Tips

■ You may use negative values for word and letter spacing, although the actual display always depends on the browser's capabilities.

■ Word and letter spacing values may also be affected by your choice of alignment.

■ Use a value of normal to set the letter and word spacing to their defaults.

■ To avoid gaping holes in justified text, use a value of 0 for letter spacing.

■ Currently, Netscape only supports text-indent.

Controlling spacing

Setting white space properties

Normally browsers will simply ignore any extra spaces or returns that you type in an HTML document. You can set certain tags to behave like the PRE tag, taking into account all this extra white space.

To set white space properties:

1. Type **white-space:**.

2. Type **pre** to have browsers take all extra spaces and returns into account.

Or type **nowrap** to keep all elements on the same line, except where you've inserted BR tags.

Or type **normal** to treat white space as usual.

✔ Tip

■ The PRE tag is explained in more detail on page 53.

```
<!DOCTYPE HTML PUBLIC "-//W3C//DTD HTML 4
Transitional//
EN"><HTML><HEAD><TITLE>Setting white space
properties</TITLE>
<STYLE>
H1 {white-space:pre;
    letter-spacing:.5em;
    background:green;
    color:yellow;
    font: normal 20pt "Nueva Roman", "Lithos
Regular"}

P  {text-indent:8pt;
    font: 10pt/15pt "Myriad Roman",
"Verdana"}

P.intro {text-indent:0;font: italic bold}
P.intro EM {font-style:normal}
</STYLE>
</HEAD>
<BODY>
<P class=intro>On this page, you'll learn a
little about each of our cats, and how they
have created <EM>their own</EM> style.
<H1>        Llumi,
     the
  Huntress</H1>
<P>Llumi is our sweet, but <EM>ferocious</
```

Figure 14.21 *A value of pre for white space means that the browser will conserve all extra spaces and returns that you type in the HTML document—as if you had formatted the text with the PRE tag, but without the monospace font.*

Figure 14.22 *Netscape supports the white-space property while Explorer does not.*

Setting white space properties

```
code.html

<!DOCTYPE HTML PUBLIC "-//W3C//DTD HTML 4
Transitional//
EN"><HTML><HEAD><TITLE>Aligning text</
TITLE>
<STYLE>
H1 {text-align:center;
    letter-spacing:.5em;
    background:green;
    color:yellow;
    font: normal 20pt "Nueva Roman", "Lithos
Regular"}

P   {text-align:justify;
    text-indent:8pt;
    font: 10pt/15pt "Myriad Roman",
"Verdana"}

P.intro {text-indent:0;font: italic bold}
P.intro EM {font-style:normal}
</STYLE>
</HEAD>
<BODY>
<P class=intro>On this page, you'll learn a
little about each of our cats, and how they
have created <EM>their own</EM> style.
<H1>Llumi, the Huntress</H1>
<P>Llumi is our sweet, but <EM>ferocious</
EM> hunter-kitty. Maybe it's because she was
```

Figure 14.23 *Set the default alignment for each tag by using the text-align marker.*

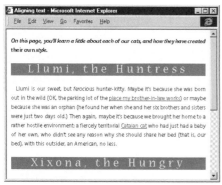

Figure 14.24 *Here I've centered the headlines and justified the P paragraphs.*

Aligning text

You can set up certain HTML tags to be always aligned to the right, left, center, or to be justified, as desired.

To align text:

1. Type **text-align:**.

2. Type **left** to align the text to the left.

Or type **right** to align the text to the right.

Or type **center** to center the text in the middle of the screen.

Or type **justify** to align the text on both the right and left.

✔ Tip

■ If you choose to justify the text, be aware that the word spacing and letter spacing may be adversely affected. For more information, consult *Controlling spacing* on page 243.

Aligning text

Underlining text

Style sheets let you underline text and get rid of underlining (say, with links). You can also add a line over the text or through it.

To underline text:

1. Type **text-decoration:**.

2. To underline text, type **underline**.

Or, for a line above the text, type **overline**.

Or, to strike out the text, type **line-through**.

To get rid of underlining, overlining, or strike through text:

1. Type **text-decoration:**.

2. Type **none**.

✔ Tips

■ You can eliminate the lines from tags that normally have lines (like U, STRIKE, DEL, INS, or A) or from tags that you've formatted earlier with lines with another style.

■ Most graphic designers hate underlining and consider it a relic from the typewriter age. Such designers might want to use the *none* option for text-decoration. However, the links will have to be marked in some other way (background color, perhaps) or nobody will know to click on them.

■ If you do get rid of the underlining below your links, make sure you also eliminate underlining under visited links, active links, and hovering *(see page 232)*.

```
                  code.html
<STYLE>
H1 {text-align:center;
    letter-spacing:.5em;
    background:green;
    color:yellow;
    font: normal 20pt "Nueva Roman", "Lithos
Regular"}

P  {text-align:justify;
    text-indent:8pt;
    font: 10pt/15pt "Myriad Roman",
"Verdana"}

P.intro {text-indent:0;font: italic bold}
P.intro EM {font-style:normal}

A:link {background:yellow;
        color:green;
        text-decoration:none}
A:visited {background:orange;
color:yellow;text-decoration:none}
A:hover {background:red;color:white;text-
decoration:none}
A:active
{background:white;color:black;text-
decoration:none}
</STYLE>
</HEAD>
```

Figure 14.25 *In this example, I've decided to highlight links with color and thus have chosen to eliminate the underlining.*

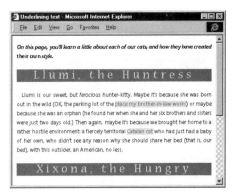

Figure 14.26 *If you really hate underlining, style sheets make it easy to get rid of it—and replace it with something that makes your links stand out without making them ugly.*

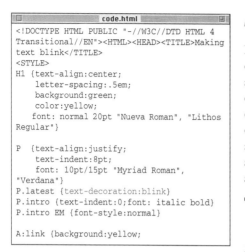

```
                code.html
<!DOCTYPE HTML PUBLIC "-//W3C//DTD HTML 4
Transitional//EN"><HTML><HEAD><TITLE>Making
text blink</TITLE>
<STYLE>
H1 {text-align:center;
    letter-spacing:.5em;
    background:green;
    color:yellow;
    font: normal 20pt "Nueva Roman", "Lithos
Regular"}

P  {text-align:justify;
    text-indent:8pt;
    font: 10pt/15pt "Myriad Roman",
"Verdana"}
P.latest {text-decoration:blink}
P.intro {text-indent:0;font: italic bold}
P.intro EM {font-style:normal}

A:link {background:yellow;
```

Figure 14.27 *I've created a new class of P tag and made it blink.*

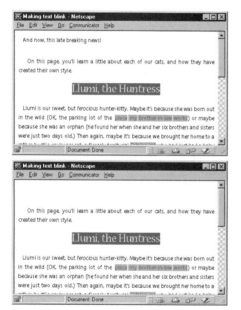

Figure 14.28 *Now you see it, now you don't. Remember though, that you'll never see text blink in Internet Explorer.*

Making text blink

Personally, I think the blink tag was one of the keys to Netscape's success. It added an element of animation to otherwise completely static pages. Nowadays, of course, you can add all sorts of moving objects to your pages, and blinking text is a bit out of fashion. But, just in case you still go for blinking, you might as well use style sheets to do it.

To make text blink:

1. Type **text-decoration:**.

2. Type **blink**.

✔ Tip

■ Although the blink option has been somewhat legitimized by its inclusion in the official specification for Cascading Style Sheets (level 2), Internet Explorer does not recognize the *blink* option. Perhaps the fact that it is a descendant of arch rival Netscape's wildly popular BLINK tag *(see page 55)* has something to do with it.

Changing the text case

You can define the text case for your style by using the text-transform marker. In this way, you can display the text either with initial capital letters, in all capital letters, in all small letters, or as it was typed.

To change the text case:

1. Type **text-transform:**.

2. Type **capitalize** to put the first character of each word in uppercase.

   Or type **uppercase** to change all the letters to uppercase.

   Or type **lowercase** to change all the letters to lowercase.

   Or type **none** to leave the text as is (possibly canceling out an inherited value).

Many fonts have a corresponding small caps variant that includes uppercase versions of the letters proportionately reduced to small caps size. You can call up the small caps variant with the font-variant marker.

To use a small caps font:

1. Type **font-variant:**.

2. Type **small-caps**.

✔ Tips

- To stop using the small caps variant for a dependent style, use **font-variant: none**.

- I've had trouble using text-transform in combination with a variety of font values *(see page 240)*. If you plan to use text-transform, I advise specifying the font values separately.

```
code.html
<!DOCTYPE HTML PUBLIC "-//W3C//DTD HTML 4
Transitional//
EN"><HTML><HEAD><TITLE>Changing the text
case</TITLE>
<STYLE>
H1 {text-transform:uppercase;
    text-align:center;
    letter-spacing:.5em;
    background:green;
    color:yellow;
    font-size: 20pt;
    font-weight: normal;
    font-family: "Nueva Roman", "Lithos
Regular"}

P  {text-align:justify;
    text-indent:8pt;
    font: 10pt/15pt "Myriad Roman",
"Verdana"}
P.intro {text-indent:0;font: italic bold}
```

Figure 14.29 *I've decided to display the headers in all uppercase letters.*

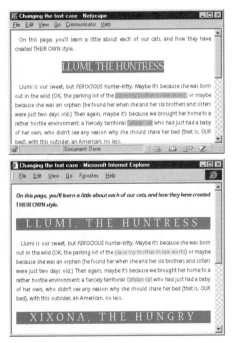

Figure 14.30 *You can see how important it is to test your pages with both browsers. Although both support the text-transform property, the fact that Netscape (above) doesn't support letter-spacing might make you decide not to display the headers in uppercase letters.*

Changing the text case (sidebar)

Layout with Styles

```
                  code.html
<!DOCTYPE HTML PUBLIC "-//W3C//DTD HTML 4
Transitional//EN">
<HTML><HEAD><TITLE>Displaying elements</
TITLE>
<LINK REL=stylesheet HREF="llumxixo.css">
</HEAD>
<BODY>
<P class=intro>On this page, you'll learn a
little about each of our cats, and how they
have created <EM>their own</EM> style.
<H1>Llumi, the Huntress</H1>
<IMG SRC="llumineu.gif" ALT="Llumi in the
snow">
<IMG SRC="llumgesp.gif" ALT="Llumi in the
jungle">
<P>Llumi is our sweet, but <EM>ferocious</
EM> hunter-kitty. Maybe it's because she was
born out in the wild (OK, the parking lot
```

Figure 15.1 *This is the document I use for most of this chapter. Notice that I have linked the page to an external style sheet that contains the formatting from Chapter 14, Formatting Text with Styles, in order to keep the focus on what we're doing* here.

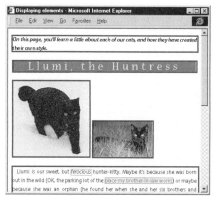

Figure 15.2 *Each element has its own box. Some boxes are block-level and automatically start a new paragraph (like the text paragraphs and header). Others are inline and do not start a new paragraph (like the EM element containing the word "ferocious").*

Every item that you create with cascading styles sheets is enclosed in an invisible box. You can control the size, color, and spacing of the box, as well as the way it flows with respect to other objects on the page.

An element's box may be *block-level* (thereby generating a new paragraph) or *inline* (not generating a new paragraph).

There are three special areas of the box that you can control. First, surrounding the contents is a space called the *padding*. You can control the padding's width. Around the padding is the *border*. The border can also be colored and thickened, and can also have texture. Around the border is a transparent space called the *margin*. Although you can't color the margin, you can change its width and height, thereby controlling the position of the elements on the page.

Some layout styles, especially percentage values, depend on an element's parent. A *parent* is the element that contains the current element. For example, the BODY might contain H1 and P tags, and thus is a parent to them. However, if the BODY is sectioned into DIV tags and the P tags are enclosed in one of the DIVs, then the DIV is the P's parent (and the BODY is the DIV's parent). Finally, the P tag might contain an EM, and, in turn, be its parent.

Offsetting elements within the natural flow

Each element has a natural location in a page's flow. Moving the element with respect to this original location is called *relative positioning*. The surrounding elements are not affected—at all.

To offset elements within the natural flow:

1. Type **position: relative;** (don't forget the semi-colon).

2. Type **top**, **right**, **bottom**, or **left**.

3. Type **:v;**, where *v* is the desired distance that you want to offset the element from its natural location, either as an absolute or relative value (10 pt, or 2em, for example).

4. Repeat steps 2 and 3 for each direction, as desired.

✔ Tips

■ The "relative" in *relative positioning* refers to the element's original position, not the surrounding elements **(Figure 15.5)**. You can't move an element with respect to other elements. Instead, you move it with respect to where it used to be. Yes, this is important!

■ The other elements are not affected by the offsets—they flow with respect to the *original* containing box of the element, and may even be overlapped.

■ To flow text around an image, the image must be positioned relatively.

■ Including **position: relative** enables offsets. Without it, the offsets may not work. (In IE4, they definitely won't.)

```
code.html
<STYLE>
IMG {position:relative;top:0;left:0}
IMG.off {position:relative;top:-40;left:30}
</STYLE>
</HEAD>
<BODY>
<P class=intro>On this page, you'll learn a
little about each of our cats, and how they
have created <EM>their own</EM> style.
<H1>Llumi, the Huntress</H1>
<IMG SRC="llumineu.gif" ALT="Llumi in the
snow">
<IMG SRC="llumgesp.gif" ALT="Llumi in the
jungle" CLASS=off>
<P>Llumi is our sweet, but <EM>ferocious</
EM> hunter-kitty. Maybe it's because she was
```

Figure 15.3 *The offsets for a relatively positioned element are with respect to where the element would have gone had you omitted the offsets. They don't have any relationship to other elements on the page.*

Figure 15.4 *All the images in this document are flowed relatively in their natural positions, like the left image. In addition, the* off *class image (the right one) is offset 40 pixels up (notice the baselines are not aligned) and 30 pixels to the right (notice the big space between the images).*

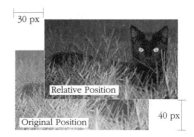

Figure 15.5 *An element is moved with respect to its natural position in the flow, not with respect to other elements.*

```
code.html
<!DOCTYPE HTML PUBLIC "-//W3C//DTD HTML 4
Transitional//
EN"><HTML><HEAD><TITLE>Positioning
elements</TITLE>
<LINK REL=stylesheet HREF="llumxixo.css">
<STYLE>
IMG {position:absolute; left:0; top:0}
</STYLE>
</HEAD>
<BODY>
<P class=intro>On this page, you'll learn a
little about each of our cats, and how they
have created <EM>their own</EM> style.
<H1>Llumi, the Huntress</H1>
<IMG SRC="llumineu.gif" ALT="Llumi in the
snow">
<IMG SRC="llumgesp.gif" ALT="Llumi in the
jungle">
<P>Llumi is our sweet, but <EM>ferocious</
EM> hunter-kitty. Maybe it's because she was
born out in the wild (OK, the parking lot of
```

Figure 15.6 *You can apply the* position *property to any element. In this example, with offsets of 0 for both top and left, the images will appear at the upper-left corner of the parent element, in this case the BODY.*

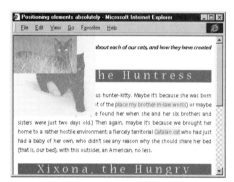

Figure 15.7 *Absolutely positioned elements are taken out of the flow—and as you can see here, the rest of the elements flow as if the images were not there, creating overlapped and covered elements. You can use offsets to determine the exact position of the elements—and avoid or control overlapping, as desired.*

Positioning elements absolutely

The elements in your Web page generally flow in the order in which they appear. That is, if the IMG tag comes before the P, the image appears before the paragraph. This is called the normal flow. You can take elements out of the normal flow—and position them *absolutely*—by specifying their precise position with respect to their parent element.

To absolutely position elements:

1. Type **position:absolute;** (don't forget the semi-colon).

2. Type **top**, **right**, **bottom**, or **left**.

3. Type **:v;**, where *v* is the desired distance that you want to offset the element from its parent element, either expressed as an absolute or relative value (10 pt, or 2em, for example), or as a percentage of the parent element.

4. Repeat steps 2 and 3 for each direction, as desired.

✔ Tips

■ For more information on parent elements, see page 249.

■ Because absolutely positioned elements are taken out of the flow of the document, they can overlap each other. (This is not always bad.)

■ If you don't specify an offset for an absolutely positioned item, the item appears in its natural position (after the header in this example), but does not affect the flow of subsequent items.

Positioning elements in 3D

Once you start fiddling with relative and absolute positioning, it's quite possible to find that your elements have overlapped. You can choose which element should be on top.

To position elements in 3D:

1. Type **z-index:**.

2. Type **n**, where *n* is a number that indicates the element's level in the stack of objects.

✔ Tips

■ The higher the z-index, the higher up the element will be in the stack.

■ You can use both positive and negative values for z-index.

```
┌────────────────── code.html ──────────────────┐
<HTML><HEAD><TITLE>Positioning elements in
3D</TITLE>
<LINK REL=stylesheet HREF="llumxixo.css">
<STYLE>
IMG {position:absolute}
</STYLE></HEAD><BODY>
<P class=intro>On this page, you'll learn a
little about each of our cats, and how they
have created <EM>their own</EM> style.
<H1>Llumi, the Huntress</H1>
<IMG SRC="llumineu.gif" ALT="Llumi in the
snow">
<IMG SRC="llumgesp.gif" ALT="Llumi in the
jungle" STYLE="z-index:-1">
<DIV STYLE="position:relative;left:200;
width:240">
<P>Llumi is our sweet, but <EM>ferocious</
EM> hunter-kitty. Maybe it's because she was
```

Figure 15.8 *By using a negative value for the second image's z-index, I ensure that it will be placed below other images. (I also adjusted the width of the DIV so that it wouldn't overlap the images in this example.)*

Figure 15.9 *The second image is underneath the first one and thus cannot be seen.*

Positioning elements in 3D

```
code.html
<!DOCTYPE HTML PUBLIC "-//W3C//DTD HTML 4
Transitional//
EN"><HTML><HEAD><TITLE>Positioning
elements</TITLE>
<LINK REL=stylesheet HREF="llumxixo.css">
<STYLE>
IMG {display:none}
</STYLE>
</HEAD>
<BODY>
<P class=intro>On this page, you'll learn a
little about each of our cats, and how they
have created <EM>their own</EM> style.
<H1>Llumi, the Huntress</H1>
<IMG SRC="llumineu.gif" ALT="Llumi in the
snow">
<IMG SRC="llumgesp.gif" ALT="Llumi in the
jungle">
<P>Llumi is our sweet, but <EM>ferocious</
EM> hunter-kitty. Maybe it's because she was
born out in the wild (OK, the parking lot
```

Figure 15.10 *Setting the IMG tag to display none means that any images inserted in the HTML document (like the two shown here) will be hidden from the visitor.*

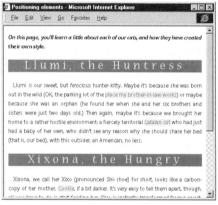

Figure 15.11 *The images are nowhere to be seen. Notice that the remaining elements flow right over the space where the images would have been displayed. It's as if the images were not part of the HTML document at all.*

Displaying and hiding elements

The display property is useful for hiding or revealing particular elements depending on the visitor's browser, language preference, or other criteria. You can also set elements to display as block-level or inline. Or you can display an element as a list item—even without the LI tag.

To specify how elements should be displayed:

1. Type **display:**.

2. Type **none** to hide the given elements.

Or type **block** to display the element as a block-level (thus starting a new paragraph).

Or type **inline** to display the element as inline (not starting a new paragraph).

Or type **list-item** to display the element as if you had used the LI tag *(see pages 125–131)*.

✔ Tips

■ If you use **display:none**, no trace remains of the hidden element in the browser window. There is no empty space.

■ The **display:none** definition, combined with scripts, is ideal for hiding elements that belong to one of several versions contained in the same HTML document.

Setting the height or width for an element

You can set the height and width for most elements, including images, form elements, and even blocks of text. If you have several elements on a page that are the same size, you can set their height and width simultaneously. This information helps browsers set aside the proper amount of space necessary and thus view the rest of the page—generally, the text—more quickly.

To set the height or width for an element:

1. Type **width:w**, where *w* is the width of the element, and can be expressed either as an absolute value or as a percentage of the window width.

2. Type **height:h**, where *h* is the height of the element, and can be expressed only as an absolute value.

✔ Tips

■ Using a percentage value for the width and height properties is a little tricky. If you are used to the WIDTH and HEIGHT attributes for the IMG tag, you might think 50% means half of the original image size. Not so. It means half of the width *of the browser window*—no matter what the original width of the image was.

■ You cannot set the WIDTH property for most text tags (like P and H1). To set the width of a block of text, enclose your P or H1 tags (or whatever) in DIV tags.

```
code.html
<HTML><HEAD><TITLE>Positioning elements
relatively</TITLE>
<LINK REL=stylesheet HREF="llumxixo.css">
<STYLE>
IMG {position:relative;top:0;left:0}
IMG.off {position:relative;top:-40;left:30}
</STYLE>
</HEAD>
<BODY>
<DIV STYLE="position:relative; left:100;
width:200">
<P class=intro>On this page, you'll learn a
little about each of our cats, and how they
have created <EM>their own</EM> style.</DIV>
<H1>Llumi, the Huntress</H1>
<IMG SRC="llumineu.gif" ALT="Llumi in the
snow">
<IMG SRC="llumgesp.gif" ALT="Llumi in the
jungle" CLASS=off>
<P>Llumi is our sweet, but <EM>ferocious</
```

Figure 15.12 *For this example, I've created a DIV section (since the width property doesn't work with P and H1 tags, among others).*

Figure 15.13 *The DIV section is restricted to a width of 200 pixels.*

```
┌──────────── code.html ────────────┐
<HTML><HEAD><TITLE>Setting the border</
TITLE>
<LINK REL=stylesheet HREF="llumxixo.css">
<STYLE>
IMG {position:relative;top:0;left:0;border:
thick double green}
IMG.off {position:relative;top:-40;left:30}
</STYLE>
</HEAD>
<BODY>
<DIV
STYLE="position:relative;left:100;width:200
">
<P class=intro>On this page, you'll learn a
little about each of our cats, and how they
have created <EM>their own</EM> style.</DIV>
<H1>Llumi, the Huntress</H1>
<IMG SRC="llumineu.gif" ALT="Llumi in the
snow">
<IMG SRC="llumgesp.gif" ALT="Llumi in the
```

Figure 15.14 *Here I've applied the border prop-*
erty to the IMG tag so that all images will have a
thick double green border.

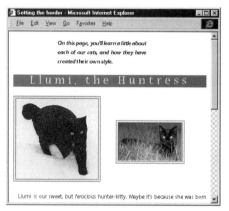

Figure 15.15 *Double borders are something you*
can not achieve with HTML tags alone.

Setting the border

You can create a border around an element and then set its thickness, style, and
color. If you've specified any padding *(see*
page 257) the border encloses both the
padding and the contents of the element.

To set the border:

1. Type **border**.

2. If desired, type **-top**, **-bottom**, **-left**, or
-right, (with no space after **border**) to
limit where the border should go.

3. If desired, type **thin**, **medium**, **thick**, or
an absolute value (like **4 px**) to deter-
mine the thickness of the border.
Medium is the default.

4. If desired, type **none**, **dotted**, **dashed**,
solid, **double**, **groove**, **ridge**, **inset**, or
outset to determine the border style.

5. If desired, type **color**, where *color* is
either one of the 16 color names or is
expressed as described on page 312.

✔ Tips

■ You can define any part of the border
individually. For example, you can
use **border-left-width:5** to set just the
width of just the left border. Or use
border-color:red to set just the color
of all four sides. The twenty different
properties are border-style (border-
top-style, border-right-style, etc.),
border-color (border-top-color, etc.),
border-width (border-top-width, etc.),
and border (border-top, etc.)

■ If you don't set the color of the border, the browser should use the color
you have specified for the element's
contents *(see page 241)*.

Adding padding around an element

Padding is just what it sounds like: extra space around the contents of an element but inside the border. Think of Santa Claus' belly—nicely padded, while being held in by his belt (the border). You can change the padding's thickness, but not its color or texture.

To add padding around an element:

1. Type **padding**.

2. If desired, type **-top**, **-bottom**, **-left**, or **-right**, (with no space after **padding**) to limit the padding to one side of the object.

3. Type **:x**, where *x* is the amount of desired space to be added, expressed in units or as a percentage of the parent element.

✔ Tips

■ There are several shortcuts available for setting the padding values. You can use **padding: t r b l** to set the top, right, bottom, and left values at once, in that order (with just a space separating each value). Or **padding: v h** to set the top and bottom values (v) equally and the right and left values (h) equally. Or type **padding: t h b** to set the top value (t), the left and right values to a single value (h), and then the bottom value (b). Or type **padding: a**, where *a* is the value for all sides.

■ The values may be expressed in absolute terms or as a percentage of the corresponding width in the parent element.

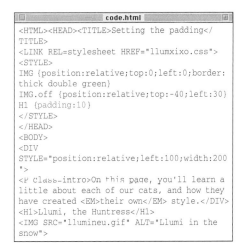

```
code.html
<HTML><HEAD><TITLE>Setting the padding</
TITLE>
<LINK REL=stylesheet HREF="llumxixo.css">
<STYLE>
IMG {position:relative;top:0;left:0;border:
thick double green}
IMG.off {position:relative;top:-40;left:30}
H1 {padding:10}
</STYLE>
</HEAD>
<BODY>
<DIV
STYLE="position:relative;left:100;width:200
">
<P class-intro>On this page, you'll learn a
little about each of our cats, and how they
have created <EM>their own</EM> style.</DIV>
<H1>Llumi, the Huntress</H1>
<IMG SRC="llumineu.gif" ALT="Llumi in the
snow">
```

Figure 15.16 *I've added some padding to the header to create a larger background around the text.*

Figure 15.17 *Ten pixels of padding have been added all around the text in the header.*

```
                  code.html
<HTML><HEAD><TITLE>Setting the margin</
TITLE>
<LINK REL=stylesheet HREF="llumxixo.css">
<STYLE>
IMG {position:relative;top:0;left:0;border:
thick double green}
IMG.off {position:relative;top:-30;left:30}
H1 {padding:10;margin:30}
</STYLE>
</HEAD>
<BODY>
<DIV
STYLE="position:relative;left:100;width:200
">
<P class=intro>On this page, you'll learn a
little about each of our cats, and how they
have created <EM>their own</EM> style.</DIV>
<H1>Llumi, the Huntress</H1>
<IMG SRC="llumineu.gif" ALT="Llumi in the
snow">
```

Figure 15.18 *To indent an element on all sides, increase the size of its margins.*

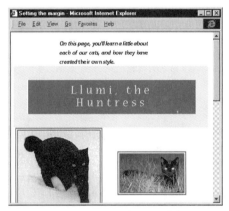

Figure 15.19 *Increasing the size of the margin (the transparent space around the header) means there isn't enough room to fit the header on one line.*

Setting the margins around an element

The margin is the amount of transparent space between one element and the next, in addition to and outside of any padding *(see page 256)* or border *(see page 255)* around the element.

To set an element's margins:

1. Type **margin**.

2. If desired, type **-top**, **-bottom**, **-left**, or **-right**, (with no space after **margin**) to limit where space should be added.

3. Type **:x**, where *x* is the amount of desired space to be added, expressed in units or as a percentage of the width of the corresponding value of the parent element.

✔ Tips

■ You can also use **margin: t r b l** to set the top, right, bottom, and left values at once, in that order (with just a space separating each value). Or **margin: v h** to set the top and bottom values (v) equally and the right and left values (h) equally. Or type **margin: t h b** to set the top value (t), the left and right values to a single value (h), and then the bottom value (b). Last but not least, you can type **margin: a**, where *a* is the value to be used for all sides.

■ The values may be expressed in absolute terms or as a percentage of the corresponding width in the parent element.

■ Margin values for absolutely positioned boxes are specified with the offset properties—top, bottom, right, and left *(see page 251)*.

Aligning elements vertically

If you have elements (like images) on your page that you would like aligned in the same way, you can use the vertical-align property to set the tag, or a class of the tag, accordingly.

To position text:

1. Type **vertical-align:**

2. Type **baseline** to align the element's baseline with the parent's baseline.

Or type **middle** to align the middle of the element with the middle of the parent.

Or type **sub** to position the element as a subscript of the parent.

Or type **super** to position the element as a superscript of the parent.

Or type **text-top** to align the top of the element with the top of the parent.

Or type **text-bottom** to align the bottom of the element with the bottom of the parent.

Or type **top** to align the top of the element with the top of the tallest element on the line.

Or type **bottom** to align the bottom of the element to the bottom of the lowest element on the line.

Or type a percentage of the line height of the element, which may be positive or negative.

```
code.html
<HTML><HEAD><TITLE>Aligning elements
vertically</TITLE>
<LINK REL=stylesheet HREF="llumxixo.css">
<STYLE>
IMG {position:relative;top:0;left:0;border:
thick double green;vertical-align:top}
IMG.off {position:relative;left:30}
H1 {padding:10;margin:30}
</STYLE></HEAD><BODY>
<DIV STYLE="position:relative;left:100;
width:200">
<P class=intro>On this page, you'll learn a
little about each of our cats, and how they
have created <EM>their own</EM> style.</DIV>
<H1>Llumi, the Huntress</H1>
<IMG SRC="llumineu.gif" ALT="Llumi in the
snow">
<IMG SRC="llumgesp.gif" ALT="Llumi in the
jungle" CLASS=off>
<P>Llumi is our sweet, but <EM>ferocious</
```

Figure 15.20 *I've eliminated the top offset from the off class images in order to show the full effect of vertically aligning all the images on this page.*

Figure 15.21 *The images are aligned with respect to their top edges.*

```
code.html
<STYLE>
IMG {position:relative;top:0;left:0;
border: thick double green; vertical-
align:middle; float:left}
IMG.right {float:right}
H1 {padding:10;margin:30}
</STYLE></HEAD><BODY>
<DIV STYLE="position:relative;left:100;
width:200">
<P class=intro>On this page, you'll learn a
little about each of our cats, and how they
have created <EM>their own</EM> style.</DIV>
<H1>Llumi, the Huntress</H1>
<IMG SRC="llumineu.gif" ALT="Llumi in the
snow">
<P>Llumi is our sweet, but <EM>ferocious</
EM> hunter-kitty. Maybe it's because she was
born out in the wild (OK, the parking lot of
the <A HREF="commonwealth.htm">place my
brother-in-law works</A>) or maybe because
she was an orphan (he found her when she and
her six brothers and sisters were just two
days old.) Then again, maybe it's because we
brought her home to a rather hostile
environment:
<IMG SRC="llumgesp.gif" ALT="Llumi in the
jungle" CLASS=right>
a fiercely territorial <A
HREF="cookie.html">Catalan cat</A> who
```

Figure 15.22 *Please note that I moved the second image (llumgesp.gif) lower down on the page for aesthetic reasons.*

Figure 15.23 *By default, images will allow text to flow to the right. Images that belong to the "right" class, like the image of Llumi in the grass, will let text flow to the left.*

Wrapping text around elements

You can define your images (or other elements) so that text always wraps around them to the left or right, down both sides, or never at all.

To wrap text around elements:

1. Type **float:**.

2. Type **left** if you want the element on the left and the text to flow to its right.

Or type **right** if you want the element on the right and the text to flow to its left.

✔ Tips

■ Remember, the direction you choose applies to the element you're floating, not to the text that flows around it. When you **float: left**, the text flows to the right, and vice-versa.

■ The trick to making text flow between elements is to always put the image directly before the text that should flow next to it.

■ For more information about flowing text between images, consult *Wrapping text around images* on page 83. The CSS properties work the same way as the regular HTML tags.

Stopping text wrap

When you flow text around images with HTML tags, you can create a line break that effectively stops text from flowing. With style sheets you can mark a particular tag so that other elements (like text) can not flow around it.

To stop text wrap:

1. Type **clear:**.

2. Type **left** to stop the flow until the left side is clear of all elements.

Or type **right** to stop the flow until the right side is clear of elements.

Or type **both** to stop the flow until both sides are clear.

Or type **none** to continue the flow.

✔ Tips

■ If you're like me and can never correctly answer 50-50 Trivial Pursuit questions like "Which hand is God holding out to Adam in the Sistine Chapel, his right or his left?", then perhaps this clarification will be useful: When you use **clear: right**, you mean you want to stop text flow *until the right is clear*. Confusingly, the result is that the left *looks clear*. Look at Figure 15.25 again. That big space on the left next to the second image only appears because the text must stop flowing until the right is clear. At that point, the text continues to flow again.

■ The use of the clear style is analogous to the BR tag with the CLEAR attribute *(see page 85)*.

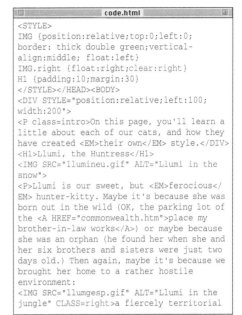

```
                    code.html
<STYLE>
IMG {position:relative;top:0;left:0;
border: thick double green;vertical-
align:middle; float:left}
IMG.right {float:right;clear:right}
H1 {padding:10;margin:30}
</STYLE></HEAD><BODY>
<DIV STYLE="position:relative;left:100;
width:200">
<P class=intro>On this page, you'll learn a
little about each of our cats, and how they
have created <EM>their own</EM> style.</DIV>
<H1>Llumi, the Huntress</H1>
<IMG SRC="llumineu.gif" ALT="Llumi in the
snow">
<P>Llumi is our sweet, but <EM>ferocious</
EM> hunter-kitty. Maybe it's because she was
born out in the wild (OK, the parking lot of
the <A HREF="commonwealth.htm">place my
brother-in-law works</A>) or maybe because
she was an orphan (he found her when she and
her six brothers and sisters were just two
days old.) Then again, maybe it's because we
brought her home to a rather hostile
environment:
<IMG SRC="llumgesp.gif" ALT="Llumi in the
jungle" CLASS=right>a fiercely territorial
```

Figure 15.24 *To keep text from flowing to the left of the second image, I've added the clear:right definition to the images that belong to the right class.*

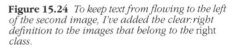

Figure 15.25 *When you clear right, you actually generate an empty (clear) space to the left, since the flow must stop until the right side is clear.*

Stopping text wrap

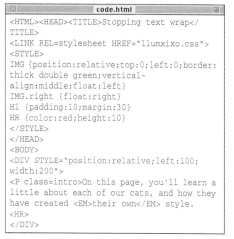

```
┌─────────────────────────────────────┐
│▦▦▦▦▦▦▦▦  code.html  ▦▦▦▦▦▦▦▦▦▦▦│
├─────────────────────────────────────┤
│<HTML><HEAD><TITLE>Stopping text wrap</│
│TITLE>                                │
│<LINK REL=stylesheet HREF="llumxixo.css">│
│<STYLE>                               │
│IMG {position:relative;top:0;left:0;border:│
│thick double green;vertical-          │
│align:middle;float:left}              │
│IMG.right {float:right}               │
│H1 {padding:10;margin:30}             │
│HR {color:red;height:10}              │
│</STYLE>                              │
│</HEAD>                               │
│<BODY>                                │
│<DIV STYLE="position:relative;left:100;│
│width:200">                           │
│<P class=intro>On this page, you'll learn a│
│little about each of our cats, and how they│
│have created <EM>their own</EM> style.│
│<HR>                                  │
│</DIV>                                │
└─────────────────────────────────────┘
```

Figure 15.26 *You can add color to horizontal lines (as shown here), or to any other element—except images.*

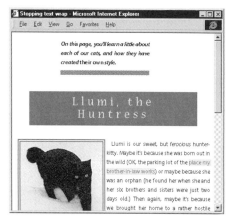

Figure 15.27 *The horizontal line shown below the first paragraph is red. Don't believe me? Check out the Web site (see page 21). Notice that the line has the same width as the paragraph of text that it follows. That's because it belongs to the DIV which we limited to 200 pixels wide (see page 254).*

Changing the foreground color

You can change the color of any element, including horizontal lines, form elements, and tables.

To change the foreground color:

1. Type **color:**.

2. Type **colorname**, where *colorname* is one of the 16 predefined colors.

Or type **#rrggbb**, where *rrggbb* is the hexadecimal representation of the desired color.

Or type **rgb(r, g, b)**, where *r*, *g*, and *b* are integers from 0-255 that specify the amount of red, green, or blue, respectively, in the desired color.

Or type **rgb(r%, g%, b%)**, where *r*, *g*, and *b* specify the percentage of red, green, and blue, respectively, in the desired color.

✔ Tips

■ If you type a value for r, g, or b higher than 255 it will be replaced with 255. Similarly a percentage higher than 100% will be replaced with 100%.

■ You can also use the color property to change the color of text. For more information, consult *Setting the text color* on page 241.

■ Changing the foreground color of an image doesn't have any effect. (You'll have to do that in an image editing program.) You can, however, change the background color (that is, what will appear through transparent areas). For more information, consult *Changing the background* on page 262.

Changing the background

The background refers not to the background of the entire page, but to the background of a particular tag. In other words, you can change the background of any element—including images, form elements, and tables.

To change the background color or image:

1. Type **background:**.

2. Type **transparent** or **color**, where *color* is a color name or hex color.

3. If desired, type **url(image.gif)**, to use an image for the background.

If desired, type **repeat** to tile the image both horizontally and vertically, **repeat-x** to tile the image only horizontally, **repeat-y** to tile the image only vertically or **no-repeat** to not tile the image.

If desired, type **fixed** or **scroll** to determine whether the background should scroll along with the canvas.

If desired, type **x y** to set the position of the background image, where *x* and *y* can be expressed as a percentage or as an absolute distance. Or use values of *top*, *center*, or *bottom* for *x* and *left*, *center*, and *right* for *y*.

✔ Tips

- Set the background for the BODY tag to create a background for the entire page.

- If you specify both a color and a URL for the background, the color will be used until the URL is loaded, and will be seen through any transparent portions of the background image.

```
code.html
<!DOCTYPE HTML PUBLIC "-//W3C//DTD HTML 4
Transitional//
EN"><HTML><HEAD><TITLE>Changing the
background</TITLE>
<LINK REL=stylesheet HREF="llumxixo.css">
<STYLE>
IMG {position:relative;top:0;left:0;
border: thick double green; vertical-
align:middle;float:left}
IMG.right {float:right}
H1 {padding:10;margin:30}
HR {color:red;height:10}
BODY {background:url(llumgesp.gif)}
P {background:white;padding:5}
</STYLE></HEAD><BODY>
<DIV STYLE="position:relative;left:100;
width:200">
<P class=intro>On this page, you'll learn a
little about each of our cats, and how they
have created <EM>their own</EM> style.
```

Figure 15.28 *I've added the background property to the BODY tag to create a background for the entire page. To keep the text legible, I added a white background to all the P tags (which will be added to and may override any P definitions from the external style sheet).*

Figure 15.29 *I'm continually amazed at how ugly I can make a page look by simply adding a background. Note that since the background image is smaller than the browser window, the image is automatically tiled to fill the window. Oh joy.*

```
                  code.html
<!DOCTYPE HTML PUBLIC "-//W3C//DTD HTML 4
Transitional//
EN"><HTML><HEAD><TITLE>Controlling
overflow</TITLE>
<LINK REL=stylesheet HREF="llumxixo.css">
<STYLE>
IMG {position:relative;top:0;left:0;border:
thick double green;vertical-
align:middle;float:left}
IMG.right {float:right}
H1 {padding:10;margin:30}
HR {color:red;height:10}
BODY {background:url(llumgesp.gif)}
P {background:white;padding:5}
</STYLE></HEAD><BODY>
<DIV STYLE="position:relative;left:100;
width:100; height:100;overflow:scroll">
<P class=intro>On this page, you'll learn a
little about each of our cats, and how they
have created <EM>their own</EM> style.
```

Figure 15.30 *After limiting the height to 100 pixels, I used the overflow property to keep the text block the desired size while enabling visitors to access the hidden contents with scroll bars.*

Figure 15.31 *Scroll bars appear both below and to the right of the DIV section.*

Figure 15.32 *If you set overflow to hidden, no scroll bars appear, and the extra contents can not be viewed by your visitors.*

Determining where overflow should go

If you make an element's box smaller than its contents with the height and width properties *(see page 254)*, the excess content has to go somewhere. You can decide where it should go with the overflow property.

To determine where overflow should go:

1. Type **overflow:**.

2. Type **visible** to expand the element box so that its contents fit. This is the default option.

   Or type **hidden** to hide any contents that don't fit in the element box.

   Or type **scroll** to add scroll bars to the element so that the visitor can access the overflow if they so desire.

✔ **Tip**

■ If you don't specify the overflow property, excess content will flow below (but not to the right of) the element's box. This is one of the reasons that assigning a height to text sometimes seems like it has no effect. (The other reason is that the height and width properties have no effect on many text tags, like P and H1. See page 254 for details.)

Clipping an element

You can create a window that only reveals a particular section of the element. Currently, the window must be a rectangle, but the idea is that other shapes will be available in future revisions of CSS.

To clip an element:

1. Type **clip: rect(**.

2. Type **t r b l**, where *t*, *r*, *b*, and *l* are the top, right, bottom, and left coordinates of the rectangular portion of the element that you want to display **(Figure 15.35)**.

3. Type the final **)**.

✔ Tips

■ Presently, an element has to be positioned absolutely *(see page 251)* before you can clip it.

■ Remember not to add commas between the offset values.

■ The offset values can be absolute (3px) or relative (3em).

■ Clipping does not just affect the element's content. It also hides padding and borders.

```
                    code.html
<HTML><HEAD><TITLE>Clipping elements</
TITLE>
<LINK REL=stylesheet HREF="llumxixo.css">
<STYLE>
IMG {position:relative;top:0;left:0;border:
thick double green;vertical-
align:middle;float:left}
IMG.right {float:right}
IMG.clip
{position:absolute;top:150;clip:rect(0 180
130 40)}
H1 {padding:10;margin:30}
HR {color:red;height:10}
BODY {background:url(llumgesp.gif)}
P {background:white;padding:5}
</STYLE></HEAD><BODY>
<DIV STYLE="position:absolute;left:100;
width:200;clip:rect(0 50 100 0)">
<P class=intro>On this page, you'll learn a
little about each of our cats, and how they
```

Figure 15.33 *Here are two examples of clipping. The clipping information from the image means we will start at the very top (0) and go down 130 pixels. Then we'll start at pixel 40 and go across to the right until pixel 180.*

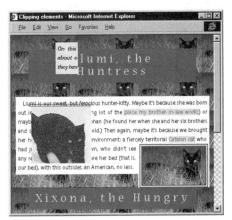

Figure 15.34 *There must be a useful way to implement clipping, but I haven't found it yet. Certainly hiding bits of text and images isn't it.*

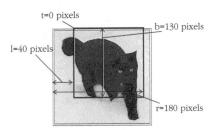

Figure 15.35 *The values for left and top are the parts you clip out. The right and bottom values minus the left and top determine what remains.*

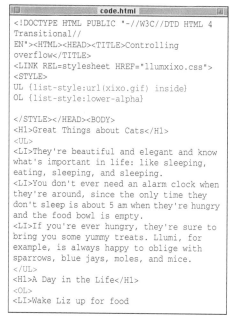

```
code.html
<!DOCTYPE HTML PUBLIC "-//W3C//DTD HTML 4
Transitional//
EN"><HTML><HEAD><TITLE>Controlling
overflow</TITLE>
<LINK REL=stylesheet HREF="llumxixo.css">
<STYLE>
UL {list-style:url(xixo.gif) inside}
OL {list-style:lower-alpha}

</STYLE></HEAD><BODY>
<H1>Great Things about Cats</H1>
<UL>
<LI>They're beautiful and elegant and know
what's important in life: like sleeping,
eating, sleeping, and sleeping.
<LI>You don't ever need an alarm clock when
they're around, since the only time they
don't sleep is about 5 am when they're hungry
and the food bowl is empty.
<LI>If you're ever hungry, they're sure to
bring you some yummy treats. Llumi, for
example, is always happy to oblige with
sparrows, blue jays, moles, and mice.
</UL>
<H1>A Day in the Life</H1>
<OL>
<LI>Wake Liz up for food
```

Figure 15.36 *Here I've set the bullet for unordered lists to an image (yes, it's a cat). I've also decided to number ordered lists with lowercase letters.*

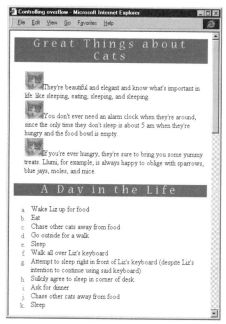

Figure 15.37 *Being able to choose your own bullets for unordered lists is so cool!*

Setting list properties

There are several bullet styles for unordered lists, and several number styles for numbered lists. You can set these styles globally with the list-style marker.

To set list properties:

1. Type **list-style:**.

2. If desired, to set the list item marker to a solid, round circle, type **disc**.

   Or type **circle** to use an empty, round circle.

   Or type **square** to use a solid square.

   Or type **decimal** to use arabic numerals (1, 2, 3, etc.).

   Or type **lower-alpha** to use lowercase letters (a, b,c, etc.).

   Or type **upper-alpha** to use uppercase letters (A, B, C, etc.).

   Or type **lower-roman** to use lowercase Roman numerals (i, ii, iii, etc.).

   Or type **upper-roman** to use uppercase Roman numerals (I, II, III, etc.).

   Or type **url(image.gif)**, where *image.gif* is the URL of the image that you want to use as a marker for your lists.

3. If desired, type **outside** to hang the marker to the left of the list items. Type **inside** to align the marker flush left together with all the other lines in the list item paragraph.

✔ Tip

■ The **outside** value won't create hanging indents properly if you use big images for bullets like I did in Figure 15.37. Until it does, **inside** looks better.

Specifying page breaks

At some point, your visitors may decide to print your Web page. Most browsers will automatically adjust the contents on a page in order to best fit the paper size the visitor has chosen in the Page Setup dialog box. With CSS2 you can specify exactly where you want the page to break when your visitor goes to print it out.

To specify a page break after a given tag:

Type **page-break-after:always**.

To specify a page break before a given tag:

Type **page-break-before:always**.

To remove page breaks:

Type **page-break-after:auto** or **page-break-before:auto**.

```
code.html
<!DOCTYPE HTML PUBLIC "-//W3C//DTD HTML 4
Transitional//
EN"><HTML><HEAD><TITLE>Setting page
breaks</TITLE>
<LINK REL=stylesheet HREF="llumxixo.css">
<STYLE>
UL {list-style:url(xixo.gif) inside}
OL {list-style:lower-alpha}
H1 {page-break-before:always}

</STYLE>
</HEAD>
<BODY>
<H1 STYLE="page-break-before:auto">Great
Things about Cats</H1>
<UL>
<LI>They're beautiful and elegant and know
what's important in life: like sleeping,
eating, sleeping, and sleeping.
```

Figure 15.38 *To make each list print on a separate page, I've added a page break to the header tag. To avoid creating an empty page before the first header, I've used a local style to override the page break in the first header.*

Specifying page breaks

Scripts 16

Scripts are little programs that add interactivity to your page. You can write simple scripts to add an alert box or a bit of text to your page, or more complicated scripts that load particular pages according to your visitor's browser or change a frame's background color depending on where they point the mouse. Because scripts are perfect for moving elements around on a page, they are the backbone of dynamic HTML, also known as DHTML.

Most scripts are written in JavaScript, which was developed by Netscape Communications (the same folks who created Netscape Navigator and Netscape Communicator). That's because JavaScript is the scripting language that is supported by most browsers, including Communicator and Explorer. VBScript, developed by Microsoft, currently works only with Explorer for Windows.

Of course, there are entire books written about JavaScript and VBScript—and some very fine ones indeed, including *Java-Script for the World Wide Web: Visual QuickStart Guide, 2nd Edition* by Dori Smith and Tom Negrino, and *VBScript for the World Wide Web* by Paul Thurrott. In this chapter, rather than talking about how to write scripts, I'll stick to explaining how to insert those scripts, once created, into your HTML documents.

Adding an "automatic" script

There are two kinds of scripts—those that are executed without the visitor having to do anything and those that react to something the visitor has done. The first group might be called "automatic scripts" and are executed by the browser when the page is loaded. You can have as many automatic scripts as you like on a page. They will run in the order they appear. (The second group, "triggered scripts", is discussed on page 270.)

To add an automatic script:

1. In your HTML document, type **<SCRIPT**.

2. Type **TYPE="content_type"**, where *content_type* notes the script's format and language. Use **text/javascript**, **text/vbscript**, **text/tcl**, etc.

3. Type **>**.

4. Type the content of the script.

5. Type **</SCRIPT>**.

✔ Tips

■ The LANGUAGE attribute, formerly used to indicate the script's language, has been deprecated in HTML 4 in favor of TYPE. If you have trouble with older browsers, you might try using both attributes.

■ Because some older browsers don't understand the SCRIPT tag, they simply ignore it and then display whatever is between the <SCRIPT> and </SCRIPT> tags as if it were regular text. Ugh! In order to hide scripts from these errant browsers, consult *Hiding scripts from older browsers* on page 273. Also, check out the tip at the bottom of page 269.

Figure 16.1 *A script may appear anywhere in your HTML document, however, where it appears determines when it will be executed.*

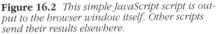

Figure 16.2 *This simple JavaScript script is output to the browser window itself. Other scripts send their results elsewhere.*

Adding an "automatic" script

```
                   script.txt
document.write("Visca Catalunya!")
```

Figure 16.3 *Here I've created an independent text file with the same script as in Figure 16.1. I can reference this external script from inside any HTML document.*

```
                   code.html
<HTML><HEAD>
<TITLE>Simple Scripts</TITLE>
</HEAD>
<BODY>

<SCRIPT TYPE="text/javascript"
SRC="extscript.txt">
</SCRIPT>

<P>Here's the rest of the page.
</BODY></HTML>
```

Figure 16.4 *The SRC attribute not only references the script, it also automatically hides it from browsers that don't recognize the SCRIPT tag.*

Figure 16.5 *External scripts are no different from internal ones. But they are often much more convenient.*

Calling an external automatic script

If you use a script in several different Web pages, you'll save time (and avoid typos) by linking the script to each page instead of typing it in each.

To call an external automatic script:

1. Type **<SCRIPT**.

2. Type **TYPE="content_type"**, where *content_type* notes the script's format and language. Use **text/javascript**, **text/vbscript**, **text/tcl**, etc.

3. Type **SRC="script.url"**, where *script.url* is the location on the server of the external script.

4. If desired, type **CHARSET=code**, where *code* is the official name for the set of characters used in the external script.

5. Type **>**.

6. Type **</SCRIPT>**.

✔ Tips

- Using external scripts is a great way to keep older browsers from displaying your scripts as text. Since they don't understand the SCRIPT tag, they ignore it (and the SRC attribute) completely. Use NOSCRIPT to give those visitors using the older browsers an idea of what they're missing *(see page 274)*.

- Explorer 4 for Macintosh does not yet support external scripts. Explorer 4 for Windows has no problem with them.

Triggering a script

Sometimes you won't want a script to run until the visitor does something to trigger it. For example, perhaps you want to run a script when the visitor mouses over a particular picture or link, or when a page is loaded. These actions—mousing over or loading a page—are called *intrinsic events*. There are currently 18 predefined intrinsic events. You use them as triggers to determine when a script will run.

To trigger a script:

1. Create the HTML tag that the intrinsic event depends on **(Figure 16.16)**.

2. Within the tag created in step 1, type **EVENT**, where *event* is an intrinsic event as defined below **(Fig. 16.17)**. Unless otherwise noted, most events can be used with most HTML tags.

ONLOAD occurs when a browser loads a page or frameset. **ONUNLOAD** occurs when it unloads. They can be used in the BODY or FRAMESET tags.

ONCLICK occurs when the visitor clicks an element. **ONDBLCLICK** occurs when they double click it.

ONMOUSEDOWN occurs when the visitor points at an HTML element and presses the mouse button down. **ONMOUSEUP** occurs when they let go.

ONMOUSEOVER occurs when the visitor simply points at an element. **ONMOUSEMOVE** occurs when the visitor moves the pointer that is over an element. **ONMOUSEOUT** occurs when the visitor moves the pointer away from the element.

ONSELECT occurs when the visitor selects some text in a form element.

```
code.html
<HTML>
<HEAD>
<TITLE>Triggering scripts</TITLE>
</HEAD>
<BODY>

What <A HREF="time.html">time</A> is it?

<P>Here's the rest of the page.
</BODY>
</HTML>
```

Figure 16.6 *First, create the HTML tag that the intrinsic event depends on. In this case, I want the script to occur when a visitor clicks the link. Therefore, I have to start with the link tag.*

```
code.html
<HTML>
<HEAD>
<TITLE>Triggering scripts</TITLE>
</HEAD>
<BODY>

What <A HREF="time.html"
ONCLICK="alert('Today is '+ Date())">time</A> is it?

<P>Here's the rest of the page.
</BODY>
</HTML>
```

Figure 16.7 *The event name and the script itself go right inside the HTML tag. Make sure to enclose the script in double quotation marks.*

Figure 16.8 *A triggered script doesn't run until the visitor completes the required action. In this case, they have to click the link.*

Figure 16.9 *Once the visitor clicks the link, the script runs. In this case, an alert appears, giving the current date and time.*

ONFOCUS occurs when the visitor selects or tabs to an element. **ONBLUR** occurs when the visitor leaves an element that was "in focus".

ONKEYPRESS occurs when the visitor types any character in a form element. **ONKEYDOWN** occurs even before the visitor lets go of the key and **ONKEYUP** waits until the visitor lets go of the key. As you might imagine, these only work with form elements that you can type in.

ONSUBMIT occurs when the visitor clicks the submit button in a form *(see page 192)*. **ONRESET** occurs when the visitor resets the form *(see page 194)*.

ONCHANGE occurs when the visitor has changed the form element's value and has left that element (by tabbing out or selecting another).

3. Next, type **="script"**, where *script* is the actual script that should run when the event occurs.

✔ Tips

- ■ If your script requires quotation marks, use single quotation marks so that they're not confused with the quotation marks that enclose the entire script (in step 3).

- ■ For a complete listing of which intrinsic events work with which HTML tags, consult the table on page 322.

Triggering a script

Creating a button that executes a script

HTML 4 offers a new kind of button, not restricted to a FORM element *(see page 182)* that you can add to your Web page. You can associate the button with a script to give your visitor full control over when the script should be executed.

To create a button that executes a script:

1. Type **<BUTTON TYPE="button"**.

2. Type **NAME="name"**, where *name* is the identifier for the button.

3. Type **ONCLICK="script"**, where *script* is the code (usually JavaScript) that will run when the visitor clicks the button.

4. If desired, type **STYLE="font: 14pt Lithos Regular; background:red"** (or whatever) to change the appearance of the text on the button.

5. Type **>**.

6. If desired, type the text that should appear on the button.

7. Type **</BUTTON>**.

✔ Tips

■ You can use other intrinsic events with buttons, but ONCLICK makes the most sense.

■ You can also add images to buttons. Simply insert the image between the opening and closing BUTTON tags (that is, after step 5 or 6).

■ You can also use buttons with forms *(see pages 193 and 195)*.

```
code.html
<HTML><HEAD>
<TITLE>Associating scripts with a button
</TITLE></HEAD>
<BODY>

<BUTTON NAME="Check Time"
ONCLICK="alert('Today is '+ Date())"
STYLE="font: 14pt Lithos
Regular;background:white;color:red">What
time is it?</BUTTON>
</BODY>
</HTML>
```

Figure 16.10 *Notice that the script is the same as the one used in the example in Figure 16.7. The style information here is optional, but it does make the button stand out. I also could have added an image.*

Figure 16.11 *Although the BUTTON tag is a standard part of HTML 4, only Explorer 4 for Windows currently supports it (with or without scripts).*

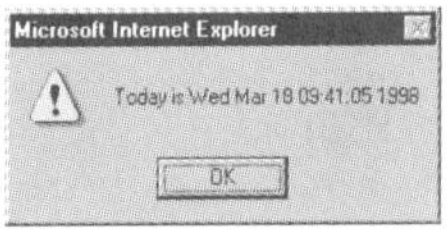

Figure 16.12 *A click on the button executes the script, as shown here.*

Figure 16.13 *This is Mosaic 1. Because it doesn't understand the SCRIPT tag, it ignores it and prints out the script as if it were regular text. Ugly!*

```
                  code.html
<HTML><HEAD><TITLE>Hiding scripts from old
browsers</TITLE>

<SCRIPT TYPE="text/javascript">
<!--
myMsg = "This is a scrolling message. It'll
keep going around the status area until you
leave this window."
i=0

function scrollMsg() {
  frontPart = myMsg.substring(i,myMsg.length)
  backPart = myMsg.substring(0,i)
  window.status=frontPart + backPart
  if (i < myMsg.length) {
      i++
      }
      else {
      i=0
      }
      setTimeout("scrollMsg()",50)
      }
// -->
</SCRIPT>
</HEAD>
<BODY onLoad="scrollMsg()">
<P>Here's the rest of the page.
</BODY></HTML>
```

Figure 16.14 *This JavaScript script comes from Dori Smith and Tom Negrino's* JavaScript for the World Wide Web: Visual QuickStart Guide.

Figure 16.15 *By commenting out the script, it is hidden from old browsers like this one. (Hey, it may not handle scripts, but this old version of Mosaic displays normal pages without trouble and runs on less than 1Mb of RAM.)*

Hiding scripts from older browsers

Older browsers don't always understand the SCRIPT tag. If they don't, they'll just ignore it and display your script as if it were part of the body of the HTML document. To keep that from happening, it's a good idea to use commenting to hide scripts from older browsers.

To hide scripts from older browsers:

1. After the initial SCRIPT tag, type **<!--**.

2. Write the script as usual.

3. Right before the final SCRIPT tag, type your scripting language's comments symbol. For JavaScript, type **//**. For VBScript, type **'** (a single quotation mark). For TCL, type **#**.

4. If desired, add text to remind yourself why you're typing all these funny characters. Something like **end comments to hide scripts from old browsers** will work just fine.

5. Type **-->**.

✔ Tips

■ The code in step 1 and in step 5 is for hiding the script from the browsers. The code in step 3 is for keeping the final --> from being processed as part of the script, and thus must be specific to the particular scripting language you're using.

■ I have to admit I had a hard time finding a browser old enough not to understand scripts. Hiding scripts is recommended, but I'm not sure it's essential.

Adding alternate information

If you give your visitors access to information through scripts, you may want to provide an alternate method of getting that data if your visitor uses a browser that can't run the scripts.

To add alternate information for older browsers:

1. Type **<NOSCRIPT>**.

2. Type the alternate information.

3. Type **</NOSCRIPT>**.

✔ Tips

■ If a browser doesn't understand the SCRIPT tag, what hope is there that it will understand NOSCRIPT? Actually it won't. It will completely ignore it and treat its contents as regular text—which is what you want. Only the browsers that understand SCRIPT (and thus can run the script) will understand NOSCRIPT as well. And they'll *ignore* the contents of the NOSCRIPT tag—which is also what you want. Clever, indeed.

■ The contents of the NOSCRIPT tag are only displayed if the browser doesn't support scripting or if the visitor has turned off scripting in the Preferences dialog box. But, the NOSCRIPT tag will not help if the browser doesn't support the scripting language or if there is a problem with the script.

```
<HTML><HEAD><TITLE>Hiding scripts from old
browsers</TITLE>
<SCRIPT TYPE="text/javascript">
<!--
myMsg = "This is a scrolling message. It'll
keep going around the status area until you
leave this window."
i=0

function scrollMsg() {
 frontPart = myMsg.substring(i,myMsg.length)
 backPart = myMsg.substring(0,i)
 window.status=frontPart + backPart
 if (i < myMsg.length) {
    i++
    }
    else {
    i=0
    }
    setTimeout("scrollMsg()",50)
    }
// END HIDING SCRIPT -->
</SCRIPT>
<NOSCRIPT>
Your browser isn't running scripts, so you
can't see the great ticker going on in the
status bar.
</NOSCRIPT>
</HEAD>
<BODY onLoad="scrollMsg()">
<P>Here's the rest of the page.
</BODY></HTML>
```

Figure 16.16 *The NOSCRIPT tag helps you take care of visitors who use really old browsers.*

Figure 16.17 *If your visitor uses a browser that doesn't support scripts (like Mosaic, shown here), they'll get a message explaining what's missing.*

Figure 16.18 *Or if your visitor has turned off JavaScript support (in Communicator here), the NOSCRIPT text will clue them in to the problem.*

Adding alternate information

```
┌──────────── code.html ────────────┐
<HTML>
<HEAD>

<TITLE>Setting the default scripting
language</TITLE>

<META HTTP-EQUIV="Content-Script-Type"
CONTENT="text/javascript">

</HEAD>
<BODY>

<SCRIPT>
document.write("Visca Catalunya! -- which
means Long Live Catalonia!")
</SCRIPT>

<P>Here's the rest of the page.
</BODY>
</HTML>
└───────────────────────────────────┘
```

Figure 16.19 *The META tag is always placed in the HEAD section of your HTML document. Notice that it is no longer necessary to specify the scripting language within the SCRIPT tag.*

Figure 16.20 *Specifying the scripting language in the META tag saves time and reduces the possibility for errors. The result, though, is not changed.*

Setting the default scripting language

According to the HTML 4 specifications, if you don't say what language you're using, your Web page is "incorrect". If you're including several scripts on a page, you can set the default scripting language for all of them in one fell swoop.

To set the default scripting language:

1. In the HEAD section of your HTML document, type **<META HTTP-EQUIV= "Content-Script-Type"**.

2. Then type **CONTENT="type"**, where *type* indicates the default format and language for your scripts. Use **text/ javascript** for JavaScript, **text/vbscript** for VBScript and **text/tcl** for TCL.

3. Type **>**.

✔ Tip

■ The scripting language indicated with the TYPE attribute in the SCRIPT tag *(see page 268)* overrides the META tag specification. That means you can set the default scripting language, but still use scripts written in other languages, if desired.

Setting the default scripting language

Extras

In this chapter, you'll find a collection of special touches you can give your Web pages to set them apart from the crowd (or to make them fit in better by following the latest trends).

Perhaps the best advice included in this chapter *(see page 278)* is to take a gander around the Web and see what other designers are up to. With each passing day, Microsoft and Netscape Communications add more extensions to their already burgeoning HTML specifications, enabling designers to push beyond current limits. By keeping your eye on the Web, you'll be among the first to find out about these new tags, and about the new ways to combine them on your pages.

Next, don't take anything at face value. Tables are a perfect example. In the printed world, they're perfect for conveying rows and columns of numbers. In the Web world, they can do so much more *(see pages 284 and 285)*. Many other HTML tags can also be stretched beyond their original use. Be creative! Hopefully, this chapter will give you a good start.

The inspiration of others

One of the easiest ways to expand your HTML fluency is by looking at how other page designers have created *their* pages. Luckily, HTML code is easy to view and learn from. However, text content, graphics, sounds, video, and other external files may be copyrighted. As a general rule, use other designers' pages for inspiration with your HTML, and then create your own contents.

To view other designers' HTML code:

1. Open their page with any browser.

2. Choose View Source (in the View menu in Netscape), or View (in the View menu in Internet Explorer).

3. The browser will open the helper application you have specified for text files and show you the HTML code for the given page.

4. If you wish, save the file with the text editor for further study.

✔ Tips

■ You can also save the source code by selecting File > Save As and then HTML Source in the Format pop-up menu in the dialog box that appears.

■ If you find something out there on the Web that you can't figure out, drop me an e-mail (how@cookwood.com) and make sure you enclose the URL of the amazing page. I'll see if I can decipher it for you.

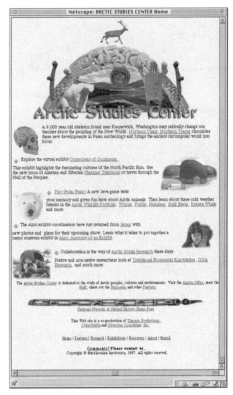

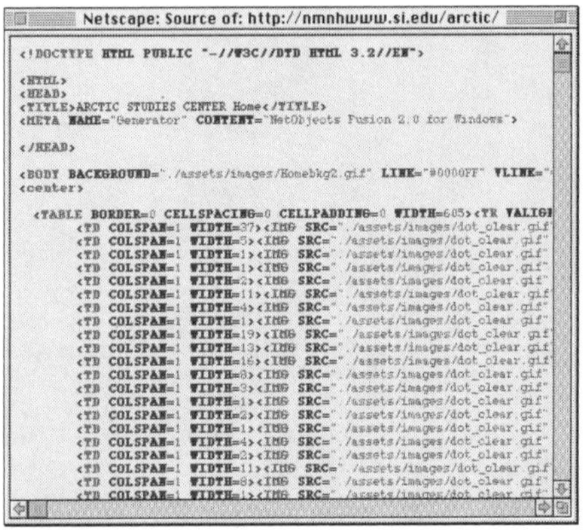

Figure 17.1 *This is the Smithsonian's very classy Arctic Studies Center (www.nmnhwww.si.edu/arctic/). That caribou up at the top is trotting along, and the images are very nicely organized with the text. How did they do it? Look at the source code in Figure 17.2.*

Figure 17.2 *When you select View Source, the page's HTML code is revealed.*

```
          code.html
<p> You are visitor number: <IMG SRC =
"/cgi-bin/Count.cgi?dd=E|df=user4/lcastro/
WWW/data/index.dat" > since March 7, 1996.
```

Figure 17.3 *This is what the code looks like to create the counter on my ISP. Notice that there is an image tag that calls a CGI script. I've also added some explanatory text so that people know what the counter references. (Of course, this script won't work for you unless you have the same ISP that I have.)*

Figure 17.4 *The counter is created at the bottom of the page and is updated automatically each time the page is loaded. Don't forget though, that loaded is not the same as visited. If I reload this page five times, the counter will go up, but I'll still only have visited it once.*

Creating a counter

It's nice to know that folks have been stopping by to see your masterpiece, once it's up and running. Many people use a special CGI script called a *counter* to tally each visit. Although CGI scripts are a bit beyond the scope of this book, I can point you in the right direction.

To create a counter:

1. First, contact your ISP. Ask them if they allow counters. If they do, they'll probably have a FAQ page that explains how to add one to your site.

2. If your ISP allows CGI scripts but doesn't have a ready-made counter, you can write your own. If you don't program, try Matt's Script Archive (www.worldwidemart.com/scripts).

3. Finally, you can use a public counter. Like other "free" services, you pay for this type of counter by including advertising on your site. You might try a service like Pagecount (www.page-count.com) or do a search on AltaVista for other "free" counters.

✔ Tips

- You can usually set the initial value for a counter. Keep that in mind when you marvel at the incredible numbers other sites seem to be attracting.

- Many ISPs offer more sophisticated visit analysis that goes way beyond a simple number. They'll tell you where visitors came from, what time they came, where they went on your site, and much more.

- You can also use search engines like AltaVista to find free guestbooks, e-mail, and even Web hosting.

Changing a link's status label

When a visitor points to a link, usually the link's URL appears in the status area of the browser window. If you want something else to appear there, you can use this easy technique to add your own status label.

To change a link's status label:

1. Create the link as usual. For more details, consult Chapter 7, *Links*.

2. In the link tag, type **ONMOUSEOVER ="window.status='**. (First double quotes, then a single one.)

3. Type the text that you want to appear in the status area of the browser window when the visitor points at the link.

4. Type **'; return true"**. (That's *single quote, semi colon,* and then the rest.)

✔ Tips

- Yes, this is JavaScript, not pure HTML. But you can still do it. (Hey, this *is* the *Extras* chapter...)

- Make sure you do not use any quotation marks or apostrophes, single or double, in the text entered in step 3.

- Explorer also supports the use of this technique to add labels to images. Simply add the line to the IMG tag **(Figure 17.7)**. For some reason, Communicator doesn't allow it.

```
                    code.html
<HTML><HEAD>
<TITLE>Status bar labels</TITLE>
</HEAD><BODY>

<IMG SRC="../images/Noho.GIF" ALT="Main
Street, Northampton" ALIGN=LEFT WIDTH="384"
HEIGHT="256" BORDER="0" HSPACE="5"
VSPACE="0" ONMOUSEOVER="window.status='Main
Street, Northampton'; return true">

<A HREF="noho.html"
ONMOUSEOVER="window.status='Click here for
more exciting information about
Northampton'; return true">Northampton</A>
is a great place to viist.
</BODY>
</HTML>
```

Figure 17.5 *You have to be careful with quotation marks. Use double quotes to enclose the whole script, single quotes to enclose the text that will appear, and no other quotes anywhere.*

Figure 17.6 *Adding the ONMOUSEOVER line to links gives visitors extra information before they actually click the link.*

Figure 17.7 *Internet Explorer also supports the ONMOUSEOVER event in image tags. (Netscape currently doesn't.)*

```
code.html
<HTML><HEAD>
<TITLE>Souped up mailto links</TITLE>
</HEAD><BODY>

Write me a <A
HREF="mailto:me@cookwood.com?subject=Your
cats">letter</A> about my cats!
</BODY>
</HTML>
```

Figure 17.8 *Notice that there is no space between the end of the e-mail address and the question mark that begins the extra information. Further, spaces are allowed in the subject line but quotation marks are not.*

Figure 17.9 *The souped up mailto tag looks like a regular link.*

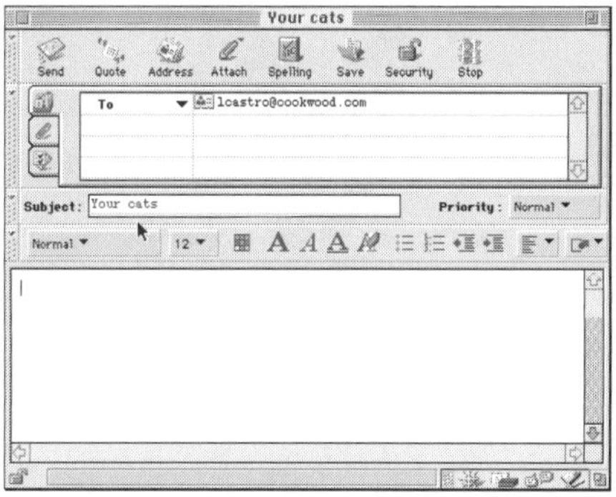

Figure 17.10 *But when you click it, the Subject line is automatically filled out.*

Souping up mailto links

When a visitor clicks a mailto link, the browser switches to a mail client and opens a new message window, pre-addressed with the recipient as defined in the mailto link *(see page 114)*. You can add information to the mailto link to automatically set the subject, cc, and bcc lines as well.

To soup up mailto links:

1. Type **<A HREF="mailto:joe@site.com**, as usual.

2. Type **?subject=topic**, where *topic* is the text you want to appear in the subject line.

   Or type **?cc=person@site.com**, where *person@site.com* is the e-mail address of the person you want to be cc'd automatically.

   Or type **?bcc=person@site.com**, where *person@site.com* is the e-mail address of the person you want to be bcc'd automatically.

3. Finally, type the closing **"**.

✔ Tips

- This is not standard HTML, nor does any browser claim to support it. Nevertheless, it does work with Explorer and Communicator on both Macs and Windows.

- Keep in mind that the visitor can change the subject, cc, or bcc lines as they wish. This technique only starts them off as you want them.

- Explorer can handle all the variables at once. Communicator only allows one at a time.

Souping up mailto links

Creating drop caps

Some of the best tricks are the simplest. Since you can't always be sure which fonts your visitors have installed, you can create an image file of the capital letter, make it transparent, and insert it before the rest of the paragraph.

To create a drop cap:

1. In an image editing program, create the capital letter, in any font you choose, for your drop cap. Save it in GIF format and make it transparent *(see pages 62 and 68)*.

2. In your HTML document where you want the drop cap to appear, type **<IMG SRC="dropcap.gif"** where *dropcap.gif* is the location on the server of the image created in step 1.

3. Type **ALIGN=left** so that the text that follows wraps around the drop cap.

4. Type the final **>** to finish the IMG definition.

5. Type the text that should appear next to the drop cap. Generally, next to a drop cap, it is a good idea to type the first few words in all caps.

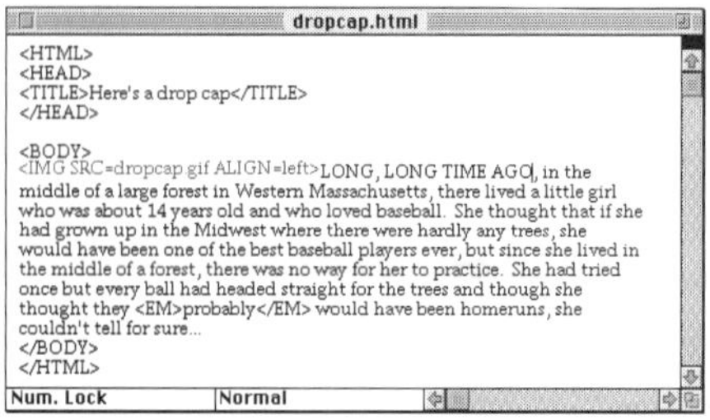

Figure 17.11 *Use the ALIGN=left attribute to wrap the text around the drop cap.*

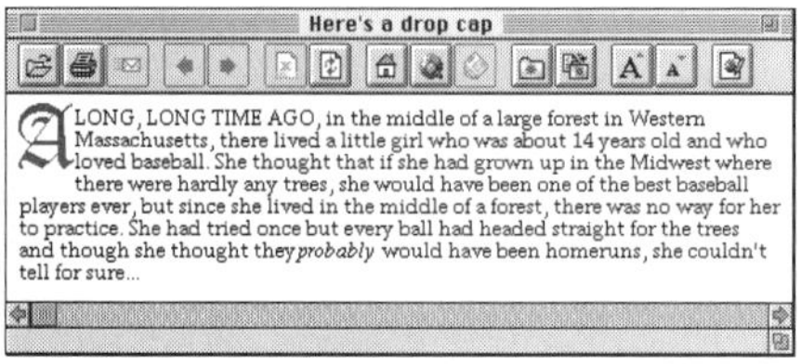

Figure 17.12 *Drop caps are ideal for books or stories.*

Creating drop caps

Figure 17.13 *You can create a vertical bar on the left side of the page by inserting an image and using the ALIGN=left attribute.*

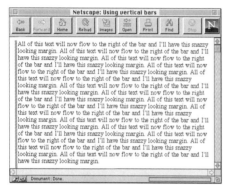

Figure 17.14 *It doesn't really matter if the vertical bar is longer than the text. It will simply continue down the page.*

Using vertical rules

It's easy to create horizontal rules in an HTML document. Creating vertical rules, along the left or right margin, for example, is only slightly more complicated.

To create a vertical rule:

1. In Photoshop, or other image editing program, create a bar of the desired color and width, and about 500 pixels high.

2. In the HTML document, place the cursor above the text that should be alongside the vertical bar.

3. Type **<IMG SRC="verticalbar.gif"** where *verticalbar.gif* is the location on the server of the vertical bar created in step 1.

4. *Either* type **ALIGN=left** to place the vertical bar along the left margin *or* type **ALIGN=right** to place it along the right margin.

5. Type the final **>** to complete the IMG definition.

6. Type the text that should appear alongside the vertical rule.

✔ Tips

■ You can create a narrow column of text by inserting a transparent vertical rule on either side of the body of your page. You can also use transparent GIFs to adjust the spacing between paragraphs, and even between words.

■ Another easy way to make a vertical rule is to create a two-column table and then specify a background color for the left column.

Creating buttons with tables

Buttons made out of images sometimes take a maddening amount of time to appear on the screen. If your user has images turned off, they may never appear at all. One solution is to create navigational buttons with tables. The technique is simple: create a table and change the background color of each cell, that is, button.

To create buttons with tables:

1. Create a table as described in Chapter 9, *Tables*.

2. The button cells might look like this: **<TD BGCOLOR=red ALIGN=middle> <A HREF="link.html"><FONT SIZE=+3 COLOR=black>Click me</FONT> </A></TD>**.

✔ Tips

■ Make sure the text that should appear in the cell is large enough to stand out. For more information, consult *Changing the text size* on page 47.

■ Use contrasting colors for both the background and the text that appears in the cell. For more information, consult *Changing the text color* on page 50 and *Changing a cell's color* on page 150.

■ Use a different colored background or image for each cell.

```
buttons.html
<!DOCTYPE HTML PUBLIC "-//W3C/DTD HTML 3.2//EN">
<HTML><HEAD><TITLE>Buttons</TITLE></HEAD>
<BODY BGCOLOR=#fce503>
<TABLE CELLPADDING=5 CELLSPACING=0 WIDTH=100%>
<TR>
<TH BGCOLOR="#F3D7E3" NOWRAP><A HREF="openingpage.html">City
Tour</A>
<TH BGCOLOR="#F6D5C3" NOWRAP><A HREF="market1.html">Market</A>
<TH BGCOLOR="#D8E9D6" NOWRAP><A
HREF="arch1.html">Architecture</A>
<TH BGCOLOR="#D1C9DF" NOWRAP><A HREF="sports1.html">Sports</A>
<TH BGCOLOR="#D4EBF9" NOWRAP><A
HREF="natlism1.html">Nationalism</A>
<TH BGCOLOR="#CECDB4" NOWRAP><A
HREF="language1.html">Language</A>
</TR>
</TABLE>
```

Figure 17.15 *In this example, all the text is black, but each cell/button is a different color.*

Figure 17.16 *The cells of the one-row table, when colored differently, look just like little buttons—but they load much more quickly than images. This page is used in the examples described in Chapter 10, Frames.*

Figure 17.17 *You can change the alignment, font size, font color, and background color of a cell. All of these properties help define that area of your page.*

Figure 17.18 *You could get this effect with images and text wrapped around them, but each time you changed the text, you'd have to adjust the images. In the table, the number cells adjust automatically according to how much text is used in the cell/paragraph to its right.*

Using tables for layout

Tables are ideal for spacing elements on your page exactly as you wish. You can use them like an invisible grid supporting your elements. For example, you might want to make a numbered list, with oversized numbers aligned with each section.

✔ Tips

- Use the ALIGN attribute within cell definitions to control how the contents will appear in the cell.

- You can divide information visually by a judicious use of background color for the cells. Don't be afraid to change the text color as well.

- Tables also have the advantage of expanding to fit the window when it's resized, something images won't do.

- Generally, when using tables for layout, you shouldn't use a border. That way, the table is invisible to the user while the structure of the table keeps the elements on the page in tune.

Using tables for layout

A shortcut for creating HTML tables in Word

Creating tables by hand can be a pain. It's hard to see where to put each element and you have to type TD and TR over and over again. Here's a way to convert a table from Word (both Mac and Windows versions) into an HTML table.

To convert a Word table into HTML:

1. Create a table in a separate document using Microsoft Word (for Macintosh or Windows).

2. Select the entire table and choose Table > Convert Table to Text **(Figure 17.20)**.

3. In the dialog box that appears, choose Tabs **(Figure 17.21)**. Your table now consists of individual paragraphs (which correspond to each row) separated by returns. Each element is separated by a tab **(Figure 17.22)**.

4. With the cursor at the top of the document, select Edit > Replace.

5. In the Find What box, type **^p** to search for every occurrence of a new paragraph (that is a new row).

6. In the Replace With box, type **^p<TR><TD>** (without spaces). The ^p is optional, since extra returns will be ignored by the browser. It makes the HTML document easier to edit.

7. Click Replace All.

8. In the Find What box, type **^t** to find every occurrence of a tab (a new cell).

9. In the Replace With box, type **^t<TD>**. Again, the ^t is optional and simply allows for easier editing here in Word.

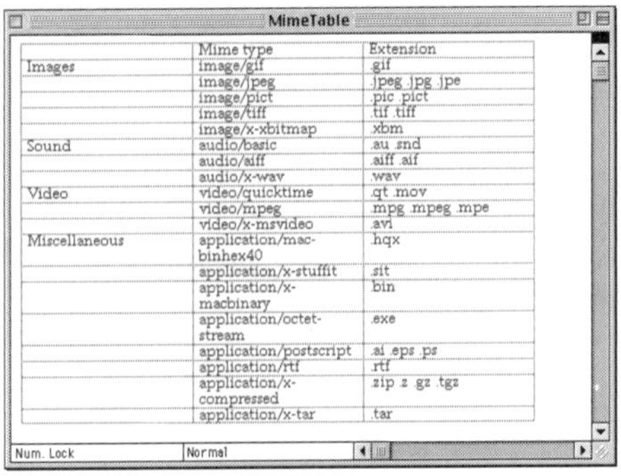

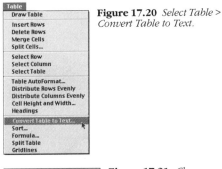

Figure 17.19 *It is much easier to create a table in Microsoft Word than by hand with HTML.*

Figure 17.20 *Select Table > Convert Table to Text.*

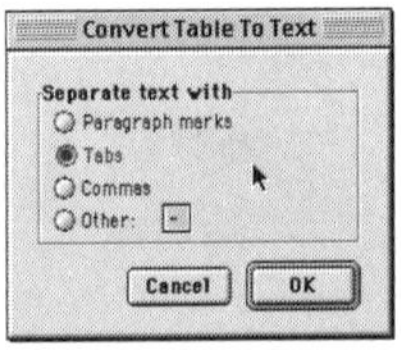

Figure 17.21 *Choose Tabs in the Convert Table to Text dialog box.*

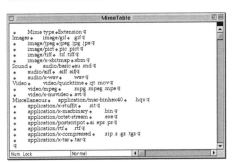

Figure 17.22 *Each row of the table is converted into a separate paragraph. The cells in each row are separated by tabs.*

A shortcut for creating HTML tables in Word

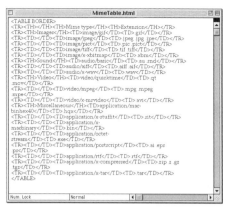

Figure 17.23 *After a few search and replace operations, the table is transformed into HTML code.*

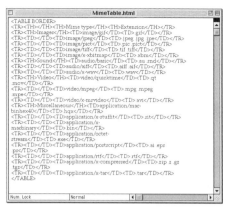

Figure 17.24 *The table looks great in the browser.*

10. Click Replace All.

11. At the very beginning of the document, type **<TABLE><TR><TD>**. Include any table attributes, as desired *(see pages 89-98)*.

12. At the very end of the document, you may find extra blank lines of TRs and TDs. Eliminate them. Type **</TABLE>** after the final cell's contents.

13. Change the TDs of your header cells to THs as needed (yes, by hand). The table is now complete **(Fig. 17.23)**.

14. Choose File > Save As.

15. In the dialog box that appears, choose Text Only in the Format submenu and click OK.

16. Copy the table back into your HTML document, if necessary.

17. View your table to make sure that everything is the way you want it **(Figure 17.24)**. You may want to adjust the alignment or text formatting of individual cells.

✔ Tips

■ Save frequently and sequentially! If you decide to add a column to your table, it will help to have a copy of the Word table still lying around.

■ These illustrations are from Word 98 for Macintosh, but the technique will work in any version of Word, for Windows or Mac. Of course, since Microsoft likes to juggle commands around, you may have to search for the Convert Table to Text command. (In Word 5.1, which I confess I still use, it's called Table to Text and is in the Insert menu.)

A shortcut for creating HTML tables in Word

Creating an automatic slide show

This isn't really an extra, but it's so unusual, I didn't know quite where else to put it. You can use a special feature of the META attribute, within the BODY tag, to automatically move the reader from one page to another. If you set up a series of pages in this way, you create a Web slide show.

To create an automatic slide show:

1. In the first page, within the HEAD section, type **<META HTTP-EQUIV= "Refresh"**. (That's a regular hyphen between *HTTP* and *EQUIV.*)

2. Type **CONTENT="n;** where *n* is the number of seconds the current page should display on the screen.

3. Type **URL=nextpage.html">** where *nextpage.html* is the URL of the next page that you want the user to jump to automatically.

4. Repeat these steps for each page in the series.

✔ Tips

■ Make sure you use a display time long enough for all of your pages to appear on screen.

■ This use of the META tag works with Netscape and Internet Explorer (and may work with other browsers as well), both on Windows machines and Macs.

■ This is a great way to show a portfolio or other series of images without having to create a lot of links and buttons.

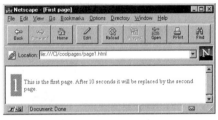

Figure 17.25 *The META tag must be in the HEAD section. It won't work if you place it anywhere else.*

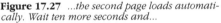

Figure 17.26 *The first page loads as usual. But wait ten seconds, and...*

Figure 17.27 *...the second page loads automatically. Wait ten more seconds and...*

Figure 17.28 *...the third page loads automatically. If you wait ten more seconds, it'll go back to page 1 (Figure 17.26) and start the whole process all over again. Of course, if you don't want it to, just leave the META tag out of the last page.*

Creating an automatic slide show

Publishing

Once you've finished your masterpiece and are ready to present it to the public, you have to publish your page on a server and help your public find a way to your door.

Your first step is to add special information to your files to make sure they get noticed (or not) on the Web. Next, test everything and make sure it works as you planned.

Then you're ready to transfer the files to the server and to change the permissions so that the files are open to the public.

Finally, you should use the services available on the Web to advertise your page so that your readers know where to find you.

Publishing

Helping visitors find your page

In the early days of the Web, surfing was rather arbitrary. You jumped to one site, found an interesting link, and jumped on. Today, surfers most often use search engines to find a page that deals with a particular topic. You can tell search engines exactly what your page is about so that if a visitor searches for that topic, there's a better chance they'll find *your* page.

To help visitors find your page:

1. In the HEAD section of your page, type **<META NAME="keywords" CONTENT="**.

2. Type a few words that concisely describe the topic discussed on your page. Separate each word with a comma and a space.

3. Type **">** to complete the META tag.

✔ Tips

■ Use a combination of very unique and more general words to describe the contents of your page. *Chihuahua* is very unique, but *dog* may also net you some visitors who didn't realize they were interested in Chihuahuas (or couldn't spell it).

■ Actually, adding misspelled keywords (in *addition* to correctly spelled ones) is not such a bad idea. You might also offer several alternative spellings for foreign words. Your aim is to match what a prospective visitor might type.

■ Most search engines offer specific tips on using the META tag to describe your site. For example, check out *http://altavista.digital.com/av/content/addurl_meta.htm.*

Figure 18.1 *Here is a page that gives a lot of information about Alpacas.*

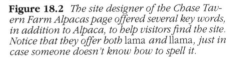

```
<HTML>
<HEAD>
    <TITLE>Chase Tavern Farm Alpacas</TITLE>
    <META NAME="keywords" CONTENT="Alpaca,
alpacas, wool, lama, llama">
    <META NAME="description" CONTENT="Chase
Tavern Farm Alpacas, Breeding Australian,
Peruvian and Chilean Alpacas since 1993.">
    <META NAME="rating" CONTENT="General">
    <META NAME="revisit-after" CONTENT="15
days">
    <META NAME="ROBOTS" CONTENT="ALL">

</HEAD>
<BODY BACKGROUND=" images/logo.gif">
```

Figure 18.2 *The site designer of the Chase Tavern Farm Alpacas page offered several key words, in addition to Alpaca, to help visitors find the site. Notice that they offer both* lama *and* llama, *just in case someone doesn't know how to spell it.*

```
code.html
<HTML>
<HEAD>
    <TITLE>Chase Tavern Farm Alpacas</TITLE>
    <META NAME="keywords" CONTENT="Alpaca,
alpacas, wool, lama, llama">
    <META NAME="description" CONTENT="Chase
Tavern Farm Alpacas, Breeding Australian,
Peruvian and Chilean Alpacas since 1993.">
    <META NAME="rating" CONTENT="General">
    <META NAME="revisit-after" CONTENT="15
days">
    <META NAME="ROBOTS" CONTENT="ALL">

</HEAD>
<BODY BACKGROUND=" images/logo.gif">
```

Figure 18.3 *You can use as many META tags as you need.*

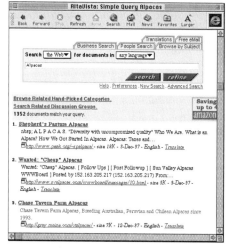

Figure 18.4 *Notice the three descriptions shown here. The first two—a lot of gobbledygook—have obviously been generated automatically from the contents at the top of the HTML document. The third—a lucid, descriptive, complete sentence about the site, was created by the site designer (see Figure 18.3).*

Controlling your page's summary

When a prospective visitor does a search at AltaVista (or wherever), a list of matches appears, each with a little summary of the page's contents. By default, the search engine uses the first few words on your page, but you can choose exactly what appears—and hopefully persuade more visitors to come to your site.

To control your page's summary:

1. In the HEAD section of your page, type **<META NAME="description" CONTENT="**.

2. Type a concise sentence or two that describes your page and hopefully persuades folks to click through.

3. Type **">** to complete the META tag.

✔ Tips

■ AltaVista limits the length of the description to 1024 characters.

■ For more information on getting noticed by search engines, and indeed by the Web public in general, consult *Getting Hits: The Definitive Guide to Promoting your Website*, by Don Sellers (Peachpit Press).

Controlling your page's summary

Controlling other information

You can also add information to your page about who wrote it, what program was used (if any) to generate the HTML code, and if it is copyrighted. However, search engines do not currently use this information, nor do browsers display it.

To control other information about your page:

1. In the HEAD section of your page, type **<META NAME="author" CONTENT="name">**, where *name* is the person who wrote the HTML page.

2. In the HEAD section of your page, type **<META NAME="generator" CONTENT="program">**, where *program* is the name of the software that created (or started) the HTML page.

3. In the HEAD section of your Web page, type **<META NAME="copyright" CONTENT="© year holder">**, where *year* is the calendar year of the copyright, and *holder* is the name of the person or entity who holds the copyright to the page.

✔ Tip

■ The generator is created automatically by Web page editors like PageMill, FrontPage, Netscape Gold, and even BBEdit, although BBEdit gives you the option to leave it out.

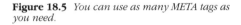

```
code.html
<HTML>
<HEAD>

<TITLE>Identifying ownership</TITLE>

<META NAME="generator" CONTENT="BBEdit 4.5">
<META NAME="author" CONTENT="Liz Castro">
<META NAME="copyright" CONTENT="&copy; 1998
Liz Castro">

</HEAD>
<BODY>
This is my page!
</BODY>
</HTML>
```

Figure 18.5 *You can use as many META tags as you need.*

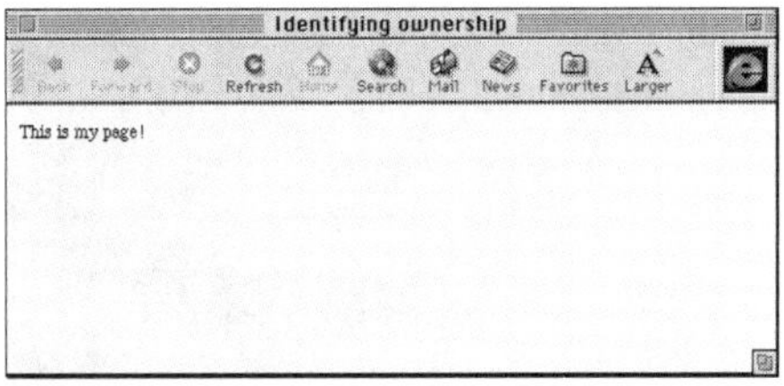

Figure 18.6 *The META information is always invisible in the browser.*

```
                    code.html
<HTML>
<HEAD>

<TITLE>Identifying ownership</TITLE>

<META NAME="generator" CONTENT="BBEdit 4.5">
<META NAME="author" CONTENT="Liz Castro">
<META NAME="copyright" CONTENT="&copy; 1998
Liz Castro">
<META NAME="robots" CONTENT="NOINDEX,
NOFOLLOW">

</HEAD>
<BODY>
This is my personal page! Here is a personal
<A HREF="personal.html">link</A>.
</BODY>
</HTML>
```

Figure 18.7 *When a search engine's robot encounters this page, it will ignore both the page and the page's links.*

Keeping search engine robots out

Search engines employ little programs called *robots* or *spiders* to hang out on the Web and look for new pages to add to the engine's index. But sometimes, you don't want search engines to know your page exists. Perhaps it's a personal page designed only for your family or an internal page for your company. You can add information to the page so that most search engine robots will stay out.

To keep search engine robots out:

1. In the HEAD section of your Web page, type **<META NAME="robots" CONTENT="**.

2. If desired, type **NOINDEX** to keep the robot from adding the current page to its index.

3. If desired, type **NOFOLLOW** to keep the robot from following the links on the page and indexing those pages.

4. Type **">** to complete the META tag.

✔ Tips

- Separate multiple values with a comma and a space.

- You can use the values ALL and INDEX to have robots add the current page (and its links) to the search engine's index. However, these are the default values and so leaving them out is the same as specifying them (but faster).

- If a page has already been indexed, you'll have to go to the search engine's Web site and look for the Remove URL page.

Testing your page

Many Web page editors offer an automatic or manual way to check your HTML syntax. Although it's a good idea to take advantage of such features, you should always test your HTML pages in at least one browser.

Inevitably you will have to make adjustments to your HTML code. You only need to forget one angle bracket for your page to look completely different from what you expected. Other times what you thought might look OK looks awful.

To test your HTML pages:

1. Open the HTML document in your text editor and check for spelling and other errors **(Figure 18.8)**.

2. Open a browser, and choose File > Open File **(Figure 18.9)**.

3. Find the Web page on your hard disk that you want to test and click Open. The page appears in the browser.

4. Go through the whole page and make sure it looks exactly the way you want it **(Figure 18.10)**. For example:

Is the formatting like you wanted?

Does each of your URLs point to the proper document? (You can check the URLs by clicking them if the destination files are located in the same relative position on the local computer.)

Are your images aligned properly?

Have you included your name and e-mail address (preferably in a mailto URL) so that your users can contact you with comments and suggestions?

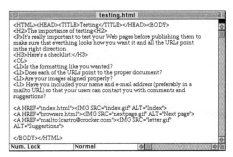

```
testing.html
<HTML><HEAD><TITLE>Testing</TITLE></HEAD><BODY>
<H2>The importance of testing</H2>
<P>It's really important to test your Web pages before publishing them to
make sure that everthing looks how you want it and all the URLs point
inthe right direction.
<H3>Here's a checklist:</H3>
<OL>
<LI>Is the formatting like you wanted?
<LI>Does each of the URLs point to the proper document?
<LI>Are your images aligned properly?
<LI> Have you included your name and e-mail address (preferably in a
mailto URL) so that your users can contact you with comments and
suggestions?

<A HREF="index.html"><IMG SRC="index.gif" ALT="Index">
<A HREF="browsers.html"><IMG SRC="nextpage.gif" ALT="Next page">
<A HREF="mailto:lcastro@crocker.com"><IMG SRC="letter.gif"
ALT="Suggestions">

</BODY></HTML>

Num. Lock            Normal
```

Figure 18.8 *Check your document for typographical errors, missing angle brackets, and other mistakes.*

```
File
New Window          ⌘N
Open Location...    ⌘L
Open File...        ⌘O
Save As...          ⌘S
Mail Document...    ⌘M
Document Information...

Page Setup...
Print...            ⌘P

Close               ⌘W
Quit                ⌘Q
```

Figure 18.9 *Choose File > Open File (the name may be slightly different depending on the browser and platform you use) in order to open the page and test it.*

```
Netscape: Testing
Back  Forward  Home  Reload  Images  Open  Print  Find  Stop    N

The importance of testing

It's really important to test your Web pages before
publishing them to make sure that everthing looks
how you want it and all the URLs point inthe right
direction.

Here's a checklist:

  1. Is the formatting like you wanted?
  2. Does each of the URLs point to the proper
     document?
  3. Are your images aligned properly?
  4.  Have you included your name and e-mail
      address (preferably in a mailto URL) so that
```

Figure 18.10 *Can you tell what's making this page look so bad?*

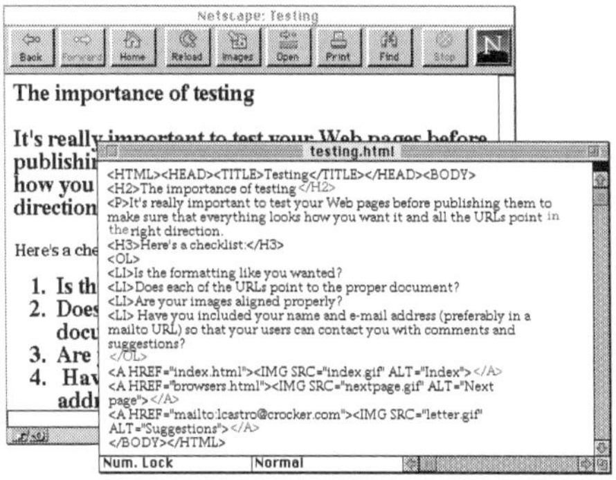

Figure 18.11 *As long as you have enough memory, you can keep the browser and the text editor open at the same time so that you can see what effects your changes are having.*

Figure 18.12 *You must save the changes to your HTML document before reloading, or else the changes will not appear in the browser.*

Figure 18.13 *Select Reload (in the View menu), or click the Reload button on the toolbar in order to show the changes.*

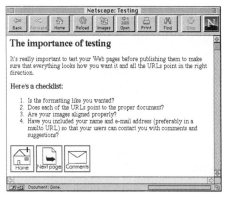

Figure 18.14 *After reloading the fixed HTML document, everything appears as it should— artistic deficiencies aside.*

5. Without closing the page in the browser, open the HTML document with a text or HTML editor. You should be able to simultaneously edit the HTML document with one program and view it with another **(Figure 18.11)**.

6. Save the changes **(Figure 18.12)**.

7. Switch back to the browser and choose Reload to see the changes **(Figures 18.13 and 18.14)**.

8. Repeat steps 1–7 until you are satisfied with your Web page. Don't get discouraged if it takes several tries.

9. Transfer the files to the server and change the permissions, if you haven't done so already *(see page 296)*.

10. Return to the browser and choose File > Open Location.

11. Type your page's URL and click Open. The page will appear in the browser.

12. With your page on the server, go through your page again to make sure everything is all right.

✔ Tip

■ If you can, use several browsers on different platforms to test your HTML documents. You never know what browser (or computer) your user is going to use. The major browsers are discussed on page 20.

Testing your page

Transferring files to the server

The steps you need to take to transfer files to the server depend on the type of server you are working with and where it is located. Many people use UNIX servers at a remote location. The easiest way to transfer your HTML files to this kind of server is an FTP program, like Fetch for Macintosh (see below), or WS_FTP for Windows *(see page 298)*. Many Web page editors offer publishing features as well. For details on publishing files to AOL or CompuServe, see page 300.

To transfer HTML files to the server with Fetch (for the Mac):

1. Open your Internet connection.

2. Open Fetch or other FTP program.

3. Choose Preferences in the Customize menu **(Figure 18.15)**, Uploading in the Topic menu of the Preferences box that appears, and make sure the Add file format suffixes option is not checked **(Figure 18.16)**.

4. Choose File > Open Connection **(Figure 18.17)**.

5. In the Open Connection window, enter the server name in the Host text box, your user name in the User ID box, your password in the Password box, and the path to the directory where you plan to save the Web pages in the Directory box **(Figure 18.18)**.

6. Click OK to open the connection. Fetch will make the connection to the server you requested and open the designated directory.

7. Make sure the correct directory where you wish to place your set of HTML files is showing in the main Fetch window **(Figure 18.19)**.

Figure 18.15 *Choose Preferences in Fetch's Customize menu to open the Preferences dialog box.*

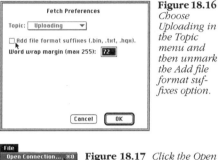

Figure 18.16 *Choose Uploading in the Topic menu and then unmark the Add file format suffixes option.*

Figure 18.17 *Click the Open Connection button or select Open Connection in the File menu to display the Open Connection window.*

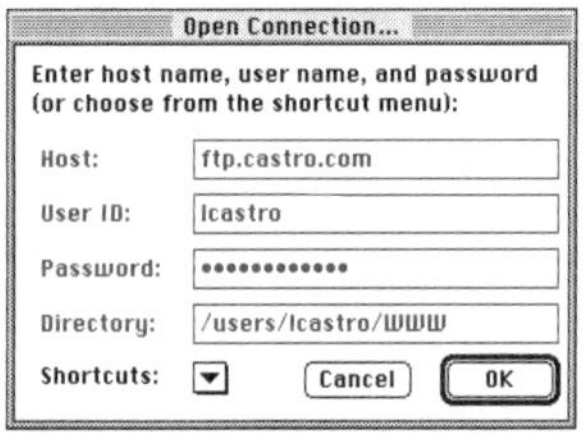

Figure 18.18 *In the Open Connection window, type the server name (Host), your User ID and password, and the directory where you want to transfer the files.*

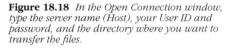

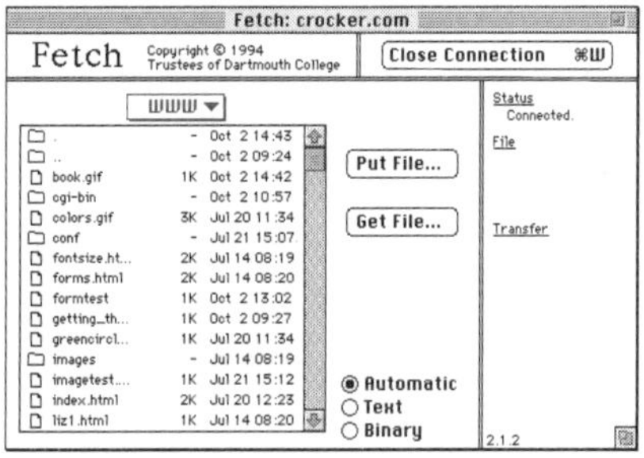

Figure 18.19 *Make sure the proper directory on the server (where you want to transfer the files) is showing in the Fetch window before transferring the files (in this case, WWW).*

Transferring files to the server

Figure 18.20 *Choose Remote > Put Folders and Files. (To transfer just one file, you can click the Put File button in the main Fetch window.)*

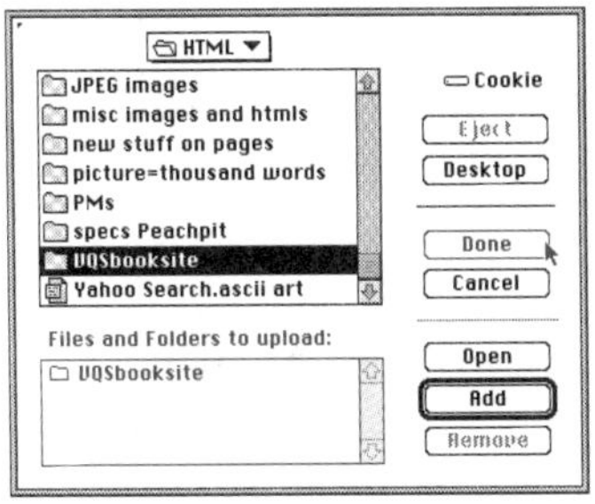

Figure 18.21 *Select each folder or file that you wish to transfer to the server and click Add. When you've finished choosing folders and files, click Done.*

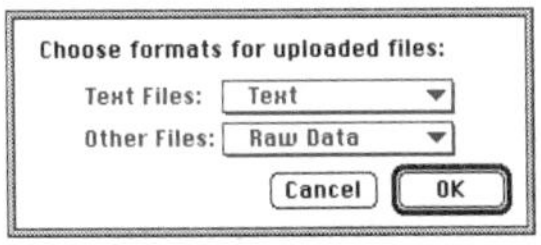

Figure 18.22 *Choose the Text format for Text files and the Raw Data format for Other Files.*

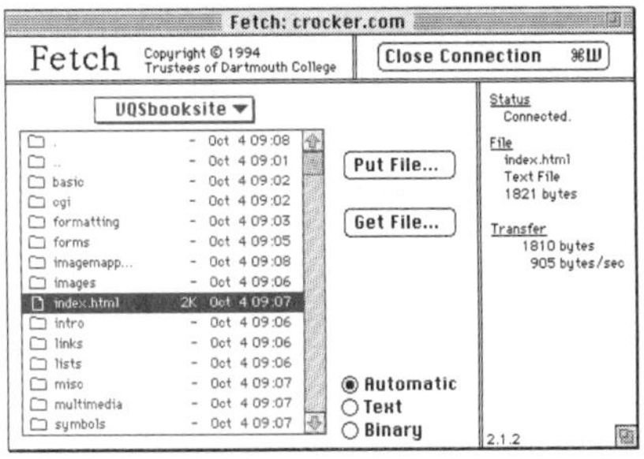

Figure 18.23 *The transferred files maintain the same hierarchy that they had on the Mac. Click Close Connection to close the connection to the server.*

8. Choose Remote > Put Folders and Files **(Figure 18.20)**.

9. In the dialog box that appears, choose the files that you wish to transfer to the server and click Add. The files will appear at the bottom of the dialog box. When you have selected all the files you wish to transfer, click Done **(Figure 18.21)**.

10. In the Choose formats dialog box that appears, select the appropriate formats for the files. Use Text for HTML and other text documents and Raw Data for other kinds of files **(Figure 18.22)**.

11. Click OK. The files will be transferred to the server and will maintain the hierarchy that they had on the local system **(Figure 18.23)**.

12. Click Close Connection to close the connection to the server.

✔ Tips

- Fetch's home page is *www.dartmouth. edu/pages/softdev/fetch.html.*

- If you have used relative URLs *(see page 29)*, these will be maintained when you transfer the entire folder or directory from your computer to the server. If you have used absolute URLs *(see page 28)*, you will have to change them to reflect the files' new locations.

Transferring files to the server

To transfer files to the server with WS_FTP (for Windows):

1. Open WS_FTP.

2. In the Session Profile dialog box that appears **(Figure 18.24)**, click New to create a new set of preferences (or select an existing profile if you've already created it).

3. Give the profile a name in the Profile Name box.

4. Enter the Host Name of the server, the Host Type (Automatic detect, if you're not sure), your User ID and Password.

5. Enter the desired directory on the server where you plan to transfer the files in the Remote Host area at the bottom of the dialog box. If you like, you can also enter the directory on the local PC from which you will transfer the files.

6. Click Save to save the profile.

7. Click OK to open the connection.

8. Click Options at the bottom of the WS_FTP window **(Figure 18.25)**.

9. Click the Extensions button **(Figure 18.26)**.

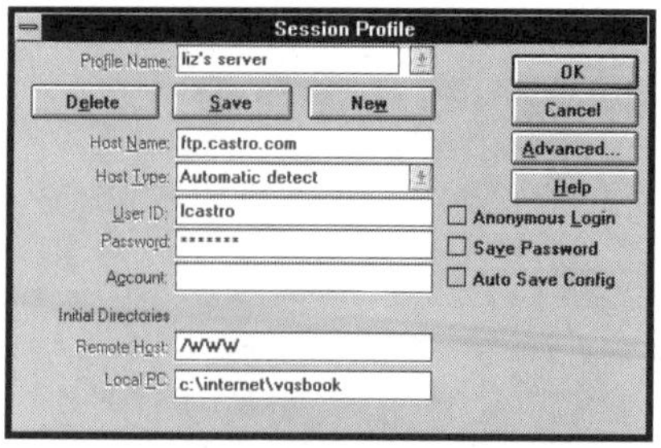

Figure 18.24 *After clicking New in WS_FTP, enter the information necessary for connecting to the server, including the server's name (Host Name), the Host type, your User ID, and password.*

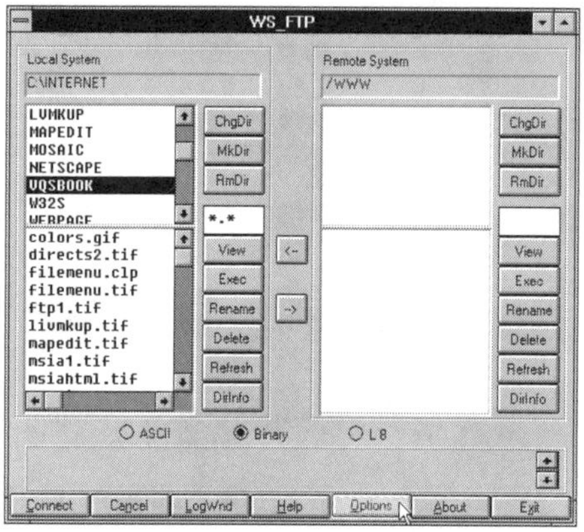

Figure 18.25 *Click Options in the bottom part of the main WS_FTP window.*

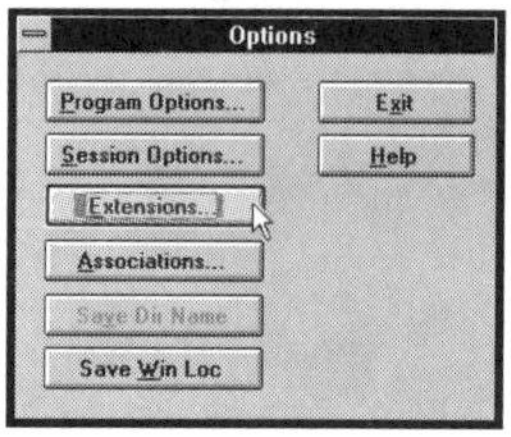

Figure 18.26 *Click the Extensions button in the Options dialog box.*

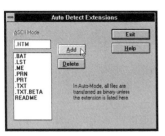

Figure 18.27 *Type* **.htm** *in the text box and then click Add so that the HTML documents will be transferred in ASCII format, even with Binary format selected in the main window.*

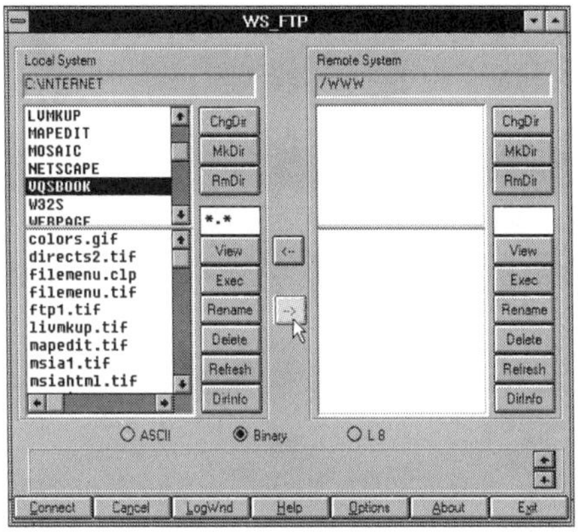

Figure 18.28 *Select the desired directory (or directories) and then click the right pointing arrow in the middle of the dialog box.*

10. Type **.htm** in the text box and click Add so that your HTML documents will be transferred in ASCII format **(Figure 18.27)**.

11. Click Exit in both dialog boxes to return to the main window.

12. Make sure the Binary radio button is selected at the bottom of the main window. This applies to all files with extensions not appearing in the Auto Detect Extensions dialog box.

13. Choose the files that you wish to transfer from the left side of the window by clicking on them. You may have to create directories on the server with the MkDir button.

14. Click the right pointing arrow to begin the transfer **(Figure 18.28)**.

15. Repeat steps 13–14 as needed.

16. Close the connection to the server.

✔ **Tips**

■ You can find WS_FTP's home page at *www.ipswitch.com/products/ws_ftp/*.

■ There are many other file transfer programs for Windows besides WS_FTP. Do a search at CNET's shareware site (www.shareware.com) if you'd prefer to use some other program.

Transferring files to the server

Transferring files to AOL or CompuServe

Even if you are a member of AOL or CompuServe you can still use the techniques described in this book to create your Web page. The only difference is how to transfer your files to their server.

To transfer files to AOL:

1. Go to keyword **myplace**.

2. Click the Upload button.

3. Type the exact name of the file, and its extension (but not the path). Click ASCII for text documents and Binary for images. Then click Continue.

4. Click Select File, and then choose the corresponding file from your hard disk and click OK.

5. Click Send to upload the file.

To transfer files to CompuServe:

1. Download and then open Publishing Wizard for Mac (GO MACPUB) or for Windows (it's included in the Home-Page Wizard; GO HPWIZ).

2. Follow the directions on each screen, choosing the files you want to upload.

✔ Tips

- The URL of your pages on AOL is *http://members.aol.com/screenname/ filename.* You can publish up to 2Mb *per screenname* (for a total of 10Mb).

- On CompuServe, your URL is *http:// ourworld.compuserve.com/home-pages/username,* where *username* is specified with the Publishing Wizard. You can publish up to 2Mb of files.

Figure 18.29 *Go to keyword* myplace *and then click the Upload button at the bottom of the screen.*

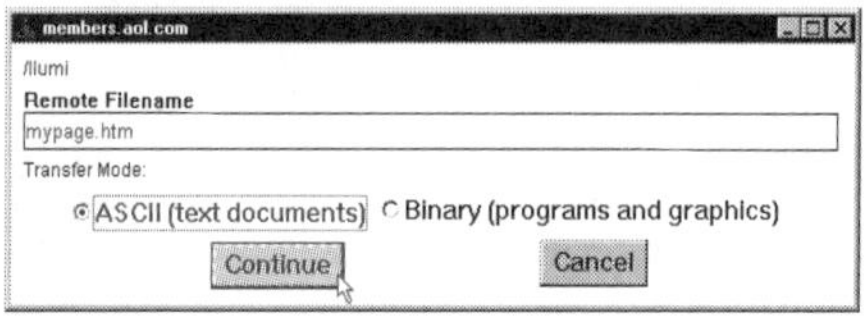

Figure 18.30 *Type the name of the file, choose ASCII or Binary, depending on the nature of the file, and then click Continue.*

Figure 18.31 *Click Select File to choose the file that you want to upload from your hard disk. Its name appears in the File box at the bottom of the screen. Then click Send to upload the file to AOL.*

Figure 18.32 *CompuServe's Publishing Wizard takes you through the transferring process step by step. Fill out each screen and click Next to continue.*

Transferring files to AOL or CompuServe

Figure 18.33 *After opening the connection with the File menu, log in by typing your user name and password.*

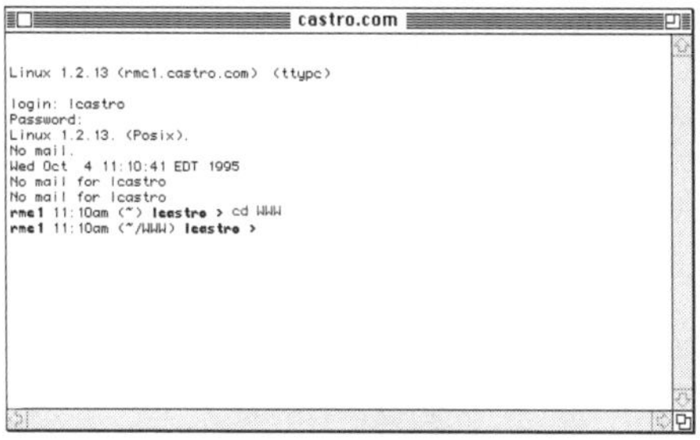

Figure 18.34 *Use the cd command to go to the directory that contains the files or directories whose permissions you wish to change.*

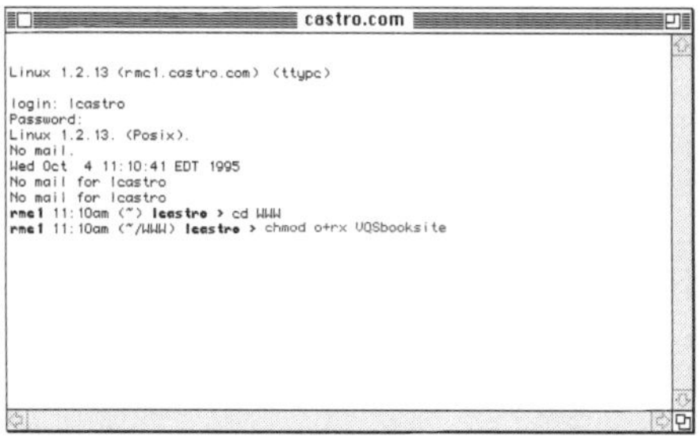

Figure 18.35 *Type* **chmod o+rx** *followed by the name of the file or directory whose permissions you wish to change.*

Changing permissions

Whether you transfer the files from a Mac or PC, or even another UNIX machine, if your server is a UNIX machine, often you will have to change the permissions of the transferred files to open access to your pages to the public. However, you may not have the necessary privileges to change the permissions. In that case, contact your server administrator.

To change permissions:

1. Open a Telnet program, like NCSA Telnet for Mac or Ewan for Windows.

2. Enter the server name in the Host box and click Connect. You will be connected to the server as if you were at a local terminal.

3. Log in with your User ID and Password **(Figure 18.33)**. Generally, you will find yourself automatically in your personal directory on the server.

4. If necessary, type **cd directory**, where *directory* is the desired directory you wish to view **(Figure 18.34)**. Type **ls** to list the directory's contents.

5. Type **chmod o+rx name**, where *name* is the name of the directory or file whose permissions will be changed **(Figure 18.35)**.

6. Type **lo** to log out.

✔ Tips

■ Type **man chmod** for more information about the chmod command.

■ HTML files and images need *read-only* permission (the *r* in o+rx); CGI scripts need *execute* permission (the *x* in o+rx).

Advertising your site

Before you start talking up your site in public, you should test it once again *(see page 294)* and make sure that everything works as it should. Once you are satisfied you can begin to recruit visitors.

To advertise your site:

1. Make sure you've added key words *(see page 290)* and a description *(see page 291)* to your site.

2. Use the Add URL fill in forms at search and indexing services like Yahoo, AltaVista, and Lycos **(Figures 18.36 and 18.37)**:

   Yahoo: *http://www.yahoo.com/docs/info/include.html*

   AltaVista: *http://altavista.digital.com/av/content/addurl.htm*

   Lycos: *http://www.lycos.com/addasite.html*

   (There are no spaces in any of these URLs.)

3. Pay a company to advertise your page for you.

4. Post a note in the moderated UseNet newsgroup *comp.infosystems.www. announce* or the unmoderated *comp.internet.net-happenings* or in newsgroups that have similar interests as your Web site.

5. Send e-mail to your associates and friends. (You can include the URL for your site in all your correspondence in a signature.)

6. Send e-mail to the creators of other sites with similar interests or topics.

Figure 18.36 *Go to the indexing service's home page and click the Add URL link. This is AltaVista. Its Add URL link is at the bottom of its home page.*

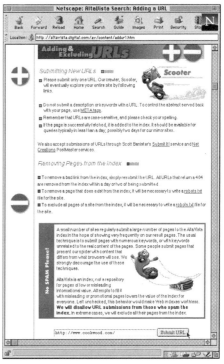

Figure 18.37 *Follow the directions on the Add URL page. In AltaVista, type the URL of your home page and then click Submit URL (at the bottom of the page).*

HTML Tools A

The lists on the following pages are by no means exhaustive. There are literally hundreds of programs, some commercial, some shareware, and some freeware, of varying quality, that you can use as you design and create your Web pages. If you don't find what you're looking for on these pages, jump to any search service on the Web (e.g., *http://altavista.digital. com*) and look for *Web tools, Web graphics,* or whatever it is you need.

HTML Editors

You can use *any* text editor to write HTML, including SimpleText or TeachText on the Macintosh, WordPad for Windows, or vi in Unix systems. The HTML code produced with these simpler programs is no different from the HTML produced by more complex HTML editors.

A simple text editor is like the most basic SLR 35 mm camera. You have to set your f-stop and aperture manually, and then focus before shooting. The dedicated HTML editors are point-and-shoot cameras: just aim and fire, for a price. They are more expensive, and generally less flexible.

What HTML editors offer	**Disadvantages of HTML editors**
Dedicated HTML editors offer the following advantages over simple text editors (of course, not every HTML editor has every feature): • they insert opening and closing tags with a single click • they check and verify syntax in your HTML and typos in your text • they allow you to add attributes by clicking buttons instead of typing words in a certain order in a certain place in the document • they offer varying degrees of WYSIWYG display of your Web page • they correct mistakes in existing HTML pages • they make it easy to use special characters	These extra features come at a price, however. Some things that may annoy you about HTML editors is that • they don't all recognize new or non-standard HTML codes (like Netscape extensions) • they don't all support forms, frames, and tables • they are more difficult to learn, and less intuitive than they promise • they cost money (all simple text editors are included free with the respective system software) • they use up more space on disk and more memory • some add proprietary information (like *their* name, for example), and tags to the HTML document • some eliminate tags that they don't understand—even if the tags are part of the standard HTML specifications

HTML Editors

HTML Editors

Name	Description	URL
Claris Home Page (M, W)	$100, WYSIWYG Editor from FileMaker, Inc. (formerly Claris Corp.). It's still not clear if Home Page will stay with FileMaker or go back to Apple.	http://www.claris.com/ products/claris/clarispage/ clarispage.html; *demo available*
Microsoft FrontPage (M, W)	$150. WYSIWYG Editor from Microsoft Corporation.	http://www.microsoft.com/ frontpage/
Adobe PageMill (M, W)	$100, Probably the most popular WYSIWYG editor for Macintosh. Also available for Windows.	http://www.adobe.com/ prodindex/pagemill/
SoftQuad HoTMetaL (M, W)	$130, WYSIWYG editor that creates standard, universal HTML. SiteMaker also available.	http://www.sq.com/products/ hotmetal/ *demo available* (Windows 95 only)
AOLpress (M, W)	America Online, WYSIWYG HTML Editor (Formerly GNNpress)	http://www.aolpress.com/ index.html *demo:* http://www. aolpress.com/download.html
BBEdit (M)	$120. Excellent HTML editor from Bare Bones Software. The most popular non-WYSIWYG HTML editor.	http://www.barebones.com *demo:* web.barebones.com/ free/free.html
Dreamweaver (M, W)	$300. Macromedia's acclaimed new WYSIWYG editor.	http://www.macromedia.com/ software/dreamweaver; *demo available*
GoLive CyberStudio (M)	$300. GoLive's professional WYSIWYG editor.	http://www.golive.com; *demo available*
NetObjects Fusion (M, W)	$300. NetObjects WYSIWYG editor for professional Web masters.	http://www.netobjects.com/ products/html/nof.html; *demo available*
World Wide Web Weaver (W)	$90, Miracle Software.	http://www.miracleinc.com/ Products/W4
Aardvark Pro (W)	$75. Distributed by TMGNetwork.	http://www.tmgnet.com/ aardvark/
ANT_HTML (W)	$40, Jill Swift; template for use with Microsoft Word (several versions and platforms).	http://telacommunications.com/ ant/antdesc.htm
HotDog Professional (W)	$150, Sausage Software. "Express" version also available	http://www.sausage.com/
Internet Assistant (M, W)	Microsoft, works with Word 6 for Windows, free	http://www.microsoft.com/ word/internet/ia/ *download:* http://www.microsoft.com/ word/internet/ia/sysreq.htm

HTML Editors

Free-use images for your pages

Name	Description	URL
Yahoo	List of sites with graphics	http://www.yahoo.com/ Computers_and_Internet/ Internet/World_Wide_Web/ Page_Design_and_Layout/ Graphics/
Hawkeye's Land of Backgrounds	Collection of background images	http://johnh.wheaton.edu/~sgill/ backgrounds.html
Paul Medoff's Hall of Doodads	Backgrounds, icons, bullets, graphics	http://ousd.k12.ca.us/ ~168webpg/iconpage.html

Graphics Tools

Name	Description	URL
GraphicConverter (M)	$35. Thorsten Lemke's image editor for Macintosh. Reads and writes an incredible array of graphics formats, including Progressive JPEG, GIF89a (Animated), etc.	http://www.lemkesoft.de/ us_gcabout.html
Adobe Photoshop (M, W)	$900. Adobe Systems' commercial image editing program. Version 4 supports Progressive JPEG, PNG, PDF, as well as GIF89a.	http://www.adobe.com/ prodindex/photoshop/ main.html. *demo*: http:// www.adobe.com/prodindex/ photoshop/demoreg.html
Paint Shop Pro (W)	JASC Software. Powerful image editing program for Windows. Commercial and shareware versions available. Supports JPEG, PNG, GIF.	http://www.jasc.com/psp.html; *download*: http://www.jasc.com/ pspdl.html
LView Pro (W)	$40. Popular shareware graphics program.	http://www.lview.com; *download*: http://www.lview.com/ down2.0.htm

Image Map Tools

Name	Description	URL
Mapedit (M, W)	$25. Thomas Boutell. Useful for both client-side and server-side image maps.	http://www.boutell.com/ mapedit

Special Symbols

You can type any letter of the English alphabet or any number into your HTML document and be confident that every other computer system will interpret it correctly. However, if your Web page contains any accents, foreign characters, or special symbols, you may have to use a special code to make sure they appear correctly on the page.

The ISO Latin-1 character set is the standard for the World Wide Web. It assigns a number to each character, number, or symbol in the set. In addition, some characters, especially the accented letters, have special names.

However, some computer systems, especially Macintosh and DOS, do not use the standard character set. That means that you could type a *é* in your HTML document and have it appear as a | (a straight vertical line) on your Web page.

To make sure accented characters and special characters appear correctly, no matter what system you write on, use the steps described on page 308 to enter them into your HTML document.

Using special symbols

The symbols numbered 32 to 126—which include all the letters in the English alphabet, the numbers and many common symbols—can be typed directly from the keyboard of any system. The symbols numbered 127 to 255 should be entered as described below.

To use special symbols:

1. Place the cursor where you wish the special character to appear.

2. Type **&**.

3. *Either* type **#n** where *n* is the number that corresponds to the desired symbol *or* type **name** where *name* is the code that corresponds to the desired symbol *(see pages 309 and 310)*.

4. Type **;**.

5. Continue with your HTML document.

✔ **Tips**

■ To create curly or smart quotes ("") on your Web page, use **“** and **”**.

■ All characters have a corresponding number. Not all characters have a corresponding name. It doesn't matter which one you use.

■ The character names are case sensitive. Type them exactly as they appear in the tables.

■ Although this system is supposed to eliminate differences across platforms, the tables illustrate that it is not 100% effective.

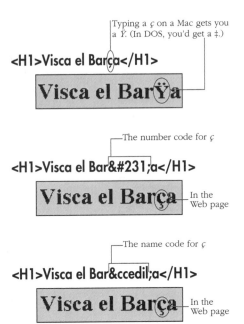

Typing a ç on a Mac gets you a Ÿ. (In DOS, you'd get a ‡.)

`<H1>Visca el Barça</H1>`

The number code for ç

`<H1>Visca el Bar&#231;a</H1>`

In the Web page

The name code for ç

`<H1>Visca el Bar&ccedil;a</H1>`

In the Web page

Figure B.1 *To display a ç properly, you must use either its number or name. It looks awful in your HTML document, but on the Web page, where it counts, it's beautiful—on any platform.*

Table I: Characters

To get this…	…type this…	…or this.	To get this…	…type this…	…or this.
à	&#224;	&agrave;	ò	&#242;	&ograve;
á	&#225;	&aacute;	ó	&#243;	&oacute;
â	&#226;	&acirc;	ô	&#244;	&ocirc;
ã	&#227;	&atilde;	õ	&#245;	&otilde;
ä	&#228;	&auml;	ö	&#246;	&ouml;
å	&#229;	&aring;	ø	&#248;	&oslash;
æ	&#230;	&aelig;	œ	&#156;	*
À	&#192;	&Agrave;	Ò	&#210;	&Ograve;
Á	&#193;	&Aacute;	Ó	&#211;	&Oacute;
Â	&#194;	&Acirc;	Ô	&#212;	&Ocirc;
Ã	&#195;	&Atilde;	Õ	&#213;	&Otilde;
Ä	&#196;	&Auml;	Ö	&#214;	&Ouml;
Å	&#197;	&Aring;	Ø	&#216;	&Oslash;
Æ	&#198;	&AElig;	Œ	&#;	*
è	&#232;	&egrave;	ù	&#249;	&ugrave;
é	&#233;	&eacute;	ú	&#250;	&uacute;
ê	&#234;	&ecirc;	û	&#251;	&ucirc;
ë	&#235;	&euml;	ü	&#252;	&uuml;
È	&#200;	&Egrave;	Ù	&#217;	&Ugrave;
É	&#201;	&Eacute;	Ú	&#218;	&Uacute;
Ê	&#202;	&Ecirc;	Û	&#219;	&Ucirc;
Ë	&#203;	&Euml;	Ü	&#220;	&Uuml;
ì	&#236;	&igrave;	ÿ	&#255;	&yuml;
í	&#237;	&iacute;	Ÿ	&#159;	*
î	&#238;	&icirc;	ç	&#231;	&ccedil;
ï	&#239;	&iuml;	Ç	&#199;	&Ccedil;
Ì	&#204;	&Igrave;	ß	&#223;	&szlig;
Í	&#205;	&Iacute;	ñ	&#241;	&ntilde;
Î	&#206;	&Icirc;	Ñ	&#209;	&Ntilde;
Ï	&#207;	&Iuml;			

* These characters don't have a name code.

Table II: Symbols

To get this...	...type this...	...or this.	To get this...	...type this...	...or this.
"	&#34;	&quot;	©	&#169;	*
#	&#35;	*	®	&#174;	*
&	&#38;	&amp;	@	&#64;	*
<	&#60;	&lt;	...	&#133;	*
>	&#62;	&gt;	"	&#147;	*
%	&#37;	*	"	&#148;	*
‰	&#137;	*	•	&#149;	*
¢	&#162;	*	°	š[1]	*
$	&#36;	*	§	&#167;	*
£	&#163;	*	¶	&#182;	*
¥	&#165;	*	º	&#186;	*
™	&#153;	*	ª	&#170;	*

* These characters don't have a name code.

[1] To get this character in Windows, type the number code º.

Colors in Hex

You can choose the color for the background of your page as well as for the text and links. Both Netscape and Internet Explorer understand sixteen predefined color names: Silver, Gray, White, Black, Maroon, Red, Green, Lime, Purple, Fuchsia, Olive, Yellow, Navy, Blue, Teal, and Aqua. Some browsers also recognize Magenta (same as Fuchsia) and Cyan (same as Aqua). Consult the inside back cover for a look at these colors.

You can also specify any color by giving its red, green, and blue components—in the form of a number between 0 and 255. To make things really complicated, you must specify these components with the hexadecimal equivalent of that number. The table on page 313 gives the corresponding hexadecimal number for each possible value of red, green, or blue.

Check the inside back cover for a full-color table of many common colors, together with their hexadecimal codes.

Finding a color's RGB components—in hex

The inside back cover contains a full-color table of many common colors and their hexadecimal equivalents. If you don't see the color you want, you can use Photoshop (or other image editing program) to display the red, green, and blue components of the colors you want to use on your page. Then consult the table on page 313 for the hexadecimal equivalents of those components.

Figure C.1 *In Photoshop, click on one of the color boxes in the toolbox to make the Color Picker dialog box appear.*

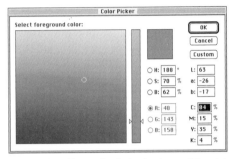

To find a color's RGB components:

1. In Photoshop, click one of the color boxes in the toolbox **(Figure C.1)**.

2. In the Color Picker dialog box that appears, choose the desired color.

3. Write down the numbers that appear in the R, G, and B text boxes. These numbers represent the R, G, and B components of the color **(Fig. C.2)**.

4. Use the table on the next page to find the hexadecimal equivalents of the numbers found in step 3.

5. Assemble the hexadecimal numbers in the form *#rrggbb* where *rr* is the hexadecimal equivalent for the red component, *gg* is the hexadecimal equivalent for the green component, and *bb* is the hexadecimal equivalent of the blue component.

Figure C.2 *Choose the desired color and then jot down the values shown in the R, G, and B text boxes. This color, a teal blue, has an R of 48 (hex=30), a G of 143 (hex=8F), and a B of 158 (hex=9E). Therefore, the hexadecimal equivalent of this color would be #308F9E.*

Figure C.3 *You can also use the Picker palette to choose colors and see their RGB components.*

✔ Tip

■ You can find instructions for specifying the background color on page 102, for specifying the text color on pages 49 and 50, and for specifying the links' color on page 123.

Hexadecimal equivalents

#	Hex.	#	Hex.	#	Hex.	#	Hex.	#	Hex.	#	Hex.	#	Hex.	#	Hex.
0	00	32	20	64	40	96	60	128	80	160	A0	192	C0	224	E0
1	01	33	21	65	41	97	61	129	81	161	A1	193	C1	225	E1
2	02	34	22	66	42	98	62	130	82	162	A2	194	C2	226	E2
3	03	35	23	67	43	99	63	131	83	163	A3	195	C3	227	E3
4	04	36	24	68	44	100	64	132	84	164	A4	196	C4	228	E4
5	05	37	25	69	45	101	65	133	85	165	A5	197	C5	229	E5
6	06	38	26	70	46	102	66	134	86	166	A6	198	C6	230	E6
7	07	39	27	71	47	103	67	135	87	167	A7	199	C7	231	E7
8	08	40	28	72	48	104	68	136	88	168	A8	200	C8	232	E8
9	09	41	29	73	49	105	69	137	89	169	A9	201	C9	233	E9
10	0A	42	2A	74	4A	106	6A	138	8A	170	AA	202	CA	234	EA
11	0B	43	2B	75	4B	107	6B	139	8B	171	AB	203	CB	235	EB
12	0C	44	2C	76	4C	108	6C	140	8C	172	AC	204	CC	236	EC
13	0D	45	2D	77	4D	109	6D	141	8D	173	AD	205	CD	237	ED
14	0E	46	2E	78	4E	110	6E	142	8E	174	AE	206	CE	238	EE
15	0F	47	2F	79	4F	111	6F	143	8F	175	AF	207	CF	239	EF
16	10	48	30	80	50	112	70	144	90	176	B0	208	D0	240	F0
17	11	49	31	81	51	113	71	145	91	177	B1	209	D1	241	F1
18	12	50	32	82	52	114	72	146	92	178	B2	210	D2	242	F2
19	13	51	33	83	53	115	73	147	93	179	B3	211	D3	243	F3
20	14	52	34	84	54	116	74	148	94	180	B4	212	D4	244	F4
21	15	53	35	85	55	117	75	149	95	181	B5	213	D5	245	F5
22	16	54	36	86	56	118	76	150	96	182	B6	214	D6	246	F6
23	17	55	37	87	57	119	77	151	97	183	B7	215	D7	247	F7
24	18	56	38	88	58	120	78	152	98	184	B8	216	D8	248	F8
25	19	57	39	89	59	121	79	153	99	185	B9	217	D9	249	F9
26	1A	58	3A	90	5A	122	7A	154	9A	186	BA	218	DA	250	FA
27	1B	59	3B	91	5B	123	7B	155	9B	187	BB	219	DB	251	FB
28	1C	60	3C	92	5C	124	7C	156	9C	188	BC	220	DC	252	FC
29	1D	61	3D	93	5D	125	7D	157	9D	189	BD	221	DD	253	FD
30	1E	62	3E	94	5E	126	7E	158	9E	190	BE	222	DE	254	FE
31	1F	63	3F	95	5F	127	7F	159	9F	191	BF	223	DF	255	FF

The Hexadecimal system

"Regular" numbers are based on the base 10 system, that is, there are ten symbols (what we call numbers): 0, 1, 2, 3, 4, 5, 6, 7, 8, and 9. To represent numbers greater than 9, we use a combination of these symbols where the first digit specifies how many *ones,* the second digit (to the left) specifies how many *tens,* and so on.

In the hexadecimal system, which is base 16, there are sixteen symbols: 0, 1, 2, 3, 4, 5, 6, 7, 8, 9, a, b, c, d, e, and f. To represent numbers greater than *f* (which in base 10 we understand as *15*), we again use a combination of symbols. This time the first digit specifies how many ones, but the second digit (again, to the left) specifies how many sixteens. Thus, 10 is one *sixteen* and no *ones,* or simply *16* (as represented in base 10).

In addition to colors, you can use hexadecimal numbers to represent special symbols in URLs. Find the corresponding number in the table on pages 309–310, convert it to hexadecimal with the above table and precede it with a percent sign (%). Thus, the space, which is number 32, and has a hexadecimal equivalent of 20, can be represented as %20.

HTML and Compatibility

Like many of the pages you'll find out on the Web, HTML is a language under construction. There are three main driving forces that determine what HTML will look like tomorrow: the World Wide Web Consortium (W3C), Netscape Communications, and Microsoft.

Theoretically, both Netscape and Microsoft have agreed to abide by the decisions of the W3C (of which they are members) in an attempt to maintain HTML's universality. However, the reality is a bit different. These two companies are in a heated battle to determine whose browser is used by the Web-surfing public. If a new extension to HTML will tip the balance in their favor, their agreement with the W3C may be at least momentarily forgotten.

On the following pages, you'll find a list of the HTML tags and attributes described in this book. In the "Vers." or *version* column, I've indicated if the tag or attribute belongs to HTML 4, or if it is only recognized by Netscape (N), by Internet Explorer (IE), or by both (N+IE). That way, you can decide if a given tag is "universal enough" for your page. If you use a tag that is not part of standard HTML 4, you might want to warn users who jump to the page that it is best viewed with a particular browser.

Deprecated tags are marked with a *D* in the Vers. column. Although the W3C doesn't recommend their use, browsers are expected to continue to support these tags for some time.

A special section at the end is devoted to intrinsic events and the HTML elements they can be associated with *(see page 322)*.

HTML Tags

TAG/ATTRIBUTE	DESCRIPTION	VERS.
--MOST TAGS--	The following attributes may be used with most HTML tags	
CLASS	For identifying a set of tags in order to apply styles (p. 228)	4
EVENT	For triggering a script (p. 270)	4
ID	For identifying particular tags for JavaScript functions and styles (p. 229)	4
STYLE	For adding local style sheet information (p. 223)	4
!--	For inserting invisible comments (p. 56)	4
!DOCTYPE	Required. For indicating version of HTML used (p. 37)	4
A	For creating links and anchors (p. 108)	4
ACCESSKEY	For adding a keyboard shortcut to a link (p. 116)	4
EVENT	For triggering a script (p. 270)	4
HREF	For specifying URL of page or name of anchor that link goes to	4
NAME	For marking a specific area of page that a link might jump to (p. 110)	4
TABORDER	For defining the order in which the Tab key takes the visitor through links and form elements (p. 117)	4
TARGET	For specifying a particular window or frame for a link (pp. 112, 113)	4
ADDRESS	For formatting the e-mail address of the Web page designer (p. 45)	4
APPLET	For inserting applets (p. 220)	4D
CODE	For specifying the URL of the applet's code	4D
WIDTH, HEIGHT	For specifying width and height of an applet	4D
AREA	For specifying coordinates of image maps (p. 120)	4
ACCESSKEY	For adding a keyboard shortcut to a particular region of the map	4
COORDS	For giving coordinates of area in image map	4
HREF	For specifying destination URL of link in area in image map	4
NOHREF	For making a click in image map have no effect.	4
SHAPE	For specifying shape of area in image map	4
TARGET	For specifying window or frame that link should be displayed in	4
B	For displaying text in boldface (p. 45)	4
BASE		4
HREF	For specifying the URL to be used to generate relative URLs (p. 113)	4
TARGET	For specifying the default target for the links on the page (p. 113)	4
BASEFONT	For specifying default font specifications throughout page (p. 46)	4D
COLOR	For specifying the default color for text	4D
FONT	For specifying the default font for text	4D
SIZE	For specifying the default size for text	4D
BGSOUND	For inserting background sound for page (p. 213)	IE
LOOP	For specifying how many times sound should play	IE
SRC	For specifying URL of sound	IE
BIG	For making text bigger than surrounding text (p. 48)	4
BLINK	For making text disappear and reappear (p. 55)	N
BLOCKQUOTE	For setting off block of text on page (p. 104)	4

Page numbers are omitted for those attributes discussed on the same page as the tag to which they belong.

TAG/ATTRIBUTE	DESCRIPTION	VERS.
BODY	For enclosing main section of page (p. 38)	4
ALINK, LINK, VLINK	For specifying color of active links, new links, and visited links (p. 123)	4D
BACKGROUND	For specifying a background image (p. 103)	4D
BGCOLOR	For specifying the background color (p. 102)	4D
LEFTMARGIN, TOPMARGIN	For specifying left and top margins (p. 92)	IE
TEXT	For specifying color of text (p. 49)	4D
BR	For creating a line break (p. 42)	4
CLEAR	For stopping text wrap on one or both sides of an image (p. 85)	4D
BUTTON	For creating buttons (pp. 193, 195, 272)	4
ACCESSKEY	For adding a keyboard shortcut to a button	4
EVENT	For associating the button with a script	4
NAME	For identifying buttons (perhaps for a JavaScript function)	4
VALUE	For specifying what kind of button to create	4
CAPTION	For creating a caption for a table (p. 137)	4
ALIGN	For placing caption above or below table	4D
CENTER	For centering text, images, or other elements (p. 99)	4D
CITE	For marking text as a citation (p. 45)	4
CODE	For marking text as computer code (p. 52)	4
COL	For joining columns in a table into a non-structural group (p. 138)	4
ALIGN	For specifying alignment of columns in column group	4
SPAN	For specifying number of columns in column group	4
COLGROUP	For joining columns in a table into a structural column group (p. 138)	4
ALIGN	For specifying alignment of columns in column group	4
SPAN	For specifying number of columns in column group	4
DD	For marking a definition in a list (p. 130)	4
DEL	To mark deleted text by striking it out (p. 54)	4
DIV	For dividing a page into logical sections (p. 230)	4
ALIGN	For aligning a given section to left, right, or center	4D
CLASS	For giving a name to each class of divisions	4
ID	For giving a unique name to a particular division	4
DL	For creating a definition list (p. 130)	4
DT	For marking a term to be defined in a list (p. 130)	4
EM	For emphasizing text, usually with italics (p. 45)	4
EMBED	For adding multimedia (and others) to pages (pp. 212, 217)	N+IE
ALIGN	For aligning controls	N+IE
AUTOSTART	For making multimedia event begin automatically	N+IE
CONTROLS	For displaying play, pause, rewind buttons	N+IE
LOOP	For determining if multimedia event should play more than once	N+IE
SRC	For specifying URL of multimedia file	N+IE
WIDTH, HEIGHT	For specifying size of controls	N+IE
FIELDSET	For grouping a set of form elements together (p. 197)	4

Page numbers are omitted for those attributes discussed on the same page as the tag to which they belong.

HTML Tags

TAG/ATTRIBUTE	DESCRIPTION	VERS.
FONT	For changing the size, face, and color of individual letters or words	4D
COLOR	For changing text color (p. 50)	4D
FACE	For changing text font (p. 44)	4D
SIZE	For changing text size (p. 47)	4D
FORM	For creating fill-in forms (p. 182)	4
ACTION	For giving URL of CGI script for form	4
METHOD	For determining how form should be processed	4
FRAME	For creating frames (p. 158)	4
BORDER	For determining thickness of frame borders (p. 168)	N
BORDERCOLOR	For determining color of frame borders (p. 167)	N
FRAMEBORDER	For displaying or hiding frame borders (p. 169)	4
FRAMESPACING	For adding space between frames (p. 171)	IE
NAME	For naming frame so it can be used as target (p. 158)	4
NORESIZE	For keeping users from resizing a frame (p. 170)	4
MARGINWIDTH, MARGINHEIGHT	For specifying a frame's left and right, and top and bottom margins (p. 165)	4
SCROLLING	For displaying or hiding a frame's scrollbars (p. 166)	4
SRC	For specifying initial URL to be displayed in frame (p. 158)	4
TARGET	For specifying which frame a link should be opened in (pp. 172, 173)	4
FRAMESET	For defining a frameset (p. 158)	4
BORDER	For determining thickness of frame borders (p. 168)	N
BORDERCOLOR	For determining color of frame borders (p. 167)	N
COLS	For determining number and size of frames (pp. 160, 161)	4
FRAMEBORDER	For displaying or hiding frame borders (p. 169)	4
FRAMESPACING	For adding space between frames (p. 171)	IE
ROWS	For determining number and size of frames (pp. 160, 161)	4
Hn	For creating headers (p. 40)	4
ALIGN	For aligning headers	4D
HEAD	For creating head section of page (p. 38)	4
HR	For creating horizontal rules (p. 90)	4
ALIGN	For aligning horizontal rules	4D
NOSHADE	For displaying horizontal rules without shading	4D
SIZE	For specifying height of horizontal rule	4D
WIDTH	For specifying width of horizontal rule	4D
HTML	For identifying a text document as an HTML document (p. 37)	4
I	For displaying text in italics (p. 45)	4
IFRAME	For creating floating frames (p. 164)	4
ALIGN	For aligning floating frames	4D
FRAMEBORDER	For displaying or hiding frame borders (p. 169)	4
NAME	For specifying the name of the floating frame, to be used as a target	4
WIDTH, HEIGHT	For specifying size of floating frame	4
SCROLLING	For displaying or hiding scrollbars (p. 166)	4
SRC	For specifying the URL of the initial page	4

Page numbers are omitted for those attributes discussed on the same page as the tag to which they belong.

HTML Tags

TAG/ATTRIBUTE	DESCRIPTION	VERS.
IMG	For inserting images on a page (p. 78)	4
ALIGN	For aligning images (p. 88) and for wrapping text around images (pp. 83, 84)	4D
ALT	For offering alternate text that is displayed if image is not (p. 79)	4
BORDER	For specifying the thickness of the border, if any (pp. 78, 118)	4D
CONTROLS	For displaying or hiding video controls (p. 218)	IE
DYNSRC	For specifying URL of video file (p. 218)	IE
HSPACE, VSPACE	For specifying amount of space above and below, and to the sides of image (p. 86)	4D
LOOP	For specifying number of repeats of video file (p. 218)	IE
LOWSRC	For specifying URL of low resolution version of image (p. 82)	N+IE
SRC	For specifying URL of image (p. 78)	4
START	For determining when video should begin (p. 218)	IE
USEMAP	For specifying the image map that should be used with the referenced image (p. 120)	4
WIDTH, HEIGHT	For specifying size of image so that page is loaded more quickly, or for scaling (pp. 80, 87)	4
INPUT	For creating form elements (pp. 183, 184, 186, 187, 190, 191, 192, 194)	4
ACCESSKEY	For adding a keyboard shortcut to a form element (p. 200)	4
CHECKED	For marking a radio button or check box by default (pp. 186, 187)	4
DISABLED	For disabling form elements (p. 201)	4
EVENT	For triggering a script with an event like ONFOCUS, ONBLUR, etc.	4
MAXLENGTH	For determining maximum amount of characters that can be entered in form element (pp. 183, 184)	4
NAME	For identifying data collected by this element	4
SIZE	For specifying width of text or password box (pp. 183, 184)	4
SRC	For specifying URL of active image (p. 196)	4
READONLY	For keeping visitors from changing certain form elements (p. 202)	4
TABORDER	For specifying the order in which the Tab key should take a visitor through the links and form elements (p. 199)	4
TYPE	For determining type of form element	4
VALUE	For specifying initial value of form element	4
INS	For marking inserted text with an underline (p. 54)	4
KBD	For marking keyboard text (p. 52)	4
LABEL	For labeling form elements (p. 198)	4
FOR	For specifying which form element the label belongs to	4
LAYER	For positioning elements (p. 100)	N
LEGEND	For labeling fieldsets (p. 197)	4
LI	For creating a list item (p. 126)	4
TYPE	For determining which symbols should begin the list item	4D
VALUE	For determining the initial value of the first list item	4D
LINK	For using an external style sheet (p. 227)	4
MAP	For creating a client-side image map (p. 120)	4
NAME	For naming map so it can be referenced later	4

Page numbers are omitted for those attributes discussed on the same page as the tag to which they belong.

HTML Tags

TAG/ATTRIBUTE	DESCRIPTION	VERS.
MARQUEE	For creating moving text (p. 219)	IE
BEHAVIOR	For controlling how the text should move (scroll, slide, alternate)	IE
DIRECTION	For controlling if the text moves from left to right or right to left	IE
LOOP	For specifying how many times the text should come across the screen	IE
SCORLLAMOUNT	For specifying amount of space between each marquee repetition	IE
SCROLLDELAY	For specifying amount of time between each marquee repetition	IE
META		4
HTTP-EQUIV	For creating automatic jumps to other pages (p. 288) and setting the default scripting language (p. 275)	4
NAME	For adding extra information to the Web page (pp. 290, 291, 292, 293)	4
NOBR	For keeping all the enclosed elements on one line (p. 106)	N+IE
NOFRAMES	For providing alternatives to frames (p. 176)	4
NOSCRIPT	For providing alternatives to scripts (p. 274)	4
OBJECT	The W3C would like this tag to eventually replace the IMG and APPLET tags. It is not currently supported very well.	4
OL	For creating ordered lists (p. 126)	4
TYPE	For specifying the symbols that should begin each list item	4D
START	For specifying the initial value of the first list item	4D
OPTGROUP	For dividing a menu into submenus (p. 189)	4
OPTION	For creating the individual options in a form menu (p. 188)	4
SELECTED	For making a menu option be selected by default in a blank form	4
VALUE	For specifying the initial value of a menu option	4
P	For creating new paragraphs (p. 41)	4
ALIGN	For aligning paragraphs	4D
PRE	For displaying text exactly as it appears in HTML document (p. 53)	4
Q	For quoting short passages of text (p. 105)	4
S	(Same as STRIKE) For displaying text with a line through it (p. 54)	4D
SAMP	For displaying sample text—in a monospaced font (p. 52)	4
SCRIPT	For adding "automatic" scripts to a page (p. 268)	4
CHARSET	For specifying the character set an external script is written in (p. 269)	4
LANGUAGE	For specifying the scripting language the script is written in	4D
SRC	For referencing an external script (p. 269)	4
TYPE	For specifying the scripting language the script is written in	4
SELECT	For creating menus in forms (p. 188)	4
NAME	For identifying the data collected by the menu	4
MULTIPLE	For allowing users to choose more than one option in the menu	4
SIZE	For specifying the number of items initially visible in the menu	4
SMALL	For decreasing the size of text (p. 48)	4
SPAN	For creating custom character styles (p. 231)	4
CLASS	For naming individual custom character styles	4
ID	For identifying particular HTML elements	4
STRIKE	(Same as S) For displaying text with a line through it (p. 54)	4D

Page numbers are omitted for those attributes discussed on the same page as the tag to which they belong.

TAG/ATTRIBUTE	DESCRIPTION	VERS.
STRONG	For emphasizing text logically, usually in boldface (p. 45)	4
STYLE	For adding style sheet information to a page (p. 224)	4
SUB	For creating subscripts (p. 51)	4
SUP	For creating superscripts (p. 51)	4
TABLE	For creating tables (p. 134)	4
BGCOLOR	For specifying the background color of the table (p. 150)	4D
BORDER	For specifying the thickness, if any, of the border (p. 141)	4
BORDERCOLOR	For specifying a solid color for the border (p. 141)	IE
BORDERCOLORDARK	For specifying the darker (shaded) color of the border (p. 141)	IE
BORDERCOLORLIGHT	For specifying the lighter (highlighted) color of the border (p. 141)	IE
CELLPADDING	For specifying the amount of space between a cell's contents and its borders (p. 152)	4
CELLSPACING	For specifying the amount of space between cells (p. 152)	4
FRAME	For displaying external borders (p. 142)	4
HEIGHT	For specifying the height of the table (p. 146)	N+IE
RULES	For displaying internal borders (p. 143)	4
WIDTH	For specifying the size of the table (p. 146)	4
TBODY	For identifying the body of the table (p. 140)	4
TD; TH	For creating regular and header cells, respectively, in a table (p. 134)	4
ALIGN, VALIGN	For aligning a cell's contents horizontally or vertically (p. 148)	4
BGCOLOR	For changing the background color of a cell (p. 150)	4D
COLSPAN	For spanning a cell across more than one column (p. 144)	4
NOWRAP	For keeping a cell's contents on one line (p. 153)	4D
ROWSPAN	For spanning a cell across more than one row (p. 145)	4
WIDTH, HEIGHT	For specifying the size of the cell (p. 147)	4D
TEXTAREA	For creating text block entry areas in a form (p. 185)	4
ACCESSKEY	For adding a keyboard shortcut to a text area	4
NAME	For identifying the data that is gathered with the text block	4
ROWS, COLS	For specifying the number of rows and columns in the text block	4
TFOOT, THEAD	For identifying the footer and header area of a table (p. 140)	4
ALIGN	For aligning the footer or header cells (p. 148)	4
TITLE	Required. For creating the title of the page in title bar area (p. 39)	4
TR	For creating rows in a table (p. 134)	4
ALIGN, VALIGN	For aligning contents of row horizontally or vertically (p. 148)	4D
BGCOLOR	For changing color of entire row (p. 150)	4D
TT	For displaying text in monospaced font (p. 52)	4
U	For displaying text with line underneath it (p. 54)	4D
UL	For creating unordered lists (p. 128)	4
TYPE	For specifying the type of symbols that should precede each list item	4D
WBR	For creating discretional line breaks in text enclosed in NOBR tags (p. 106)	N+IE

Page numbers are omitted for those attributes discussed on the same page as the tag to which they belong.

HTML Tags

Intrinsic events

An intrinsic event determines when an associated script will run. However, not every intrinsic event works with every HTML element. This table illustrates which events and tags work together. For more information on associating a script with an intrinsic event, consult *Triggering a script* on page 270.

EVENT	WORKS WITH	WHEN
ONBLUR	A, AREA, BUTTON, INPUT , LABEL, SELECT, TEXTAREA	the visitor leaves an element that was previously in focus (see ONFOCUS below)
ONCHANGE	INPUT, SELECT, TEXTAREA	the visitor modifies the value or contents of the element
ONCLICK	All elements *except* APPLET, BASE, BASEFONT, BR, FONT, FRAME, FRAMESET, HEAD, HTML, IFRAME, META, PARAM, SCRIPT, STYLE, TITLE	the visitor clicks on the specified area
ONDBLCLICK	Same as ONCLICK	the visitor double clicks the specified area
ONFOCUS	A, AREA, BUTTON, INPUT, LABEL, SELECT, TEXTAREA	the visitor selects, clicks, or tabs to the specified element
ONKEYDOWN	INPUT (of type NAME or PASSWORD), TEXTAREA	the visitor types something in the specified element
ONKEYPRESS	INPUT (of type NAME or PASSWORD), TEXTAREA	the visitor types something in the specified element
ONKEYUP	INPUT (of type NAME or PASSWORD), TEXTAREA	the visitor lets go of the key after typing in the specified element
ONLOAD	BODY, FRAMESET	the page is loaded in the browser
ONMOUSEDOWN	Same as ONCLICK	the visitor presses the mouse button down over the element
ONMOUSEMOVE	Same as ONCLICK	the visitor moves the mouse over the specified element after having pointed at it
ONMOUSEOUT	Same as ONCLICK	the visitor moves the mouse away from the specified element after having been over it
ONMOUSEOVER	Same as ONCLICK	the visitor points the mouse at the element
ONMOUSEUP	Same as ONCLICK	the visitor lets the mouse button go after having clicked on the element
ONRESET	FORM (*not* INPUT of type RESET)	the visitor clicks the form's reset button
ONSELECT	INPUT (of type NAME or PASSWORD), TEXTAREA	the visitor selects one or more characters or words in the element
ONSUBMIT	FORM (*not* INPUT of type SUBMIT)	the visitor clicks the form's submit button
ONUNLOAD	BODY, FRAMESET	the browser loads a different page after the specified page had been loaded

Index

Index

Index

Index

Index

Index